D1073958

ANALYSIS
AND
VALUATION
OF RETAIL LOCATIONS

ANALYSIS
AND
VALUATION
OF RETAIL LOCATIONS

Edwin M. Rams

RESTON PUBLISHING COMPANY, INC. / A PRENTICE-HALL COMPANY
Reston, Virginia

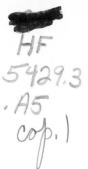
Library of Congress Cataloging in Publication Data

Main entry under title:

Analysis and valuation of retail locations.

Includes bibliographies.
1. Store location—United States—Addresses, essays,
lectures. 2. Store, Retail—Valuation—United States—
Addresses, essays, lectures. I. Rams, Edwin S.
HF5429.3.A5   338.6'042'0973   76-12594
ISBN 0-87909-033-2

© 1976 by Reston Publishing Company, Inc.
A Prentice-Hall Company
Reston, Virginia 22090

10 9 8 7 6 5 4 3 2

Printed in the United States of America

In Memory of my father
Michael S. Rams
A Retailer of Another Era

ABOUT THE AUTHOR

An urban economist-market analyst-appraiser of Washington, D.C., Edwin M. Rams has had a varied and extensive nationwide career in the real estate industry for over a quarter of a century. As consultant to business, industry, and government, his experience includes numerous studies of central business districts and suburban shopping centers, including feasibility analyses relating to the development and redevelopment of large segments of many American cities.

He is the author of four books and dozens of research papers published in American and foreign professional journals and by the National Academy of Sciences. He is a member of the International Fraternity of Lambda Alpha, honorary land economics society, of which he was International President, 1965–67, the Washington Society of Investment Analysts, and the American Institute of Real Estate Appraisers.

ACKNOWLEDGEMENTS

Special gratitude to all authors and editors for their cooperation and consent in the use of the many essays and research efforts. Time does not diminish their collective share and contribution in the building blocks of knowledge on this important subject.

Both Fred Lauterbach, MAI, and George S. Anderson provided time, energy, and know-how in running the several computer analyses that highlight a number of techniques and methodologies.

CONTENTS

SECTION
4

CONSUMER BEHAVIOR, PROFILES, AND PREFERENCES   245

PREFACE

Retail trade in the United States is a multi-billion dollar industry and represents one of several common denominators of commercial activities linking together every inhabited part of the nation. As a principal channel of distribution, retailing functions represent a national network of firms and establishments that are highly differentiated by function, size, market penetration, merchandise, goods, products, and services. The complexities of establishments range from single-product enterprises to multi-thousand inventories that represent entrepreneurial and managerial responses to consumer wants, needs, and expectations.

Retail locations, their analysis and valuation, are perceived from a comprehensive point of view. The totality of a location includes important matters of trade areas, consumer behavior patterns, locational accessability, and enterprise location costs for entry and continued viability in the retailing sector. Accordingly, locational interdependence and the casual relationships of competitors in a spatial context serve as fundamental criteria for location decision-making for the consultant and management responsible for enterprise locational situations.

This book is organized to provide a systematic study of the important aspects of retail location analysis. These facets cover urban growth considerations, the geography of retailing activities, feasibility analysis, locational attributes in a profitability framework, and consumer behavior and preferences.

Important details of retail-commercial land values and the valuation of real property interests provide parameters for retail facility costs and important guidelines for managerial implementation of this part of the decision-making process.

Section 1 of the book provides the beginning point for analysis of urban economic structure, basis for retail development, and changing socio-economic dimensions of urbanized areas. The forum serves as a foundation for subsequent detailed study of retail trade potentials and market opportunities.

Methodology for trade area delineation and criteria for feasibility of market entry, including measures of sales potentials, represents the main thrust of Section 2. Techniques and findings from a number of geographic areas cover aspects of threshold analysis of retail establishments, longitudinal analysis of trade areas, and drawing power of several different kinds of retail establishments.

A central problem of retailing involves location analysis, which is the subject of Section 3. Central city, suburban, and small city locational derivation techniques are presented. Greater insight concerning the costs of a location are considered via a buy-lease decision model that facilitates an interfacing of assumptions and consequent benefits and costs.

Section 4 articulates a key element of the retail location equation—consumer behavior, profiles and preferences. This crucial variable is examined from a number of vantage points, to wit, the discount store, small cities, department stores, and matters of time-distance and accessability.

The dimensions of land values and the determinative forces that account for intra-urban differentials are matters discussed in Section 5.

Finally, Section 6 rounds out the basic theme with techniques for the valuation of retail facilities, including the new real estate appraisal process. Important subjects of interest are leasehold interests, condemnation lease provisions, Monte Carlo simulation of an investment, and cash flow analysis. This comprehensive framework does indeed result in a total portrayal of important elements and methodology for the valuation of real property interests for retailing functions.

The encyclopedic coverage of all key ingredients to location studies and property evaluation can serve as a format for the solution of most complex problems in this area of interest. The scope of the material may provide a synthesis of subject matter for both student and researcher concerned with retail location selection.

Neither the inclusion or exclusion of related material is suggestive of any finality of techniques and methods. The dynamics of retailing serve as a constant reminder of change on the urban scene, whether attributable to technology, social mores, consumer tastes and preferences, or other critical external forces modifying the location matrix of retailing activities. The collected essays merely provide a range of research-analysis possibilities for the study of this important sector of commerce.

EDWIN M. RAMS

ANALYSIS
AND
VALUATION
OF RETAIL LOCATIONS

URBAN GROWTH AND THE GEOGRAPHY OF RETAILING ACTIVITIES

An Overview

Urban growth, including all components of an urban economy, represents important factors contributing to the presence, stability, and increasing levels of retailing functions. Since growth is a relative concept, an urban center defined and circumscribed within given limits and definitions should not be viewed in absolute terms but, rather, on a relative and comparative basis. Segmentation of an urban center, such as county versus city, or county and/or city versus the SMSA, provides an intraurban view of growth sectors within the general fabric of a community.

For example, Sibley has analyzed the incidence of greengrocers in Leicester, England, over a period of seven decades. The principal inquiry was to test the allometric law of urban growth; the research suggests validity at 250-meter rings from the core area of the city (David Sibley, *Urban Studies,* Vol. 7, Oct. 1970). This kind of study provides insight into the competitive frame of reference of retail competition in a spatial context within an internal urban center situation.

Another vantage point for the analysis of the comparative and relative retail sector growth of an urban center involves an assessment of similar-sized and/or neighboring competing urban areas. In a study of the Upper Great Lakes Region, Berry reported that where metropolitan areas are closely spaced (less than 100 miles) the respective commuting fields overlap, with the consequence that income levels and other indexes are often more favorable in the countryside between the metropolitan areas than in the cities themselves. A distance in excess of 100 miles can show evidence of declining incomes, out-migration, and so on (Brian J. L. Berry,

1

Growth Centers and Their Potential in the Upper Great Lakes Regions, Washington, D.C., Upper Great Lakes Regional Commission, May 1969). A group comparison of urban centers can indicate, aside from matters of growth, the efficiency of utilization of individual urban-oriented resources.

Three crucial dimensions, which always represent a beginning point, are population, employment, and income levels. All other urban activities are the dependent variables in an equating of status, trends, and forecasts within the general purview of urban dynamics. Manifestly, these urban measures can frequently serve as proxies to forecast ensuing urban expansion and economic activity.

In a recent study of innovation in retailing, through planned regional shopping centers, for the years 1949–1969, Yehoshua S. Cohen (*Diffusion of an Innovation in an Urban System,* University of Chicago, 1972) found that the three key variables contributing to adoption in an SMSA were (1) retail sales volume, (2) disposable income, and (3) general merchandise sales. An inhibiting force to adoption was a strong, viable central business district (CBD). However, when adoption (development) of a major regional shopping center did take place, its physical size–magnitude was of such dimensions as to compete with the CBD.

An interesting finding of this research concerned adoption of innovation by urban areas undergoing rapid change compared to slower-growing centers. As Cohen points out,

> What seems to be one of the most important results of the study is the repudiation of the hypothesis that cities that undergo rapid change will adopt the innovation before slow growing cities. In fact, in both the simple correlation analysis as well as in the stepwise multiple regression, there is no relationship whatsoever between differential rates of growth of market characteristics and the variation in times of adoption. That is, in the long run, in the 20 year period under study, the dynamics of change within the urban system are not significant in the explanation of adoption time differentials (p. 104).

The study contributes to a better understanding of the urban dynamics of metropolitan areas and related retailing activities. In retrospect, regional centers have changed the geography of store locations, the technology of physical structures and consequent modes of merchandising, and consumer behavior patterns, the latter significantly because of the interrelationship between the use of the automobile and the consumer shopping trip.

In a somewhat parallel study, A. L. Bowling and J. F. Hair, Jr.

("Structural Changes in Retailing: A Predictive Model," *Marquette Business Review,* Summer 1975) found three key variables relating to mass merchandise discounters that influence changes in retailing as a consequence of changing consumer needs and expectations: (1) knowledge on the part of the consumer, (2) discretionary purchasing power, and (3) consumer mobility.

The findings indicate that the first factor results in immediate reaction and is sustained for several years following its initial impact. The same result is significant concerning mobility. However, discretionary purchasing power has a lagged effect; that is, the present year's increase is reflected in the following year's increase in expenditures for this class of retailing functions. The implications of the findings are self-evident in relation to market entry and potential for competitive position and market share for mass merchandising ventures.

Whereas the Cohen study traced the adoption of planned regional shopping centers for a 20-year period, a recent study of 165 shopping centers (76 older and 89 randomly selected) concerned their relative economic life (*Depreciable Lives of Shopping Centers,* Touche Ross & Co., 1973, The International Council of Shopping Centers, New York). Most of the centers were constructed in the last 20 years.

Two very significant findings emerge from this survey. First, the older the shopping center, the larger the dollar investment and additions of gross leasable area required for the centers to remain competitive. For example, centers 15 years and older added about 250 percent of original gross leasable area.

The second aspect concerns the reasons as perceived by management to undertake alterations. The sample covered a total of 249 shopping centers. Reasons given, on a percentage basis, include competition (27 percent), business expansion (19 percent), outdated design (17 percent), changes in merchandising trends (9 percent), changes in trade area trends (7 percent), changes in population density (4 percent), changes in highway driving patterns (5 percent), physical decay (13 percent), other reasons (2 percent). A total of 85 percent is attributable to economic causes motivating management to undertake major alterations.

On a composite basis, 20 percent were motivated by competition, of which 16 percent were traceable to trade area changes, which triggered 9 percent to modify merchandise lines. Functional obsolescence (design) affected 17 percent of the total sample.

These several studies illustrate the dynamic nature of the retailing sector and the constant competitive stress. Accordingly, urban growth, decline, or a stagnation over time represents a principal signal of the presence or absence of opportunities for retail entry or expansion in one of several merchandise lines. Inherent in the dynamics of urbanized areas are the locational factors of retail outlets. Thus, within these basic factors the most likely and viable parameters of retail locations must be delineated.

In a historical and evolutionary framework, G. H. Wadinambiaratchi traces the stages of innovation, specialization, and so on, of retail functions, with the environment being a major and controlling factor. The details of forces that mold the retail firm, its practices and norms, provide an interesting picture of this activity in less-developed countries and industrialized society.

The essay by David J. Luck on changes in the economic base of a community and the discussion of trends in multicity complexes by John R. Lowry introduce additional considerations and measures for exploratory or definitive analysis.

Theories of Retail Development [1]

G. H. Wadinambiaratchi

This paper will briefly review some existing explanations for the development of retailing institutions and practices, discuss the implications of findings from a study in Ceylon for these explanations, and attempt to outline a modified theory of retail development.

Existing Explanations and Present Findings

McNair [20] contends that new retailing institutions start out as low-margin, low-price operations; the new type of store gradually increases its services, and simultaneously its margins, until it reaches a higher level in the price scale. At that stage another innovator starts another type of store, again at low margins and low prices, and the cycle repeats itself. This explanation has come to be known as the "Wheel of Retailing." Hollander [11] contends that social and economic environments both assist and impose limitations on the development of retailing and retail institutions. He implies, therefore, that the

Wheel of Retailing can revolve only if the environment is favorable for the successful introduction of a new technique.

Cundiff [5] contends that innovations in retailing, such as the "Wheel" theory describes, take place only in the most highly developed economies, and that other economies merely adapt these innovations. He further contends that the ability of a system to adapt innovations successfully is related directly to its level of economic development. The author's study helped identify several specific factors in the economic, social, political, and business environment that facilitate, or impose limitations on, innovations and/or adaptations of retailing institutions, methods, and techniques.

Explanations Related to Innovations in Retailing Institutions and Practices

What has come to be known as the "Wheel of Retailing" arose from a reference by McNair [20, p. 25] in 1958 to a

Reprinted from *Social and Economic Studies,* Vol. 4, December 1972, by permission of the Institute of Social and Economic Research, University of the West Indies, Jamaica, W.I.

1 This paper is based on Chapter IX of the author's unpublished Doctoral Dissertation, *Development of Food Retailing in Ceylon,* Faculty of Graduate Studies, University of Western Ontario, London, Canada, 1968. The author is grateful to Prof. D.S.R. Leighton, of the University of Western Ontario, who helped to clarify many of the issues, in numerous discussions held with him.

"more or less definite cycle in American distribution." According to McNair there are five stages in this cycle. Several observers of American and British retailing have identified developments in those countries that appear to substantiate the concept of a wheel of retailing.[2] Some of these same observers, e.g., Barger [3, pp. 51–82] and others,[3] have noted patterns of development that are not fully in accord with the wheel concept. From the patterns of development discussed by these observers two conclusions could be drawn: (a) there is fairly conclusive evidence that the wheel of retailing concept, in broad terms, does apply to retail development in economically developed and growing countries; (b) new institutions, whether innovations or adaptations from innovating countries, require certain environmental preconditions (e.g., growth) for success. Even in McNair's explanation there is the implicit assumption that the environment provides for a monopolistic opportunity and also that there is ease of entry for a new type of institution.

Hollander [11] makes a strong and direct reference to a connection between the environment and retailing:

. . . modern retailing history is often set in the framework of company history and merchant biography. . . . They concentrate upon the unique individual, the merchant prince, and his contributions to retailing. Thus they can easily overlook the environmental changes that created the merchant prince's opportunity . . . considerable grounds for believing that what the merchant can accomplish is limited by the social and economic environment.

. . . the underdeveloped economies seem to accept only certain types of retailing . . . certain Western types of retailing, particularly our modern mass marketing techniques, appear as misfits when placed in the wrong cultures. Another reason for believing in the importance of environment is the number of times the same innovation has been introduced simultaneously by a number of separate individuals. . . .

. . . our recorded retail history does seem to reveal some fairly clear-cut connections between the environment and the kinds of retailing that will be fostered.

Alderson [1, Chapter 9] believes that retail institutions and practices evolve in the process of the retailers' adjustments to heterogeneous and discrepant markets. The important variables in the retailers' environment are, to Alderson, the suppliers and the consumers. For survival, retailers must adjust to that environment by offering suitable packages of goods, services, and prices. In his view, few retailers can change their environment; new types of retailers, in a wheel pattern, can emerge but their survival depends on consumer acceptance or rejection.

Observations made by other authors suggest that the presence or absence of environmental factors could be used as explanations for the features of, or changes in, retailing.[4] From these obser-

2 Barger [3] pp. 35–36, 80, 82, 97, Converse [6], Hall et al. [10] p. 8, Holton [14], Jefferys [15], Levy [17] p. 202, Linden [18], Lockwing [19] pp. 3, 17–18, Oakes [23], Pennance and Yamey [24].

3 Converse [6], Hollander [12] pp. 11–24 and [11] pp. 441–9, Holton [14] pp. 54–55, Jefferys [15] pp. 34, 158, 235, Mueller and Garoian [21] p. 133, Pennance and Yamey [24], Shawver [25] p. 92.

4 Barger [3] pp. 35–36, 82, Boyd et al. [4] pp. 26–33, Dewey [7], Elgass [8] pp. 425–433, Holton [14] p. 53, Hall et al. [10] pp. 3, 21, 87, 96, 98, 100, 114, Jefferys [15], Leighton [14] Ch. XI, Levy [16] p. 13, Lochwing [19], Mueller and Garoian [21] p. 12, Pennance and Yamey [24], Stewart [26] pp. 47–51, Taylor [27] pp. 54–5.

vations it could be concluded that in the developed Western economies generally, the retail innovations of this century are, to a large extent, a reflection of the changes in the retailers' environment: increase in discretionary purchasing power, growth of production capacity through technological progress, growth of private automobile transportation, the movement towards suburbia, and changes in consumer attitudes.

Explanations Related to the Geographical Origins and Spread of Innovations

Cundiff [5], who looked at the adaptation, in 20 countries, of what he called "four really new operating methods" (self-service; low-markup, high-stock-turn operations; suburban planned shopping centers; and automated retailing), set up five postulates for his study:

Innovation takes place only in the most highly developed systems.

Retailers in other systems have more to gain from adoption and adaptation of developments already tried and tested in the most highly developed systems.

The ability of a system to adapt innovations successfully is related directly to its level of economic development. Certain minimum levels of economic development are necessary to support anything beyond the most simple retailing methods.

When the economic environment is favorable to change, the process of adaptation may be either hindered or helped by local demographic factors, social mores, governmental action, and competitive pressures.

The process of adaptation can be greatly accelerated by the actions of aggressive individual firms.

and, he concluded:

Retailing and the broader field of marketing are not only affected by the total economic environment, but in turn, they may themselves affect this environment. In societies with high discretionary incomes and abundant goods, there are pressures for improvement in retailing efficiency. The degree to which these economic pressures result in the evolution and adoption of new methods of retailing operations depends on the total environment (cultural acceptance or resistance of change, demographic and geographical influences, the political and legal framework, the strength of pressure groups such as business competitors and unions).

The observations made by Boyd et al. [4], Dewey [7], Elgass [8], Stewart [26], and Taylor [27] seem to support Cundiff's conclusions.

Specific Environmental Influences

The findings from the author's study established distinct relationships between *certain specific forces* in the environment and retailing institutions, methods, and techniques. Thus, the study attempted to refine the Hollander and Cundiff explanations of retail development by identifying a whole set of specific environmental factors that appear to be related to retailing development, and by further establishing the manner in which retailing is so affected. These findings showed that the relationship between the main retailing features and specific environmental forces, within Ceylon, were as follows for certain of the important variables tested:

a. The degree of product specialization of retail shops is a direct function of per capita incomes, level of economic growth, density of population, urbanization of population, and aggressiveness of manufacturers' and wholesalers' selling methods; and an inverse function of consumer preference for neighborhood shops.

b. The extent of the use of self-service is a direct function of density of population, newspaper circulation and readership, availability of trade credit, and the general level of advertising; and an inverse function of consumer preference for daily shopping in small quantities.

c. The extent of the use of fixed and marked prices is a direct function of literacy and newspaper circulation; and an inverse function of consumer preference for daily shopping in small quantities, and consumer preference for neighborhood shops.

d. The extent of the use of sophisticated margin policies is a direct function of literacy, circulation of newspapers, and aggressiveness of manufacturers' and wholesalers' selling methods; and an inverse function of consumer preference for daily shopping in small quantities, and consumer preference for neighborhood shops.

e. The extent of the use of retail advertising is a direct function of literacy; and an inverse function of consumer preference for daily shopping in small quantities, consumer preference for credit, and consumer preference for neighborhood shops.

f. The extent of the use of loss leader type selling is a direct function of literacy, newspaper readership, and the aggressiveness of manufacturers' and wholesalers' selling methods; and an inverse function of consumer preference for credit.

It is admitted that to the extent that retailers can change the environment (e.g., by changing consumer preferences through advertising), retailing will become an independent variable and the economic and social environments dependent variables. It is believed, however, that instances where the economic or social environments will be a function of retailing will be much fewer than the instances where retailing will be a function of these environmental factors.

These findings show a relationship between retailing institutions and retailing practices in Ceylon and per capita incomes, economic growth, demographic factors such as density and urbanization of population, literacy levels, circulation and readership of newspapers, availability of trade credit, selling methods of manufacturers and wholesalers, and consumer preferences, in Ceylon. Placed in the context of existing explanations of retailing,[5] these findings suggest that the existing explanations may be refined and extended by the specific environmental variables identified in this study.

From a theoretical point of view, because institutional changes are slower, it could be said that *retailing institutions* (e.g., product specialized stores) are a function of the environmental factors of the *immediate past period*. Similarly, the *retailing practices* may be said to be a function of the environmental factors of the *same period*.

Toward a Theory of Retail Development

It is useful to go back to the concept of a market as postulated by Alderson.

---

[5] The descriptive material in some works (for example Hall [10] p. 62, Mueller and Garoian [21] pp. 8, 11, 14, Nystrom [22] pp. 67–8, Pennance and Yamey [24], Shawver [25] pp. 43–4) seem to suggest that some retail institutions have evolved through increasing product and function specialization. This is essentially an extension, to the field of retailing, of the economic theory of the division of labor. Thus specialization is best treated as a process used in the development of retail institutions, rather than an explanation of retail development as such.

According to Alderson the market could be treated as an organized behavior system.[6] This concept could be used in a much broader way: the market can be conceived of as several organized behavior systems (each of a company, its competitors, suppliers, channels, and of customers) operating in the larger environment known as society. The society is composed of individuals and their formal and informal associations; organized government; and the society's culture as represented by its economy, its technology and its social, political, economic, and technological institutions (see Figure 1). The organization and operation of a marketing system is, to a large extent, conditioned by this environment, which may be thought of as outside the marketing system. The marketing system, including the retail segment of the system, is then operating in an environment of economic, technological, social, demographic, cultural, political, and legal forces.

The relationships established in

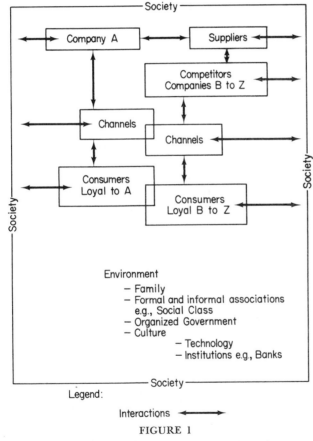

FIGURE 1

The Market Seen as a Behavior System in Society

[6] Wroe Alderson introduced the concept of the market as an organized behavior system in [2] and expanded it in [1].

Ceylon suggest the hypothesis that certain environmental conditions such as per capita incomes, economic growth, density and urbanization of population, literacy, newspaper circulation and readership, availability of trade credit, aggressiveness of manufacturers' and wholesalers' selling methods, general advertising, and sophisticated consumer preferences are a precondition for the adoption of certain "advanced" types of retail institutions and methods. It could be further hypothesized that the type of institution is a function of these environmental forces as they existed in the immediate past, and that the retailing practices are a function of these forces as they presently exist.

The wheel of retailing concept is built around the innovator. The thesis of the present paper is that both the innovator and the process he may use (e.g., specialization) are limited by the environment. If the forces in the environment permit, these retail institutions, methods, and techniques can be introduced. And as long as the forces in the environment permit, these institutions, methods, and techniques can continue to exist. There cannot, then, be an instance of "*the* best institutions, methods, and techniques," as what is most appropriate will be different from one environment to another. A retailing system can be meaningfully "advanced" or "primitive" depending only on whether the environment in which that system operates is advanced or primitive.

If this is, indeed, the case, we can speculate on the nature of this relationship in more specific terms than simply "advanced and primitive." If we identify stages of socio-economic development (as defined by the environmental variables stated in the hypothesis, above), then we should be able to predict in general terms the kind of retail pattern we will find associated with them.

Marketing, and particularly retailing, are social processes developed to handle the distribution of a society's output of goods and services. Prior to the existence of a market society, this process was called barter, and the exchange was of goods for goods, or of goods for services. With the extension of monetization, agriculture was transformed from peasants growing for exchange to farmers growing for cash, and every task (including feudal obligations) came to have a more or less fixed monetary reward. It was then, and only then, that a market society came into existence. Even today, some undeveloped economies that retain peasant agriculture and quasi-feudal non-cash obligations are not pure market societies.

All countries, according to the concept as set out in the hypothesis above, go through six stages of development: tribal, peasant, early commercial, highly commercial, early industrial, and highly industrial. Each phase is characterized by different types of agricultural and industrial production, different forms of commerce, different structures of social organization, different demographic features, different degrees of development in infra-structure, and different levels of personal incomes. During these six phases of development, the needs of the people (consumers) are different, and patterns of consumption are different. For each stage of development, the main features are as follows:

Tribal Stage

Agricultural production is for local consumption only, and industrial production is limited to crude agricultural implements; commerce is in the form of barter between individuals, and social organization is feudal; population density is low, and there is no urbanization; there is no infra-structure; the concept of income levels and their diffusion is inapplicable. During this stage consumer needs are rudimentary, and the predominant retail outlets are itinerant traders.

Peasant Stage

Agricultural production is for local and regional consumption; industrial production is limited to crude agricultural implements; commerce is in the form of barter between individuals, and organized barter; the social organization is quasi-feudal with a small upper class and very large lower class; population density and urbanization are very low; transportation and communications are primitive; general business is very primitive; literacy, and the circulation and readership of newspapers are very low; income levels are very low, and incomes are very highly skewed; consumer needs are basic. During this stage the predominant retail outlets are exchange markets, with a few itinerant traders, and fewer country storekeepers.

Early Commercial Stage

Agricultural production is for local and regional consumption; commercial crops are grown for export; industrial production is limited to crude agricultural implements; the form of commerce is organized barter and cash exchange, and powerful foreign merchant groups operate in imports, exports and retailing; social organization is quasi-feudal, with a small upper class and very large lower class; population density is low to medium and urbanization is low; transportation and communications, and business are little developed; literacy, and newspaper circulation and readership are low; income

levels are low to medium, and incomes are highly skewed; consumer needs are mostly for essentials and a few non-essentials. During this stage country storekeepers predominate with a few itinerant traders and a lesser number of general stores.

Highly Commercial Stage

Agricultural production is for local and regional consumption, and commercial crops for export; industrial production is of modern agricultural implements and of crude consumer essentials; the form of commerce is a cash exchange; powerful foreign groups operate in imports, exports, and retailing, and a small local merchant group operates in retailing; the social organization is along a small upper class, a small middle class, and a large lower class; the density and urbanization of population are medium; transportation and communications, and general business are developed; literacy and the circulation and readership of newspapers are medium; the levels of income are medium but their diffusion is skewed; consumers need more of essentials than of non-essentials. During this period the predominant retail outlets are general stores with a few product specialized stores.

Early Industrial Stage

Agricultural production is for local and regional consumption, and commercial crops are grown for export; industrial production is of modern agricultural implements and import-substitute consumer goods; the form of commerce is within a cash exchange, with a powerful foreign group operating in imports, exports and retailing, and a substantial local merchant group operating in retailing; there are small upper and middle classes and a large lower class;

population density and urbanization are high; transportation and communications, as well as general business, are highly developed; literacy, and the circulation and readership of newspapers are high; income levels are medium to high; and incomes are diffused; consumer needs for essentials and for non-essentials are about equal. In this period the predominant retail outlet is a product specialized store.

Highly Industrial Stage

Agricultural production is for local and regional consumption, and commercial crops are for export; industrial production is of modern agricultural implements and manufactured consumer goods (at this stage there is heavy industry and secondary manufacturing); commerce is on a cash exchange, and the local merchant retailing group is substantial; there is a small upper class, a large middle class, and a small lower class, population density and urbanization are very high; transportation and communication, and general business are very highly developed; literacy, and circulation and readership of newspapers are very high; income levels are high and incomes are diffused; consumers need more of non-essentials than of essentials. During this stage mass merchandising stores are the predominant retail outlets with few product specialized stores.

It will be seen that the supply factors for goods (as determined by production and importation) and the demand factors for goods (as determined by consumer needs) are different during the different stages; therefore, the dominant retail outlets will be found to be correspondingly different, both in organization and the selling methods used.

During the early stages of a country's development the retail institutions are small and undifferentiated in product or in function. During this stage many primitive retail institutions such as farmers' markets and general stores predominate. Most retailers have limited capital which curbs physical expansion or use of complex and expensive merchandising techniques. Retailers enjoy a low prestige position among the people of the community, who believe that they are making money from an occupation that is unproductive and parasitic from the community's point of view. These retailers have to take the initiative in making transactions with suppliers who are also of low status in the community, but powerful because of their financial position. During these early times, retailers believe, as do the suppliers, that demand tends to be fixed and that consumers will come to them even though they do nothing to make the consumers come to them. The consumers for their part seek only to fulfill their basic needs from their limited resources.

Production, wholesaling, and retailing in the modern profit-oriented manner started only after the 18th century, after the commercialized market societies had got under way. Profit was deemed evil and those who profited, especially from buying and selling, were accounted as vulgar. Commercialization has helped to overcome this belief, but there are some who hold this view in the most industrialized countries.

With increasing development the environment changed. Marketing and retailing evolved to meet the needs of the changing patterns of supply and demand. As the supply of goods increased in variety and quantity, and as the demands of consumers changed with their needs (which they themselves had changed with changes in the social and demographic features of the society, and with the changes in consumer incomes), there were, at each stage of development, corresponding changes in the institutions and in the methodological innovations in marketing, and especially in retailing, to sell off the supply and satisfy the demands (Figure 2).

It is the transition from a sellers' to a buyers' market, which came with extensive industrialization, that created new retailing norms; the output of the mass production facilities could be sold only through mass marketing institutions and mass marketing techniques. The increasing competition led to the development of profit-oriented management techniques for marketing and for retailing. For example, it is only in competitive societies that have adopted these modern management theories that retailers think of long-run profit maxi-

mization. These retailers in societies still wedded to the traditional economic theories think in terms of short-run profit maximization.

The process of product specialization in retailing, for example, can start only when the environmental factors are similar to those in a highly commercial society. Product specialized stores will be predominant only in early industrial societies. The wheel pattern of development can start only in early industrial societies. And mass merchandising outlets, which are really function specialized stores, can predominate only in highly industrial societies.

The environmental thesis of retail development that is presented here is applicable to retailing in any of the six phases above. Developments during the highly commercial phase are better understood if both the environmental factors and (at least partially) the spe-

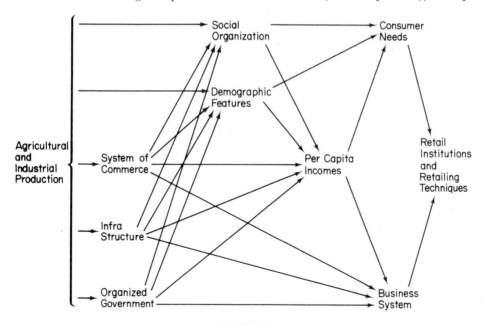

FIGURE 2

How Environmental Factors Affect Retailing

cialization process are considered. A study of developments during the early industrial phase makes it imperative that both environment and specialization be considered, as specialization is the dominant process during this phase. Additionally, a consideration of the wheel pattern promotes a better understanding of some developments during the early industrial phase. Developments during the highly industrial phase are best understood in terms of the environmental factors *plus* a consideration of the process of specialization *plus* a consideration of changes along a wheel pattern.

Retailing institutions, methods and techniques evolve *pari passu* with an evolving social structure, which in turn has evolving political, economic and business components. Certain combinations of the economic, political and business components produce specific social structures that create the need for certain retailing institutions, methods and techniques. At respective points in the development of the society, the retailers are able and willing to offer a specific package of retail institutions, methods and techniques, and also the consumers are able and willing to accept that retailing package.[7] Different countries with differing economic, political and business conditions have differing

societies, and therefore have differing retail systems. Even within the same country, different regions with differing combinations of economic, political and business conditions, and therefore with differing societies, have differing retail systems. Thus, the retail system differs with the different environments provided for retailing and a retail system changes with changes in that environment.

As has already been submitted, retailing is a social process, and a retail institution is a social institution. It is the nature of the society (politically, economically, and socially) that determines what that particular social institution can and will do in and for the society. The mandate that retailer members of a society are granted to operate a retail system will be rooted in and, therefore, circumscribed by, the political, economic, social, and business conditions in that society. The personal assets and aspirations of both the retailer and non-retailer (consumer) members of that society will therefore limit the mandate sought by retailers and the license granted by the consumers.

The retail institutions, methods and techniques must then necessarily be a function of the political, economic, social and business environments in which they operate.

REFERENCES

1. Alderson Wroe, *Dynamic Market Behaviour,* Homewood, Ill.: Richard D. Irwin, 1965.
2. ———, *Marketing Behaviour and Executive Action,* Homewood, Ill.: Richard D. Irwin, 1957.
3. Barger, Harold, *Distribution's Place in the American Economy Since 1896,* Princeton: Princeton University Press, 1955.

---

[7] For an interesting study of the retailing package approach see Gurein [9].

4. Boyd, Harper W., el Sherbini, Abdel Azziz, and Sheriff, Ahmed Fouad, "Channels of Distribution for Consumer Goods in Egypt," *Journal of Marketing,* October 1961.

5. Cundiff, Edward W., "Concepts in Comparative Retailing," *Journal of Marketing,* January 1965.

6. Converse, P. D., "Mediocrity in Retailing," *Journal of Marketing,* April 1959.

7. Dewey, Alice G., *Peasant Marketing in Java,* New York: Free Press of Glencoe, 1962.

8. Elgass, George A., "Marketing in Japan" in W. D. Stevens (ed.), *Social Responsibilities of Marketing,* Proceedings of Winter Conference, 1961 American Marketing Association, 1962.

9. Gurein, Joseph R., "Limitations of Supermarkets in Spain," *Journal of Marketing,* October 1964.

10. Hall, Margaret, Knapp, John, and Winsten, Christopher, *Distribution in Great Britain and North America,* New York: Oxford University Press, 1961.

11. Hollander, Stanley, "Retailing: Cause or Effect" in W. S. Decker (ed.), *Emerging Concepts in Marketing,* Proceedings of Winter Conference, 1962, American Marketing Association, 1963.

12. ———, "Competition and Evolution in Retailing," *Stores,* September 1960.

13. ———, "Wheel of Retailing" in H. C. Barksdale (ed.), *Marketing in Progress: Patterns and Potentials,* New York: Holt, Rinehart and Winston, Inc., 1964.

14. Holton, Richard, *Supply and Demand Structure in Food Retailing Services,* Cambridge, Mass: Harvard University Press, 1954.

15. Jefferys, James B., *Retail Trading in Britain 1850–1950,* Cambridge: Cambridge University Press, 1954.

16. Leighton, David S. R., *Merchandising and Promotional Policies of Discount Houses,* Unpublished Doctoral Dissertation, Harvard University, Graduate School of Business Administration, 1956.

17. Levy, Herman, *The Shops of Britain,* London: Routledge & Kegan Paul, 1949.

18. Linden, Fabian, "Department Stores in a Decade of Change," *Conference Board Business Record,* Vol. XV No. 7, No. 8 and No. 10.

19. Lochwing, D. A., "Resourceful Merchants," *Barrons,* Vol. 38 (Nov. 17, 1958).

20. McNair, Malcolm P., "Progress in Distribution: An Appraisal After 30 Years," *Boston Conference on Distribution,* 1958.

21. Mueller, Willard E., and Garoian, Leon, *Changes in the Market of Grocery Retailing,* Madison: University of Wisconsin Press, 1961.

22. Nystrom, Paul, *Economics of Retailing: Retailing Institution and Trends,* 3rd. ed. New York: Ronald Press Co., 1932.

23. Oakes, Ralph H., "Price Differentials for Identical Items in Chain, Voluntary Group and Independent Grocery Stores," *Journal of Marketing,* October 1949.

24. Pennace, F. G., and Yamey, B. S., "Competition in the Retail Grocery Trade 1850–1939," *Economica,* XXII (November 1955).

25. Shawver, D. L., *Development of Theories of Retail Price Determination,* Urbana: University of Illinois Press, 1956.

26. Stewart, Charles F., "Changing Middle Eastern Market," *Journal of Marketing,* January 1961.

27. Taylor, Donald A., "Retailing in Brazil," *Journal of Marketing,* July 1959.

The Changing Economic Base and Its Significance to Marketers

David J. Luck

The economic base of any community is a prime determinant of its destiny, just as the nation's economic base underlies its strength and its citizens' welfare. Many groups and individuals have professional, as well as personal, concern with the economic bases of their hometowns, regions, and nation. These should include marketers, since the size and growth of communities' economic bases bear direct relationship to market potentials. Marketing educators have several reasons for interest in this subject, on which I shall dwell later, although little attention is paid to it in the literature of the field.

There has been a marked shift in economic bases in the past fifteen years, whether viewed locally, regionally, or nationally. My intrigue with this, some four years ago, led me to study a region in the middle Mississippi and Ohio river basins. Then I was engaged by the State of Illinois in long-range projections of that state's economic base.[1] The exploration is continued in this paper relative to a broader, more diversified region, and into certain questions.

This is an empirical study of change. Its purposes may be summed up in this manner:

1. To delineate economic base changes within specified regions and among cities in those regions.
2. To inquire into certain questions, to wit:
   a. What have been the relative economic growths among cities with certain types of economic bases?
   b. How uniform have been these tendencies?
   c. Can such categorizations and trends be employed reliably in market forecasting?
   d. Among the three economic sectors, does one have primacy over the others as an economic generator?
3. What is the significance of these findings to marketers and to marketing educators?

Concepts and Methods

The conventional division of various enterprises and employments in the economic base is threefold: *(a) Primary* sector, the "underlying" industries that produce natural wealth—particularly

Reprinted from *Business Perspectives,* College of Business and Administration, Southern Illinois University, Carbondale, Summer 1968, Vol. 4, No. 4, by permission of the author and editor.

[1] D. J. Luck, *Service Industry Study of the Illinois Economic Study* (Springfield: Illinois Department of Economic and Business Development, 1967).

agriculture, mining, and fisheries; *(b) Secondary* sector, those that fabricate materials into finished products—manufacturing and construction; and *(c) Tertiary* sector, which embraces all services—utilities, transportation, trade, and consumer, business, and governmental services.

The terms "primary," "secondary" and "tertiary" connote traditional views of these sectors. A view long prevailed that economies rested mainly on primary sectors. The dominance of manufacturing and ease of importing natural materials, however, brought recognition that an economy can be very strong with reliance on the secondary sector without main dependence on its primary industries. The tertiary sector remains regarded, in the prevailing view, as wholly dependent on the two more basic sectors and not itself an independent generator of economic wealth. Services have sometimes been derogated as merely "taking in one another's washing."

I doubt whether this traditional view of the services sector is still accurate today. Some services such as insurance in a sense can be exported from a community and thus bring in revenue and support employment independently of its primary and secondary sectors. A number of services that are performed in the community bring in outside income. These may include transportation, finance, medical services, and (conspicuously) higher education. This role of services may to a degree characterize regional and national economic bases, as witnessed by tourism in the Hawaiian Islands or Switzerland. The latter country also, of course, is heavily supported by international banking.

The region chosen for this study is described on the map. It represents a "center cut" of the United States, border to Gulf. It includes both northern and southern economies—the diversified manufacturing heart of the nation, and rich agriculture from Corn Belt to cotton areas. While it lacks some of the extreme features found in the east and far west, it appears to typify most of the United States. A relevant test of its normalcy is a comparison of this total area's percentage of employment in manufacturing and in services. Its manufacturing employment, as a percentage of total employment is 31.1 per cent, which is very close to the national percentage of 31.9 per cent. Its service employment percentage is nearly as close to the nation's: 62.3 per cent versus 61.1 per cent for the United States.

Included for individual study were 170 cities or city clusters. These are all that had over 10,000 population in both 1950 and 1960, with certain exclusions. Suburban cities were excluded in some cases where data were not available, but for the largest cities their immediate counties were taken entire. Satellite cities were included individually and, where immediately adjoining central cities appeared to be highly symbiotic, they were treated as a single city.

Employment data were used to determine the economic orientation of cities' economic bases and their growths. Effects of change were appraised in terms of sales, payrolls, population, and employment. Research in this subject faces a distinct paucity of data. Only the Census of Population offers comprehensive data on industry or employment and payrolls. Comprehensive sales data, however, are found only in the Census of Business, which covers a different set of years. By averaging a largely overlapping ten-year span the census information could be computed to relate to Census of Population data. More recent and frequent payroll and employment data may be had only from Social Security records; these confront us with

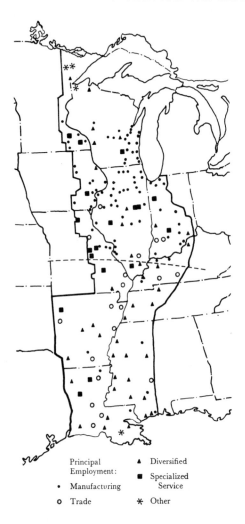

Principal
Employment: ▲ Diversified

                     ■ Specialized
• Manufacturing   Service

○ Trade   * Other

the postwar splurge of durable goods purchasing subsided around 1950. Durable goods purchasing has since had its ups and downs but with a slightly upward secular trend. Nondurables have tended to hold a declining share of consumer expenditures. Services, however, have been experiencing a nearly constant, although gradual, increase in share of expenditures. Today they have risen to 44 per cent of consumer expenditures. Continuation of this rate will find more than half of the consumer dollar going into services around 1980. As Victor Fuchs has pointed out, the United States is becoming the first predominantly service economy in the world. While incomes rise and consumers tend to become surfeited with goods, the trend to services will not abate.

Since services usually are labor-intensive, contrasted with the capital-intensiveness of the primary and secondary sectors, their share of employment exceeds considerably their share of expenditures. Since this is approaching 64 per cent of total employment nationally, many areas and cities may be expected to have 70 to 80 per cent of their employment in services. For the state of Illinois, whose service employment percentage is roughly the same as the nation's, I have projected this for 1980: more than 3 out of 4 employed persons will work for some service firm or institution.

One of my purposes is to ascertain the shift in urban economies—in direction, nature, and location. If changing orientation is to be determined, one must first categorize the meaningful types of orientation, in measurable terms. To this end, four types of city economies are identified: manufacturing cities, trade cities, specialized service cities, and diversified cities.

The factor employed to type cities, in this research, is the number em-

incomplete coverage of employments, a different situs definition than in the Census of Population, and different years covered. Despite all of these problems, I believe that valid statistical inferences are afforded by the use of these data.

Trends

The United States economy has been undergoing fundamental changes since ployed in each industry. Only three kinds of industry are large enough in any city to place it in one of the first three groups: manufacturing of all classifications, wholesale–retail trade, and "special" services whose nature is one of importing revenue from outside. Among the latter, the particular services that often are large enough to characterize a city's orientation are higher education, hospital–medical, and government. Diversified cities are those in which no industry is sufficiently large to place it in one of the three other categories.

Long examination of cities within the region studied led to this criterion for typing its economic orientation: either manufacturing or trade services, or specialized service must constitute over 24 per cent of total employment. If none equals this, the city is categorized as a diversified one.

The 170 cities were categorized for the employment distribution in 1950 and also in 1960, utilizing Census of Population data. The numbers in these years are presented in Table 1.

The Total line in Table 1 indicates a general reduction in retail and wholesale trade's share of employment, which may be related both to advancing efficiency and to the declining share of income being used to purchase goods.

Nearly two-thirds of these cities tended toward becoming more service-oriented, either generally or emphasizing specialized services. There was no general tendency, however, to decrease manufacturing orientation among those cities that were based predominantly on manufacturing in 1950. Quite the contrary, more cities which were former trade cities shifted in that direction during the decade.

Our total vertical section through the United States contains marked differences between its northern and southern parts. A distinct difference is notable north and south of a line drawn east–west lying just south of St. Louis and Owensboro, Kentucky. The northern area, as shown in Table 1, contains two-thirds of the cities; over 60 per cent of these were manufacturing-oriented in 1950. In the same year the southern area's cities were predominantly engaged in trade; only 15 per cent were manufacturing-oriented.

By 1960, more northern cities had moved toward manufacturing orientation, with three-fourths of them in this category. Trade orientation had dropped sharply due in a few cases to cities developing strongly in specialized services but, more typically, to growing manufacturing employment. The south presents only one similarity: in growth

TABLE 1

Cities Economic Orientation, 1950 and 1960

Region	Number of Cities									
	Manufacturing		Trade		Diversified		Specialized Service		Other	
	1950	1960	1950	1960	1950	1960	1950	1960	1950	1960
Total area	82	90(+ 8)	41	19(−22)	33	40(+ 7)	10	17(+7)	4	4
Northern	73	84(+11)	10	4(− 6)	18	13(− 5)	9	12(+3)	3	3
Southern	9	6(− 3)	31	15(−16)	14	29(+15)	1	5(+4)	1	1

of specialized service cities, manufacturing cities actually declined, trade orientation declined heavily, while services rose broadly and made diversified cities the principal type in the south.

These figures, as they represent only the numbers of cities with particular orientations, might give rise to erroneous inferences. For instance, manufacturing employment grew more in the southern ($+15.1$ per cent) than in the northern cities ($+13.2$ per cent), but the southern growth was well scattered among most cities and is computed on a relatively small base. Retail employment was growing in most cities but far more slowly in both northern cities ($+7.0$ per cent) and southern ($+12.8$ per cent). The greatest growth, in relative terms, was in the services outside of trade, which swelled by practically 21 per cent in these cities over the decade. It was greatest among the northern cities (which were largely manufacturing-oriented), but is concealed in Table 1 because many of these cities employ a very large proportion in manufacturing.

Analysis of Effects Associated with Economic Bases

Having seen that a considerable shift has been taking place in cities' economic bases, one would be curious how this has affected them in economic terms. I have not at this point attempted a cause-and-effect determination, but certain changes in these cities that would be marketers' chief interests have been calculated. These factors are the individual cities' changes in population, income, and retail sales during the 1950–60 interim. Table 2 categorizes the cities according to their 1960 economic bases. The median has been

TABLE 2

Economic Changes in Cities Classified by Economic Orientation from 1950 to 1960

Economic Orientation of Cities	Percentage Change from 1950 to 1960		
	Population	Aggregate Income	Retail Sales
Manufacturing	+18.5	+109	+49.9
Trade	+16.7	+125	+47.9
Specialized services	+19.6	+140	+63.0
Diversified	+20.4	+120	+63.9

Sources: Population and Median Income from *Census of Population,* 1950 and 1960 Retail Sales: Census of Business, 1949, 1954 and 1963.

chosen as the indicator of central tendency because with the small number of items in the calculations, the arithmetic means have proved to be overly influenced by extreme values.

It should be explained, in connection with Table 2, that aggregate income could be determined comprehensively only with the median incomes, given for the individual cities, multiplied by their populations. This is only an approximation of the aggregate but is the best available. No total enumeration city figures are available for 1950 and 1960 retail sales; therefore, a roughly equivalent span of time had to be approximated by first averaging the 1949 and 1954 data and then comparing the average of these two with the 1963 data for each city.

Turning to the data in Table 2, it is first apparent that generally the cities that rely most on manufacturing as their economic base had only mediocre performance in that decade. They generated substantially less income and were below average in retail sales gains. It may be surmised that this was related to the relatively slow growth of manufacturing employment; and that, despite the relatively higher wages paid in manufacturing, they were not offering the mix of attractive services that would bring income into the city or entire service expenditures from their residents. There may be a cultural explanation, too, in that their populations may be less inclined to purchase services than the other city types.

Trade cities tended to have a more lackluster performance, with poorest improvement in retail sales despite their heavier reliance on trade employment. This might well have been expected, however, on the premises that these may be cities that have blossomed less in the non-goods-related services, lack the stimulus of manufacturing export revenues, and do not offer the variety and attractiveness of services that the other cities do.

Diversified and specialized service cities are strong in service business; both therefore seem to benefit from the growth of service consumption. Specialized service cities, we should note, tend to be medium or smaller-sized cities in which one or two services that attract income stand out: for example, Rochester, Minnesota (medical–hospital); Fayetteville, Arkansas (education); Madison, Wisconsin (education–government). It is hardly surprising that these cities have not surpassed the diversified

cities in development of retail trade. The diversified cities include some of the larger cities in the overall region (for example, Louisville and New Orleans) and often have strength in one of the specialized services to buoy them (for example, DeKalb, Illinois), although such a service is not predominant.

There were, then, substantial enough differences in the performance of the service-oriented cities to give our categorization important significance. The analysis may be too gross, however, when it is considered that the northern and southern portions of the studied region have notable contrasts in their mixes of the four city types (the north being predominantly manufacturing and specialized service cities, the south largely diversified and trade cities) and in their economic environments. In Table 3 the north and south are separated for individual consideration.

Southern cities have shown consistently higher growth rates in both population and retail sales. That there is one exception (trade cities' income growth) is not surprising, for the medians of such small samples are unstable. In both north and south, specialized service cities displayed their superior performance. Diversified cities were second best in northern performance but

TABLE 3
Economic Changes in Southern and Northern Cities from 1950 to 1960

	Median Percentage Change from 1950 to 1960					
	Southern Cities			Northern Cities		
Economic Orientation	Population	Income	Retail Sales	Population	Income	Retail Sales
Manufacturing	+32.5	+176	+68.1	+17.5	+106	+46.2
Trade	+20.2	117	+55.5	+ 3.0	143	+43.9
Specialized services	+26.8	315	+76.4	+20.9	196	+63.0
Diversified	+21.3	120	+68.2	+ 5.6	111	+53.0

lagged behind manufacturing cities in the south overall. Both trade and manufacturing cities had stronger growth in the south than north, which may be attributed to the less mature stage of southern industrialization and growth. Furthermore, southern trade and manufacturing cities mainly are the minor ones, with small bases as growth centers. In general, the conclusion remains that the more service-oriented cities had markedly better growth in market opportunity.

Market forecasts after 1960 are now given on the basis of the observations of the 1950–60 trends. If these forecasts stand up, generalizations from those findings may be permissible. For this testing the only available comprehensive data are those published in *County Business Patterns*, of which I will use the 1959 and 1964 data. Drawbacks of these data must be recognized: (*a*) they represent whole counties, and therefore among the cities in our total sample we properly can include their counties only where the central city dominates the county employment; and (*b*) *County Business Patterns* publishes data of "taxable" employment and payrolls under the Social Security system, which excludes all public employment and some other service employments that are rapidly growing, thus sharply understating services' growth.

Returning to the hypotheses drawn from the 1950–1960 changes, these would lead to this forecast for cities' economic growth in the 1959–1964 period:

1. Specialized service cities would have the fastest growth in market potential.
2. Diversified and trade cities would stand second and third in growth.
3. Manufacturing cities would exhibit slowest growth.

In this analysis I would group cities according to their 1960 economic orientations. Instead of city data, as explained, I have to use their counties' data, but in each instance used the principal city dominates county employment. The median growths of the cities' counties from 1959 to 1964, using data from *County Business Patterns*, are given in Table 4.

The forecast is borne out for the leadership of specialized service cities and for the slowest performance of the manufacturing-oriented. Trade cities, however, surpassed diversified cities, which may be attributable to their faster development of manufacturing employment. A striking aspect is that the vigor of all three service-oriented types of cities carries over to greater expansion in the manufacturing sector than the manufacturing-oriented cities.

This leads to another question about

TABLE 4
Economic Changes in Counties from 1959 to 1964

Economic Orientation of County	Median Percentage Change from 1959 to 1964				
	Total Payroll	Total Employment	Service Employment	Manufacturing Employment	Manufacturing Payroll
Manufacturing	+29.0	+ 9.0	+10.4	+ 6.2	+24.9
Trade	+44.2	+15.1	+21.9	+16.7	+52.0
Specialized Services	+48.3	+17.5	+23.3	+14.6	+52.3
Diversified	+31.0	+11.9	+16.7	+ 6.2	+30.8

communities' economic growth: Is manufacturing employment and payroll really the primary cause of cities' growth, according to the traditional view? While the data do not suffice to offer a definitive answer, they do shed light in two respects:

1. The manufacturing payroll increase rate, for the 10 cities which had the fastest growth in that factor, was compared with their total payroll growth. If manufacturing is *primary* in stimulating the total local economy, then the total payroll growth rate should at least equal manufacturing payroll growth. But the contrary was found. The arithmetic mean of these counties' manufacturing payroll increase was 94.1 per cent, against only a 63.6 per cent growth in total payroll.
2. When the 21 counties with fastest total payroll growth were examined (including all with more than 50 per cent growth in the five-year span), it was found that in 10 of these counties total payroll growth exceeded the rate of manufacturing payrolls.

Therefore it appears doubtful that manufacturing is any more *primary* than services as the generator in the economic base.

Implications

The data and theses examined in this study hold some intriguing implications. We shall state these for four different disciplines.

1. For *economic base* theory. Relative to communities and possibly to much larger areas, the concept that any of the three economic sectors is "primary," "secondary," or "tertiary" appears to be highly doubtful. More accurate and useful classification and analysis perhaps should instead consider various industries and employments with regard to their ability to export their output or to bring in revenues from outside, regardless of whether they produce goods or services.
2. For *economic development*. The attitude that a community should strive to bring manufacturing industries, above all, into its economy appears obsolete in our high-level economy. Indeed "smokestack chasing," when successful, may create a community environment adverse to growth in the big and burgeoning service sector. My other study has found that there are hundreds of specialized and novel services offered in the most advanced service cities that are not yet developed in the typical city. It is suggested that the focus of industrial development be broadened to seek and encourage service businesses, too.
3. For *marketing practitioners,* two rather apparent implications emerge:
   a. That many services offer excellent sales potentials and are far from saturation. Continuing prosperity is likely to increase the demand for services far more than the demand for goods. There are so many recent successful ventures of corporations and franchisers in services that this would not be news to many alert entrepreneurs.
   b. That market research should incorporate in the analysis the factor of cities' or areas' type of economic base. It is premature to judge the weight that such a factor might be given, but its significance is evident.
4. Finally, these are the implications for *marketing education:*
   a. Consumption expenditure and market growth patterns have been undergoing vital changes. Textbooks and lectures should recognize this and be abreast of these dynamic forces.
   b. The marketing of services has been a neglected subject while the discipline has concentrated almost wholly on marketing of goods. Basic textbooks at last are beginning to devote one chapter to services marketing, but this does not appear to have entered advanced courses.

c. It is not possible to say much that is meaningful about services marketing, however, until extensive research has been conducted. Not only has hardly any research been published about services, but little heed at all—on the part of either economists or marketing scholars—has been paid to the fact that the economy has become a service one. It is time to swing the spotlight on the service sector.

The foregoing findings and interpretations are only a tentative early step. I have barely gone below the surface of some overt and limited facts. The material needs to be expanded, particularly in the time dimension, and to have further plumbing with regression analyses and measurements of the reliability and incidence of the market potentials implications. It would be very desirable, too, to bring in other influential environmental factors.

Other avenues of research are made apparent. For instance, it appears feasible to determine the degree of causation or impact of the various sectors (when sensibly categorized) on an economy. Surely various important contributions might be made with studies of the marketing functions, of the operating economics, and of the management of service enterprises. Perhaps the service sector now offers the most unexplored and fruitful area for empirical marketing studies. It may be added that not very much is known about markets and marketing on a macro scale and that a great deal more empirical and descriptive study is needed. It is profoundly hoped that these phenomena will attract the keenest and most inquisitive minds among marketing scholars.

Multiple-City Complexes: A New View of Consumer Markets

John R. Lowry

Our perspective of consumer markets generally includes population, types of areas in which the consumers live, and location of these consumer areas. Upon locating the consumer markets, perhaps the next step for most firms is the analysis of the markets in terms of potential or expected sales. Buying habits, number of buyers, and spendable income provide the means for determining these estimates or potentials of the consumer markets. However, important considerations in analyzing consumer markets are sometimes neglected. These include considerations of the location of large markets (especially the growth markets), their spatial composition, and how market areas are delineated.

The determination of consumer market areas on the basis of population statistics is generally acceptable as one of the most critical factors of a market evaluation. Although generally acceptable, immediate difficulties do arise. For instance, what are the boundaries or limits to a particular market? A political basis, such as a city or county boundary, may be used. The big problem, however, is where to draw the line that accurately separates one market from another. The concept of the central city has helped to solve this problem, but because of changes in the internal spatial composition of the markets, central city concepts are no longer as acceptable as in the past. What view, then, will give optimum knowledge about the various consumer markets? I believe that a multiple-city complex concept may be the answer.

A New View of Consumer Markets

Many of today's consumer markets are groups of integrated and interrelated cities. Multiple-city complexes usually involve a central city and a number of related cities, which are approximately equal to or exceed the size of the central city. In real terms, the multiple-city complex consists of several cities existing in a common area—this can be called a market area. Consumer buying activities and employment centers correspond more to the city of residence or contiguous city than to the central city. Consumer markets are not central cities with sprawling unlimited suburbs, nor are they composed of many people

Reprinted from *Business Perspectives*, College of Business and Administration, Southern Illinois University, Carbondale, Winter 1968, Vol. 4, No. 2, by permission of the author and editor.

living in some meaningless pattern throughout one or more counties. These markets are a complex of several cities which are bound together for the practical reasons of distribution and consumption activities, although they still exist as independent urban communities.

In the period before 1950, people did less daily traveling than they do now. At that time a metropolitan market could have been thought of as a small area with a central city and nearby cities which depend on and use the market facilities of the central city. Today, however, central city influence as a market center for the distribution of consumer goods is less important and is relative to the total trade area. The population of the area outside the central city has greatly increased in the period from 1950 to the present—especially when contrasted to the growth of the central city. These changes in the residential living habits of the population resulted in consumer buying on a much larger scale outside of the central city market places and the expansion of metropolitan markets to include greater trade areas (in terms of distances).

Rather than setting a political boundary of consumer markets or setting absolute limits to area boundaries of metropolitan markets, multiple-city complexes (MCX's) are determined according to cities that are in close proximity to each other. A general limit of about 50 miles is used as a restriction in most cases. In considering the importance of a particular city as supplying a consumer market, the population of smaller cities and areas throughout the county in which the "market city" (over 25,000 population) is located help identify the importance of the market city in serving a populated area. Therefore, the general

method of determining a multiple-city market is to define the market as a series of cities. The smaller cities and county areas that are not included in the definition are included in the population figures for determination of the relative importance of any one MCX market to another.

Multiple-City Complexes Defined

Although it would be easier to define area markets in terms of county lines or as populations expanding radially from a central city using a circular concept of a city or metropolitan trading area, it is not realistic in terms of recent metropolitan area growth. The more recent growth of population and its corresponding residential relocation have resulted in more of a suburban spread, although not necessarily radially. This growth has also resulted in a greater spread from a central city, a spread to smaller cities, and the filling in of gaps between two or more central cities or between a central city and the largest of the nearby communities. All this makes the metropolitan area resemble a network of interrelated cities, rather than a circle or a group of counties.

Several other factors should be recognized since they influence the present shape of the MCX area and trends of the MCX growth pattern. Geographical features such as mountain ranges, rivers, bays, and oceans affect the MCX pattern. Also, location of transportation systems, natural resources, and other influencing conditions, such as universities and resources, determine the MCX spread.

The MCX's consist of both major markets and minor markets. The concept of multiple-city complexes used here, however, is one of identification of relatively large scale consumer markets. Major MCX markets are those which contain over 500,000 population, while minor MCX markets contain 250,000 to 500,000 population. The cities included within the MCX are limited by two restrictions: a distance restriction and a population restriction.

DISTANCE RESTRICTIONS. Any establishment of limits to trade areas is somewhat artificial—whether using political–geographical limits, such as counties, or absolute distance limits. Since MCX's are based on clusters of cities that form a metropolitan trading area, a general distance restriction establishes the absolute limit to the trade area. The reason for the 50-mile limit is to give markets proper perspective—that of urban market areas which may be larger than one Standard Metropolitan Statistical Area (SMSA). A 50-mile limit acknowledges a large enough trade area that encompasses the usual and accepted traveling patterns of the population. The general 50-mile distance restriction covers specific directions from a "central city" (over 50,000) to another "central city," *or* to a city unit of over 25,000 population. Through this restricted coverage of specific directions, a network of basic cities is created which corresponds to population and traveling patterns. The city units as well as the central cities must belong to a general economic and social network forming a loosely contiguous and continuous market area in the multiple-city complex.

POPULATION RESTRICTIONS. Population restrictions are established for the MCX-Minor and MCX-Major; the minimum being 250,000 for the minor and 500,000 minimum for the major. For the city units of the MCX's, 25,000

is designated as a minimum size. Places smaller than 25,000 are grouped as a total figure for the counties within which the MCX's are located. The smaller places usually depend on larger communities as trade centers.

MCX TITLES. The titles to the MCX's are the two or three largest cities in the MCX metropolitan area (as defined). The use of two or three cities is based on the need for description of the MCX as a network. Therefore, Dallas and Fort Worth, Texas, identifies the MCX with the largest cities and generally describes the area covered. On the other hand, the San Francisco, Oakland, and San Jose three-city title has to be used to show the extent of that MCX. The St. Louis–East St. Louis MCX is a special situation in that the primary growth of cities in Illinois as well as those in Missouri has spread in the older pattern of radial expansion from a central city.

The 1970 Census and MCX Studies

Plans for the use and application of MCX area studies must be done in conjunction with up-to-date statistical data. Therefore, those companies planning any new type of market analysis, such as the MCX studies, need to have their activities and operations firmly established before the next census and coordinated with the new census data. In order for the individual firm to make use of MCX market area studies, a further elaboration of the MCX data must be organized. A basic plan for the application of MCX studies consists of:

1. *A definitive construction of MCX market areas.* This could be accomplished through the compilation and/or

computer analysis of population, market, and other pertinent data.

2. *Application of MCX studies to general markets.* This data can be used to provide a source reference and a guide to consumer markets.

3. *Application of MCX studies to the individual firm's market demand factors.* Based on MCX data, sales efforts and elements of supply—as needs and location of warehousing—could be coordinated into the sales and marketing plan of the firm.

This basic plan for the application of MCX studies provides general market and individual market area data. It also establishes a basis of comparison of present and future markets and marketing effectiveness. The basic plan for use of the multiple-city complex idea further provides the firm with a more factual and sounder statistical basis for the overall marketing plan.

Analysis of Four MCX's: General Markets

MCX's AND SMSA's. The metropolitan areas shown in Table 1 represent a variety of market situations. They exemplify four different settings and growth conditions, although all fit our definition of major MCX's and all are general market studies.

Individual firms, however, would start with the construction of their MCX market areas, and then collect pertinent statistical information. Next, an individual firm could determine general market areas and gather data as a general guide to consumer markets. Table 1 compares the MCX description of four market areas with the Standard Metropolitan Statistical Areas that make up the MCX. The descriptions (Table 1) and maps (Figures 1, 2, 3, 4) show that the MCX's and SMSA's do not always coincide. To take this comparison one step further, they show that SMSA's are probably not the best definition of a market area as viewed by a firm selling to consumer or industrial markets.

The statistics used for determination of the MCX's are from the *1960 Census of Population* and the Bureau of the Budget's *Standard Metropolitan Statistical Areas* (1961). When current data from the 1970 census are available, the figures for the MCX's can be updated easily. There will be some changes in the ranking of MCX's, and probably more markets will be joined together that are now thought of as separate. The MCX concept is not meant to

TABLE 1
Four MCX's and Related SMSA's

MCX	SMSA (Included in the MCX Areas)
San Francisco–Oakland–San Jose MCX (Calif.)	San Francisco–Oakland, Calif., SMSA and San Jose, Calif., SMSA
Denver–Colorado Springs MCX (Colorado)	Denver, Colorado, SMSA and Colorado Springs, Colorado, SMSA
Dallas–Fort Worth MCX (Texas)	Dallas, Texas, SMSA and Fort Worth, Texas, SMSA
St. Louis–East St. Louis MCX (Missouri–Illinois)	St. Louis, Missouri–Illinois, SMSA

replace any work done by various government agencies, but has the purpose of making the data more serviceable to those investigating potentials and planning sales in consumer markets. The concepts of SMSA's and "central cities" are used to provide a standard base for the establishment of the MCX concept.

The MCX markets are a less complex (by definition) and possibly more market-oriented version of SMSA statistics. *Census of Population* is the principal source of statistics and certain SMSA concepts and applications are used as an MCX basis. For example, the concept of the central city and SMSA designations are accepted and used. This study is principally concerned with metropolitan areas and, therefore, SMSA data and definitions correspond very well with the concepts of the MCX. SMSA's are established primarily on population and metropolitan characteristics criteria.[1] Counties are the area limits with a central city or cities of 50,000 population (or two contiguous cities which economically and socially constitute a single community, with a combined population of 50,000 or more with the smaller city having at least 15,000 population).

POPULATION OF MCX AREAS. In presenting the illustration of four MCX's, *general markets,* the specific population statistics (Table 2), are given for cities, county remainders, and total market areas. The total statistics presented are based on the population of the major cities in the MCX, all cities over 25,000 persons, and the population in cities of under 25,000 along with other persons not living in cities. Most people, however, in the "County Population Remainder" group live in towns of under 25,000 persons. The great number of people in this group may become very significant in future market studies.

Total populations (Table 2 and Figures 1–4) of the four MCX's, each MCX having over one million persons, show that they are significant market areas. An ordinary viewing of these markets as individual cities or even as SMSA's shows these areas to be of less significance as consumer markets.

CITIES WITHIN MCX's. Several questions arise concerning the cities within the MCX's. Does most of the population live in the central city? Does a large segment live in the smaller towns or in the unincorporated areas? In the

TABLE 2
Population of Multiple-City Complexes and Counties Within the MCX Market Areas

Multiple-City Complex *	Population of Cities (over 25,000)	County Population Remainder †	Total Population
San Francisco–Oakland–San Jose MCX	2,254,477	1,036,600	3,291,077
Denver–Colorado Springs MCX	683,745	389,380	1,073,125
Dallas–Fort Worth MCX	1,249,969	406,847	1,656,816
St. Louis MCX	1,099,948	1,004,721	2,104,669

* Counties within the MCX Market Area are those included in the related SMSA's (see Table 1).
† County figures include total population for counties that do not have a city over 25,000 inhabitants. For counties with cities over 25,000, the remainder of the county population is presented. Remainder of county is the population within the county that does not reside in cities of 25,000 or more inhabitants.

[1] For a more detailed explanation and listing of SMSA's, see *Standard Metropolitan Statistical Areas*, Bureau of the Budget, U.S. GPO, 1964.

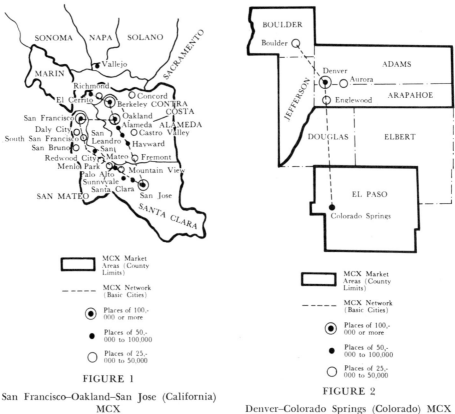

FIGURE 1

San Francisco–Oakland–San Jose (California)
MCX

FIGURE 2

Denver–Colorado Springs (Colorado) MCX

four MCX's studied, all had more than 50 per cent of their total population residing in cities of over 25,000 (see Table 3 and Figures 1–4). It is startling to note, however, that in only two of the four MCX's does the total central city population exceed 50 per cent of the total area population. Furthermore, in three of the MCX's, the "All other cities" category accounted for approximately 12 per cent of the area population (Table 3). The one exception, the San Francisco–Oakland–San Jose MCX, having 28.6 per cent in the "All other cities" category, represents an area of extremely heavy population growth.

A Tool for Marketing Management

Market determination and comparative market measures result from using multiple-city complexes as consumer market guides. Changing consumer markets and increasing competition create a constant need for better definition and evaluation of market areas. As a tool for marketing managers, the multiple-city complex concept offers a number of uses. Typical uses would include the following:

1. Identification of large consumer markets according to concentrated urban buying areas.

TABLE 3
Comparison Table of Population for MCX and Central Cities

MCX	Population	Per Cent of Total
San Francisco–Oakland–San Jose		
Central Cities:		
San Francisco	740,316	22.5
Oakland	367,548	11.2
San Jose	204,196	6.2
Total central cities	1,312,060	39.9
All other cities (over 25,000)	942,417	28.6
County remainders (cities under 25,000 and county residents)	1,036,600	31.5
Total MCX	3,291,077	100.0
Denver–Colorado Springs MCX		
Central Cities:		
Denver	493,887	46.0
Colorado Springs	70,194	6.5
Total central cities	564,081	52.5
All other cities (over 25,000)	119,664	11.2
County remainders	389,380	36.3
Total MCX	1,073,125	100.0
Dallas–Fort Worth MCX		
Central Cities:		
Dallas	679,684	41.0
Fort Worth	356,268	21.5
Total central cities	1,035,952	62.5
All other cities (over 25,000)	214,017	12.9
County remainders	406,847	24.6
Total MCX	1,656,816	100.0
St. Louis MCX		
Central Cities:		
St. Louis, Mo.	750,026	35.6
East St. Louis, Ill.	81,712	3.9
Total central cities	831,738	39.5
All other cities (over 25,000)	268,210	12.7
County remainders	1,004,721	47.8
Total MCX	2,104,669	100.0

Source: Census of Population, 1960.

2. Indication of potential large-scale consumer markets by showing urban growth trends.

3. Provision for better allocations of sales and promotional funds based on accurate consumer market analysis.

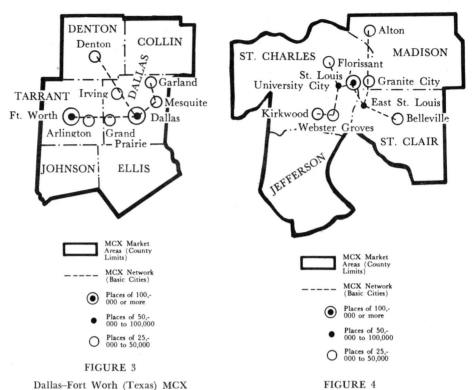

MCX Market Areas (County Limits)

MCX Network (Basic Cities)

● Places of 100,-000 or more

• Places of 50,-000 to 100,000

○ Places of 25,-000 to 50,000

FIGURE 3

Dallas–Fort Worh (Texas) MCX

MCX Market Areas (County Limits)

MCX Network (Basic Cities)

● Places of 100,-000 or more

• Places of 50,-000 to 100,000

○ Places of 25,-000 to 50,000

FIGURE 4

St. Louis–East St. Louis (Missouri-Illinois) MCX

4. Measurement for determining marketing effectiveness by allowing comparison of markets.

The marketing manager must take a realistic approach to present and potential market areas in order to compete effectively. This realistic approach calls for a rational conceptualization of markets in terms of people: where they live, work, and buy. Seeing markets as individual cities, county areas, and trading areas based on political subdivisions—as most census data show them—no longer represents an accurate conceptualization of consumer markets. The multiple-city complex concept is a step toward developing a current and modern view of these markets.

TRADE AREA STUDIES— FEASIBILITY ANALYSIS

The long-term structuring of a shopping center facility, involving various kinds of assets, represents a formidable commitment and confidence in the socioeconomic fabric of the supporting trade area. For it is axiomatic that the kind, quality, and stability of the community as a whole, and the sector or trade area contained therein, are fundamental and primary to the decision to invest, for equity and mortgage interests, in an existing or contemplated retail facility.

Basic Factors

Four basic factors require close scrutiny for the qualitative ranking of trade areas: (1) population, (2) income levels, (3) retail expenditures, and (4) competition. Requisite thresholds are required in both number and kind of population for different merchandise lines merely to survive. Consequently, the composition of population and its density in a time–distance framework represent important parameters for potential accessibility and consumer attraction and patronage.

Income levels, including their rate of change and relative structures, indicate the depth and quality of market segments and real or potential discretionary income. Therefore, subtle visible changes in neighborhood maintenance and corresponding resultant attitudes in the area can represent and be forerunners of emerging upside or downside trends. The neighborhood or sector of a community is essentially part of a larger organism (the urbanized area), but nevertheless has to a degree its own tempo and character. These highly subjective attributes spell more than numbers per se (census, trade journals, etc.). A proper reading can in some instances identify unserved and specialized viable market segments.

Expenditure patterns, where they can be ascertained, reflect the lifestyles and values of the residents. Again, the evidence may be subtle, but the differences might signify important opportunities or caution signals for certain kinds of retail ventures. As noted earlier, perception and subjective evaluation, in addition to identified and quantified retail expenditures, may be most important.

Finally, the kind, quality, scale, and locational attributes, in terms of access and immediate and connecting environment, represent the last of the four factors in the equation of trade area potentials, viability, continuity, and related opportunity.

A reasonable marshaling of the appropriate and pertinent evidence relating to these factors, followed by synthesis, can provide a forum for trade area study and analysis. Such a synthesis can then serve as a basis for the interfacing of a specific location, a retail activity, and the probable influence and interaction between the firm and its most likely customers. From this flows a relative opportunity index, which indicates the feasibility of proceeding with or abandoning plans for entry. This synthesis represents the basis of trade area analysis; only the means and level of sophistication of inquiry and study reflect the random variables.

The Gravity Model Analysis

The gravity model of retail gravitation formulated by William J. Reilly (*Retail Gravitation,* New York: Pilsbury Publishers, Inc., 1931) mirrors and is a manifestation of the least-effort attribute of human behavior. Assuming a freedom of choice and compelling need for goods, the Reilly formula, which equates attraction directly to population size and inversely to the square of the distance, develops a breaking point based on automobile highway distance. At that time, in the context of city size–location–highway networks, the "law" indicated significant predictability as to the outer limits of trade areas. More recently, David B. MacKay ("Measuring Shopping Patterns," *Geographical Analysis,* Oct. 1973), utilizing trend-surface methods, suggests something less than equipotential penetration of trade involving a supermarket in the Midwest.

In more recent years, L. W. Ellwood ("Estimating Potential of a Shopping Center," *Appraisal Journal,* Vol. 22, 1954) reformulated Reilly's law in the context of the size (square feet) of a retail district and the square of the driving-time distance from related residential districts. The attraction of a retail center (D) then takes the form S/D^2, where S represents the area concentration of retail facilities and D^2 is the driving-time distance (calculated into 5-minute driving-time units). The breaking point (BP) then can be computed from the following formula:

$$BP = \frac{\text{distance from A to B}}{+ \sqrt{\text{size A/size B}}}$$

While the Ellwood formulation approaches the retail flow and attraction of consumers from another vantage point, it serves basically as a first proximation of location potentials. One element requiring attention is the psychology of access to retail centers. That is, aside from driving time, what kind of environment must be traversed and passed through to reach a given shopping center? In some cases this may represent an overriding factor from the standpoint of consumer behavior vis-à-vis a specific shopping facility.

Feasibility Analysis

The concept of feasibility relates to two aspects concerning retail location developments: market feasibility and financial feasibility. The central question of potential consumer trade must first be ascertained, including matters of capture rates of market potential; this must be sufficient to support a projected retail outlet or group of outlets.

Financial feasibility addresses itself to the associated costs, such as rental or cost of facility, for a proposed establishment and the matching of probable gross revenues, profit margins, and so on, to determine if the levels are realistic to support the venture.

As an illustration, Table 1 outlines the basis of a proposed regional shopping center investment analysis. Each component must be closely calculated to provide as clear a picture as possible of the most likely and realistic return on the investment.

Data from Table 1 can then be matched with the available financing to provide additional insight into the financial feasibility of the center. Most financing is predicated on the guaranteed part of the net revenues. Therefore, overage rents are imputed to equity and capitalized at higher rates, thus recognizing the uncertainty and risk of excess rent.

The study of the composition of communities and their respective economic base usually is a forerunner of trade area studies.

TABLE 1
Pro Forma Investment Analysis

Total Investment: $26,303,000.00

Income and Expenses

Income	
Guaranteed rents	$2,218,800
Services	30,000
Standby charges	150,000
Guaranteed rent, total income	$2,398,800
Expenses	
Taxes, insurance, maintenance	$510,000
Management	70,000
Promotion	30,000
Contingencies	20,000
Vacancy (8%), except major anchor tenants	108,000
	$738,000 [a]
Net operating income at guaranteed rent	$1,660,800 [b]
Overage income at 75% of stabilized sales	356,700 [c]
Net operating income (1st year)	$2,017,500
Overage income after 1st year	744,800 [d]
Net operating income at stabilized sales	$2,762,300

---

[a] Ratio of expenses to guaranteed total rental income = 30.8%.
[b] Ratio of net operating income (guaranteed) to total investment = 6.3%.
[c] Ratio 1st year overage to net guaranteed rental = 44.8%.
[d] Ratio net operating income (after 1st year) to investment = 10.5%.

In a detailed study, Roy Kass provides a classification system for a large number of communities. Extending some of the work of Applebaum and Nelson, J. D. Forbes and W. T. Ziemba's theme of the "least effort" of human behavior serves as a basis to measure the drawing power of a supermarket.

Peter Simons's overview on the shape of a trading area is quite extensive and provides persuasive arguments as to why the trade area is basically circular in form.

Two essays represent different approaches to the same problem of trade area potentials: the grid and census tract map technique of William Applebaum, and the study of thresholds of population and incidence of retail functions, including the range of a good, of Michael S. Noble, Ronald F. Bush, and Joseph F. Hair. Both represent multi-vantage point techniques appropriate to retail location feasibility studies.

In a study of the Cleveland area, Avery M. Guest develops a

model for testing a hypothesis of family location based on family attributes and composition. Criteria developed for identifying kinds and types of families in urbanized areas are compared to those findings of researchers concerned with spatial research. The Columbus–Springfield, Ohio, market is examined via a longitudinal study by William B. Wagner.

Joseph B. Mason and Charles T. Moore point out in their analysis of assumptions relating to trade areas that socioeconomic profiles do not account for all the variability of trade area consumers.

Collectively, the essays serve as a foundation of techniques and methods for retail potential studies and the development of retailing facilities feasibility analysis.

A Functional Classification of Metropolitan Communities

Roy Kass

The concept of functional specialization attempts to identify the role of the community's local economic production in the larger economy. Both theoretically and empirically, the functional specialization attributed to a community should reflect the activities which integrate it with the larger social system. The pattern and distribution of economic activity varies among communities in our society. Some communities provide a relatively narrow range of goods or services for their own use or for that of the economy as a whole; other communities have a widely based production capacity and provide a broad range of goods and services for their own needs and those of the general economy. The term "function" is used to refer to economic activities and economic organization. Thus all activities that are concerned with the maintenance of the community and with its niche in the larger system of communities are included. Noneconomic functions such as cultural, religious or historic symbolism attached to a community are not included in the discussion of functional specialization.

It is interesting to note that, although flows of energy, information or material must have a destination as well as an origin, the concept of functional specialization considers a community solely in its role as origin of the flow. Virtually all systems for classifying functional specialization consider communities in terms of their export activities. Communities are classified according to the functions or activities performed within them which generate a net in-flow of payment from the larger economy. Maintenance functions which are common to all communities are generally not accounted for except to distinguish them from export functions. Goods or services which must be purchased from sources outside the community are never taken into consideration. Thus, while the national economy is integrated by a system of flows, classification schemes of functional specialization only identify a community as an originating node in these flows.

A common criticism of functional classification of communities is that the objectives of the classification systems and their efficacy for further investigation are often difficult to establish (Smith, 1965a, p. 546). Duncan and his collaborators (Duncan et al., 1960) have noted that the purposes of the various

Reprinted from *Demography*, Vol. 10, No. 3, August 1973, by permission of the author and editor.

authors who have introduced each new design for a system of determining the functional specialization of communities have "seldom been made explicit and often times little is done with them after they are finished" (p. 35). If the various functional types can be thought to represent different contexts for social life, the effects of these contexts should be examined. If the point of a classification system is the presentation of a pedagogic or heuristic scheme, it should be accepted as just that.

The classification system introduced in this paper was devised during an investigation of differentials in population characteristics between metropolitan communities. That study was primarily concerned with the impact of a community's functional specialization on its population characteristics. Before introducing the new procedure, a synopsis of major literature pertaining to the problem of functional classification is in order.

Five basic approaches to the quantitative identification of communities' functional specialization can be seen in the literature. Each presents a general conceptual framework and operational procedure for separating the activity in a community which is oriented toward maintaining its population from that which is oriented toward integrating the community with the larger social system. These five different approaches may be labeled as: (1) a taxonomy based on absolute constraints; (2) a classification system based on the normal distribution; (3) a system based on the minimally necessary level of activity for a community's viability; (4) a system based on the relative proportion of activity in the community; and (5) a system based on the "industrial profile" of the community.

Each of these procedures operationally defines the specialized func-

tions of a community in a different way. The basic procedures involved are predicated on different underlying frameworks for separating a community's maintenance activities from its export activities. Harris's (1943) classification system uses a series of absolute constraints to determine the single category representing the "activity of greatest importance to the community" (p. 86). The constraints were said to have been developed following an analysis of "cities of well-recognized types" although neither those cities nor the procedures used in the development of the constraints have been identified. Nelson's (1955) classification system makes use of the empirical distribution of activities within the several communities of interest. Based on the distribution of the percentages of the labor force employed in each of the selected industries, the system classes a community as specialized in a given function if the percentage of its labor force involved in the function is at least equivalent to one standard deviation above the mean for all communities of interest.

Alexandersson's (1956) system uses the percentage of the labor force equivalent to that observed in the lowest fifth percentile among the communities of interest as the delineation point between maintenance and export activities for each selected function. For each industry, if the percentage of a community's labor force is found to be at least five percentage points above this necessary proportion, the community is said to be specialized in that industry (Alexandersson, 1956, p. 22).

Duncan and Reiss (1956, p. 218), recognizing that a community's maintenance requirements are related to its size, developed a classification system based on a comparison of the level of activity in a given industry in a community with that in other communities of comparable size. The criterion measures for determining specialization in a function were: values above the top quintile in the distribution of percentage of the labor force employed in manufacturing for specialization in that activity; values above the top quartile in the distribution of per capita sales for specialization in trade activity; and values above the top decile in the distribution of the percentages of the communities' labor forces employed in each other sector for other selected functions (Duncan and Reiss, 1956, pp. 215–252 passim). No explanation for selection of the various indices of relative activity level was offered. Indeed, the authors stated that their choice of the different criterion levels was "somewhat arbitrary" (Duncan and Reiss, 1956, p. 223).

Duncan and his colleagues (Duncan et al., 1960) presented the fifth major approach to the problem of classifying a metropolitan community's function: the industrial profile. The industrial profile of a community was said to consist of all industries in which the community specialized. These industries were identified by means of the location coefficient for industrial composition of the labor force. A community's location coefficient for an industry is the ratio of the proportion of the community's labor force employed in that industry to the corresponding proportion in the national labor force. If, for a given industry, this coefficient is greater than unity, that industry is said to be a net exporter of the specified goods or services and is included in the community's industrial profile (Duncan et al., 1960, pp. 199–211).

Some communities may be specialized in more than one function. Others may be diversified in that they do not

specialize in any particular function. Past discussion of functional specialization has, for the most part, failed to adequately deal with the problem of multifunctional communities. All of the classification procedures mentioned, except the absolute constraints approach offered by Harris, allow a community to be classed as specialized in more than one function. However, when actually applying the procedures, it may be seen that they do so by allowing the communities to be singly specialized in more than one function, not by attempting to deal with the total configuration of functions in which the communities are specialized (cf. Nelson, 1957; Duncan and Reiss, 1956).

Examining communities on the basis of their total configuration of functions can add insights into the impact of functional specialization; this simply cannot be attained through the single function approaches. If the major approaches discussed are used to classify communities and then the communities are aggregated into similar groups, there are inherent problems in operationally comparing communities of different types. Independent comparisons of communities of different types cannot be made. It is possible, for instance, to compare communities with high levels of activity in retail trade with other communities and to compare communities with high levels of activity in finance with other communities. However, since the two categories are not mutually exclusive, communities may be specialized in both. Thus, the two groups cannot be compared with each other.

There obviously is much more involved in the character of urban communities than can be accounted for on the basis of differences in their economic functions. Some of the other important factors may be the community's size, its age and the region in which it is located. These factors can be exclusively determined. It seems desirable to practicably categorize communities into mutually exclusive groups of communities more similar to each other than to communities not in the group. An approach to this problem which takes account of the total configuration of functions in the communities is now offered.

For the purposes of this discussion eight broad groups of functions will be used: (1) durable goods manufacturing; (2) nondurable goods manufacturing; (3) retail trade; (4) wholesale trade; (5) transportation; (6) finance; (7) education; and (8) public administration. These groups were chosen because it was thought that they represented the functions which integrated the communities into an interdependent system.

The location coefficients for the several industry groups are used to indicate the relative amount of activity in each. Data concerning employment levels in these selected industries in the 212 Standard Metropolitan Statistical Areas of the early 1960's are available from the 1960 Census of Population (U.S. Bureau of the Census, 1963). The problem is to determine groupings of communities sharing common configurations of total functional activity.

The value of the location coefficient for each function is well defined in each community. For any given community, some of these values may be high, others low, while still others can lie in a middle range. We may speak of a community's combination of values for activity in all of the functions together as that community's "function profile." This profile is simply the combination of values of the separate functions' location coefficients.

Categorizing the communities according to their whole configuration of functions entails analytically identifying groups of communities with similar function profiles. If we were to dichotomize the activity level in each of the eight selected functions, then the communities would have eight functions, with a two-level score representing specialization or nonspecialization. In order to allow for all possible configurations of functional activity, we would need 2^8, or 256, categories in our classification system. This would allow for all possible combinations, ranging from one in which the community was specialized in all eight of the selected activities to one in which the community was not specialized in any of them. Although the empirical fact of a community being specialized in all of the selected functions is very unlikely to occur, it is a logical possibility since the selected functions do not represent an exhaustive partition of the whole labor force. The approach offered in this paper does not necessitate dichotomizing the activity level into a binary state. Furthermore, it hopefully will reduce to a manageable task the job of dealing with many possible combinations of functions. Rather than starting with a preconceived set of categories, the procedures offered will empirically identify groups of communities with a similar total configuration of functions.

The basic problem in arranging the communities into these groups lies in combining them in such a way that the communities in a group are more like each other than like the communities not included in that group. It may be that this exercise results in some groups being large, containing many communities, while others contain only two or three communities. Furthermore, there may well be unique communities whose function profiles simply are not like those of any others. In this situation, the procedure should not force them into a group, rather it should recognize their uniqueness.

Communities may be classed in the manner suggested by use of cluster analysis procedures for pattern recognition. The basic approach is explained at length in *Cluster Analysis* by Tryon and Bailey (1970). The authors refer to the approach as "object analysis" since the items being examined are the observed objects themselves, rather than the variables measured in the objects. The objective of this procedure is a determination of mutually exclusive sets of objects. The algebraic manipulations involved are directly analogous to those normally used in correlation analysis and the subsequent cluster analysis of the correlation matrix. In object analysis, the basic data matrix from which the correlations are calculated is the transpose of the data matrix usually examined when investigating the relationship between variables. Performing a cluster analysis on the matrix of correlations between these objects results in groups of objects whose profiles are more similar to those of others in the group than to the profiles of objects not included in the cluster.

In our case where the objects are the metropolitan communities and the variables are the location coefficients for each of the eight functions, the resultant clusters are the empirically derived groupings of communities according to their mutual similarity of functions. The clusters extracted from the intercorrelations between the communities' profiles represent a parsimonious attempt to identify natural groups of communities with similar profiles. As was mentioned earlier, there may be unique communities which do not fall into a set. In such a case, the community is simply not part of a classificatory type.

The procedure for identifying the clusters of communities started with a matrix of correlations between the communities' function profiles. The clusters of communities were extracted from these correlation matrices by the cluster analysis program of the OSIRIS computer program package distributed by the Institute for Social Research (n.d.) at the University of Michigan. The actual program used was modified at the University of Cincinnati Computer Center for use on their equipment.

In identifying the members of each cluster, the first pair of communities selected were those which had the highest positive correlation in the matrix. The minimum value allowed for this "highest correlation," which would allow the start of a cluster, was arbitrarily set at 0.70. Once the initial two communities were identified, the minimum correlation of each of the remaining communities with the initial two was determined.

The community having the highest minimum positive correlation with the first two communities was chosen as the third member of the cluster, provided that this minimum value was greater than an again arbitrarily selected value of 0.30. The fourth community was identified in a similar way, except that the minimum correlation of each remaining community was with the three member communities.

It is important that only communities whose function profiles are positively correlated are entered into the same cluster. A number of applications of cluster analysis are blind to directionality. The fact of high levels of interrelationships is important in those applications, rather than the direction of those correlations. However, for the pattern recognition purposes involved in this application, the direction of the correlations is important. We do not want to combine communities whose function profiles are mirror images of each other.

The process continued, adding more communities to the cluster, until one of three events occurred to stop it. (1) All of the available communities could be identified as members of the cluster, in which case no additional members would be sought. (2) If none of the available communities had positive correlation with all of the communities previously identified as members of the cluster, no others would be added to the cluster. (3) The procedure would stop if the highest minimum correlation of the available communities with the communities identified as belonging in the cluster was below the 0.30 level chosen for inclusion.

Once a cluster was completed, the communities identified as members of that cluster were removed from consideration as possible members for any other cluster. This means that a community may appear in, at most, one of the identified clusters. The entire procedure for identification of clusters continued until all commnuities had been brought into some cluster or the highest correlation between unclustered communities was less than the level necessary for the initiation of a new cluster (Institute for Social Research, n.d., pp. 327–328).

Using this clustering approach, communities were classed according to their whole configuration of functional activity: their profiles of location coefficients in eight functions. The groupings were determined separately for each of five classes: (a) 50,000–100,000; (b) 100,000–250,000; (c) 250,000–500,000; (d) 500,000–1,000,000; and (e) 1,000,000 and over. These size classes,

based on a log scale, are used repeatedly in the literature. By grouping communities in the same size class on the basis of their function profiles, it is possible to determine whether there are some configurations of functional specialization found in all size classes of metropolitan communities and whether some other configurations are found only in certain size classes.

This procedure identifies clusters of communities with similar function profiles. However, it does not describe the profiles. In order to ascertain the distinguishing attributes of the clusters, the function profiles of communities in each cluster were examined. The mean values of relative employment level in each of the functions were calculated for the communities in each of the clusters. These means were examined to determine the pattern, or configuration, of functions which distinguished communities in the cluster.

Using these procedures, thirty-one clusters of communities were identified. A number of basic profile patterns are repeated throughout the five size classes. These may be thought to represent basic configurations of industrial activity under which the metropolitan communities of the United States in 1960 may be classed. As was anticipated, there were some communities whose eight-member function profiles were not sufficiently similar to others in the same size class to be clustered using the given constraints. Of the 212 metropolitan communities, twenty-four were unclustered. These communities are listed in the Appendix, Table A-1, together with communities belonging to each of the identified clusters.

The function profiles of the thirty-one clusters, on examination, had enough in common that they could be combined into twelve groups, or classes, having similar patterns of functional activity. This identification process was conducted by examining the mean normalized values of the several profile elements within each cluster. A function was arbitrarily said to be distinguishing for a cluster if the within-group mean for the location coefficient was greater than unity. This would signify that the mean value within the cluster was more than one standard deviation above the national mean. The national means and standard deviations for the location coefficients of the eight selected functions may be found in Table 1.

The mean values for each profile element in two of the clusters were all less than one standard unit. In these two cases, the first was among the communities between 500,000 and 1,000,000 and the other, among the communities of 1,000,000 or more. Assignment has been to categories which most closely resemble their relative activity in the several functions. In the first case the relative activity in retail and finance were both much greater than in any other functions, while in the latter case, the greatest emphasis was found to be in the manufacture of nondurable goods and in finance.

The twelve patterns of functions in which the communities had a relatively high level of activity were:

1. Durable goods manufacture
2. Nondurable goods manufacture
3. Retail trade
4. Wholesale trade
5. Transportation
6. Education
7. Public administration
8. Nondurable goods manufacture and education together
9. Nondurable goods manufacture and finance together
10. Retail trade and finance together
11. Retail trade and wholesale trade together
12. Wholesale trade and public administration together.

Appendix Tables A-2 through A-7 contain the means and ranges of values for each of the elements in the function profiles for the thirty-one clusters which were identified. In order that the activity level in each of the functions be comparable to each other, the location coefficients have been normalized against their respective national means and standard deviations.

Only one pattern of functional activity, a relatively high level of employment only in durable goods manufacture, was found in all five size

TABLE 1

Means and Standard Deviations of Location Coefficients for Selected Industrial Groups: 212 Standard Metropolitan Statistical Areas, 1960

Function	Mean	Standard Deviation
Durable goods manufacture	100.9	72.1
Nondurable goods manufacture	101.4	62.4
Retail trade	104.9	36.1
Wholesale trade	105.6	13.4
Transportation	103.6	35.0
Finance	92.2	29.8
Education	104.6	46.6
Public administration	109.9	74.5

Source: Derived from U.S. Bureau of the Census, 1963, Part 1, Table 9 and State Reports, Table 75.

classes. A high level of employment in public administration by itself was a distinguishing characteristic in all but the smallest size class of communities. A pattern of relatively high employment only in the manufacture of non-durable goods distinguished clusters in all but the largest size class. All of the other configurations of activity occurred in only one or two of the size classes.

Each of the function profiles represents a set of functional niches occupied by the metropolitan communities. While the single function approach to functional classification allows a statement concerning whether or not a community was specialized in a given function, the cluster approach provides a mechanism for identifying patterns of configurations of all the functions in the communities. The results of the analysis performed suggest that there were twelve such major patterns in the metropolitan communities of the United States in 1960.

The clustering approach reduced the job of identifying the communities having similar configurations of functions in which they were specialized to a manageable size. The distinguishing characteristics of the clusters could be single- or multi-functional. No preconceived criteria or prior selection of specific functions in which communities were specialized was necessary.

The proposition may be made that a classification procedure for communities should allow a number of "statements not only about the characteristics used in the operational evaluation of the community but also about other characteristics of the community which are thought to be important" (Smith, 1965a, p. 546).

As mentioned earlier, this procedure was devised during an investigation of differentials in population characteris-

tics between metropolitan communities. For the purposes of that objective, the classification procedure is worthwhile if the groups resulting from its application allow better statements about these differentials than do the groups resulting from the other procedures. A straightforward way of ascertaining whether the clusters do a better job of distinguishing communities on the basis of their population characteristics is to examine the characteristics' values within the several clusters. This may be done through the analysis of what may be called the "characteristic profile."

Each population characteristic has a distribution of values among the metropolitan communities. The mean value of this distribution is the value of the characteristic representative of all the metropolitan communities. In the same way, one may think of the distribution of population characteristics among the communities in a cluster. The mean of these values for each characteristic is representative of the cluster just as the national mean is representative of all metropolitan communities as a whole. Similarly, we can ascertain the mean value of each population characteristic within communities specialized in each of the single functions. The values of the population characteristics within the clusters of communities and among the groups of communities specialized in each of the functions considered separately provide a vehicle by which the distinguishing ability of the two approaches may be determined.

A profile with wide variation in its values represents a group that distinguishes well between the various population characteristics. The values of some characteristics are high while those of others are low. A profile with a narrow range of variation, on the other hand, does not distinguish as well between the various characteristics. While it is possible to state that a group of communities whose characteristics profile has wide variation has a population composition that is sharply different from that of the nation as a whole, a group whose characteristics profile has a narrow range of variation need not necessarily be similar to the nation as a whole.

If the mean value of the profile of normalized population characteristics values is not close to zero, signifying that the values of the characteristics in the group were close to those of the national means, the mere fact of little variation between the separate elements of the profile obviously would not mean that the group was representative of the nation as a whole. Rather, the group of communities would have had values in all characteristics that were uniformly above or below the national mean.

An exercise such as that has been carried out for some twenty population characteristics, comparing the utility of the clustering approach with that of the single specialization approach. The results indicate that groups of communities having similar total configurations of functions are better distinguished from the national level than are communities grouped together on the basis of their common specialization in single functions.

The approach to classification offered in this paper is generalizable to a wide range of applications, in which entire configurations of characteristics are thought desirable in the classification of the objects analyzed. The groups resulting from this approach are empirically derived groups which may, as was found in the study reported in this paper, have theoretical as well as statistical significance.

TABLE A-1
Size and Cluster Type of SMSA's: 1960

Community	Size	Type
Abilene, Texas	100–250	Retl/whls
Akron, Ohio	500–Mill.	Ndur. gds.
Albany, Georgia	50–100	Whls/puba
Albany–Schenectady–Troy, New York	500–Mill.	Public adm
Albuquerque, New Mexico	250–500	Public adm
Allentown–Bethlehem–Easton, Pennsylvania– New Jersey	250–500 (B)	Ndur. gds.
Altoona, Pennsylvania	100–250	Transport.
Amarillo, Texas	100–250	Retl/whls
Ann Arbor, Michigan	100–250	Education
Asheville, North Carolina	100–250 (B)	Ndur. gds.
Atlantic City, New Jersey	100–250	No cluster
Atlanta, Georgia	Million +	Retl/fin.
Augusta, Georgia–South Carolina	100–250 (B)	Ndur. gds.
Austin, Texas	100–250 (A)	Education
Bakersfield, California	250–500	Public adm
Baltimore, Maryland	Million +	Public adm
Baton Rouge, Louisiana	100–250	Educ/ndur
Bay City, Michigan	100–250	Dur. gds.
Beaumont–Port Arthur, Texas	250–500 (A)	Ndur. gds.

TABLE A-1—Continued

Community	Size	Type
Billings, Montana	50–100	Wholesale
Binghamton, New York	100–250 (A)	Ndur. gds.
Birmingham, Alabama	500–Mill.	Retl/fin.
Boston, Massachusetts	Million +	No cluster
Bridgeport, Connecticut	250–500	Dur. gds.
Brockton, Massachusetts	100–250 (B)	Ndur. gds.
Brownsville–Harlingen–San Benito, Texas	100–250	Retl/whls
Buffalo, New York	Million +	Dur. gds.
Canton, Ohio	250–500	Dur. gds.
Cedar Rapids, Iowa	100–250	Dur. gds.
Champaign–Urbana, Illinois	100–250 (A)	Education
Charleston, South Carolina	100–250 (A)	Public adm
Charleston, West Virginia	250–500 (A)	Ndur. gds.
Charlotte, North Carolina	250–500 (A)	Retl/fin.
Chattanooga, Tennessee–Georgia	250–500 (A)	Ndur. gds.
Chicago, Illinois	Million +	Dur. gds.
Cincinnati, Ohio–Kentucky	Million +	Ndur/fin.
Cleveland, Ohio	Million +	Dur. gds.
Colorado Springs, Colorado	50–100	Whls/puba
Columbia, South Carolina	250–500	Public adm
Columbus, Georgia–Alabama	100–250 (B)	Ndur. gds.
Columbus, Ohio	500–Mill.	No cluster
Corpus Christi, Texas	100–250	Retl/whls
Dallas, Texas	Million +	No cluster
Davenport–Rock Island–Moline, Iowa–Illinois	250–500	Dur. gds.
Dayton, Ohio	500–Mill.	No cluster
Decatur, Illinois	50–100	No cluster
Denver, Colorado	500–Mill.	Retail
Detroit, Michigan	Million +	Dur. gds.
Des Moines, Iowa	250–500 (B)	Retl/fin.
Dubuque, Iowa	50–100	No cluster
Duluth–Superior, Minnesota–Wisconsin	250–500	Transport.
Durham, North Carolina	100–250	Educ/ndur
El Paso, Texas	250–500	Public adm
Erie, Pennsylvania	250–500	Dur.gds.
Eugene, Oregon	100–250	No cluster
Evansville, Indiana–Kentucky	100–250	No cluster
Fall River, Massachusetts–Rhode Island	100–250 (B)	Ndur. gds.
Fargo–Moorhead, North Dakota–Minnesota	100–250	Retl/whls
Fitchburg–Leominster, Massachusetts	50–100	Ndur. gds.
Flint, Michigan	250–500	Dur. gds.
Ft. Lauderdale–Hollywood, Florida	250–500	No cluster
Fort Smith, Arkansas	50–100	No cluster
Fort Wayne, Indiana	100–250	Dur. gds.
Fort Worth, Texas	500–Mill.	Retl/fin.
Fresno, California	250–500 (A)	Retl/fin.
Gadsden, Alabama	50–100	Dur. gds.
Galveston–Texas City, Texas	100–250	Transport.

TABLE A-1—Continued

Community	Size	Type
Gary–Hammond–East Chicago, Indiana	500–Mill.	Dur. gds.
Grand Rapids, Michigan	250–500	Dur. gds.
Great Falls, Montana	50–100	Wholesale
Green Bay, Wisconsin	100–250 (B)	Ndur. gds.
Greenville, South Carolina	100–250 (B)	Ndur. gds.
Greensboro–High Point, North Carolina	100–250 (B)	Ndur. gds.
Hamilton–Middletown, Ohio	100–250	No cluster
Harrisburg, Pennsylvania	250–500	Public adm
Hartford, Connecticut	500–Mill.	No cluster
Honolulu, Hawaii	500–Mill.	Public adm
Houston, Texas	Million +	Retl/fin.
Huntington–Ashland, West Virginia–Kentucky–Ohio	250–500	Transport.
Huntsville, Alabama	100–250 (B)	Public adm
Indianapolis, Indiana	500–Mill.	Retl/fin.
Jackson, Michigan	100–250	Dur. gds.
Jackson, Mississippi	100–250 (B)	Education
Jacksonville, Florida	250–500 (A)	Retl/fin.
Jersey City, New Jersey	500–Mill.	Ndur. gds.
Johnstown, Pennsylvania	250–500	Dur. gds.
Kalamazoo, Michigan	100–250 (B)	Ndur. gds.
Kansas City, Missouri–Kansas	Million +	Retl/fin.
Kenosha, Wisconsin	100–250	Dur. gds.
Knoxville, Tennessee	250–500 (A)	Ndur. gds.
Lake Charles, Louisiana	100–250 (B)	Ndur. gds.
Lancaster, Pennsylvania	250–500 (B)	Ndur. gds.
Lansing, Michigan	250–500	No cluster
Laredo, Texas	50–100	Wholesale
Las Vegas, Nevada	100–250 (A)	Public adm
Lawrence–Haverhill, Massachusetts–New Hampshire	100–250 (A)	Ndur. gds.
Lawton, Oklahoma	50–100	Whls/puba
Lewiston–Auburn, Maine	50–100	Ndur. gds.
Lexington, Kentucky	100–250 (A)	Education
Little Rock–North Little Rock, Arkansas	100–250	Retl/whls
Lima, Ohio	100–250	Dur. gds.
Lincoln, Nebraska	100–250 (B)	Education
Lorain–Elyria, Ohio	100–250	Dur. gds.
Los Angeles–Long Beach, California	Million +	Dur. gds.
Louisville, Kentucky–Indiana	500–Mill.	Ndur. gds.
Lowell, Massachusetts	100–250 (A)	Ndur. gds.
Lubbock, Texas	100–250	Retl/whls
Lynchburg, Virginia	100–250 (A)	Ndur. gds.
Macon, Georgia	100–250 (A)	Public adm
Madison, Wisconsin	100–250 (A)	Education
Manchester, New Hampshire	50–100	Ndur. gds.
Memphis, Tennessee	500–Mill.	Retail
Meriden, Connecticut	50–100	Dur. gds.
Miami, Florida	500–Mill.	Retail
Midland, Texas	50–100	Wholesale
Milwaukee, Wisconsin	Million +	Dur. gds.

TABLE A-1—Continued

Community	Size	Type
Minneapolis–St. Paul, Minnesota	Million +	Retl/fin.
Mobile, Alabama	250–500	Public adm
Monroe, Louisiana	100–250	Retl/whls
Montgomery, Alabama	100–250 (A)	Public adm
Muncie, Indiana	100–250	Dur. gds.
Muskegon–Muskegon Heights, Michigan	100–250	Dur. gds.
Nashville, Tennessee	250–500 (B)	Retl/fin.
New Bedford, Massachusetts	100–250 (A)	Ndur. gds.
New Britain, Connecticut	100–250	Dur. gds.
New Haven, Connecticut	250–500	No cluster
New London–Groton–Norwich, Connecticut	100–250 (A)	Ndur. gds.
New Orleans, Louisiana	500–Mill.	Retail
New York, New York	Million +	Retl/fin.
Newark, New Jersey	Million +	Ndur/fin.
Newport News–Hampton, Virginia	100–250 (B)	Public adm
Norfolk–Portsmouth, Virginia	500–Mill.	Public adm
Norwalk, Connecticut	50–100	Ndur. gds.
Odessa, Texas	50–100	Wholesale
Ogden, Utah	100–250 (A)	Public adm
Oklahoma City, Oklahoma	500–Mill.	Public adm
Orlando, Florida	250–500 (A)	Retl/fin.
Omaha, Nebraska–Iowa	250–500 (B)	Retl/fin.
Patterson–Clifton–Passaic, New Jersey	Million +	Ndur/fin.
Pensacola, Florida	100–250 (A)	Public adm
Peoria, Illinois	250–500	Dur. gds.
Philadelphia, Pennsylvania–New Jersey	Million +	Ndur/fin.
Phoenix, Arizona	500–Mill.	No cluster
Pittsburgh, Pennsylvania	Million +	Dur. gds.
Pittsfield, Massachusetts	50–100	Dur. gds.
Portland, Maine	100–250	Retl/whls
Portland, Oregon–Washington	500–Mill.	Retail
Providence–Pawtucket, Rhode Island–Massachusetts	500–Mill.	No cluster
Provo–Orem, Utah	100–250 (A)	Education
Pueblo, Colorado	100–250	Dur. gds.
Racine, Wisconsin	100–250	Dur. gds.
Raleigh, North Carolina	100–250 (B)	Education
Reading, Pennsylvania	250–500 (B)	Ndur. gds.
Reno, Nevada	50–100	Wholesale
Richmond, Virginia	250–500 (B)	Retl/fin.
Roanoke, Virginia	100–250	Transport.
Rochester, New York	500–Mill.	Dur. gds.
Rockford, Illinois	100–250	Dur. gds.
Saginaw, Michigan	100–250	Dur. gds.
Salt Lake City, Utah	250–500 (A)	Retl/fin.
San Angelo, Texas	50–100	Wholesale
San Antonio, Texas	500–Mill.	Public adm
San Bernardino–Riverside–Ontario, California	500–Mill.	Public adm
San Diego, California	Million +	Public adm
San Jose, California	500–Mill.	Dur. gds.

TABLE A-1—Continued

Community	Size	Type
San Francisco–Oakland, California	Million +	No cluster
Sacramento, California	500–Mill.	Public adm
Santa Barbara, California	100–250 (B)	Education
Savannah, Georgia	100–250	Transport.
Scranton, Pennsylvania	100–250 (B)	Ndur. gds.
Seattle, Washington	Million +	No cluster
Shreveport, Louisiana	100–250	Retl/whls
Sioux City, Iowa	100–250	Retl/whls
Sioux Falls, South Dakota	50–100	Retail
South Bend, Indiana	100–250	Dur. gds.
Spokane, Washington	250–500 (A)	Retl/fin.
Springfield, Illinois	100–250 (A)	Public adm
Springfield, Missouri	100–250	Retl/whls
Springfield, Ohio	100–250 (B)	Public adm
Springfield–Chicopee–Holyoke, Massachusetts	250–500 (B)	Ndur. gds.
St. Joseph, Missouri	50–100	Retail
St. Louis, Missouri–Illinois	Million +	Ndur/fin.
Stamford, Connecticut	100–250	No cluster
Steubenville–Weirton, Ohio–West Virginia	100–250	Dur. gds.
Stockton, California	100–250 (A)	Public adm
Syracuse, New York	500–Mill.	Dur. gds.
Tacoma, Washington	250–500	Public adm
Tampa–St. Petersburg, Florida	500–Mill.	Retail
Terre Haute, Indiana	100–250	Transport.
Texarkana, Texas–Arkansas	50–100	No cluster
Toledo, Ohio	250–500	Dur. gds.
Topeka, Kansas	100–250 (A)	Public adm
Trenton, New Jersey	100–250 (B)	Public adm
Tucson, Arizona	100–250 (B)	Education
Tulsa, Oklahoma	250–500	Transport.
Tuscaloosa, Alabama	100–250 (A)	Education
Tyler, Texas	50–100	No cluster
Utica–Rome, New York	250–500	No cluster
Waco, Texas	100–250 (B)	Education
Waterloo, Iowa	100–250 (A)	Ndur. gds.
Washington, D.C.–Maryland–Virginia	Million +	Public adm
Waterbury, Connecticut	100–250	Dur. gds.
West Palm Beach, Florida	100–250	No cluster
Wheeling, West Virginia–Ohio	100–250	Dur. gds.
Wichita, Kansas	250–500	Dur. gds.
Wichita Falls, Texas	100–250 (A)	Public adm
Wilkes Barre–Hazelton, Pennsylvania	250–500 (A)	Ndur. gds.
Wilmington, Delaware–New Jersey	250–500 (A)	Ndur. gds.
Winston-Salem, North Carolina	100–250 (B)	Ndur. gds.
Worcester, Massachusetts	250–500	Dur. gds.
York, Pennsylvania	100–250 (A)	Ndur. gds.
Youngstown–Warren, Ohio	500–Mill.	Dur. gds.

Source: Derived from Tables A-2 through A-7 and U.S. Bureau of the Census, 1963, State Reports, Table 75.

TABLE A-2
Mean, Minima and Maxima of Standardized Function Profiles for Clusters (Durable Goods Manufacture) of Communities

Durable Goods Manufacture

Element	50–100 Mean	Min.	Max.	100–250 Mean	Min.	Max.	250–500 Mean	Min.	Max.	500–Mill. Mean	Min.	Max.	Million Plus Mean	Min.	Max.
Durable goods manufacture	1.41	0.50	2.46	1.72	0.61	2.97	1.39	0.77	2.91	1.44	0.57	2.31	1.07	0.54	1.67
Nondurable goods manufacture	0.06	−.50	.46	−.57	−1.15	.42	−.44	−1.16	.43	−.43	−.98	−.08	−.26	−.73	.17
Retail trade	−1.31	−1.51	−1.05	−.77	−1.84	.44	−.27	−1.17	.94	−.80	−1.58	−.09	−.01	−.29	.33
Wholesale trade	−.35	−1.02	.13	−.41	−1.69	.90	−.38	−1.55	.15	−.91	−1.17	−.54	−.59	−.91	−.40
Transportation	−1.04	−1.37	−.51	−.49	−1.58	.91	−.45	−1.30	.51	−.53	−1.05	−.18	−.06	−.41	−.56
Finance	−.56	−.99	−.29	−.88	−1.79	.51	−.48	−1.33	.46	−.47	−1.11	.21	.04	−.51	.79
Education	−.56	−.82	−.40	−.36	−.69	.70	−.37	−.61	−.07	.07	−.55	.86	−.44	−.65	−.25
Public administration	−.52	−.60	−.43	−.74	−.91	−.38	−.67	−.88	−.30	−.57	−.78	−.37	−.40	−.49	−.31
Number of communities	3			18			11			5			7		

Source: Derived from Table 1 and U.S. Bureau of the Census, 1963, State Reports, Table 75.

51

TABLE A-3

Mean, Minima and Maxima of Standardized Function Profile for Clusters (Nondurable Goods Manufacturing) of Communities

	Nondurable Goods Manufacturing												
	50,000–100,000			100,000–250,000						250,000–500,000						500,000–Million		
	Mean			Cluster A			Cluster B			Cluster A			Cluster B			Mean		
Element	Min.	Mean	Max.	Min.	Mean	Max.	Min.	Mean	Max.	Min.	Mean	Max.	Min.	Mean	Max.	Min.	Mean	Max.
Durable goods manufacture	−1.02	−0.25	0.29	0.12	0.44	0.96	−1.17	−0.65	−0.15	−0.89	−0.54	−0.01	0.52	0.73	1.07	0.03	0.08	0.17
Nondurable goods manufacture	.57	2.69	4.50	.56	1.39	2.70	.80	1.90	4.23	.98	1.51	2.03	.73	1.09	1.52	.48	1.31	2.28
Retail trade	−1.40	−.73	−.11	−1.30	−.91	−.06	−.99	−.37	.62	−1.07	−.30	.39	−1.08	−.77	−.35	−.83	−.25	.15
Wholesale trade	−1.78	−1.21	−.65	−1.58	−1.11	.17	−1.62	−.30	1.60	−1.19	−.36	.30	−1.46	−1.16	−.46	−1.91	−.92	−.25
Transportation	−1.46	−1.10	−.62	−1.34	−.84	−.31	−1.21	−.48	.76	−.47	−.09	.97	−1.09	−.76	−.47	−.20	.81	2.11
Finance	−1.37	−.57	.54	−1.40	−1.05	−.72	−1.37	−.54	.24	−.99	−.52	.40	−1.44	−.74	.40	−.78	.30	1.47
Education	−.83	−.58	−.13	−.83	−.35	.44	−.89	−.23	.97	−.53	−.22	.44	−.72	−.43	.00	−.94	−.71	−.56
Public administration	−.83	−.58	−.38	−.80	−.42	.00	−.82	−.41	.26	−.70	−.45	−.15	−.88	−.66	−.34	−.77	−.44	−.24
Number of communities	4			8			12			6			4			3		

Source: Derived from Table 1 and U.S. Bureau of the Census, 1963, State Reports, Table 75.

TABLE A-4
Mean, Minima and Maxima of Standardized Function Profiles for Clusters (Retail Trade, Wholesale Trade, Transportation and Education) of Communities

Element	Retail Trade 50,000–100,000			Retail Trade 500,000–Million			Wholesale Trade 50,000–100,000			Wholesale Trade 100,000–250,000			Transportation 250,000–500,000			Education 100,000–250,000 Cluster A			Education 100,000–250,000 Cluster B		
	Mean	Min.	Max.	Mean	Min.	Max.	Mean	Min.	Max.	Mean	Min.	Max.	Mean	Min.	Max.	Mean	Min.	Max.	Mean	Min.	Max.
Durable goods manufacture	−1.04	−1.17	−0.92	−0.66	−0.91	−0.29	−1.11	−1.26	−0.74	−0.68	−1.08	−0.41	−0.21	−0.71	0.39	−0.47	−1.15	0.52	−0.76	−0.97	−0.56
Nondurable goods manufacture	.91	.30	1.51	−.37	−.80	−.04	−.88	−1.25	−.40	.41	−.10	.62	−.50	−.73	−.25	−.71	−1.11	.19	−.68	−1.51	−.07
Retail trade	2.13	1.72	2.54	1.22	.30	1.89	.89	−.16	2.76	−.06	−.99	.47	−.03	−.13	.11	−.85	−1.98	.14	.26	−.55	.93
Wholesale trade	.53	.44	.63	.80	.24	1.96	1.52	−.08	3.00	.46	.16	1.02	.61	.29	1.17	−.11	−1.56	.75	.43	−.55	1.65
Transportation	.50	.39	.61	.99	−.07	2.09	.69	−.15	1.63	3.02	1.03	7.13	1.65	1.14	2.23	−.83	−1.10	−.47	−.23	−.87	.63
Finance	.13	−.45	.71	.92	.31	1.43	.17	−.80	1.02	−.27	−1.23	.65	−.41	−.83	.36	−.52	−1.33	.55	.84	−.03	1.48
Education	−.44	−.89	.00	−.27	−.58	.21	−.18	−.45	−.05	−.21	−.53	.35	−.14	−.43	.25	3.89	1.19	7.66	1.13	.56	1.93
Public administration	−.49	−.53	−.47	−.06	−.43	.51	.02	−.79	1.16	−.45	−.68	−.16	−.45	−.66	−.15	.08	−.73	1.36	.19	−.06	.73
Number of communities	2			6			7			5			3			7			6		

Source: Derived from Table 1 and U.S. Bureau of the Census, 1963, State Reports, Table 75.

TABLE A-5
Mean, Minima and Maxima of Standardized Function Profiles for Clusters (Public Administration) of Communities

	Public Administration														
	100,000–250,000						250,000–500,000			500,000–Million			Million Plus		
	Cluster A			Cluster B											
Element	Min.	Mean	Max.	Min.	Mean	Max.	Min.	Mean	Max.	Min.	Mean	Max.	Min.	Mean	Max.
Durable goods manufacture	−1.26	−0.86	−0.19	0.37	0.86	1.20	−1.10	−0.76	−0.13	−1.05	−0.60	0.01	−1.14	−0.16	0.35
Nondurable goods manufacture	−1.16	−.42	.80	−.99	−.62	.06	−1.06	−.36	.08	−1.03	−.62	.20	−1.08	−.72	−.09
Retail trade	−1.31	−.28	.34	−1.50	−1.35	−1.26	−.66	.17	.57	−.31	.43	1.27	−1.16	−.73	−.32
Wholesale trade	−.43	.22	1.84	−1.41	−.74	−.33	−1.03	.23	1.44	−.68	.34	1.49	−1.37	−.55	.25
Transportation	−.51	.33	2.68	−1.54	−.87	−.47	−.42	.42	1.42	−.31	.19	.83	−.85	−.28	.35
Finance	−.99	−.09	1.35	−1.46	−1.00	−.78	−.63	.14	.82	−.48	.15	.81	.22	.49	.73
Education	−.80	−.26	.12	−.33	.07	.91	−.52	.10	.37	−.31	.07	.36	−.35	−.04	.14
Public administration	.04	1.71	5.11	.02	1.12	2.32	.45	1.52	3.11	1.07	2.13	3.68	.41	2.40	5.82
Number of communities	10			4			7			7			3		

Source: Derived from Table 1 and U.S. Bureau of the Census, 1963, State Reports, Table 75.

TABLE A-6

Mean, Minima and Maxima of Standardized Function Profiles for Clusters (Nondurable Goods Manufacture, Education, Retail Trade and Finance) of Communities

Element	Nondurable Manufacture and Education 100,000–250,000			Retail Trade and Finance 250,000–500,000 Cluster A			Cluster B			500,000–Million			Million Plus		
	Min.	Mean	Max.	Min.	Mean	Max.	Min.	Mean	Max.	Min.	Mean	Max.	Min.	Mean	Max.
Durable goods manufacture	-1.13	-1.10	-1.07	-0.98	-0.69	-0.47	-0.85	-0.71	-0.64	0.23	0.41	0.53	-0.47	-0.33	-0.05
Nondurable goods manufacture	.65	1.10	1.55	-.85	-.50	.42	.11	.32	.66	-.81	-.50	-.17	-.13	.03	.48
Retail trade	-.91	-.52	-.14	.98	1.67	2.60	.70	1.13	1.47	.49	.65	.74	1.18	1.55	1.92
Wholesale trade	-1.27	-.50	.26	.05	.73	1.17	-.30	-.05	.37	-.21	.09	.36	-.95	-.17	.06
Transportation	-1.19	-.91	-.62	-.70	.45	1.11	.22	.86	2.32	.11	.27	.43	.55	.88	1.51
Finance	-.14	-.06	.03	-.22	1.07	2.61	1.04	2.21	3.92	.19	.70	1.20	.62	1.42	2.54
Education	1.90	2.01	2.13	-.64	-.16	.28	-.56	-.20	.18	-.66	-.45	-.31	-.63	-.38	.07
Public administration	-.66	-.24	.19	-.69	-.08	.54	-.28	.01	.24	-.52	-.24	-.02	-.70	-.24	.02
Number of communities	2			6			4			3			5		

Source: Derived from Table 1 and U.S. Bureau of the Census, 1963, State Reports, Table 75.

TABLE A-7

Mean, Minima and Maxima of Standardized Function Profiles for Clusters (Retail and Wholesale Trade, Wholesale Trade and Public Administration, Nondurable Goods Manufacture and Finance) of Communities

	Retail and Wholesale 100,000–250,000			Wholesale and Public Adm. 50,000–100,000			Nondurable Mfg. and Finance Million Plus		
		Mean			Mean			Mean	
	Min.		Max.	Min.		Max.	Min.		Max.
Durable goods manufacture	−1.24	−0.95	−0.62	−1.23	−1.08	−0.94	0.19	0.30	0.49
Nondurable goods manufacture	−1.02	−.38	.51	−1.08	−.68	.03	.31	.60	1.19
Retail trade	.47	1.58	2.53	−.89	−.37	.63	−.16	.17	.55
Wholesale trade	.29	1.44	2.05	1.10	1.92	3.18	−1.35	−.82	−.34
Transportation	−.12	.68	1.57	−.43	−.33	−.21	−.26	.09	.58
Finance	−.91	.21	1.20	−.22	.35	1.25	.32	.66	1.53
Education	−.43	.14	1.16	.00	.65	1.56	−.62	−.53	−.46
Public administration	−.55	−.17	.27	1.05	1.32	1.80	−.64	−.37	−.14
Number of communities		12			3			5	

Source: Derived from Table 1 and U.S. Bureau of the Census, 1963, State Reports, Table 75.

REFERENCES

Atchley, Robert C. 1967. A Size-Function Typology of Cities. Demography 4:721–733.

Alexandersson, Gunnar. 1956. The Industrial Structure of American Cities. Lincoln: University of Nebraska Press.

Bollens, John C., and Henry J. Schmandt. 1965. The Metropolis: Its People, Politics and Economic Life. New York: Harper & Row.

Bruce, Grady D., and Robert E. Witt. 1971. Developing Empirically Derived City Typologies: An Application of Cluster Analysis. The Sociological Quarterly 12:238–246.

Duncan, Otis Dudley, and Albert J. Reiss. 1956. Social Characteristics of Urban and Rural Communities, 1950. New York: John Wiley & Sons.

————, Richard W. Scott, Stanley Lieberson, Beverly Duncan, and Hal H. Winsborough. 1960. Metropolis and Region. Baltimore: The Johns Hopkins Press.

Executive Office of the President, Bureau of the Budget. 1963. Standard Metropolitan Statistical Areas. Washington, D.C.: Government Printing Office.

Gibbs, Jack P. 1967. Urban Research Methods. Princeton: Van Nostrand Company.

Hadden, Jeffrey K., and Edgar F. Borgatta. 1965. American Cities: Their Social Characteristics. Chicago: Rand McNally & Company.

Harris, Chauncy D. 1943. A Functional Classification of Cities in the United States. Geographical Review 33:86–99.

Institute of Social Research, University of Michigan, n.d. Osiris Users Manual. Ann Arbor: Survey Research Center, University of Michigan.

Kass, Roy. 1972a. A Functional Classification of Metropolitan Communities. Unpublished paper presented at the annual meeting of the Population Association of America, Toronto, Canada.

————. 1972b. The Impact of Functional Specialization on Population Characteristics of Metropolitan Communities. Unpublished Ph.D. thesis, Brown University.

Kneedley, Grace M. 1945. Functional Types of Cities. In The Municipal Yearbook. Chicago: International City Managers Association.

Maxwell, J. W. 1965. The Functional Structure of Canadian Cities. Geographical Bulletin 7:79–104.

Nelson, Howard J. 1955. A Service Classification of American Cities. Economic Geography 31:189–210.

————. 1957. Some Characteristics of the Population of Cities in Similar Service Classifications. Economic Geography 38:95–108.

Pfouts, Ralph W. 1960. The Techniques of Urban Economic Analysis. West Trenton: Chandler-David Publishing Company.

Reiss, Albert J. 1957. Functional Specialization of Cities. Pp. 555–575 in Paul K. Hatt and Albert J. Reiss (eds.), Cities and Society. New York: The Free Press.

Smith, Robert H. T. 1965a. Method and Purpose in Functional Town Classification. Annals of the American Association of Geographers 55:539–548.

————. 1965b. The Function of Australian Towns. Tijdschrift voor Economische en Sociale Geografe 56:81–92.

Steigenga, W. 1955. A Comparative Analysis and a Classification of Netherland Towns. Tijdschrift voor Economische en Sociale Geografe 46:105–119.

Tyron, Robert C., and Daniel E. Bailey. 1970. Cluster Analysis. New York: McGraw-Hill.

Ullman, Edward L., and Michel F. Dacey. 1960. The Minimum Requirements Approach to the Urban Economic Base. Papers and Proceedings of the Regional Science Association 6:175–194.

U. S. Bureau of the Census. 1962 .County and City Data Book: 1962. (A Statistical Abstract Supplement). Washington, D.C.: Government Printing Office.

————. 1963. U. S. Census of Population: 1960. Vol. I, Characteristics of the Population. Washington, D.C.: Government Printing Office.

————. 1966a. Census of Business: 1963. Vol. 2, Retail Trade: Area Statistics. Washington, D.C.: Government Printing Office.

————. 1966b. Census of Business: 1963. Vol. 5, Wholesale Trade: Area Statistics. Washington, D.C.: Government Printing Office.

————. 1966c. Census of Manufacturers: 1963. Vol. 3, Area Statistics. Washington, D.C.: Government Printing Office.

Estimation of Supermarket Drawing Power: An Extension of Location Theory and Practice

J. D. Forbes and W. T. Ziemba

Introduction

The establishment of new business locations are very important capital investment decisions for some types of retailers. Supermarket chains, franchisers, gasoline companies, department stores, banks and other population specific sellers of goods and services spend large amounts of money and devote much management time to the insurance of "good" location decisions. These decisions have been intuitive to a large degree except in a few specific cases.

A major reason for the lack of structure in making this type of a decision is the lack of an adequate theory by which the structure of the decisions could be improved. Also it is believed by many practitioners that the informational and computing costs of using more sophisticated models does not justify their use. We will argue below that in many situations this is not the case.

This paper presents empirical evidence to show that Applebaum's method for structuring location decision conforms to Zipf's principle of least effort. Furthermore, it provides the means for estimating the relative attractiveness of retail stores, rapidly and inexpensively, with data which are relatively easy to collect.

Background

In 1949 Zipf advanced the principle of least effort in human behavior and used spatial phenomena to illustrate that "since human beings, after all, are the elements of the social group and, in providing the action of the group with least effort, they will make the group action one of least effort (p. 415)." This principle underlies the justification for almost all investigations of human spatial behavior. Olsson (1965) has provided an excellent summary of the myriad ways in which that principle and similar ideas have been applied and tested over the years.

The use of the theory in store location is the specific area of interest to this paper. Little theory has been used in locating retailing facilities in the past. Only one piece of theory specific to store location (Huff, 1963) has been found. However, most of the general theory of location can be applied to the store location problem.

Reprinted from *The Annals of Regional Science,* Vol. V, No. 2, December 1971, by permission of the authors and editor.

Management has been relatively slow in applying theory to practice. This is partly due to the fact that the necessary operations research expertise has been lacking in most of the firms where location decisions are important. Several national oil companies have had the operations research expertise in their organizations and the application of this expertise to the location problem has significantly improved their decisions in this area.

Two published methods of store location which are used to some degree by practitioners to assist in making location decisions have been found. The method published by Nelson (1958) has much intuitive insight into the location problem. However, the specification of the data use for the method is vague and tends to leave the reader unsure of how to proceed.

A second method of store location was given by Applebaum (1966). While the article describing the Applebaum model does not have the richness and intuitive insights which Nelson's book does, it does specify how store location decisions are made along with the method. This method is amenable to statistical verification and the remainder of this paper is devoted to a description of the Applebaum location procedure and the conversion of data collected by this method into a form which is recognizable as conforming to the principle of least effort.

Location Practice—A Description of the Analog Method

Two types of data are collected to estimate sales with the analog method, First, in-store interviews are conducted to determine where customers live and the size of their purchase. This is done by obtaining an address and then determining the lineal distance from the place of residence to the store. Secondly, circular distance rings are drawn to encompass the $0-\frac{1}{4}$, $\frac{1}{4}-\frac{1}{2}$, $\frac{1}{2}-\frac{3}{4}$, $\frac{3}{4}-1$, $1-1\frac{1}{2}$, $1\frac{1}{2}-2$, and $2\frac{1}{2}-3$ mile distance categories. Through the use of map overlays and other data sources the total population in each distance ring is determined. These two types of data are used to compute the analogs via:

$$DP_i = \frac{n_i}{N} \tag{1}$$

and

$$S_i = \frac{DP_i \cdot WS}{TP_i} \tag{2}$$

where DP_i = drawing power is the percentage of the store's customers obtained from distance category i

S_i = weekly sales per capita in distance category i

n_i = number of customers in sample of store customers from distance category i

N = total number of customers sampled

WS = weekly sales of the market

TP_i = total population in distance category i

i = (1) $0-\frac{1}{4}$ miles, (2) $\frac{1}{4}-\frac{1}{2}$, (3) $\frac{1}{2}-\frac{3}{4}$, (4) $\frac{3}{4}-1$, (5) $1-1\frac{1}{2}$, (6) $1\frac{1}{2}-2$, (7) $2-2\frac{1}{2}$, (8) $2\frac{1}{2}-3$

$$\text{ESC} = \sum_{i=1}^{8} S_i \cdot \text{TP}_i \qquad (3)$$

$$\text{TES} = \frac{\text{ESC}}{b} \qquad (4)$$

where ESC = calculated estimated sales

TES = total estimated sales

$$b = \sum_{i=1}^{8} \text{DP}_i$$

= the percent of sales up to and including the three mile category. In practice this varies with the location of the store. Typical values are .6 to .9. See Figure 1. In Equation (4) if the value for b was .85 then ESC would be 85% of the total sales estimate

The values of S_i are called analogs. They represent the sales per capita of persons within each distance ring and typically decline rapidly from the nearest to the farthest ring. The calculation in (4) using the parameter b is a catch-all to estimate sales to customers outside the three mile radius of the stores. For smaller stores this calculation rep- resents a small proportion (ten percent or less) of total sales. In larger stores this adjustment can be 30 to 40 per- cent. The error involved in such a cal- culation is not known. Cumulative S_i's are plotted in Figure 1.

To use the method, the location analyst is presented with a possible site location. From his data bank he gathers

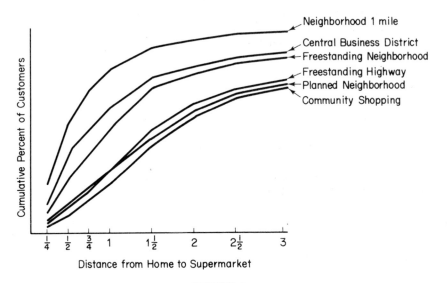

FIGURE 1

Drawing Power for Types of Supermarkets

population and income information for the concentric rings specific to the new location. He then searches his analog information bank and tries to find a set of analogs from a store which has characteristics—competition, income level, population, store size, etc. —similar to the proposed store. He then uses these analogs and the population and income data for the proposed site to produce an estimate of sales. If an appropriate analog set is not found he uses his experience to modify existing analogs to fit the proposed site.

The use of the Bureau of Labor Statistics data on family food purchases in conjunction with income information provides cross-checks on the validity of total food sales within the area under analysis and the reasonableness of supermarket sales. In practice this cross-check is usually very àccurate.

Through the use of the analog method, decision makers in the firm become more analytical in their evaluation of location from both a tactical as well as a strategic point of view. In addition to using the analogs to predict sales, the data is also useful to managers in evaluating the effects of location on their own and competitive outlets. Future location strategy can be simulated by forecasting growth areas and doing long-range planning to take advantage of the growth potential.

The managerial implications of using such a model in forms where location decisions can be important to the long-range viability of the organization are very important but are outside the scope of this paper.

Technical Problems with the Method

The most serious technical problem with using Applebaum's method is the fact that the criteria for choosing "ap-

propriate" analogs are left to the location maker. In practice the analogs are adjusted until they "look right." Experienced location analysts usually make good decisions with this method. However, it is difficult to learn from experience and to satistically identify where problems occur with this method.

It is felt that using data from many decisions could be helpful in removing individual aberrations in analogs and thereby increase the generality of the accumulated information. The remainder of this paper is concerned with restructuring information collected for use with Applebaum's procedure into a form which is more amenable to statistical analysis and naive empirical application.

Location Theory—An Exposition of a Modified Theory of Least Effort

Zipf's law states that, other things being equal, persons will go to the closest geographic location to obtain goods or services. This idea underlies much of location theory and is the basis of the mathematical derivations in this section of the paper.

The most common theories of human spatial behavior have, in their formulation, a monotone decreasing decay function. Hence customers go to the closest geographic location where perceived distance is some non-decreasing function of actual distance. For example, a store four miles away may be perceived as being more than twice as far away as a store two miles distant. If the relation is a power function with exponent two, then the perceived distance of the two stores would be in the ratio of 2^2 to 4^2 or 4 to 16. In other words, the store four miles away appears to be four times farther away than the store two miles from the buyer.

If the value of the exponent is known, then the spatial behavior of people and competitors can be predicted.

The distance effect is assumed to be

$$\frac{1}{D^\lambda} \qquad (5)$$

In an environment where people are spread over a geographic area the probability of a person patronizing store i is assumed to be

$$\frac{1/D_i^\lambda}{\sum\limits_{j=1}^{N} (1/D_j^\lambda)} \qquad (6)$$

Formula (6) assumes for stores of equal size, i.e., one unit, that the probability of patronizing store i is proportional to the customer's distance from store i and all other possible alternatives, where it is assumed that each D_j is at least one. Note that P_i is invariant under scale changes in the D_j.

For distances of 1, 2, 3, . . . units in radius, (6) is

$$P_i = \frac{1/D_i^\lambda}{1/1^\lambda + 1/2^\lambda \cdots + 1/n^\lambda + \cdots} \qquad (7)$$

for fixed decay factor λ. Note that the limiting term in the denominator of (7) is zero; i.e., assuming $\lambda > 0$, $\lim\limits_{D\to\infty} (1/D^\lambda) = 0$. This latter extreme case indicates that one will choose the outlet that, as λ gets large, is closest to his home with probability approaching one.

It is useful for the analysis to be presented here to consider alternative decay functions such as those illustrated in Figure 2. For high values of λ the distance effect is much greater than for low values.[1] A fitting of actual date to the generalized λ formula allows de-

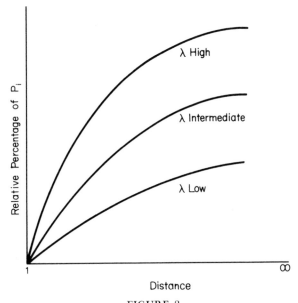

Relative Percentage of P_i

Distance

λ High

λ Intermediate

λ Low

FIGURE 2

Relationship Between P_i and Distance

[1] A recent article by Bucklin (1971) presents an interesting exposition on this matter. He also applies a new analytical technique which may be of value to the problem of store choice.

termination of spatial behavior for the types of stores for which data are available. Notice the striking resemblance between Figures 1 and 2.

To estimate sales from each distance using Applebaum's technique one may allocate a proportion of weekly sales to each ring by using the proportion of people in his in-store sample to represent the proportion of sales from each of the rings. This mixes income levels with population and makes assumptions about sales per customer, which, while empirically useful, is not conducive to identifying where the analyst erred in applying judgment. In addition to the latter, the theory leads one to feel that one should see a declining probability of patronage with increasing distance. To do this Applebaum's data must be transformed as follows:

$$\frac{\dfrac{\begin{array}{c}\text{Probability of a person}\\\text{in the store is from}\\\text{distance ring } i\\ \mathbf{DP}_i\end{array}}{\left(\begin{array}{c}\text{Number of people in}\\\text{distance ring } i\\ A_i\end{array}\right)}}{\displaystyle\sum_{i=1}^{N}\frac{\mathbf{DP}_i \cdot N}{A_i}} = P_i$$

where P_i = probability of person at A_i patronizing the store, $i = 1, \ldots, N$. The model hypothesizes that the P_i are generated via equation (6) and hence a stochastic specification of the model is

$$P_i = \frac{1/D_i^{\lambda}}{\displaystyle\sum_{i=1}^{N}(1/D_i^{\lambda})} + \epsilon_i \qquad (8)$$

where the ϵ_i is the unobserved error in equation $i, i = 1, \ldots, N$.

Now if one wishes to calculate the best λ via least squares, one must

$$\text{minimize } \phi(\lambda) = \sum_{i=1}^{N} \epsilon_i^2$$

$$= \sum_{i=1}^{N} \left(P_i - \frac{1/D_i^{\lambda}}{\displaystyle\sum_{i=1}^{N}(/D_i^{\lambda})}\right)^2 \qquad (9)$$

Since, for some types of stores, a substantial percentage of customers live beyond three miles, it was considered useful to provide a ninth estimation point. Consequently the cumulative percent of customers graph shown as Figure 1 was projected to 100 percent. We arbitrarily selected $4\frac{3}{4}$ miles as the center point of a concentric ring beyond which no customers would come. Population in that ring was said to have been equal to the population density of the ring closest to it (A_8) and P_9 was computed from these data.[2] There were then two sets of data, 8 normalized actual observations and 8 plus i computed observations which, since DP_9 was equal to $1 - \Sigma\ DP_i$, $i = 1$, ..., 8, did not need to be normalized.

Estimating λ

The values of λ for six store types for the two sets of data were estimated using Box's simplex method for function minimization (1965). The simplex method is a very efficient and simple method to implement for minimization problems. For the problem at hand involving only one unknown parameter, it works essentially as follows. Choose two values of λ, say λ_1 and λ_2, $\lambda_1 < \lambda_2$, evaluate ϕ at each of these points and also at their average $\lambda_a = (\lambda_1 + \lambda_2)/2$. Find the maximum of $[\phi(\lambda_1),\ \phi(\lambda_2)]$. This locates the worst point. Now as long as this worst point is not better

---

[2] A discussion of the data available for estimating λ in the discussion section below will support this procedure.

than the point λ_a one reflects a distance away from the worst point. More specifically, suppose $\phi(\lambda_2) > \phi(\lambda_1)$ and λ_2 is the worst point; one moves to the point $\lambda_3 = \lambda_2 - \alpha(\lambda_2 - \lambda_a)$ for a given α, normally 1.3. The process continues utilizing λ_1 and λ_3 as depicted in Figure 3 until the value of ϕ at each of the three points is within some given tolerance.

In practice one uses several values of λ at each iteration instead of just two and a variable α. The simplex method is a relatively ad hoc approach, however, because ϕ is not convex or even quasi-convex; it proved superior to other methods because of its speed and the fact that one could try several sets of starting values of λ if it was suspected that the λ^* obtained was a local rather than a global minima. In actual fact the method worked admirably and the maximum number of iterations needed to obtain a solution for any of 204 estimates made was fourteen (using a tolerance of 10^{-5} on ϕ).[3, 4]

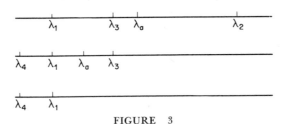

FIGURE   3

[3] Only the λ for the averaged data are reported in this paper. A working paper contains the λ values for 96 individual store estimates. A copy of this working paper by the present authors is cited in the references and is available on request.

[4] There are at least two variants of (9) that one might use to estimate λ. Namely, one might minimize

$$\psi(\lambda) = \sum_{i=1}^{N} \left(P_i \sum_{i=1}^{D} \frac{1}{D_i{}^\lambda} - \frac{1}{D_i{}^\lambda} \right)^2$$

This function is ill-conditioned and some preliminary computer runs indicated that λ tends to ∞ (indicating that all terms in the expression for ψ are getting smaller and smaller) since $\lim_{\lambda \to \infty} \psi(\lambda) = 0$. In the second variant one lets

$$u = \left(\sum_{i=1}^{N} \frac{1}{D_i{}^\lambda} \right)^{-1}$$

and minimizes

$$\psi(\mu, \lambda) = \sum_{i=1}^{N} \left(P_i - \mu \frac{1}{D_i{}^\lambda} \right)^2$$

This approach is less efficient than minimizing ϕ since the information that

$$\mu = \left(\sum_{i=1}^{N} \frac{1}{D_i{}^\lambda} \right)^{-1}$$

is not taken into account, but one might suspect that it would be easier to minimize than ϕ and would give substantially the same results. However, even though the λ^*'s obtained were nearly the same as those obtained by minimizing ϕ this method proved to be computationally far less efficient.

It is expected that the estimated value of λ for the store having the least ability to draw customers from far away (a store located in a neighborhood area with competition within one mile) would have the highest value of λ. Likewise, stores in community shopping centers should have the lowest λ value. In fact the order of having the highest cumulative percent of customers in three miles should be the order for the values of λ. It can be seen in Table 1 and in Figure 4 that this order was obtained except that the λ values for planned neighborhood centers were more like the freestanding neighborhood centers and C. B. D. locations than freestanding highway and community shopping centers. In Figure 4 only three of the six λ values have been plotted to reduce confusion.

Discussion

The estimates of store drawing power provided by the simplex method seem to conform to location theory. It remains to apply the estimates obtained to data which will allow a test of the parameters (λ*) produced as an estimating technique for supermarket sales. The purpose of this paper was to produce these estimates from data collected for a similar problem with a technique which, to the authors' knowledge, has not been applied to this problem class before.

It is felt that the pooling of data from stores of the same type in different areas cancels out aberrations at individual stores, varying population densities and things such as local traffic access, etc.

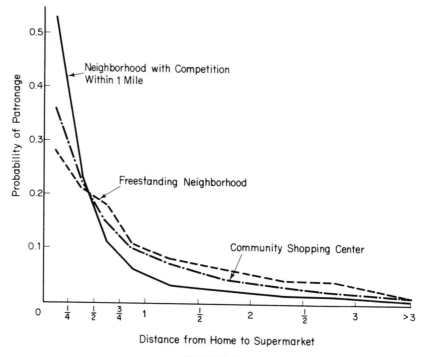

FIGURE 4

Estimated Relationship Between Distance and Patronage

TABLE 1
Estimated Probabilities of a Person Patronizing a Type of Store by Distance of Residence from That Store

Distance from Store (miles)	Community Shopping Center (n = 16)		Planned Neighborhood Center (n = 15)		Freestanding Highway (n = 10)		Freestanding Neighborhood (n = 29)		Central Business District (n = 11)		Neighborhood Competition Within 1 mile (n = 17)	
	9 points	8 points	9 points	8 points	9 points	8 points	9 points	8 points	9 points	8 points	9 points	8 points
0–¼	.28	.28	.39	.39	.28	.29	.36	.37	.38	.38	.53	.53
¼–½	.21	.21	.17	.17	.21	.21	.22	.22	.19	.19	.23	.24
½–¾	.18	.18	.12	.12	.16	.16	.15	.15	.11	.12	.11	.11
¾–1	.11	.11	.10	.10	.14	.14	.10	.10	.08	.08	.06	.06
1–1½	.08	.08	.08	.08	.09	.09	.07	.07	.08	.08	.03	.03
1½–2	.06	.06	.06	.07	.06	.06	.04	.04	.07	.07	.02	.02
2–2½	.04	.05	.03	.04	.03	.03	.03	.03	.05	.05	.01	.01
2½–3	.04	.04	.03	.03	.02	.02	.02	.02	.03	.03	.01	.01
Over 3	.01		.01		.01		.01		.01		.00	
Computed λ value	.64	.61	.88	.86	.66	.63	.86	.84	.86	.85	1.29	1.28
r^2	.934	.947	.985	.988	.993	.993	.974	.978	.991	.992	.984	.985

67

The data for this study are from a chain of supermarkets. In many cases the three mile distance ring is in rural farmlands. This can be seen in the data since total population should increase with each distance ring if the density of population remains constant over the area. This happens because the area of each concentric ring is larger than the previous one. In the data for this paper, such was not the case. In an urban area, where all stores are surrounded by relatively high population densities, the values for λ should be higher than those estimated here because the tail of the cumulative probability distribution would approach zero more rapidly due to an increased probability of intervening shopping opportunities as distance increases.

In the case of the present data, oftentimes areas farther away from the store are rural and therefore contain no alternative grocery stores. For data for stores in a large metropolitan area, with its concomitant increase in alternative shopping sites and higher transportation friction, higher λ values would most likely be the result.

In summary, it has been shown that through a simple transformation an estimation of the λ value in Huff's model can be estimated from data collected in a grocery store according to a procedure outlined by Applebaum. A simplex method for estimating these values was found efficient and effective. The distribution of probabilities of patronage conform to Zipf's principle of least effort.

Conclusions

The following conclusions may be drawn from the study:

1. It is possible to estimate the drawing power of stores through information on the origin of customers gathered in those stores.
2. The type of measures of distance decay which were estimated conform with Zipf's principle of least effort and as theorized by Huff's formulation of the standard gravity model.
3. Supermarket drawing power is affected by location.
4. A simplex algorithm for function fitting is an efficient and effective method of estimating the distance effect exponent.
5. It may be possible to use this technique to study the usage of other people–based activities and systems of activities.

REFERENCES

Applebaum, William, "Methods for Determining Store Trade Areas, Market Penetration, and Potential Sales," *Journal of Marketing Research,* Vol. 3, No. 2 (May 1966), pp. 127–141.

Box, M. J., "A New Method of Constrained Optimization and a Comparison with Other Methods," *Computer Journal,* 7 (1965), 42–52.

Bucklin, Louis P., "Trade Area Boundaries: Some Issues in Theory and Methodology," *Journal of Marketing Research,* Vol. 8, No. 1 (Feb. 1971), pp. 30–37.

Forbes, J. D., and Ziemba, W. T., *Estimation of Supermarket Drawing Power: An Extension of Location Theory and Practice,* Working Paper No. 60, Faculty of Commerce and Business Administration, University of British Columbia, Vancouver, 1971.

Huff, David L., *A Probabilistic Analysis of Consumer Spatial Behavior*, Division of Research, Graduate School of Business Administration, University of California, Los Angeles, 1963.

Nelder, J. A., and Mead, R., "A Simplex Method for Function Minimization," *Computer Journal*, 7 (1965), 308.

Nelson, R. L., *The Selection of Retail Locations*, McGraw-Hill Book Co., New York, 1958.

Olsson, Gunnar, *Distance and Human Interaction*, Bibliography Services No. 2, Regional Science Research Institute, Philadelphia, 1965.

Zipf, George Kingsley, *Human Behavior and the Principle of Least Effort*, Addison-Wesley Press, Inc., Reading, Mass.

The Shape of Suburban Retail Market Areas: Implications from a Literature Review

Peter L. Simons

Specifying the shape of a retail market area is a potentially useful way of summarizing the general characteristics of the distribution of customers around a store or shopping center. However, most specifications of shape are two-dimensional (spatial) generalizations based on a single market area boundary which represents the points of origin of customers. Conventionally, these points of origin are taken to be customers' homes. A major fault of these spatial generalizations is that little or no attention is paid to the relative importance of patronage with increasing distance from retail outlets.

Descriptions of shape are an important part of the geometrical tradition in geography,[1] where shape is used to summarize a wide range of spatial patterns. There are also theoretical reasons for the interest of geographers[2] (and others) in shape. In the case of retail market areas, central place theory and the gravity model are central elements in the voluminous literature. These theories[3] give some insight into the spatial shape of market areas since they are quite explicit about the origins of patronage of shopping centers. However, the theories are in direct conflict in what they say about the structure, or third dimension, of retail market areas.

This article is, then, concerned with two interrelated problems: the failure of traditional measures of shape to incorporate a third dimension, and the conflict between the theories relevant to the third dimension in retailing. In the first section of the article, a single spatial shape is established and those factors likely to distort it are identified by a literature review; the review also defines the nature of the conflict between the theories in the third dimension. The second section of the article considers the implications of this con-

---

Reprinted from the *Journal of Retailing*, Vol. 49, No. 4, Winter 1973–1974, by permission of the author and editor.

[1] P. Haggett, *Locational Analysis in Human Geography* (London: Edward Arnold, 1966), pp. 15–16.

[2] B. J. Blair and T. H. Biss, "The Measurement of Shape in Geography: An Appraisal of Methods and Techniques," *Bulletin of Quantitative Data for Geographers,* No. 11 (London: Department of Geography, Nottingham University, 1967), p. 1.

[3] It seems justified to consider the gravity model as a theory rather than an empirical regularity in view of the recent article by J. H. Niedercorn and B. W. Bechdolt, "An Economic Derivation of the Gravity Law of Spatial Interaction," *Journal of Regional Science,* Vol. 9, No. 2 (August 1969). A comment and reply are contained in Vol. 10, No. 3 (December 1970).

flict by outlining the complexity of the problem of theoretically specifying a single structure for market areas, particularly in suburban areas.

Theoretical Shape of Market Areas

Theoretical ideas about the spatial shape of retail market areas were initiated by Christaller [4] and Lösch. [5] They concurred that the basic shape is a circle, although they modified this shape to a hexagon in order to achieve consistency in their theoretical systems. Subsequent theoretical modifications allowed for variations in population density [6] and in transport costs. [7]

Empirical studies that consider the spatial shape of market areas suggest that this basic shape is affected by competition [8] (including intervening opportunity), [9] by varying population density and income, [10] and by physical barriers to movement. [11] It is worth noting that barriers to movement may also be nonphysical; that is, an individual's knowledge or perception of an area may create subjective barriers that are only slightly less effective than physical barriers. For example, perceptual barriers are inherent in the use of reference nodes (place of residence) and of an orientation node (the CBD) to explain urban search behavior. [12] Barriers of this kind also underlie the suggestion that, in the case of retail market areas, "consumers tend to move towards a dominant centre [say the CBD] and will not bypass a centre to reach another of comparable facility. . . ." [13] The net effect of all these distorting factors on the basic shape of retail market areas is that "visually the trading areas are *elliptical,* with the *longer axis* tending away from the CBD" [my italics]. [14]

Actually, the market area shapes that

---

[4] W. Christaller, *Central Places in Southern Germany* (Englewood Cliffs, N.J.: Prentice-Hall, Inc., 1966).

[5] A Lösch, *The Economics of Location* (New Haven, Conn.: Yale University Press, 1954).

[6] W. Isard, *Location and Space Economy* (Cambridge, Mass.: M.I.T. Press, 1956), pp. 272–73.

[7] M. L. Greenhut, "The Size and Shape of the Market Area of the Firm," *Southern Economic Journal,* 19 (1952), 40–41.

[8] W. Applebaum and S. B. Cohen, "The Dynamics of Store Trading Areas and Market Equilibrium," *Annals of Association of American Geographers,* 51, No. 1 (March 1961), 81–83.

[9] S. A. Stouffer, "Intervening Opportunities: A Theory Relating Mobility and Distance," *American Sociological Review,* Vol. 5 (December 1940). J. Simmons, "The Changing Pattern of Retail Location," Research Paper No. 92 (Chicago: Department of Geography, University of Chicago, 1964), pp. 140–44.

[10] B. J. L. Berry and H. G. Barnum, "Aggregate Relations and Elemental Components of Central Place Systems," in *Readings in Economic Geography,* R. H. T. Smith et al. (eds.) (Chicago: Rand McNally, 1968), pp. 306–7. D. L. Thompson, "Analysis of Retailing Potential in Metropolitan Areas," Research Paper (Berkeley, Calif.: Institute of Business and Economic Research, University of California, 1964), Chapter 3. P. Scott, *Geography and Retailing* (London: Hutchinson, 1970), pp. 61–67.

[11] Applebaum and Cohen, "The Dynamics of Store Trading Areas," pp. 80–81. B. J. L. Berry, "Commercial Structure and Commercial Blight" (Chicago: Research Paper No. 85, Department of Geography, University of Chicago, 1963), pp. 69–71.

[12] L. A. Brown and J. Holmes, "Search Behavior in an Intra-Urban Migration Context: A Spatial Perspective," Discussion Paper No. 5 (Columbus, Ohio: Department of Geography, Ohio State University, 1970). See also K. Lynch, *The Image of the City* (Cambridge, Mass.: M.I.T. Press, 1960), pp. 72–83 for a general discussion of nodes and landmarks.

[13] Scott, *Geography and Retailing,* p. 61.

[14] Applebaum and Cohen, "The Dynamics of Store Trading Areas," p. 80.

Applebaum and Cohen call ellipses only approximate that shape. Study of their maps suggests that the minor axis of the "ellipse" more often than not passes through the major axis near the focal point farthest from the dominant center (see Figure 1). Also that the store or shopping center tends to be near the focal point closest to the dominant center.[15] These variations from the "pure" elliptical shape are a result of: decreasing population density with increasing distance from a dominant center[16]; easier accessibility to and from dominant centers because of the radial pattern of transport routes which exists in most cases; and the need to service all areas which causes the width of a market area to increase with increasing distance from the dominant center or orientation node. It is interesting to note that if a set of these irregular ellipses is converted to irregular hexagons, the result is a replica of that developed by Isard when he adjusted Lösch's regular hexagons.[17]

Thus it can be seen that the hypoth-esized shape of a retail market area is dependent upon the assumptions made. At the highest level of generalization, the basic theoretical shape is a circle. The key assumption underlying this suggested shape, in the case of a single market area, is that there will be a "limit of feasibility" for patronizing a retail outlet (whatever its characteristics). An additional assumption of equal accessibility in all directions from the outlet(s) means that the "limit of feasibility" will form the circumference of a circle.

Central place theory, which considers the multimarket area case, contains a further assumption that, in effect, redefines the "limit of feasibility," but does not change the basic shape. To be specific, the assumption of rational spatial actions (which incorporates the principle of least effort) places the boundary of each market area halfway between a central place[18] and the nearest central places of the same order in the hierarchy. Since central places of the same order are equi-

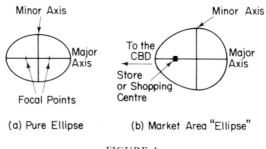

(a) Pure Ellipse   (b) Market Area "Ellipse"

FIGURE 1

Difference Between a Pure Ellipse and the Elliptical
Shape of Empirical Market Areas

[15] See also the maps by B. J. L. Berry, *Geography of Market Centers and Retail Distribution* (Englewood Cliffs, N.J.: Prentice-Hall, Inc., 1967), p. 55.

[16] Research in this area is reviewed in Haggett, *Locational Analysis in Human Geography,* pp. 154–58.

[17] Isard, *Location and Space Economy,* pp. 272–73.

[18] Precedents for equating retail centers with central places are widespread in the literature, although it is realized that they are not quite the same conceptually.

distant from each other, the conclusion that a circle is the basic shape of market areas is not affected.

Regarding the third dimension, or structure, of market areas, it follows from the assumption of rational actions that each central place has 100 percent drawing power (or penetration) within the market areas defined by central place theory. Little more that is related to the structure of market areas can be derived from central place theory.

The major source of ideas about the structure of retail market areas is research based upon the gravity model. Essentially, the gravity model suggests that the relative volume of purchases by consumers at a store, and the frequency of trips to a store, is a function of the size of the store (or shopping center) and of the distance between the store and the origin of a purchasing trip. This model underlies the work of Reilly,[19] Fetter,[20] and the Hysons,[21] among others, while Huff[22] incorporated probabilistic notions. The gravity principle is also implicit in Golledge's[23] zones of advantage and disadvantage, in Stouffer's[24] concept of intervening opportunity, in Nelson's[25] idea of suburban shopping centers a

"interceptors," in Rushton's[26] work on indifference curves and consumer space preferences, and in the almost universal subdivision of retail market areas into primary, secondary, and fringe areas.[27] In fact, it is fair to claim that, despite its problems,[28] the gravity concept is the most pervasive theory currently used in Economic Geography.

If central-place theory and the gravity model are used to construct theoretical solids to represent the shape of retail market areas in three dimensions, the solids that result are quite different. A right-circular cone, with a base extending almost to the nearest centers of similar size, is the approximate shape one would expect if more recent versions of the gravity model were able to operate undisturbed in all directions from a retail node (Figure 2a). A cone is only an approximate representation of the "pure" form of the gravity model because the inverse distance exponent used in the model results in a curved slope (rather than a straight line) to represent structure. For example, squaring distance leads to a convexo-concave slope with increasing distance from a retail node. Indirect support for a curved slope is outlined

[19] W. J. Reilly, "Methods for Study in Retail Relationships," Research Monograph No. 4 (Austin, Texas: Bureau of Business Research, University of Texas, 1929).

[20] F. A. Fetter, "The Economic Law of Market Areas," *Quarterly Journal of Economics*, Vol. 28 (1924).

[21] C. D. Hyson and W. P. Hyson, "The Economic Law of Market Areas," *Quarterly Journal of Economics*, Vol. 64 (1950).

[22] D. L. Huff, "A Probabilistic Analysis of Shopping Center Trade Areas," *Land Economics* (1963); "Defining and Estimating a Trading Area," *Journal of Marketing*, Vol. 28, No. 3 (1964). R. Gambini, D. Huff, and G. F. Jenks, "Geometric Properties of Market Areas," *Papers and Proceedings of Regional Science Association*, Vol. 20 (1968).

[23] R. G. Golledge, "Conceptualizing the Market Decision Process, *Journal of Regional Science*, Vol. 7, No. 2 (Supplement), (1967), p. 244.

[24] Stouffer, "Intervening Opportunities."

[25] R. L. Nelson, "The Selection of Retail Location" (Chicago: F. W. Dodge, 1958), p. 26.

[26] G. Rushton, "Analysis of Spatial Behavior by Revealed Space Preference," *Annals of Association of American Geographers*, Vol. 59, No. 2 (June 1969); "Behavioral Correlates of Urban Spatial Structure," *Economic Geography*, Vol. 47, No. 1 (January 1971).

[27] For example, see Berry (1967), "Commercial Structure," p. 127.

[28] Haggett, *Locational Analysis in Human Geography*, pp. 37–39.

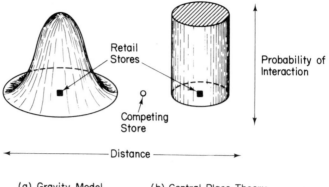

(a) Gravity Model   (b) Central Place Theory

FIGURE 2

Theoretical Market Area Shapes in Three
Dimensions

by Bucklin,[29] while a detailed discussion of empirical results that support such a slope is undertaken by Thorpe and Nader.[30]

In the case of central-place theory, a circular cylinder (Figure 2b) is a result of the assumptions of rational spatial actions, equal accessibility, and a uniform population distribution. Also, there is an implicit assumption of equal interaction by individuals with a central place. The base of the cylinder has a radius of half the distance to competing nodes of similar size.

The main differences between these theoretical solids are portrayed by Figures 2 and 3. Figure 2 depicts the "ideal shapes" in relation to a single competing store positioned relative to both shapes, while Figure 3 illustrates the differences between the shapes in a cross-sectional format. The vertical axis (or height of the shapes) may represent either probability of interaction or pro-portion of sales or expenditure by consumers.

Problem of Identifying a Single Theoretical Structure

It is apparent that the most obvious differences between the ideal shapes occur in the structure of market areas. These differences in structure are a result of the sharp boundaries between market areas which are part of central place theory, whereas the gravity model, more realistically, allows for extensive overlap between market areas. It is tempting to dismiss these differences by claiming that they result from the assumption of rational spatial action in central place theory. While this may be so, the differences between the shapes have other implications that are worth consideration. Of prime importance are the reality of the rational action as-

[29] L. P. Bucklin, "The Concept of Mass in Intra-Urban Shopping," *Journal of Marketing*, 31, No. 4, Part 1 (October 1967), 42.

[30] D. Thorpe and G. R. Nader, "Customer Movement and Shopping Centre Structure—A Study of a Central Place System in North Durham," *Regional Studies*, Vol. 1 (1967).

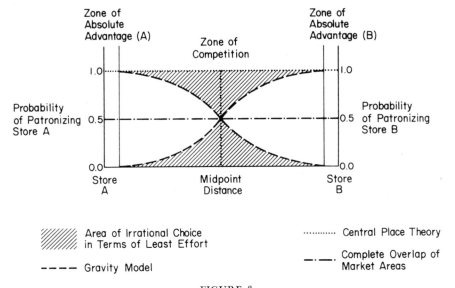

FIGURE 3

Cross Section of Market Area Between Two Competing Stores (Assuming
No Other Stores)

sumption and the related problem of generalizing about the structure of retail market areas or, more specifically, about the shape of the cross-sectional curve.

To date, in this article, no distinction has been made between the interurban and suburban situations. While it can be argued that the sharp boundaries drawn by classical central place theorists are often arbitrary, empirical results indicate that divisions between consumer patronage of centers are quite distinct in rural areas.[31] These results indicate that distance is an important influence on consumer choice in rural areas and that an assumption of rational spatial action may have some relevance in such situations. So it seems reasonable to suggest that, in the interurban case, the shape of the profile derived from central place theory may be an adequate first approximation of the structure of retail market areas.

In contrast, a more complex situation exists in suburban areas largely because population densities are higher. These higher densities make it possible for retail stores to achieve acceptable levels of sales within an area much smaller than that enclosed by the maximum distance consumers are willing to travel to purchase a particular good: in central place theory terms, a central place's threshold area is very much less than the range area of the goods it supplies. The result, in surburban areas, is that retail facilities are duplicated within the range area of other stores, market areas overlap extensively, and a

31 For example, see Berry (1967), *Geography of Market Centers,* pp. 11–12, 17. N. G. Sharp, *Case Studies of Rural Shopping, Northern New South Wales* (Australia: Unpublished doctoral thesis, Department of Geography, University of Sydney, 1967).

high degree of irrational choice, in terms of the least effort principle, is present. Consequently, consumers' "revealed preferences are most affected by the variety of goods and services," [32] and distance is relatively less important as a factor in consumer choice within cities.

These complications do not alter the conclusion that the basic plan shape of a market area is a circle. Even in metropolitan areas, there will be feasibility limits (of distance) for patronage of a center and, assuming equal accessibility in all directions and that the probability of visiting a store does not change with direction from the store, so a circle will still be the basic spatial shape.

However, it is more difficult to identify a single cross-sectional shape for the suburban case. At first sight it may seem that the gravity model achieves the objective of a single profile shape because it allows for overlap between the market areas and for competition between centers.[33] There are several reasons why such a claim is too simplistic; these include empirical studies by Garrison and Marble, who concluded that trip frequency is not a function of distance over relatively short distances,[34] problems inherent in the gravity model itself, and ideas expressed by Golledge [35] and by Bucklin.[36] The last three points will be considered in sequence.

Despite the inherent problems of the gravity model outlined by Haggett [37] and Carrothers,[38] the usual opinion of the gravity model is that it is a surprisingly accurate empirical generalization. On the contrary, the "accuracy" of the model is usually a result of "calibrating" the model to fit particular situations; that is, the distance exponent is adjusted to the data being analyzed. It is hardly surprising that this kind of procedure has led to large variations in distance exponent values. (Even Reilly found that the exponent varied between 0.0 and 12.5.[39]) However, variations in the exponent when estimated in such a fashion are not solely attributable to the independent variable of distance. What is happening, in fact, is that distance operates as a kind of error term for all other independent variables; it is an error term for variables in the equation and for others in the area being studied. Therefore, the supposed "accuracy" of the gravity model is largely a result of an almost classic example of circular reasoning.[40]

Unfortunately, no independent method of estimating the distance exponent for particular situations has been developed. The utility-based derivation of the gravity model by Neidercorn and Bechdolt [41] is of no assistance, while Huff clearly derives the distance exponent for areas and commodities

---

[32] Berry (1967), *Geography of Market Centers,* p. 88.

[33] Huff (1964), "Probabilistic Analysis of Shopping Center Trade Areas," p. 37.

[34] Reported in W. Bunge, *Theoretical Geography* (Lund: C. W. K. Gleerup, 1966), p. 151.

[35] Golledge, "Conceptualizing the Market Decision Process."

[36] L. P. Bucklin, "Trade Area Boundaries: Some Issues in Theory and Methodology," *Journal of Marketing Research,* Vol. 8, No. 1 (February 1971).

[37] Haggett, *Locational Analysis in Human Geography,* pp. 37–40.

[38] G. P. Carrothers, "An Historic Review of the Gravity and Potential Concepts of Human Interaction," *Journal of American Institute of Planners,* 22 (1956), pp. 94–102.

[39] Reported in Scott, *Geography and Retailing,* p. 169.

[40] For a discussion of the need to predesignate hypotheses see F. C. Mills, *Introduction to Statistics* (New York: H. Holt and Company, 1956), p. 211.

[41] Neidercorn and Bechdolt, "An Economic Derivation of the Gravity Law."

from data for the area.[42] It should be remembered that Huff's work is regarded as the most advanced form of development of the gravity model. Hence it may be concluded that a different profile shape exists for every commodity in every retail store—no single profile shape has been identified in either empirical or theoretical research.

Further, Golledge's work on behavior, and particularly that on learning theory, suggests that market area profiles vary through time. He combines the central place theory and gravity model profiles in a series of probability curves, and argues that in the zone of maximum advantage (depicted for an early learning stage in Figure 3) it is absolutely certain that a consumer will visit the retail outlet specified. The result is a form of stereotype (repetitive) behavior which is the logical result of the learning process. However, rational behavior, in terms of least effort, is only one of a number of possible behavioral strategies [43]: stereotype behavior may include regular patronage of more than one store.

Beyond the zone of maximum advantage is the zone of competition where the probability of patronage decreases in the manner suggested by the gravity curve. Also decreasing is "the possibility of finding evidence of the one-center least effort syndrome . . ." [44] as a result of increasing uncertainty as to the outcome of shopping trips and of the need to be aware of opportunities over a larger area.

Therefore, in the context of this article, Golledge is suggesting that the "area" of irrational choice in Figure 3

will decrease as the learning process continues and stereotype behavior becomes established. Over time, the probability of regular patronage will increase at greater distances from the store. The implication is that, in general, the least-effort behavioral strategy will become more common as learning proceeds. On the basis of Golledge's ideas no comment can be made about changes over time in the relationship between the proportion of sales and distance because varying behavioral strategies are possible.

So the spatial extent of the zone of maximum advantage will increase through time, according to Golledge. At any particular point in time a market area is the aggregate of the behavior patterns of individual consumers who are at different stages in the learning process, or who have settled into one of the stereotype behavior patterns.

These general conclusions must be slightly modified in the case of suburban retail market areas. In urban areas, the duplication of retail facilities, the high degree of overlap of market areas, and the high level of accessibility of consumers to retail facilities is likely to mean that the least-effort behavioral strategy will not be important in the choice of a particular center. In fact, it seems likely that zones of maximum advantage are unlikely to be strongly developed because relatively few stores or shopping centers have substantial areas around them in which all possible consumers visit them regularly.

Infinite possible variations in the shape of the cross sections of suburban market areas lead, inevitably, to sup-

[42] Huff, "Defining and Estimating a Trading Area" (1964), p. 37.

[43] P. Kotler, "Behavioral Models for Analyzing Buyers," *Journal of Marketing*, Vol. 29, No. 4 (1965).

[44] Golledge, "Conceptualizing the Market Decision Process," p. 246.

port for the conclusion reached by Bucklin. He identified two extreme profiles: a vertical (least-effort) profile where distance provides maximum protection and a horizontal profile where distance from a store does not affect the probability of visiting it; the latter represents complete overlap in that the competing stores each attract 50 percent of sales in Figure 3. The degree of overlap is related to "the importance of finding the right price, quality, and service when buying and to the perception that these vary among retail outlets."[45] The inference is that the greater the effort consumers are willing to make to purchase a particular good, the greater the overlap in market areas.

While the vertical profile obviously corresponds to the central place theory case identified earlier and the gravity model is applicable between the two extremes, a theoretical base for the other extreme is more obscure. In his chapter on "differentiation of the product," Chamberlin [46] identified spatial (location) and product differentitation components of monopoly. It is suggested that the product differentiation component (perhaps the term "store differentiation" is more appropriate here) is relevant to the horizontal profile. If a store is successfully differentiated (that is, it is seen to be unique by consumers), then distance is unlikely to provide protection except insofar as feasibility limits[47] eventually appear. As a result, customers may be expected to make some effort to patronize their preferred store and the extent of overlap between market areas will be complete. Com-

peting, similarly differentiated, stores will attract those consumers not patronizing the first store.

Interestingly, the spatial monopoly component of Chamberlin's ideas is applicable to the vertical profile. Here perfect competition is assumed and so all stores are seen to be similar by consumers. Consequently, convenience becomes a decisive explanatory factor and consumers patronize the nearest store. The coexistence of monopoly and competition is a crucial element in Chamberlin's exposition and is also important in understanding market area profiles.

From Chamberlin's work it seems reasonable to infer that the location strategies of retail firms may depend upon the effort consumers are willing to make to purchase goods. If little effort can be expected, then the location strategy should be either to obtain a spatial monopoly by locating as far as possible from competitors, or to select a location which will "intercept" a sufficient proportion of a competitor's customers. The obvious analogy of the former strategy is the explanation in central place theory of the location of a low-order center in relation to three equal higher-order centers. Alternatively, if consumers make an effort to purchase a store's goods, a site near competitors is desirable in order to facilitate comparison.

Bucklin follows a similar line of reasoning when he suggests that the shape of the profile will be reasonably consistent for each product.[48] This line of argument is, of course, an extension of the convenience–comparison goods dichotomy which has not been used so

[45] Bucklin, "The Concept of Mass in Intra-Urban Shopping," p. 31.

[46] E. H. Chamberlin, *The Theory of Monopolistic Competition* (Cambridge, Mass.: Harvard University Press, 1960), pp. 61–63.

[47] Golledge, "Conceptualizing the Market Decision Process," p. 241.

[48] Bucklin, "The Concept of Mass in Intra-Modern Shopping," p. 31.

often in recent years; this dichotomy has always really been a surrogate for consumer effort. The difficulty in using this distinction between goods is that individuals are willing to make varying efforts to purchase the same good. Both Bucklin's work and the preceding comments derived from Chamberlin's theory do not adequately resolve the problem of variations in individual effort.

Concluding Statement

There can be no doubt that at the highest level of generalization, the basic plan shape of retail market areas is a circle. This conclusion does not change in the light of Golledge's work on learning theory or Bucklin's research on market area overlap. It simply means that not all consumers in a potential market area are customers and that customers may have different purchasing patterns, including regular patronage of other stores. The summary description of the plan shape must still be the circle.

However, it is not possible to identify a single profile shape indicative of the structure of retail market areas. The indeterminant nature of the structural dimension is a result of variations in the importance of distance and in the effort consumers are willing to make to purchase goods. Existing theory in this area is either poorly developed (Chamberlin), too restrictive (central place theory) or has conceptual problems (the gravity model).

There are a number of areas of research potential that may lead to the resolution of these problems. First, it may be possible to develop a method of deriving the distance exponent of the gravity model which does not depend on data relevant to a specific area. Such an approach would presumably be based upon the effort consumers are willing to make to purchase a good and on the nature of the spatial structure in which the purchasing decision is made. Secondly, the use of the bivariate normal distribution as a theoretical solid representing retail market areas is an attractive possibility. Empirical work referred to earlier supports such a shape, but there is a need to justify, in theoretical terms, why customers should be normally distributed around a shopping center. Finally, recent work on consumer images of stores and shopping centers [49] indicates the nature of differentiations between retail outlets. The extent to which these differences are associated with variations in consumer effort remains to be established.

[49] L. L. Berry, "The Components of Department Store Image: A Theoretical and Empirical Analysis," *Journal of Retailing,* Vol. 45, No. 1 (Spring 1969).

W. Lazer and A. G. Wyckham, "Perceptual Segmentation of Department Store Markets," *Journal of Retailing,* Vol. 45, No. 2 (Summer 1969).

Methods for Determining Store Trade Areas, Market Penetration, and Potential Sales

William Applebaum

Determining Trade Areas and Market Penetration

Customer Spotting Techniques

An existing store's trade area is determined by a technique known as "customer spotting" [6]. This technique involves interviewing a representative sample of customers in a store to obtain their addresses and information on shopping habits. If one useful interview is obtained for every $100 of weekly store sales, each interviewed customer statistically represents $100. Locating ("spotting") each interviewed customer on a map gives a cartographic view of the store's trade area.

Circles or zones with radii of $1/4$, $1/2$, $3/4$, 1 mile, etc., are drawn from the store site on the map. The number of spotted customers in each zone is determined and computed as a ratio (percentage) of the total called "drawing power."

Store sales are assumed to be proportionate to location of customers (an assumption that involves some margin of error), and therefore the percentage of sales the store gets from each zone is the same as the drawing power ratio.[1] If 20 percent of a store's spotted customers come from the 0–$1/4$ mile zone and the store has $30,000 sales each week, then $6,000 sales are assumed to come from this zone.

By using a population dot map, one

Reprinted from the *Journal of Marketing Research,* Vol. III, May 1966, published by the American Marketing Association, by permission of the author and editor.

[1] The author has tested the validity of this assumption, based on 7,584 customer interviews obtained in eight supermarkets on a Thursday and Saturday. The weekly value of a customer was calculated by multiplying the actual customer's sales transaction by the number of weekly store visits, as reported by the customer. The results were:

Zone of Customer's Residence (miles)	Weekly Value Index
.00–.25	1.00
.25–.50	.96
.50–.75	.93
.75–1.00	.93
	.94

can determine the population within each zone and compute sales per capita [1]. In the above example, if there are 3,000 people within the 0–¼ mile zone, the store's weekly per capita sales from this zone are $2.00.

A space–distance approach, this zonal method treats all space within a zone equally. It is known that when distance from the store site increases beyond some variable point, customers are not drawn equally from all parts of the zone. In some cases a store may have many customers from one section of a zone and none from another section. Two major factors affecting directional drawing power of a store are topography and competition.

Primary, Secondary and Tertiary Trade Areas

Store location analysts frequently subdivide a store's trade area into primary, secondary and tertiary (or fringe) areas. Such subdivisions are typically related to automobile travel time, or time–distance, and are particularly useful for studying large planned shopping center sites. Little published quantitative empirical data are available to support the validity and usefulness of travel time intervals delineating trade area subdivisions.

For analytical purposes, a store's trade area can be subdivided meaningfully using customer spotting and supplementary data. By refining and extending the zonal or space–distance approach, greater precision is possible in measuring (1) the store's trade area, (2) the total sales potential of the area, and (3) the market share (penetration) that the store gets from within the different parts of its trade area.

To get practical statistical measurements for evaluating store performance in relation to opportunity, the primary trade area must be thought of as a geographic *core* from which a store gets the most business. Hence, a ratio of store sales from the core area to total store sales must arbitrarily be set. The author has found that the core trade area of metropolitan supermarkets generally accounts for 60 to 70 percent of the store's customers. This is the area generally closest to the store and with the highest density of customers to population (also with the highest per capita sales), and with minimum overlapping of trade areas of sister stores operated by the same company.

Therefore, if one chooses to delineate the primary trade area of a store, he must arbitrarily decide on a ratio of sales to total–60, 65, 70 percent, or some other amount. If he chooses 60 percent of total sales, the primary trade area would be defined as the core area closest to the store, with the highest density of customers to population and from which the store gets 60 percent of its total sales.

Similarly, the secondary trade area is that area adjoining the primary trade area with the next highest ratio of customers to population and from which the store gets 15, 20, or 25 percent of its sales. The tertiary (or fringe) trade area would be defined as the residual portions of the store's trade area.

Subdividing Trade Areas

The technique for subdividing a trade area assumes that topographic maps, population, land use, competition, and customer spotting data are avaliable. (See Figures 1, 2, and Table 1.) A demonstration of this technique is presented in the following actual supermarket example in which names are disguised, and no topographic or competition maps are shown to avoid disclosure.

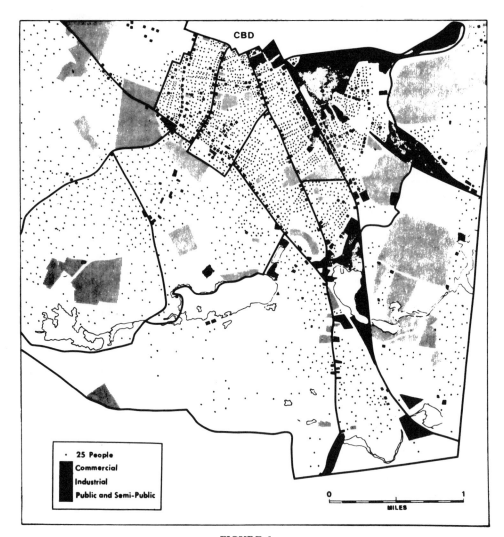

FIGURE 1

Population and Land Use—Southtown

The steps in the procedure are:

1. Place a grid of ¼ × ¼ mile squares (or smaller squares for greater precision) along coordinate lines on a population and land-use map. Line up a point where four grid squares meet over the corresponding store site on the map. Determine and record the population in each square.

2. Place the same grid over the customer spotting map on which each spotted customer equals $100 weekly sales. If the scale of this map is different from the population and land-use map, use different scale grids to correspond to the scales of these maps. Count the number of spotted customers in each square, multiply this by $100 and enter the dollar amount in the square. This is

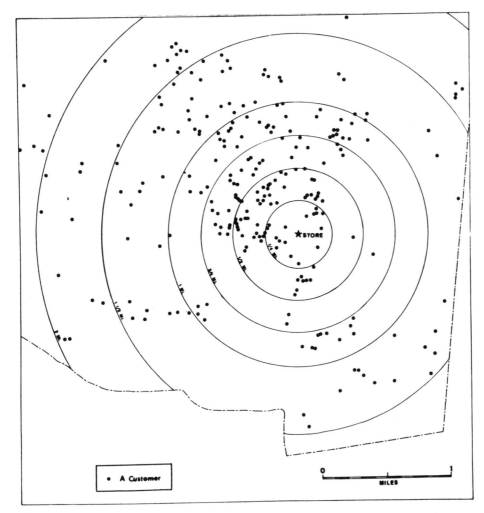

FIGURE 2

Customer Spotting—Store 12—Southtown

the store's weekly sales in the square.

3. Divide the weekly sales by the population in the square. The quotient is the store's weekly per capita sales. Record this quotient in the square. (See Figure 3.)

4. The primary trade area in this case is defined to represent 60 percent of the store's total sales. Adjusted weekly sales are estimated at $32,000, based on 320 customers spotted (Table 1). Hence 60 percent of 320, or 198 customers, are allocated to this trade area. Beginning with the squares on the grid nearest to the store (Fig. 3), include those squares that show the highest weekly per capita sales, in descending order, until the required number of customers (198 in this case) is accounted for. (Sales divided by 100 equals number of customers in a square.) Check off each grid square to be included.

5. Superimpose the grid on the population and land-use map and examine carefully

TABLE 1
Customer Spotting Data

Summary Data

Store address:	1500 S. Plum St., Southtown	Date opened:	July 6, 1955
Store number:	12	Income:	Medium
Location type:	Large business district	Parking:	120 cars
Sales area:	15,000 sq. ft.	Customers interviewed:	320+
Date spotted:	October 18, 1963	Price index:	121.5
Adjusted weekly sales:	$32,000	Sales/sq. ft.	$2.66/$2.13

Survey Data [a]

Customer Type		Store Visits per Week			Mode of Travel		Length of Patronage		Departments Shopped	
Female	63%	1	time	10%	Ride	94%	1st time	3%	All	79%
Male	21	1	time	48	Walk	6	1 year	4	GM	5
Couples	16	2	times	26	—		1 to 2 years	3	GP	8
Children	—	3–5	times	14		100%	2 to 3 years	5	MP	2
	—	6 and over		2			3 to 5 years	9	G	4
	100%						5+ years	9	M	2
				100%			Since opening	67	P	—
								100%		100%

Per Capita Sales Estimates

Zone (miles)	Customers	Drawing Power	Sales	Population	Per Capita Sales	Cumulative D.P.	P.C.S.
.00–.25	17	5.3%	$ 1,700	1,525	$1.11	5.3%	$1.11
.25–.50	56	17.5	5,600	5,900	.95	22.8	9.8
.50–.75	38	11.9	3,800	6,575	.58	34.7	.79
.75–1.00	53	16.6	5,300	9,925	.53	51.3	.64
1.00–1.50	70	21.9	7,000	23,375	.30	73.2	.52
1.50–2.00	41	12.8	4,100	36,725	.11	86.0	.33
Beyond	28	8.7	2,800				
Out of town	17	5.3	1,700				
	320	100.0%	$32,000				

a Base is 320 interviews.

each of the *peripheral* squares checked off for inclusion. Examine simultaneously the topographic map. Pencil in the boundary line of the primary trade area, making adjustments in the line for significant physical or man-made barriers, non-residential land uses and

breaks in the continuity of residential use (distribution of population).

6. Superimpose the grid on the customer spotting map, and see whether the penciled boundary line of the primary trade area includes all the spotted customers within the peripheral squares

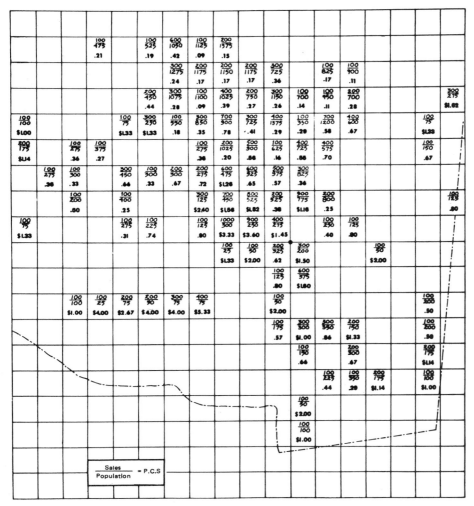

FIGURE 3

Per Capita Sales Grid—Store 12

checked off for inclusion. Make minor adjustments in the line necessary to include some spotted customers omitted in the adjustments of the line drawn in Step 5. This is the final 60 percent boundary line which should be transferred to the customer spotting map or a transparent overlay. (See Figure 4.)

7. The secondary trade area is derived by the same procedure as the primary. In the present example, the secondary trade area includes 20 percent of the store's

customers who, in this case, all live to the north and west.

8. If Figure 4 is superimposed on a competition map, the blunting effect of competition on the store's primary and secondary trade area can be seen.

Measuring Markets Penetration

Market share is the proportion of total potential sales that a store or a com-

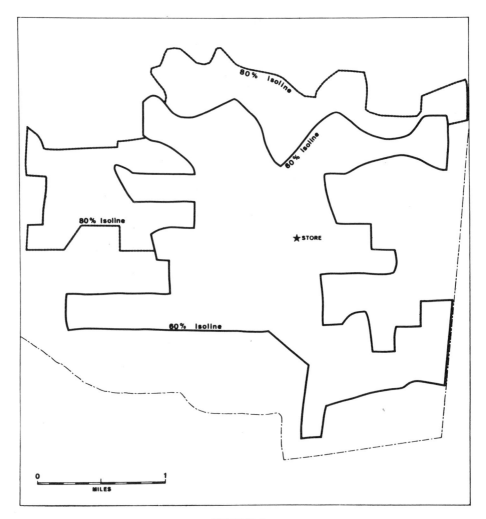

FIGURE 4

Primary and Secondary Trade Areas—Store 12

pany obtains from a given area. We can express this as

$$\text{Market share} = \frac{\text{Store's sales per capita}}{\text{Per capita sales potential}}.$$

The information needed for measuring market share (or market penetration) is the same as for subdividing trade areas, plus some additional data by Census tracts.

The first three steps in the procedure are the same as those for subdividing trade areas. If the subdividing has already been done, there is no need to repeat these steps.

4. Prepare a Census tract map of the store's trade area. From the *U.S. Census of Population and Housing* determine the number of people in each Census tract, the average number of people per

family and the median income. Enter these data inside each tract. From the Bureau of Labor Statistics' 1960–61 *Consumer Expenditures and Income* reports, determine (in this case) the per capita weekly home food expenditures

for the corresponding income group, and enter the figures in each Census tract.[2] (See Figure 5.)

5. Decide what intensities of market penetration are meaningful for analysis.

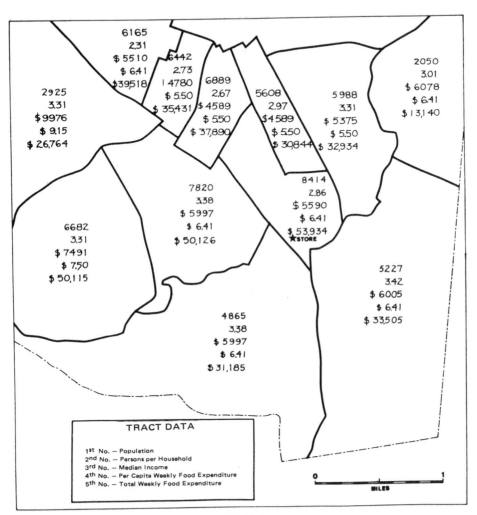

FIGURE 5

Census Tracts—1960—Southtown

[2] Consumer expenditure data for 1960–61 are published for each of four regions, for each of 45 cities and for the total rural nonfarm population. Thus for greater refinement, the researcher can use the published consumer expenditure data for the geographic area closest to the location being studied, as is done in this article.

In this case four degrees of penetration were measured, as shown below:

Share of Market	Intensity of Penetration
5 to 9.99%	1
10 to 19.99%	2
20 to 29.99%	3
30% and over	4

6. Superimpose a grid on Figure 5 and draw on it the Census tract boundaries. Classify the Census tracts by income group. (In this case, as given in Table 2.) Color or shade each Census tract on the grid by income group classification. (See Figure 6.)

7. Refer to Figure 3, which gives within the grid squares the store's weekly per capita sales. Superimpose the grid prepared in Step 6 on Figure 3. Compare the store's per capita sales shown in Figure 3 with the data shown in Table 2. Classify and record each square according to the market share (intensity of penetration) the store gets from that square. For example, if the family median income within the square is $7,235, the per capita weekly food expenditures are $7.50 (Table 2). If the store's per capita weekly sales within that square are $1.21, the store's market share is 16.2 percent, between 10 and 19.99 percent, and its classification code is 2.

Figure 6 shows the intensity of penetration for all squares with five percent or more market share.

8. Pencil in on Figure 6 tentative isolines of 5, 10, 20 and 30 percent penetration, to include the squares which fall within the four intensity-of-penetration classifications.[3] A square which fails to qualify, but is positioned between two

TABLE 2
Market Penetration Values

Median [a] Family Income	Per Capita Weekly Home Food Expenditures [b]	Per Capita Home Food Expenditures When Share of Market Is:			
		5 percent	10 percent	20 percent	30 percent
High					
$8,000 and over	$9.15	$.46	$.92	$1.84	$2.76
Medium high					
6,500–7,999	7.50	.38	.75	1.50	2.25
Medium					
5,500–6,499	6.41	.32	.64	1.38	2.02
Medium low					
4,500–5,499	5.50	.28	.55	1.10	1.65
Low					
Under $4,500	4.20	.21	.42	.84	1.26

[a] Average family—3.5 persons.
[b] In 1960; BLS index of food prices 116.5.
Note: If at the time of customer spotting the BLS index of food prices is more than 5 percent different from the 1960 index (116.5), then adjust, accordingly, the figures in this table. For example, if the BLS index is 130.2, then the $9.15 becomes $10.23, etc.

$$\frac{X}{\$9.15} = \frac{130.2}{116.5} \quad \text{or} \quad X = \$10.23$$

Some analysts may wish to make adjustments for smaller changes in the BLS index.

[3] Isolines are lines of the same or equal weight, value or measurement.

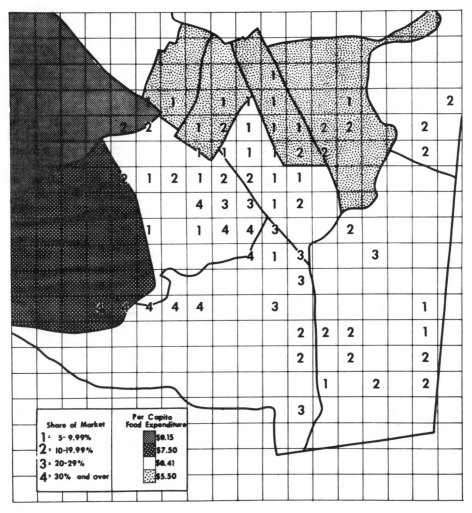

FIGURE 6

Share of Market Grid—Store 12

squares which do, should be included. Segments of trading areas that are isolated islands because of barriers or other discontinuities either can be included with nearby areas of similar market penetration, or can be left standing as islands.

9. Put the grid with the tentative isolines on the population and land-use map and modify these lines to correspond more realistically to the distribution of population on the map. Unpopulated areas may be excluded.

10. As a final check, put the above grid on the customer spotting map to make sure no spotted customers within a qualifying square have been left out in the adjustments of the isolines. Correct the isolines if this is the case. Transpose the final isolines onto a transparent overlay. (See Figure 7.)

11. By superimposing Figure 7 on a com-

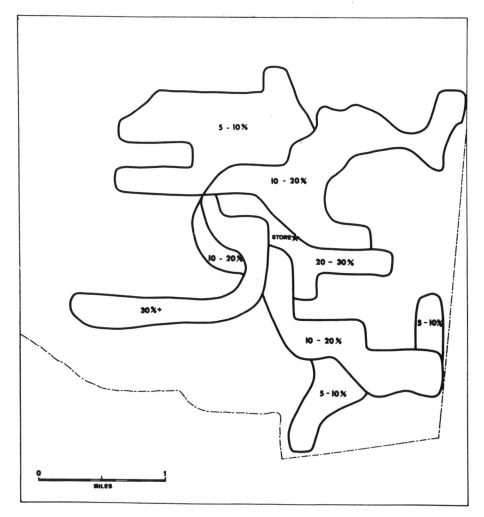

FIGURE 7

Market Penetration—Store 12

petition map one is able to discern the effect of competition on the store's market penetration.

Determining Market Penetration by Census Tracts

The data which are developed in customer spotting, subdividing trade areas and measuring market penetration can be used to determine the market penetration of stores for individual Census tracts. An illustration of such an analysis is given in Figure 8.

Similarly, market penetration can be determined for primary and secondary trade areas. Such determinations also give per capita sales.

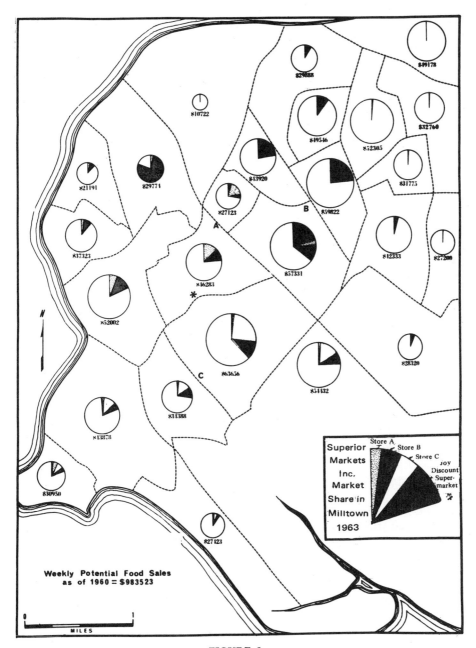

FIGURE 8

Potential Food Sales and Market Share Secured by Superior Markets Inc.—1963

An Analog Method for Estimating Potential Store Sales

The Analog—A Research Tool

The method for estimating potential store sales presented here depends partly on *quantified experience,* and partly on *subjective judgment.* The more quantified experience available, the less one needs to depend on subjective judgment. By quantified experience is meant empirical measurements of store sales in relation to known market factors, consumer shopping behavior patterns and store characteristics. Similar stores and similar market factors make for approximately analogous situations.

When the store characteristics, market factors, consumer shopping behavior and sales are statistically quantified and related, this record of experience becomes an *analog*—a benchmark for reference.

Through the classification of stores, location types and their tributary trade areas, store sales performance can be differentiated and, from this, analogs can be set up [3, 4]. Store sales potentials for proposed new sites are then projected using analogs as measurement standards.

Since neither are two sites exactly alike, nor are the market factors in one situation exactly like those in another situation, subjective judgment is needed in using analogs. Furthermore, market factors, consumer shopping behavior and store characteristics change [5]. Since analogs developed yesterday may not be completely valid tomorrow, subjective judgment is required in using and projecting into the future yesterday's quantified experience.

A firm's public acceptance (image) can and generally does vary from one region to another. Differences in acceptance cause differences in market share a store is able to achieve. Two identical stores with similar market potentials, but with different public acceptance (images), will have different per capita sales. Such differences in per capita sales produce different analogs. This is the only quantitatively meaningful difference in image.

Analogs (Table 3) are developed from customer spotting, trade area analyses and market penetration measurements.[4] Companies with many stores in many areas are in the best position to develop their own analogs and to

TABLE 3
Customer Spotting Data—Analog

Summary Data			
Store address:	1300 E. Duane Ave., Northtown	Adj. weekly sales:	$43,500
Location type:	Neighborhood (near core area)	Store number:	5
Opened:	October, 1951	Income:	Medium
Customers interviewed:	435	Parking:	119
Store sales:	$52,850—average 16 weeks	Checkouts:	6
Sales area:	12,800 sq. ft.	Price index:	121.5
Date spotted:	October 18, 1963	Sales/sq. ft.	$4.40/$3.62

[4] Table 3 for Store No. 5 contains the same kind of information as Table 1 contains for Store No. 12 *and* additional data on the primary trade area of Store No. 5.

Survey Data [a]

Customer Type		Store Visits per Week			Mode of Travel		Length of Patronage		Department Shopped	
Female	76%	1	year	8	Ride	57%	1st time	1%	All	58%
Male	17	1	time	21	Walk	43	1 time	8%	GM	8
Couples	7	2	times	27		—	1–2 years	5	GP	15
Children	—	3–5	times	40		100%	2–3 years	6	MP	1
	—	6 and over		4			3–5 years	10	G	15
	100%						5+ years	26	M	1
				100%			Since opening	44	P	2
								100%		100%

Per Capita Sales Estimates

Zone (miles)	Customers	Drawing Power	Sales	Population [b]	Per Capita Sales	Cumulative D.P.	P.C.S.
.00–.25	161	37%	$16,100	6,700	$2.40	37%	$2.40
.25–.50	126	29	12,600	15,800	.80	66	1.28
.50–.75	48	11	4,800	22,900	.21	77	.76
.75–1.00	26	6	2,600	22,000	.12	83	.34
Beyond	74	17	7,400			100	
	435	100%	$43,500				

Primary Trade Area [c]

Population: 20,400

PTA food sales potential: $130,800

All supermarkets' shares of PTA potential: [e]

Per capita home food expenditures: $6.41

Store's share of PTA potential: 24%

Supermarket Competition Within Primary Trade Area

Name and Address [d]	Distance from Own Store (miles)	Store Age	Sales Area (sq. ft.)	Check-outs	Cars Parking	Estimated Sales	Sales/ Sq.Ft.	Sales Within PTA
Q—Chain	.25–.50	25	3,240	3	0	$ 14,000	$4.32	$ 7,000
R—Chain	.25–.50	12	11,230	6	95	42,500	3.78	21,750
Competing supermarkets		19	14,470	9	95	56,500	3.91	28,750
Own store		12	12,800	6	119	52,850	4.40	31,710
All supermarkets		16	27,270	15	214	109,350	3.64	60,460 [e]

[a] Base is 435 interviews.

[b] Population as of 1960 census, stable since 1950, partly Jewish within .50 mile radius of store.

[c] Primary trade area is 60 percent of total. All sales figures are for the time of customer spotting, *unadjusted*.

[d] Names and addresses intentionally omitted.

[e] To the east of Store 5's PTA, .75 to 1 mile away, are located three competing supermarkets. One of these is an independent discount supermarket with estimated weekly sales of $75,000; the other two supermarkets (one chain and the other independent) have estimated weekly sales, $40,000 and $27,500, respectively. These three units are estimated to secure between $45,000 and $50,000 weekly sales from within Store 5's PTA.

update them. The analogs of one firm may or may not fit another firm in the same business even though both operate their stores in the same areas. On the other hand, an objective comparative study of the analogs of many companies would yield valuable information for scientifically estimating store sales [2].

The rest of this article shows how analogs are used in estimating potential store sales. The illustration is an actual case with names and places disguised.

The Problem

In the fall of 1963, Bull's Supermarkets made a survey to determine the sales potential of a store at or near Lincoln and Baker Streets. Management had long sought to establish a store in that area but "the problems of putting together the right property parcels were enormous and the cost would be very high." The key question was: How

much business could Bull's realistically expect to do there?

Three of Bull's present supermarkets, all large volume, successful stores (Figure 9), secured a total of $17,900 weekly (as determined by customer spotting) from the area which was estimated to be the total trade area of a store at that location. Bull's sales penetration of the trade area was considered weak and unsatisfactory by the management.

Store A, completely renovated two years ago, was located in a large business center and served an area of medium and medium-high income. Store sales in 1962 were $3,384,511 and pretax profits were $136,741, or 4.047 percent.

Store B was an old, well-kept store. It had a near monopoly neighborhood location in a very densely populated apartment house area of medium income near the state university. Store

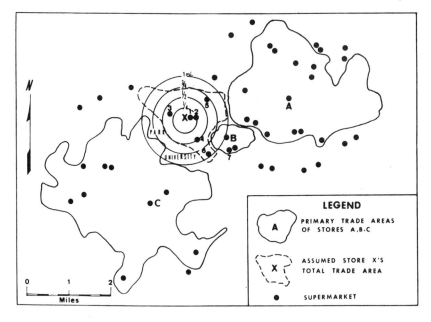

FIGURE 9

Store Trade Areas and Competition

sales in 1962 were $2,704,120, and pre-tax profits were $109,787 or 4.06 percent.

Store C, which was three years old and freestanding on a major highway, served a high income community. Store sales in 1962 were $2,626,007, and pre-tax profits were $79,043 or 3.017 percent.

A new Bull's Supermarket at the location under consideration (X in Figure 9) would take part of the $17,900 business which Stores A, B and C were doing in Trade Area X. Also, a new store would reduce the profits of the three stores. Would the incremental profit justify the investment? The answer to this question was the sales potential for a Bull's Supermarket at Location X.

Calculation of the Sales Estimate

Bull's location research analyst examined the firm's Customer Spotting Data Analogs which contained all known, pertinent information about Bull's Supermarkets and their trade areas. Three analogs were selected as approximating the market factors of Location X. One of these is shown in Table 3.

The Location Sales Projection for X was developed as shown in Table 4 based on data obtained by field surveys of the trade area, analogs and internal records. The analyst applied cautious, subjective judgment in using all the available quantified data.

The Location Sales Projection is designed to be self-explanatory. All the estimates shown near the top of the exhibit are subsequently supported by statistical data, detailed calculations and explanatory notes. Thus, the firm has a complete record of how the analyst made the sales estimate for the proposed location. The anticipated sales and profit losses of the three sister stores A, B and C were discounted in the same manner.

The Computed Drawing Power developed for Location X will typically vary from the Estimated Drawing Power. If this variation is quite marked, the analyst must re-examine both the Estimated Drawing Power and the Estimated Per Capita Sales. Perhaps some market factors were not evaluated adequately, and some adjustments would result in a better fit. Limitations of the analogs used may cause a poor fit. If so, the analyst must exercise subjective judgment.

The Location Sales Project serves as a record against which actual customer spotting results are checked when a store is established at the proposed location. The analyst can "check on himself" and learn how to apply his know-how to future situations.

Since the dynamics of the marketplace may cause an analog to become dated, analogs should be revised as conditions change. From analogs the analyst can learn of changes in market factors and their effect on the store's performance. The analyst will keep his analog tools sharp and will become more skillful in using them. Some firms update their analogs regularly; at least one supermarket chain does it annually.

When a proposed location is evaluated for a store differing in major respects from existing stores (a discount supermarket inside a free-standing discount house, for example), and the analyst has no analogs, the best he can do is use his own judgment based on past experience.

Analogs and Merchandising

Analogs are benchmarks for appraising a store's sales performance compared with similar company stores under analogous market conditions. Market information developed in each analog (Table 3) about customer shopping habits and competitors can be useful for store merchandising and promotion decisions.

TABLE 4
Location Sales Projection

Summary Data

Address: At or near W. Lincoln Ave. and S. Baker St. (marked X on Figure 1)
Location type: Neighborhood (near core area)
Total trade area population: 32,500 [a]
Per capita home food expenditure: $6.00
All supermarkets' share of total trade area potential: 70 percent
Estimated weekly sales for Store X: $40,910 (increase due to population growth not anticipated)
Estimated Store X's share of PTA potential: 23% (average of 3 analogs, 21 percent)
Estimated effect on sister stores: Sales loss $7,150 weekly; profit loss $18,590 annually
Estimated ride customers: 75 percent
Income: Medium ($5,654)
Food sales potential: $195,000
Price index: 121.5
Date: November 18, 1963

Survey Data on Competing Supermarkets (location moves by competitors not expected)

Name and Address	Distance from Location (miles)	Store Age	Sales Area (sq. ft.)	Check-outs	Cars Parking	Estimated Sales	Sales/ Sq. Ft.	Sales from Trade Area
1. Independent	Within .25	12	7,500	4	88	$30,000	$4.00	$30,000
2. Chain N	Within .25	13	7,800	4	56	20,000	2.56	20,000
3. Independent	.25 to .50	1	3,400	3	0	13,500	3.97	13,500
4. Independent	.50 to .75	8	5,000	2	24	12,000	2.40	12,000
5. Chain K	.50 to .75	13	11,025	8	175	47,500	4.32	28,500
6. Independent	.75 to 1	25	4,000	3	0	20,000	5.00	8,000
7. Chain F	Nearly 1.50	12	11,232	6	95	42,500	3.79	14,875
		12	49,957	30	438	$185,500	$3.69	$126,875
Own Store B	1 to 1.25	12	12,800	6	119	52,850	4.40	10,200 [b]
		12	62,757	36	557	$238,350	$3.78	$137,075

Analogs Used in Estimating Sales Potential

Zone (miles)	Population of Analog				Drawing Power of Analog				Per Capita Sales of Analog			
	5	8	15	Avg.	5	8	15	Avg.	5	8	15	Avg.
.00–.25	6,900	3,400	6,450	5,500	37%	29%	34%	34%	$2.40	$1.79	$1.47	$1.89
.25–.50	15,800	8,200	11,450	11,800	29	27	31	29	.80	.72	.75	.76
.50–.75	22,900	12,500	18,350	17,900	11	17	12	13	.21	.30	.19	.23
.75–1.00	22,000	10,300	12,000	13,800	6	9	6	7	.12	.17	.13	.14
Beyond					17	18	17	17				

Application of Above Analogs to Location X

Zone (miles)	Population at Location X [c]	Estimated Drawing Power [d]	Estimated per Capita Sales [e]	Estimated Weekly Sales	Computed Drawing Power [f]
.00 to .25	4,700	30%	$2.00	$ 9,400	28%
.25 to .50	12,900	30	.76	9,804	29
.50 to .75	23,000	15	.22	5,060	15
.75 to 1.00	36,300	10	.12	4,356	13
		———		———	
		85%		$28,620	
Beyond		15		5,051	15
		———		———	———
		100%		$33,671	100%

Estimated sales at current prices $40,910 [g]

Estimated Effect of Store X on Sister Stores

	Sales from Trade Area X Weekly	
Store	Present	Projected
B	$10,200	$ 5,600
A	5,300	3,550
C	2,400	1,600
	———	———
	$17,900	$10,750
		40,910
		51,660
		—17,900

Net new sales from Trade Area X	$33,760
Estimated annual sales loss of sister stores	$371,800
Estimated annual profit shrink at 5 percent [h]	18,590

[a] Population as of 1960; increased 5 percent between 1950 and 1960; slight growth since; area practically built up. To east of Location X, mostly all multiple dwelling residential; many small families.

[b] In addition, own stores C and A, 2 and 2.50 miles respectively from Location X, secure $7,700 weekly from this trade area.

[c] Population in the trade area is expected to remain stable over the next decade; thereafter it may decline very slightly.

[d] Estimated drawing power modified slightly from average of analogs, in view of population density, pattern of population distribution, and shape of projected trade area. Very large population in zones .50 to .75 and .75 to 1 mile is expected to produce, proportionately, more customers to total than in average of analogs.

[e] Estimated per capita sales in 0 to .25 mile zone increased above average of analogs, in view of medium income of the population surrounding Location X; however, kept lower than at Analog 5 because of competing supermarkets within this zone. Per capita sales in .50 to .75 and .75 to 1 mile zones slightly reduced below average of analogs because of competition from own Store B.

[f] The computed drawing power is a check on the reliability of the Estimated Drawing Power. In this case the computed drawing power is very close to the estimated in all zones except .75 to 1 mile.

[g] Current BLS index of food prices is 121.5. Hence, $33,671 multiplied by this index is $40,910.

[h] "Rule of thumb" basis applied by the firm to such sales believed to be conservative.

REFERENCES

1. William Applebaum, "A Technique for Constructing a Population and Urban Land Use Map," *Economic Geography,* 28 (July 1952), 240–3.
2. ———, "Can Store Location Research Be a Science?", *Economic Geography,* 41 (July 1965), 234–7.
3. ———, "Chain Store Location Strategy and the Store Profit S-Curve," in *New Directions in Marketing,* Proceedings American Marketing Association (June 1965), 283–94.
4. ———, "Store Performance in Relation to Location and Other Characteristics," *Chain Store Age,* 41 (November 1965), E14–6.
5. ———and Saul B. Cohen, "The Dynamics of Store Trading Areas and Market Equilibrium," *Annals of the Association of the American Geographers,* 51 (March 1961), 73–101.
6. ——— and Richard F. Spears, "How to Measure a Trading Area," *Chain Store Age,* 27 (January 1951), 15–7, 33–4.

Threshold Analysis and the Community Location Decision

Michael S. Noble, Ronald F. Bush, and Joseph F. Hair, Jr.

In the past, and even today in sparsely developed regions of the world, fairs and markets have been the beginning of permanent centers of trade. Buyers and sellers appear at an appointed time and place to conduct trade with each other. A "market day" in which farmers, artisans, and craftsmen gather to exchange their goods and services is still quite common throughout much of the world. As population increases and becomes more stable, the concentration of purchasing power causes the development of a permanent center of trade [5].

A considerable body of research, referred to as central place theory, has been developed in an attempt to explain some of the characteristics of these trade centers. Theorists believe that, rather than occurring by chance, economic, geographic, political, and social pressures ensure some ordering principles in the development of centers of trade. Their theories provide an explanation for such things as the number and distribution of trade centers throughout an area, their size, and the goods and services they may offer as a result of that size [1, 2, 5, 6, 8, 10].

The purpose of this article is to extend previous threshold analysis research, a concept in central place theory, by presenting empirical findings of a threshold study conducted in the southwestern United States. Former researchers have suggested that the threshold values generated in previous studies may be "geographic specific" [11]. No such analysis, insofar as the writers are aware, has been performed in the Southwest. This article will (1) briefly review the concept of threshold analysis and its usefulness in business; (2) present empirical findings on the application of threshold analysis to 55 selected businesses in 85 centers of trade in the southwestern United States; and (3) provide some suggestions for future threshold research.

Threshold Analysis

Threshold analysis, introduced by Berry and Garrison [3, 4], is a concept that has been developed to facilitate the study of centers of trade. Succinctly, threshold analysis estimates whether there are too many or too few types of a particular business in a given community based on the community's population size.

The threshold population of a type

Published by permission of the authors.

of business refers to the minimum number of customers (population) necessary to provide a sales volume sufficient for a good (type of business) to be offered profitably. Hurlebaus and Fulton [9] and Douglass and Mason [7] have examined threshold analysis for its application as a tool in business studies of the economic potential of a community. Knowledge of the threshold population necessary for a particular type of business can aid the businessman and the community planner. With reference to the applicability of threshold analysis, Douglass and Mason suggest that

Perhaps the most significant use of the concept of threshold population in marketing is as a screening device in the selection of retail locations for given types of businesses. For example, national or regional franchise chains should find it to their benefit to utilize threshold data as a first initial step in choosing potential communities for new outlets [7, p. 40].

The businessman may utilize threshold information to estimate the economic feasibility of another business outlet among various alternative communities. Also, since the successful services located in a community influence its ability to attract capital and main-tain a stable economy, city planners could encourage or discourage the development of certain businesses based on threshold information.

Research Procedure

For the purposes of this study, communities in the states of Arizona, Nevada, New Mexico, and Utah were selected on a random basis to provide as large and representative a sample as resources permitted. Although some judgment was involved in the sampling procedures, the sampling method was intended to ensure a complete array of population sizes.[1] The range of population of the sample was from 4 to 12,462.[2] A mail questionnaire was sent to the major, or other appropriate town representative, which asked the respondents for the number of each of the 55 businesses within their respective community. Information from 85 communities was utilized in developing the threshold information for this study.

Data Analysis

Previous studies in the area of threshold analysis, particularly those by Berry

[1] In threshold analysis it is important to provide a sample of communities whose population sizes approximate a continuum. This is necessary to avoid problems arising from attenuated regression, which result in distorted threshold values. The problem may be overcome with very large random samples. In this study the authors found it necessary to randomly resample communities within certain population categories to ensure a sample with a continuum of population sizes.

[2] Due to agglomeration effects discovered by other researchers, the sample in this study was confined to communities having populations of 20,000 or less. Agglomeration effects are inter-industry linkages, which grow more complex as city size increases and, as a result, seriously distort threshold values. As a city grows, it begins to expand its role as an exporter of services. Smaller communities in the surrounding area, incapable of supporting specialized skills in, for example, finance, medicine, or education, begin to depend on the larger city for these services. With sufficient growth a large metropolitan area may provide highly specialized services for the entire nation. The city's own population, therefore, is no longer an indicator of the types and numbers of businesses it is capable of supporting. This study has also been confined, for similar reasons, to the analysis of the 55 businesses most often found in the small community.

and Garrison [3, 4], have shown that the best single curve describing the relationship between population and number of businesses is an exponential growth curve. Accordingly, the equation for such a curve, which is $P = A(BN)$, where P is the population, N is the number of businesses, and A and B are the parameters being estimated, was utilized in the present research. In addition, a conversion was performed to provide a regression equation in the form of $\log P = \log A + N \log B;$ this equation was fitted by the least-squares method.

Threshold Values for the Southwest

The threshold values for the selected businesses of 85 communities in Arizona, Nevada, New Mexico, and Utah are shown in Table 1. The column on

TABLE 1
Threshold Values for Southwestern Communities

	A	*B*	*Threshold Population*
Service station	295.36	1.21	357.6
Restaurant	286.32	1.30	372.1
Motel	312.21	1.32	412.1
Beauty salon	259.20	1.63	423.0
Grocery store	288.33	1.52	437.7
Tavern	286.14	1.53	438.3
Insurance Agency	265.90	1.73	460.4
Lawyer	264.99	1.74	461.9
Physician	260.28	1.88	488.3
Real estate	264.12	1.98	523.8
Auto parts	254.08	2.51	638.1
Barber shop	304.02	2.13	648.1
Public accountant	406.33	1.77	718.5
Women's clothing	285.56	2.62	748.0
Furniture store	434.61	1.73	752.4
New car	253.62	2.97	754.1
Clothing store	537.96	1.41	758.3
Dentist	265.47	3.12	827.6
Drugstore	308.68	2.72	840.4
TV store	228.76	4.11	940.3
Shoe repair	796.35	1.19	943.9
Appliance store	335.10	2.84	953.3
Laundromat	292.32	3.55	1,039.0
Bowling alley	654.42	1.60	1,044.7
Electrical repair	291.26	3.62	1,054.8
General store	447.99	2.56	1,147.8
Used car	258.46	4.55	1,177.2
Savings & loan	822.08	1.44	1,180.5
Bank	274.30	4.43	1,216.5
Dry cleaners	242.67	5.09	1,234.3
Hardware store	310.45	4.08	1,267.2
Liquor	313.18	4.20	1,316.2
Lumberyard	271.42	4.88	1,323.9
Variety store	273.19	4.95	1,352.1

TABLE 1—Continued

	A	B	Threshold Population
Men's clothing	405.60	3.36	1,362.1
Building materials	386.74	3.57	1,380.9
Department store	208.46	6.66	1,388.5
Hotel	351.39	4.13	1,450.4
Loan agency	217.48	7.06	1,536.1
Tire repair	357.09	4.32	1,544.1
Feed store	385.06	4.39	1,691.9
Jewelry store	269.67	6.98	1,882.6
Movie	329.40	6.78	2,234.6
Florist	228.46	9.96	2,276.5
Taxi	395.86	6.19	2,449.7
Sporting goods	277.57	9.87	2,740.1
Farm equipment	261.46	17.47	4,567.3
Mortuary	276.20	19.37	5,349.0
Optometrist	232.36	26.16	6,078.7
Clinic	288.50	22.46	6,479.8
Hospital	303.32	26.32	7,983.9
Photo	250.33	35.09	8,785.2
Veterinarian	289.46	42.34	12,256.4
Stationery	251.47	48.91	12,298.5
Radio station	269.31	119.31	32,131.7

the left of the table gives the value for A, which represents the population value where the regression line crosses the y axis. The threshold population represents the population value of the regression equation where the x axis is equal to 1. The B value is the slope of the line and represents the minimum required population increase before an additional business of the same kind is likely to be successful. The required population increase may be found by multiplying the B value by the threshold population. A restaurant, for example, requires a minimum population of 372.1 to exist. The required population necessary to add another restaurant to the community would be $372.1 \times 1.30 = 483.6$. Thus, a population increase of 483.6 is necessary for two restaurants to be successful in a trade center.

Expected Versus Actual Number of Businesses

A comparison of the expected number versus the actual number of businesses for a sample of three communities with different populations is shown in Table 2. In instances when the expected and actual number of businesses vary, it may be because (1) the center of trade, due to its idiosyncracies, may be able to support more or fewer businesses than is normal (e.g., a center of trade located on a major highway system may be able to support a very large number of service stations), (2) the population of the center of trade has expanded or contracted rapidly, resulting in more or fewer businesses than expected, or (3) the center of trade is drawing from an area, either larger or smaller, than a center its size would normally attract.

TABLE 2
Actual Versus Expected Businesses

Type of Business	Community A Population 1,193		Community B Population 3,587		Community C Population 8,915	
	Expected	Actual	Expected	Actual	Expected	Actual
Service station	3	3	10	15	24	20
Grocery store	2	2	8	6	20	13
General store	1	1	3	0	7	2
Bank	0	1	2	2	7	3
Beauty salon	2	2	8	7	21	15
Restaurant	3	9	9	8	23	9
Drugstore	1	1	4	2	10	5
Insurance agency	2	0	7	11	19	8
Physician	2	1	7	4	18	7
Dentist	1	1	4	2	10	2
Lawyer	2	1	7	5	19	15
Furniture store	1	1	4	2	11	6
Auto parts	1	1	5	2	13	4
Feed store	0	0	2	2	5	4
Real estate	2	3	6	2	17	12
TV store	1	0	3	0	9	4
Dry cleaners	0	2	2	2	7	5
Farm equipment	0	0	0	3	1	6
Hardware store	0	2	2	3	7	1
Variety store	0	1	2	1	6	3
Motel	2	0	8	18	21	5
Florist	0	1	1	1	3	3
Electrical repair	1	1	3	2	8	2
Lumberyard	0	1	2	2	6	2
Optometrist	0	0	0	1	1	1
Veterinarian	0	0	0	1	0	1
Laundromat	1	2	3	2	8	3
Used car	1	1	3	0	7	2
New car	1	1	4	4	11	4
Loan agency	0	0	2	0	5	2
Jewelry store	0	0	1	1	4	1
Radio station	0	0	0	1	0	1
Department store	0	0	2	0	6	8
Mortuary	0	1	0	1	1	1
Hospital	0	0	0	1	1	1
Clinic	0	1	0	0	1	1
Tire repair	0	0	2	2	5	4
Stationery	0	0	0	3	0	2
Photo	0	1	0	1	1	2
Sporting goods	0	2	1	0	3	2
Shoe repair	1	0	3	1	9	1
Bowling alley	1	1	3	0	8	1
Savings & loan	1	0	3	0	7	1
Taxi	0	1	1	1	3	1
Public accountant	1	1	4	7	12	8

TABLE 2—Continued

Type of Business	Community A Population 1,193		Community B Population 3,587		Community C Population 8,915	
	Expected	Actual	Expected	Actual	Expected	Actual
Clothing store	1	1	4	3	11	8
Hotel	0	0	2	6	6	0
Barber	1	0	5	3	13	4
Appliance store	1	1	3	1	9	6
Movie	0	1	1	1	3	1
Liquor	0	3	2	0	6	6
Tavern	2	10	8	7	20	1
Women's clothing	1	1	4	2	11	3
Building materials	0	0	2	2	6	2
Men's clothing	0	0	2	1	6	1

For some businesses, the *area of dominant influence* may be a more valid predictor of threshold population than the actual population of the center of trade. A radio station is an obvious example since its threshold number is 32,131.7, which exceeds the size of any center of trade sampled. Whether or not this is true poses an interesting question for future research.

Threshold Value, Market Entry, and a Goods Order and Range

Theorists of centers of trade maintain that centers exist in a hierarchy rather than a continuum and that discrete separations exist between centers of trade and what businesses they can support [1, 10]. For example, a center of trade with only a gas station and grocery store may not be able to support a drugstore until it increases in population. When it is capable of supporting the latter, however, it also may be capable of supporting a physician, an insurance agency, and a furniture store. As a result of this hierarchy, centers of trade and goods have order and range.

High-order goods are generally "shopping goods" purchased infrequently and for which the consumer is willing to travel longer distances (the goods "range") to a relatively higher ordered center of trade. Low-order goods are generally less expensive and are purchased more frequently with little consumer travel (range). The higher the order of a good, for example, furniture, the fewer the establishments that provide it and the greater the cost and the conditions for entering the market place. Conversely, the lower the order of a good, for example, bread, the greater the number of establishments and the lower the cost and conditions necessary for entry [5].

The different threshold and B values, then, generally provide a relative ranking of the order of a good (or business) and for the cost and ease of market entry for a business. For example, the cost of opening and the difficulty of market entry for a hospital, even a small one, are, as its threshold value reflects, much greater than, say, for a service station. The threshold population required for a hospital is 7,983.9; the threshold population for a service station is only 357.6.

Discussion

The threshold values of this study show some rather wide variations when compared with those found by other researchers. The studies by Berry and Garrison [3, 4] and by Douglass and Mason [7] are somewhat limited, however, the former because only those communities with a population of 3,000 and below were included in the sample, and the latter because the research data were not based on an array of communities with different population sizes.

Due to the completeness of their data, the study by Hurlebaus and Fulton [9] offers the best comparison. In some instances the threshold population values found in the present study are quite close to those found by Hurlebaus and Fulton. There remains, however, a considerable difference in a number of the threshold values. Some of the variation is likely due to the geographical differences between the South and Southwest. For example, in the South farms are both more numerous and smaller than farms in the Southwest.[3] The threshold value for a farm equipment dealer in the South, because of a larger market, should then be lower than that for a farm equipment dealer in the Southwest. The threshold value for a farm equipment dealer in the Tennessee Valley is 1,803, whereas in the Southwest it is 4,567.3. These empirical findings lend credence to Schettler's hypothesis that threshold values are "geographic specific" [11]. Additional variation in threshold values may be due to the differences in the definitions of the particular business functions by the various researchers and the respondents themselves.

The geographical variation in threshold values generated thus far is but one limitation of threshold analysis. The potential user of threshold information should be forewarned that threshold values should be used only as general guidelines from which finer decisions may be made only after the consideration of the qualitative dimensions of the community that may affect a specific business. Regarding this, Hurlebaus and Fulton wrote,

Of course, the threshold population technique does not eliminate the need for study of individual investment possibilities. While it would be highly unusual for a town with an actual number of, for example, drug stores greater than the expected number to be a good economic environment for adding another establishment providing the same service, such a possibility cannot be dismissed only on the basis of a threshold analysis. Nevertheless, the "screening" value of the [threshold] analysis should not be underestimated [9, pp. 14–15].

In conclusion, threshold analysis represents an extension of the theory of centers of trade and identifies the minimum population number necessary for the survival of a particular business. That number is the lower limit of the range of the goods or services that the business offers. Threshold analysis, consequently, may be used to determine the additional population necessary for a particular business to be successfully repeated in a community. Threshold analysis also identifies the economies of scale and the ease and cost of market

---

[3] The average number of farms and their acreage in the states of Georgia, Tennessee, Alabama, and Mississippi in 1969 was 55,750 and 191, respectively. The average number of farms and their acreage in the states of Arizona, New Mexico, Utah, and Nevada in 1969 was 8,250 and 4,111, respectively [12].

entry of different businesses. For these reasons, it is evident that threshold analysis offers much potential as a tool in making community location decisions. Consequently, the authors suggest that additional threshold research be undertaken in other relatively homogeneous geographical areas to provide businessmen in these areas with meaningful threshold values.

REFERENCES

1. Baskin, C. W. (translator). *Central Places in Southern Germany,* by Walter Christaller. Englewood Cliffs, N.J.: Prentice-Hall, Inc., 1966.
2. Berry, B. J. L. *Geography of Market Centers and Retail Distribution.* Englewood Cliffs, N.J.: Prentice-Hall, Inc., 1967.
3. Berry, B. J. L., and Garrison, W. L. "A Note on Central Place Theory and the Range of a Good." *Economic Geography* 34 (1958): 304–311.
4. Berry, B. J. L., and Garrison, W. L. "The Functional Bases of the Central Place Hierarchy." *Economic Geography* 34 (1958): 145–154.
5. Berry, B. J. L., and Pred, A. *Central Studies: A Bibliography of Theory and Applications.* Philadelphia: Regional Science Research Institute, 1961.
6. Brush, J. "The Hierarchy of Central Places in Southwestern Wisconsin." *The Geographical Review* 43 (1953): 380–402.
7. Douglass, Robert, and Mason, J. B. "Threshold Analysis as a Tool in Economic Potential Studies and Retail Site Location: An Illustrative Application." *The Southern Journal of Business* 7 (Aug. 1972): 48.
8. Gaplin, C. "The Social Anatomy of an Agricultural Community." Research Bulletin 34. Madison, Wis.: Agricultural Experiment Station, University of Wisconsin, May 1915.
9. Hurlebaus, J. F., and Fulton, R. Jr. "Community Size and the Number of Businesses and Services." *Tennessee Survey of Business* 3 (July 1968): 5, 14, 15.
10. Losch, A. *The Economics of Location,* translated by W. H. Woglom and W. E. Stolper. New Haven, Conn.: Yale University Press, 1954.
11. Schettler, C. "Relation of City Size to Economic Services." *American Sociological Review* 8 (1943): 60–62.
12. *U. S. Bureau of the Census, Statistical Abstract of the United States: 1973* (94th ed.), Washington, D.C., 1973.

Patterns of Family Location

Avery M. Guest

Human ecologists have been primarily interested in how metropolitan population growth and size affect the distribution of land uses in relationship to the Central Business District (CBD), and how these in turn affect the distribution of types of population, such as higher status persons, in relationship to the CBD. There has been some confusion, however, on the issue of whether the spatial organization of the city is determined by short-run competitive pressures for central land or by the past growth of the city.

The importance of short-run competition is emphasized in the work of Hawley (1950). He argues that large metropolitan areas have vigorous competition for central land, which is highly valued for its centrality to transportation points and all parts of the city. Central land prices are driven up by the bidding, and only those activities willing and able to pay the central rents locate near the CBD. According to Hawley (p. 280), businesses and industries, particularly, outbid other activities for the central land. Recreational and residential activities, with little economic power, are apt to be driven out of the CBD. Furthermore, the residential land which is found near the CBD must be developed inten- sively, since most residents of the city could not afford large tracts of central land. Thus, residential areas around the CBD in large cities would be expected to have a large number of dwellings- per-acre of residential land, and each residential unit would have little internal space, or few rooms-per-dwelling. Using this basic theory about the segregation of land uses in large cities, Hawley has argued that the congestion or high intensity of land use around the CBD drives higher status persons to the outskirts.

Other human ecologists, while not seriously disagreeing with the above analysis, have placed more emphasis on past growth of the city as a determinant of land use patterns. In short, the age of a neighborhood may affect other neighborhood characteristics independently of short-run competition. In fact, the relationship between distance from the CBD and the characteristics of neighborhoods may be partially due to the fact that old neighborhoods are located close to the CBD. Thus, Wins- borough (1963) has shown how age affected neighborhood density in Chicago independently of distance from the CBD. This finding can be interpreted within the context of improved trans- portation technology (primarily the au-

Reprinted from *Demography,* Vol. 9, No. 1, February 1972, by permission of the author and editor.

tomobile), which has permitted persons to live at low density far from their work-place. Beverly Duncan (1964) has shown how old Chicago neighborhoods are particularly apt to be located near manufacturing employment. Much of the tendency for manufacturing activity to be centrally located may be due to a former dependence on water transport facilities which were located near the CBD. The development of rail and motor transport has allegedly permitted the decentralization of manufacturing.

Human ecologists, on the whole, have been more interested in applying their theory of the segregation of land uses to the location of higher status persons and racial and ethnic groups than to types of families. Nevertheless, Burgess (1963), perhaps the best known human ecologist, argued that homeless men and unmarried young adults would be found disproportionately near the center of cities whereas married couples with children would be found disproportionately toward the outskirts of cities. Burgess' predictions appeared related to the availability of large, single family dwellings on the outskirts for families in the childbearing stage and to the availability of small, multiple unit housing in the area around the CBD for homeless men and unrelated one- or two-person households.

Burgess' (1963, p. 64) observation that "The larger the city, the more differentiated its areas and its family types" was fully consistent with ecological theory. However, it was often difficult to determine from Burgess' work whether he subscribed to views emphasizing short-run competition or previous growth as important in determining the spatial organization of the city.

The validity of the Burgess viewpoint about the importance of space for family location has been clearly demonstrated. For instance, Rossi (1955) showed for a sample of Philadelphia families that intraurban mobility was most characteristic of two types of families, those in the childbearing period in search of housing space and those who had completed childbearing and were seeking less space.

There is also ample evidence to suggest that age and site features of neighborhoods, integral to human ecology theories, affect the distributions of types of families. In regard to site, David Riesman (1957) has suggested that one of the prime causes of suburbanization, primarily among families in the childbearing period, has been flight from the "industrialism" of the central city and the drawing power of the green spaces on the outskirts. In his study of Toronto suburbs, Clark (1966) found that both housing space and age were important in predicting the location of types of families. Younger families with children were primarily found in newly developed, single unit areas, whereas older families, often through the childbearing stage, were found in older suburbs. Clark's analysis would suggest that neighborhoods pass through life cycles in which newly built housing is inhabited by newly formed families whereas older housing tends to have families who have "aged" with the neighborhood. This pattern is also suggested by Hoover and Vernon (1962, pp. 219–226) in their study of the New York Metropolitan Region.

Using ideas of the human ecologists, we have thus suggested theoretical justification for a model of family distribution in old, large metropolitan areas. As indicated in Figure 1, this model shows distance from the CBD affecting Site (recreational and industrial land uses) and the distribution of housing

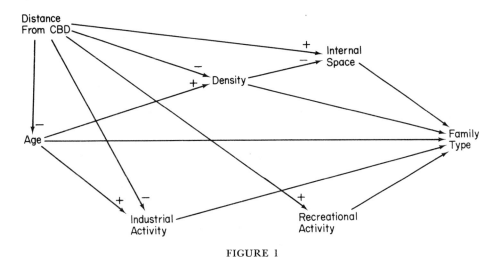

FIGURE 1

Hypothesized Model of Family Location

by Age or period of development and Space (dwellings-per-area and rooms-per-dwelling). In turn, these variables affect the distributions of types of families. If past growth of the city is important for present structure, Age may also have an effect on the distributions of types of families through its effect on density and location of industrial activity, independent of distance. Finally, we have included a path from dwellings-per-acre to rooms-per-dwelling, since most low density, single unit housing seems to be larger in size than multi-dwelling apartment housing.

This model will be evaluated with the statistical technique of path analysis, using census tract data drawn from the 1960 and 1963 statistical reports for the Cleveland, Ohio, Metropolitan Area. Cleveland, old and large in population, represents the type of place where the arguments of the human ecologists could be validly tested. Families will be characterized by their stage in the married life cycle and by the presence of a married couple in the household.

Our model is admittedly limited in the sense that we have not included all variables which might affect the location of family types. The effects of some of these variables, such as tract racial composition, owner occupancy status, and rent and housing evaluation levels, have been discussed elsewhere (Guest, 1970, pp. 57–81). In general, except for race, these other variables had little partial relationship with the proportions of various family types once the effects of the Age, Space, and Site variables had been controlled. When the model was run separately for black tracts, the results were similar although less clear.

In the next section, we shall operationalize the six types of families to be used in the empirical analysis. Following this, we shall test our model and discuss the results.

Family Types

We defined six types of families or pseudo-families on the basis of available 1960 data. Four types represent idealized stages in the life cycle of married couples: Young Couples, husband under 45 with no children under 18 at home; Young Families, husband under 45 with children under 18 at home; Old Families, husband over 45 with children under 18 at home; Old Couples, husband over 45 with no children under 18 at home. The other two types of families, Single Heads and Primary Individuals, do not contain married couples as heads of the household. In Single Head families, there are relatives (perhaps some children) living together, while Primary Individual living units generally consist of one to three unrelated individuals.

The number of each of the four types of married couples is based on data reported for a 25 percent sample of all married couples (U.S. Bureau of the Census, 1962, Table P-1). For Cleveland, the same table also shows that 98 percent of all married couples have their own households.

While a typical married couple will move through these four stages of Young Couple, Young Family, Old Family, and Old Couple, it appears that many married couples (as defined by the U.S. Census Bureau) would not follow such an idealized pattern. Most of these problems with the data are discussed elsewhere by Edwards (1970).

The other two types of families, Single Heads and Primary Individuals, are based on a census household or living unit definition. Most of these two types of households are headed by persons from broken marriages, single adults, and widowed persons, particularly the latter. Census data for the U.S. population in 1960 showed that 46.9 percent of Single Heads and 47.2 percent of Primary Individuals households were headed by widowed persons, presumably elderly in age (U.S. Bureau of the Census, 1964, Table 2).

To control for variation in population size of census tracts, we have operationalized each family type as a percentage of the total of the six family types in the tract. This poses some problems in interpreting the results of the statistical analysis, since the six types are logically interrelated—knowledge of the proportions of five types in a census tract automatically indicates the proportion of the sixth type. However, without this standardization procedure, the results of the regression analysis or path analysis would have become confounded with population size.

As Table 1 shows, it is indeed true that these family types vary with distance from the Cleveland CBD. Young Families and Old Families in the mature childbearing stage are found disproportionately on the outskirts of Cleveland, while Single Heads and Primary Individuals are found more often near the center. Old Couples, presumably just through the childbearing period, are somewhat decentralized, although the relationship with distance is slightly curvilinear. The peak concentrations occur near the outskirts, but there is a clear drop in concentration in the last two-mile-distance zones. The sixth family type, Young Couples, presumably about to begin childbearing, shows little relationship with distance from the CBD.

However, it should be emphasized that most of the variance in each family type is left unexplained by linear distance from the CBD. We were unable to find significant other spatial patterns, such as sectoral or location in relationship to Lake Erie, that might account for much more of the variance in the family types.

These relationships between distance and the proportion of each family type are generally consistent with our ex-

TABLE 1

Mean Proportion of Family Types by One Mile Distance Zones from Cleveland CBD [a]

Zone	Family Type					
	Young Couples	Young Families	Old Families	Old Couples	Single Heads	Primary Indiv.
0–1 (13)	5.7	16.7	5.2	12.0	10.5	50.8
1–2 (35)	7.5	25.3	8.0	16.4	17.0	25.6
2–3 (46)	8.1	27.6	8.7	20.3	14.6	20.5
3–4 (47)	8.3	27.6	9.6	23.7	12.8	17.8
4–5 (46)	7.3	25.2	11.2	27.6	11.6	16.9
5–6 (44)	6.3	28.8	13.0	28.9	9.6	13.3
6–7 (35)	6.0	32.3	13.9	29.1	8.3	10.4
7–8 (28)	8.0	41.1	13.4	23.3	6.7	7.4
8 plus (59)	6.5	39.6	14.8	25.4	6.1	7.5
Grand mean (353)	7.2	30.4	11.4	24.1	10.8	16.1
Standard deviation	3.0	10.7	4.8	7.1	4.9	12.7
Zero-order r with linear distance from CBD	—.10	.52	.54	.43	—.65	—.60

[a] Number of tracts in parentheses.

pectations. Given that families with children, Young Families and Old Families, should be attracted to the outskirts by the presence of recreational activity and spacious housing, we would expect them to be particularly decentralized. Young Families might also be decentralized through the use of new housing. Single Heads and Primary Individuals should be particularly centralized by their use of the small space of central housing. Furthermore, since these families are often headed by elderly widowed persons, they might be found particularly in old housing near the city center. There may be some propensity for widows to live in the neighborhood where they lived as spouses in families with children. The relatively strong propensity for Old Couples to be decentralized is somewhat surprising, given the fact that they should have fewer space needs than families in the childbearing stage and that they might be found in the old housing near the city center. On the

other hand, the weak relationship between the proportion of Young Couples and distance from the CBD is generally expected. Location in areas of new housing might lead to their decentralization. But this family type should have little tendency to locate in reference to Site or Space. Some of these families might seek large amounts of space in preparation for childbearing, whereas others would seek small amounts for their current minimal needs.

The Model

In this section, we shall test the model outlined in Figure 1 by first determining whether the model of the relationships among the distance, Age, Space, and Site variables has empirical support. We shall then determine whether the model can account for the relationships among the distance and family type variables. And finally, we shall show how various paths explain the centralization or decentralization of various family types.

In interpreting the results, it should be remembered that the analysis is based on cross sectional data. Since some of the human ecologists' arguments are based on propositions about change over time, it would be valuable to have a longitudinal analysis. However, data on family composition of tracts for decades before 1960 are not in readily analyzable form.

In testing our original model, we drew data on Age and Space characteristics from Table H-1 of the census tract report (U.S. Bureau of the Census, 1962). Distance from the census-defined CBD was estimated in terms of one mile concentric zones. Site characteristics were drawn from a special 1963 survey (Cleveland-Seven County Transportation Land Use Study, 1968).

The sample will consist of 353 census tracts found in the Cleveland Standard Metropolitan Statistical Area (SMSA), consisting of Cuyahoga and Lake Counties. Fourteen census tracts were eliminated from the analysis because they had fewer than 100 persons, had significant institutionalized populations, or lacked data on Site characteristics.

Our tool of analysis, path analysis, can help in handling two principal tasks: (a) determining whether the structural variables account for the relationships between distance from the CBD and the proportions of family types, and (b) showing the relative importance of various paths in accounting for these relationships. Thus, as an example, we can try to reproduce the correlation between linear distance from the CBD and the proportion of Young Families, and then we can show whether the decentralization of new areas or the decentralization of low density housing is more important in accounting for the location of Young Families. These two tasks can be accomplished by using the fundamental theorem of path analysis, $r_{ij} = \Sigma \ p_{iq} r_{jq}$, where i and j denote two variables in the system and the index q runs over all variables from which paths lead directly to variable X_i. Some of the basics of path analysis are explained by O. D. Duncan (1966). The basic inputs into the model, the zero order correlations among variables, are shown in Table 2. Since some of the correlations among variables are quite high, there are clearly problems in distinguishing the effects of one variable from the effects of another. The distance and Age and the distance and density (dwellings-per-area) variables are particularly associated. The same problem was found when alternative measures of Age were used, such as period of housing build-up.

Since the dependent variables in the analysis are the variances of the family type proportions, the reader should be aware that we are not showing how a specific level of density, for instance, affects the proportion of a certain family type. Our concern is explaining the variance that exists, not the amount of the variance. As Table 1 shows, some of the family types tend to have much more variance than others, particularly Young Families and Primary Individuals. However, this issue is not the concern of the present study.

In testing our original model, paths were generally kept if the path coefficients equaled at least .10 and the correlations between most pairs of variables could be closely reproduced. As we shall shortly note, paths had to be added where their absence would mean large differences between implied and actual correlations.

As predicted, Age and distance both

TABLE 2
Zero Order Correlations of Structural Characteristics and Family Types

Selected Characteristics	Age [a]	Internal Space [b]	Density [c]	Industrial [d]	Recreational [e]
Age	—				
Internal space	−.31	—			
Density	.66	−.65	—		
Industrial	.22	−.36	.30	—	
Recreational	−.25	.17	−.31	−.15	—
Distance	−.74	.55	−.82	−.30	.29
Young couples	.07	−.29	.20	.20	−.08
Young families	−.65	.36	−.53	−.01	.11
Old families	−.44	.67	−.66	−.24	.16
Old couples	−.12	.65	−.44	−.35	.12
Single heads	.61	−.27	.59	.15	−.30
Primary individuals	.53	−.74	.67	.19	−.08
Mean value	.70	5.1	2.2	−4.8	−5.7
Standard deviation	.34	.9	1.3	2.0	1.8

[a] Age—proportion of household units built before 1940.

[b] Internal space (rooms-per-dwelling)—mean number of rooms per household unit.

[c] Density (dwelling-per-acre)—natural logarithm of number of household units per acre of residential land.

[d] Industrial—natural logarithm of proportion of total land area in industrial uses.

[e] Recreational—natural logarithm of proportion of total land area in recreational open spaces such as parks and golf courses.

made independent contributions to residential density (see Figure 2), although the effect of Age was quite small. In other words, there is little evidence that neighborhood Age had much effect on areal density independent of distance from the CBD. It is also noteworthy that our model could almost perfectly reproduce the correlations among Age, industrial, and recreational variables by the paths from distance to each of these variables. Therefore, we dropped the hypothesized path from Age to the industrial variable.

Our original model also had to be revised by adding paths from the Age and industrial variables to internal space, rooms-per-dwelling. Without these paths, there were serious differences between the implied and actual correlations for several pairs of variables in the model. Our additional paths suggest that older areas tend to have more

internally spacious housing than newer areas, and that industrial areas have smaller living units than nonindustrial areas. The reasons for these clear relationships are not readily explainable. As a result of these multiple paths to rooms-per-dwelling, distance from the CBD has both negative and positive impact on the internal space of housing.

Given this basic empirical model, we can undertake our two most important tasks: (a) explaining the correlations between distance from the CBD and the proportions of family types, and (b) indicating the strengths of various paths in explaining these correlations. We shall discuss each of these in turn.

As Table 3 shows, our model does an excellent job of reproducing correlations between job of reproducing correlations between distance from the CBD and the proportions of various family types, particularly in regard to

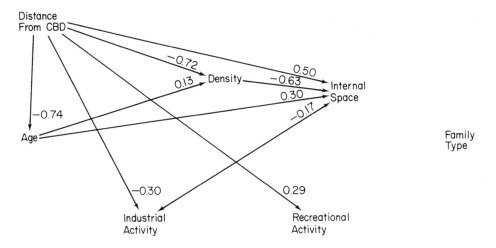

All path coefficients were at least three times as large as their standard errors.
Lines or paths to family types are not shown.

Relationship	Actual r	Implied r	Coefficients of Determination (R^2) for Dependent Variables	
a. Age....Industrial	0.22	0.22	a. Age	0.55
b. Age....Recreational	−0.23	−0.21	b. Density	0.68
c. Recreational....Internal Space	0.09	0.14	c. Internal Space	0.50
d. Industrial....Recreational	−0.12	−0.08	d. Industrial	0.09
e. Density....Industrial	0.30	0.22	e. Recreational	0.08
f. Density....Recreational	0.31	−0.21		

FIGURE 2

Actual Model of Family Location

Young Families, Old Families, and Primary Individuals. Of the other three types, only Old Couples and Single Heads had clear relationships with distance from the CBD. The failure of the model in predicting completely the spatial location of Single Heads could not be attributed to exclusion of variables such as tract racial composition or housing evaluation levels.

For Old Couples, we believe the difference between the actual and the implied correlation is primarily due to curvilinear relationships with distance from the CBD. Using the structural variables in a regression equation, one can generate predicted proportions of

Old Couples for each mile distance zone and compare them with the actual proportions. When this analysis was done, there was almost no difference between the actual and the predicted proportions for any mile zone.

Now, let us turn to our second principal task, showing how different paths lead to the centralization or decentralization of various family types. The direct effects of each predicting variable are shown in Table 3, and the effects of various paths from distance to family types are shown in Table 4.

In general, the most important variables for predicting the proportions of family types are those relating to Age

TABLE 3
Standardized Partial Regression Coefficients (Path Coefficients) for Effects of Structural Variables on Location of Family Types [a]

Variable	Family Type					
	Young Couples	Young Families	Old Families	Old Couples	Single Heads	Primary Indiv.
Age	—.06	—.60	—.11	.19	.37	.31
	(.07)	(.05)	(.05)	(.05)	(.05)	(.04)
Internal space	—.24	.21	.46	.53	.09	—.63
	(.07)	(.05)	(.05)	(.05)	(.05)	(.04)
Density	.04	—.08	—.30	—.18	.37	.13
	(.08)	(.07)	(.06)	(.07)	(.07)	(.05)
Industry	.11	.21	.04	—.15	—.02	—.12
	(.06)	(.04)	(.04)	(.04)	(.04)	(.03)
Recreation	—.03	—.07	—.03	.00	—.12	.12
	(.06)	(.04)	(.04)	(.06)	(.04)	(.03)
R^2	.09	.50	.55	.46	.46	.67
Implied r with distance	—.16	.53	.56	.35	—.55	—.60
Actual r with distance (353 tracts)	—.10	.52	.54	.43	—.65	—.60

[a] Standard errors in parentheses.

TABLE 4
Values for Paths from Distance to Family Types

Selected Variables	Family Type					
	Young Couples	Young Families	Old Families	Old Couples	Single Heads	Primary Indiv.
Di–Ag	.04	.44	.08	—.14	—.27	—.23
Di–De–Ro	—.11	.09	.21	.24	.04	—.28
Di–Ag–Ro	.05	—.05	—.10	—.12	—.02	.14
Di–Ro	—.05	.04	.09	.11	.02	—.13
Di–Ag–De–Ro	—.01	.01	.03	.03	.01	—.04
Di–In–Ro	—.01	.01	.02	.03	.00	—.03
Di–De	—.03	.06	.22	.13	—.27	—.09
Di–Ag–De	.00	.01	.03	.02	—.04	—.01
Di–In	—.03	—.06	—.01	.05	.01	.04
Di–Re	—.01	—.02	—.01	.00	—.03	.03
Sum	—.16	.53	.56	.35	—.55	—.60

Symbols: Di—distance from CBD, Ag—age, Ro—internal space or rooms–per–dwelling, De—density or units–per–acre, In—industrial activity, Re—recreational activity.

and Space. Site features play a very small role. The model demonstrated that for Young Families, Old Families, and Pri-mary Individuals the effects of distance are transmitted through age of housing and density. For Young Couples, Old

Couples, and Single Heads, distance apparently has an effect on location independent of other variables. Of course, Young Couples showed little variation with distance in the first place, and we have already suggested that most of the failure of our model in regard to Old Couples may be due to curvilinear relationships with linear distance from the CBD.

The Space variables generally have the strongest direct and indirect effects on the location of family types. The direct effect of internal space or rooms-per-dwelling is particularly impressive. Young Families, Old Families, and Old Couples show fairly clear tendencies to be located in areas of internally spacious housing, while Young Couples and Primary Individuals are located disproportionately in the opposite types of areas. Most of the effect of the internal space variables is transmitted through the distance–density relationship. In short, much of the tendency for Young Families, Old Families, and Old Couples to be found on the outskirts may be attributed to the existence there of low density, spacious housing. Young Couples and Primary Individuals are centralized for the opposite reasons. Density or dwellings-per-area also has a strong direct effect on location for Old Families, Old Couples, and Single Heads, independent of the number of rooms-per-dwelling. The first two family types are partially decentralized due to their use of low density housing on the outskirts, regardless of the number of rooms-per-dwelling, whereas Single Heads are partially centralized due to their use of high density housing, regardless of its other characteristics. These results, then, suggest that much of the distribution of families is simply a function of differential intensity of residential land use.

Age of area has strong direct effects on the location of three types of families. Young Families are found particularly in new areas, while Primary Individuals and Single Heads, often widowed persons, are found particularly in old areas. Thus, much of the tendency for these families to be centralized or decentralized may be explained by the location of old housing near the city center and new housing on the outskirts, regardless of the other characteristics of housing. Since Age has little effect on density, very little centralization or decentralization of family types may be attributed to indirect effects of Age. There is some tendency for Age to operate indirectly through the rooms-per-dwelling variable, but we have little understanding of why this should occur.

Although the effects are small, Site features actually operate opposite to expectations for some family types. For instance, Young Families and Old Families are found particularly in areas of industry and little recreation when other ecological variables are controlled, It should be emphasized, however, that the effects are very weak.

Given this model, we may now summarize the reasons for centralization or decentralization of types of families.

Young Families and Old Families are decentralized, but apparently for somewhat different reasons. Young Families are on the outskirts primarily due to the presence of relatively new housing, while Old Families are there because of low density housing.

Both Primary Individuals and Single Heads are found toward the CBD because they live in old areas. Primary Individuals are also particularly centralized because of residence in high density areas; density is less important for Single Heads.

Of the other two types, only Old Couples had much relationship to distance from the CBD. In this case, paths have noticeably opposite effects. Thus, Old Couples are decentralized due to residence in low density areas but centralized due to residence in older areas; that is, there are forces pulling them toward both the center and outskirts of Cleveland. There is also some tendency for location in new neighborhoods to decentralize Young Couples, whereas location in high density neighborhoods tends to centralize them.

A composite model of the distribution of families in relationship to the CBD would indicate whether the tendency of various types of families to live in the same or different neighborhoods could be due to attraction or repulsion by the same ecological features. To determine whether this is true, we can compare the actual correlations between the proportions of each family type over the census tracts with the correlations implied by our model. As Table 5 shows, the implied correlations are generally similar in sign to the actual, although the levels of relationship often differ substantially. For instance, while the tendency of

Young Families and Primary Individuals to locate in different areas can be explained partially by neighborhood characteristics (basically Age and Space variables), there is also a very large unexplained difference between them. At this point, we cannot say why this difference occurs.

Summary and Discussion

It is clear that the arguments of the human ecologists are valuable for understanding the location of types of families in the metropolis. Much of the tendency for family types to be located close to or distant from the CBD may be explained through the distance–density and distance–Age relationships. In fact, the tendency for Young Families and Old Families to be decentralized and for Primary Individuals to be centralized can be almost completely explained by the model.

Given the massive evidence (Muth, 1969) that population densities decline in a fairly regular manner with distance from the CBD, one would expect generally similar patterns of family distribution in most American metropolitan

TABLE 5
Implied and Actual Correlations Among Family Types [a]

Family Type	Family Type					
	Young Couples	Young Families	Old Families	Old Couples	Single Heads	Primary Indiv.
Young couples	—	.06	—.40	—.38	.11	.03
Young families	—.07	—	.28	—.14	—.39	—.73
Old families	—.19	.40	—	.47	—.41	—.63
Old couples	—.21	.16	.43	—	—.25	—.43
Single heads	.08	—.42	—.35	—.16	—	.21
Primary individuals	.20	—.48	—.59	—.44	.38	—

[a] Actual above diagonal; implied below.

areas. Indeed, we (Guest, 1970) have shown that patterns of family distribution in sixteen other metropolitan areas are generally similar to those found in Cleveland.

The direct effect of areal Age on patterns of family location may indicate the importance of the neighborhood life cycle in understanding the distribution of population. Neighborhoods, regardless of their housing and Site characteristics, may indeed pass through life cycles in their family composition, from Young Families to Old Couples, Primary Individuals, and Single Heads. This, of course, has been only suggested, not demonstrated, by the model. While areal Age may exert a direct effect on family location, there is little evidence that it has much indirect effect through other variables.

The ecologists' model would suggest that patterns of family distribution in relationship to the CBD should be most distinct in the largest metropolitan areas, whether for reasons stemming from the greater competition for central land or from the generally old age of the area around the CBD. However, we have elsewhere (Guest, 1970, p. 162) correlated (for Cleveland and the sixteen other metropolitan areas) population size with the predicted change in the proportion of each family type for each mile distance zone from the CBD. This analysis showed that the proportions of Young Families and Old Families increased most rapidly with distance from the CBD in the smallest places, while the proportions of Single Heads and Primary Individuals decreased most rapidly with distance from the CBD in the smallest places. This result was consistent with Muth's (1969, p. 152) finding that the density gradient changed most rapidly in the smallest places. While these results seem to be contradictory to current ecological

theory, we have no present explanations. Obviously, more research is needed into the process of neighborhood change as cities age and grow in population.

While this paper has been directed toward an analysis of family location in terms of human ecology theory, it is perhaps appropriate to note the relationship of our results to the other major tradition of urban spatial research, factorial ecology. For a full analysis of factorial ecology, see Rees (1970). The factorial ecologists, in numerous studies of the organization of U.S. cities, have produced at least two principal dimensions of urban differentiation, socioeconomic status and family status. These dimensions have resulted from the application of factor analytic techniques to matrices of correlations among population and housing characteristics for census tracts. The factorial ecologists have generally produced a family status dimension that indicates the joint presence (or absence) in tracts of low female labor force participation, high fertility, a young age structure, and single unit housing.

In regard to our analysis, the family status dimension probably corresponds most closely to the disproportionate presence in certain tracts of Young and Old Families and the absence of Single Heads and Primary Individuals. As Table 5 shows, there is some tendency for Young and Old Families to be found together in tracts not inhabited by Single Heads and Primary Individuals. And, of course, the presence or absence of single unit, or low density, housing on the family dimension is consistent with our finding that the residential density pattern has a strong effect on the location of families. Furthermore, the factorial ecologists have found that the family dimension varies concentrically with distance from the CBD, in a manner consistent with the variation of Young and Old Families and Single Heads and Primary Individuals.

Beyond this clear similarity, our results diverge. Most importantly, our results suggest that patterns of family location cannot be completely, or even primarily, summarized by one dimension, family status. The generally low intercorrelations among the types of families would suggest that most neighborhoods are apt to have a relatively wide range of family types. Furthermore, there are multiple interrelations of Age, Site, and Space variables which produce the locations of various types of families. It would also seem that the factorial ecologists have been particularly neglectful of the role of past urban growth or areal age in determining the location of families.

To us, exciting research questions center around the effects of historical, technological, and population processes in determining the structure of the city. Human ecology has a long tradition of theory and analysis from which this search may be continued. The factorial ecologists have barely begun.

An important recent series of articles on factorial ecology (Berry, 1971) indicates an awareness of some of my criticisms. For instance, various authors recognize the possibility that family location patterns cannot be summarized neatly in one dimension, that housing age or period of construction affects the types of families in a neighborhood, and that general location patterns of types of families must be understood as products of the city's past growth. This suggests the probability that there is convergence in the work of factorial ecology and human ecologists.

REFERENCES

Berry, Brian J. L. (ed.). 1971. Comparative Factorial Ecology. Special Issue of Economic Geography 47, No. 2.

Burgess, Ernest. 1967. The growth of the city. In Robert E. Park, Ernest W. Burgess, and Roderick D. McKenzie (eds.), The City. Chicago: University of Chicago Press.

————, Harvey J. Locke, and Mary Margaret Thomas. 1963. The Family. New York: American Book Co.

Clark, S. D. 1966. The Suburban Society. Toronto: University of Toronto Press.

Cleveland-Seven County Transportation–Land Use Study. 1968. Supported by the commission of that name. Cleveland, Ohio.

Duncan, Beverly. 1964. Variables in urban morphology. In Ernest W. Burgess and Donald J. Bogue (eds.), Contributions to Urban Sociology. Chicago: University of Chicago Press.

Duncan, Otis Dudley. 1966. Path analysis: sociological examples. American Journal of Sociology 72:1–16.

Edwards, Ozzie L. 1970. Patterns of residential segregation within a metropolitan ghetto. Demography 7:185–193.

Guest, Avery M. 1970. Families and Housing in Cities. Unpublished Ph.D. dissertation, University of Wisconsin, Madison.

Hawley, Amos H. 1950. Human Ecology: A Theory of Community Structure. New York: Ronald Press.

Hoover, Edgar M., and Raymond Vernon. 1962. Anatomy of a Metropolis. New York: Anchor Books.

Muth, Richard F. 1969. Cities and Housing. Chicago: University of Chicago Press.

Rees, Richard. 1970. Concepts of social space: toward an urban social geography. In Brian J. L. Berry and Frank E. Horton (eds.), Geographical Perspectives on Urban Systems. Englewood Cliffs, N.J.: Prentice-Hall, Inc.

Riesman, David. 1957. The suburban dislocation. Annals of the American Academy of Political and Social Science 314:123–146.

Rossi, Peter. 1955. Why Families Move. Glencoe, Ill.: The Free Press.

United States Bureau of the Census. 1962. U. S. Censuses of Population and Housing: 1960. Census Tracts. Final Report PHC(1)-28. Washington, D.C.: Government Printing Office.

———. 1964. U. S. Census of Population: 1960. Subject Reports. Persons by Family Characteristics. Final Report PC(2)-4B. Washington, D.C.: Government Printing Office.

Winsborough, Hal H. 1963. An ecological approach to the theory of suburbanization. American Journal of Sociology 68:565–570.

A Longitudinal Study of Retail Gravitation Between Columbus and Springfield, Ohio

William B. Wagner

An empirical study of the Springfield and Columbus, Ohio, trading areas for various goods and services was concluded in August, 1972. Consisting of three separate surveys, it extended over a period of eight years and five months. It is thought to be the first extensive longitudinal study designed to test two methods of retail trading area determination, namely: (1) Reilly's Law of Retail Gravitation, and (2) the geographic midpoint. In addition, circulations of Springfield and Columbus newspapers were correlated with the trading areas of these cities.

As stated above, this study tested Reilly's Law which states, "Two cities attract retail trade from an intermediate city or town in direct proportion to the populations of the two cities and in inverse proportion to the square of the distances [1] from these two cities to the intermediate town." [2] Although the original intent of the Law was to measure the trading areas of fashion goods for sizable trading centers surrounded by rural areas, it has often been considered applicable to both highly urbanized as well as sparsely populated areas. In fact, if adequate care is taken, it has been deemed applicable to the sale of service and convenience goods by some experts. [3]

Originally, Reilly formulated the Law from data derived from measuring the sales of leading stores of all the larger cities in Texas, house-to-house interviewing of consumer buying habits, and retail stock checking in different sized cities and towns. [4] Some twenty years later Douglas employed five different methods, including the Law, to measure the retail trading area of Charlotte, North Carolina. [5] In comparison with the analysis of credit records, analysis of bank deposits,

---

Reprinted from the *Bulletin of Business Research,* The Ohio State University, Vol. XLIX, No. 2, February 1974, by permission of the author and editor.

1 Distance via the most direct improved automobile highway.

2 William J. Reilly, *The Law of Retail Gravitation* (New York: The Knickerbocker Press, 1931), p. 9.

3 Paul D. Converse, Harvey W. Huegy, and Robert V. Mitchell, *The Elements of Marketing,* 6th edition (Englewood Cliffs, N.J.: Prentice-Hall, Inc., 1958), pp. 31–32.

4 For a description of the entire study see William J. Reilly, *Methods for the Study of Retail Relationships* (Austin: University of Texas, 1929).

5 Edna Douglas, "Measuring the General Retail Trading Area—A Case Study: I," *Journal of Marketing,* XIII, No. 4 (April, 1949), pp. 481–497; and Edna Douglas, "Measuring the General Retail Trading Area—A Case Study: II," *Journal of Marketing,* XIV, No. 1 (July, 1949), pp. 46–60.

analysis of traffic flows, and analysis of population, she found the Law provided a "remarkably accurate delineation of the Charlotte retail trading area." [6]

Reynolds, in a study conducted in southwestern Iowa, concluded that the Law accurately determined trading areas for shopping goods; however, in a study covering the entire state of Iowa he thought the Law was ineffective.[7]

The three studies conducted by the author tested the Law for sizable trading centers surrounded by rural areas for thirteen different consumer goods and services to determine whether or not it would be possible to determine accurately the trading areas of items for which it was originally intended (i.e., shopping goods) as well as convenience and specialty goods and services. The studies attempted to test certain hypotheses:

1. Reilly's Law is more effective than the geographic midpoint in determining the trading areas for all goods and services surveyed.
2. The amount of purchasing varies according to the type of good or service (i.e., convenience, shopping, and specialty) and such purchasing patterns are relatively stable over time.
3. Newspaper circulations parallel the general trading area of the city of publication.

Sampling Procedure [8]

In March, 1964, two samples each consisting of fifty respondents (households) were selected from the area between Columbus and Springfield, Ohio. One sample (Sample A) was centered around the *breaking point* determined through an application of Reilly's Law and, using U.S. Highway 40 as the straight line connecting the centers of the cities in question, located thirty-one miles from Columbus and thirteen miles from Springfield.[9] The other sample (Sample B) was centered around the *geographic midpoint* located one-half the distance between Springfield and Columbus, or twenty-two miles from each. The same two samples were used in July, 1967 (Samples AA and BB) and in August, 1972 (Samples AAA and BBB).

Findings

Data analysis reveals that the true breaking point differs according to type of good or service. For purposes of illustration, a comparison between shopping patterns for a convenience good (i.e., groceries) and a shopping good (i.e., work and school clothes) is provided.

Convenience goods and services are

---

[6] *Ibid.,* p. 60.

[7] Robert B. Reynolds, "A Test of the Law of Retail Gravitation," *Journal of Marketing*, XVII (January, 1953), pp. 273–277.

[8] The sampling procedure employed was developed by Dr. James L. Heskett, formerly of The Ohio State University and presently at Harvard University; Dr. William Morgenroth, formerly of The Ohio State University and presently at the University of South Carolina; and the author.

[9] Samples A, AA, and AAA were centered around a breaking point determined by an equation (formula) derived from Reilly's Law to yield the theoretically correct point between the two

cities in question. Application of the formula ($\dfrac{D}{1 + \sqrt{Px/Py}}$ = Miles from City Y, where D is the

distance between Cities X and Y, Px is the population of City X, and Py is the population of City Y) to the case in question results in a breaking point located approximately thirty-one miles from Columbus, or thirteen miles from Springfield.

normally defined as those which customers prefer to purchase on short notice, with a minimum amount of effort, and, most characteristically of all, at a convenient location. These items typically have the smallest trading areas as there are a greater number of establishments handling them relative to stores concentrating on selling shopping or specialty goods. In addition, customers of these goods usually have a frequent need for replenishment. Groceries meet these requirements well. Analysis of grocery purchase patterns indicates that the Columbus and Springfield trading areas for groceries were smaller than the trading areas for other items. The total number of respondents doing the majority of their grocery shopping in the cities were relatively few. As shown in Tables 1 and 2, the number of respondents purchasing grocery items in either of the two cities in all three surveys was very small, and in almost all of these cases the head of the household was employed in the city where the purchases were made. These findings coincide with those found in Doherty's classic study of the Boston retail area in which he concluded that the food (i.e., grocery) market was highly decentralized and not served by a few important centers, as was true with shopping and specialty goods.[10]

Shopping goods command higher prices than convenience goods, and the potential purchaser usually makes several trips to a variety of stores to inspect them before arriving at a final decision. Quality, style, suitability and price provide common bases for comparison. And sales are commonly dependent upon consumer taste. Accordingly, it is logical to infer that these goods should

have larger trading areas than their convenience counterparts. In the "work and school clothes" classification as an example, Springfield attracted 66 percent in Sample A, 74 percent in Sample AA, and 56 percent in Sample AAA; it attracted only 2 percent in Sample B, 4 percent in Sample BB, and 0 percent in Sample BBB. Columbus, on the other hand, garnered 10 percent, 16 percent, and 22 percent in Samples A, AA, and AAA, respectively; 42 percent, 60 percent, and 68 percent in Samples B, BB, and BBB bought this type of clothing in Columbus. The raw data from which these calculations are made are shown in Tables 1 and 2.

In sum, 76 percent in Sample A, 90 percent in Sample AA, and 78 percent in Sample AAA shopped for nonfashion clothing in one of the two cities; 44 percent in Sample B, 64 percent in Sample BB, and 68 percent in Sample BBB bought this item in Springfield or Columbus, indicating clearly the wider trading area for work and school clothes (v. groceries).

Findings on Retail Trading Area Determination Techniques

Reilly's Law, as discussed earlier, was tested by formulating a sample around the breaking point determined by a formula derived from the Law. If the principle underlying the Law was correct, the number of respondents buying goods and services in Springfield would equal the number purchasing in Columbus. Thus, the null hypothesis is that no difference exists in the two groups (Springfield and Columbus buyers) in that the proportion of Springfield buyers who purchase convenience goods

[10] Richard P. Doherty, "The Movement of Concentration of Retail Trade in Metropolitan Areas," *Journal of Marketing*, V, No. 4 (April, 1941), p. 395.

TABLE 1
Item Demand by Time and Place of Purchase
(Breaking Point)

Type of Goods or Service	Springfield Responses			Columbus Responses		
	Sample A 1964	Sample AA 1967	Sample AAA 1972	Sample A 1964	Sample AA 1967	Sample AAA 1972
Convenience Goods and Services						
Groceries	8	6	11	0	0	0
Barber	16	19	16	0	0	0
Doctor (gen. medical)	15	16	14	1	0	2
Total	39	41	41	1	0	2
Shopping Goods (non-durable)						
Work and school clothes	33	37	28	5	8	11
Dress clothes	30	30	31	5	8	10
Total	63	67	59	10	16	21
Shopping Goods (durable)						
Television sets	24	25	26	2	4	1
Washers	23	21	23	2	3	4
Automobiles (two most recent)	35	49	39	4	2	4
Total	82	95	88	8	9	9
Shopping and Specialty Services						
Motion pictures	17	24	18	4	3	2
Sporting events	3	5	5	2	1	0
Music events	1	5	5	3	4	3
Restaurants	17	23	23	7	9	8
Total	38	57	51	16	17	13
Overall Shopping Measure						
Christmas Shopping	32	32	31	4	9	13
Total	32	32	31	4	9	13

and services is the same as the proportion of Columbus buyers who purchase convenience goods and services, and that this holds true for shopping and specialty items as well.

An analysis of data from the samples centered around the breaking point shows Springfield as the much stronger of the two cities in pulling power. In all three studies, as shown in Table 1, significantly more trade gravitated to Springfield. Concerning convenience goods and services, Columbus has almost no pulling power in the barber, general medical service, and grocery categories. In the case of shopping

TABLE 2
Item Demand by Time and Place of Purchase
(Geographic Midpoint)

Type of Goods or Service	Springfield Responses			Columbus Responses		
	Sample B 1964	Sample BB 1967	Sample BBB 1972	Sample B 1964	Sample BB 1967	Sample BBB 1972
Convenience Goods and Services						
Groceries	0	1	0	3	4	3
Barber	0	1	0	2	4	2
Doctor (gen. medical)	1	0	0	3	5	3
Total	1	2	0	8	13	8
Shopping Goods (non-durable)						
Work and school clothes	1	2	0	21	30	34
Dress clothes	2	1	2	25	33	38
Total	3	3	2	46	63	72
Shopping Goods (durable)						
Television sets	1	0	1	12	11	23
Washers	1	1	1	9	8	17
Automobiles (two most recent)	5	4	3	14	13	16
Total	7	5	5	35	32	56
Shopping and Specialty Services						
Motion pictures	4	1	5	17	22	16
Sporting events	0	0	0	7	6	9
Music events	1	0	0	4	9	4
Restaurants	1	1	4	21	20	24
Total	6	2	9	49	57	53
Overall Shopping Measure						
Christmas Shopping	3	3	1	31	33	36
Total	3	3	1	31	33	36

goods, Springfield has appreciably more purchasing power in television sets, washers, and automobiles. In other words, respondents preferred to buy all durable shopping goods tested in Springfield by a wide margin. *The degrees of difference point out the ineffectiveness of the Law in practice.*

Regarding nonconvenience services, including restaurant and various entertainment forms, Springfield again drew considerably more than Columbus with respect to patronage of restaurants, motion pictures, and sporting events. Only in the case of music events, in which the number of responses was very small, was there any question as to Springfield's advantage in purchasing power.

Springfield's dominance in the selling of all other goods and services sampled was supported through the use of the sign test. This test pointed out that the differences were significant at the .001 level for every good and service category with the exception of music events.

Another key question revolves around the geographic midpoint's effectiveness in delineating trading areas. Table 2 clearly indicates that the pulling power of Columbus was appreciably stronger than that of Springfield for all categories of goods and services, i.e., convenience, shopping, and specialty. It is important to note the almost complete lack of Springfield responses for all items in each of the three studies. Through employment of the sign test, differences in the relative buying power of Columbus are shown to be significant at the .001 level for all items except barbers and groceries, both of which had only a few total responses.[11]

Findings on the Newspaper Circulation–Trading Area Relationship

Newspaper advertising affects the flow of trade. To the extent that this is true, it is possible to determine trading areas by plotting the circulation of newspapers in competing cities. Of course, the effect of direct mail such as mail-order catalogs, along with radio, television, and the overlapping circulation of competing newspapers in the area between the cities must be acknowledged. Data regarding newspaper subscriptions indicate the close parallel between newspaper circulation and trading areas.

Subscriptions to the various newspapers remained relatively constant from 1964 through 1972. It is evident that Springfield newspapers were read by considerably more people in the sample centered around the breaking point determined by Reilly's Law, i.e., Samples A, AA, and AAA. Springfield sellers likewise monopolized this market.

In the sample centered around the geographic midpoint, Columbus newspapers and sellers dominated. However, the degree of dominance by Columbus sellers in this sample was less than that of the Springfield merchants in the breaking point sample, partially because it: (1) had a geographic center only four miles north of London, Ohio, the largest city between Springfield and Columbus, and one with several very progressive merchants; and (2) required longer average driving times per shopping trip due to the greater distance to and traffic in Columbus.

Conclusions

As hypothesized, with respect to measuring retail trading areas for the thirteen goods and services surveyed, the geographic midpoint proved ineffective. In the samples centered around the midpoint (i.e., Samples B, BB, and BBB), Columbus held a significant advantage. This is partially attributable to the fact that although as the larger city Columbus has considerably more traffic congestion and parking problems, it provides a much greater selection of merchandise in terms of style, quality, and price. Furthermore, there are many more shopping centers in the Columbus

---

[11] The sign test indicates that the difference in the relative purchasing power of Columbus and Springfield concerning both barbers and groceries is significant at the .05 level in this sample.

metropolitan area, including several that offer easy access for sample respondents from the west.

Concerning services, Columbus has a greater number and variety of establishments, including amusements and forms of recreation. Hotels, motels, and restaurants of all kinds abound. Also, it offers a wide variety of indoor and outdoor motion pictures and theatrical productions. Sporting events at the college and professional level can be enjoyed. Other agglomerating forces, such as the large number of industrial, educational, and governmental institutions, contribute to the extension of Columbus trading areas for all goods and services beyond the geographic midpoint located about twenty-two miles from Columbus.

Reilly's Law of Retail Gravitation also proved inadequate as a means of accurate determination of trading areas. Analysis of the Springfield and Columbus responses in the sample located around the breaking point resulted in a rejection of the null hypothesis, i.e., there was no difference in the two groups (Columbus and Springfield buyers) in that the proportion of Springfield buyers who buy shopping goods is the same as the proportion of Columbus buyers who buy shopping goods, and that this holds true for convenience and specialty items as well. Differences were found to be significant at the .001 level by the sign test; the only exception was in the case of music events.

Population, as an indicator of a city's size, is employed in most applications of the formula derived from Reilly's Law. It is important to note, however, that it is often overemphasized when the formula is used, particularly in cases where wide variations in population exist. In a case where one city is twenty-five times as large as another and they are located sixty miles apart, a breaking point located ten miles from the smaller city and fifty miles from the larger one would exist. And this, of course, is unrealistic even for shopping goods. In other words, the larger the difference in city size, the greater the inaccuracy of Reilly's Law. The Law's effectiveness is also hampered by increases in the distance figure employed in the formula.

Based on the foregoing, trading areas for Columbus merchants offering any of the thirteen goods and services surveyed extend past the midpoint located twenty-two miles from Columbus. Yet none of the trading areas extend to the breaking point located thirty-one miles from Columbus. The actual or true breaking point for all goods and services analyzed, therefore, lies somewhere within the nine-mile area between 22 and 31 miles from Columbus. As the relative strength in pulling power of each city in the sample located closest to it is unquestioned for almost all, if not all, goods and services sampled, a point one-half the distance between the midpoint and breaking point might be a better approximation.

Empirical investigation of respondents' purchasing patterns as well as subscriptions to local newspapers showed a close relationship between trading areas and newspaper circulations, as originally hypothesized. With both purchasing behavior and newspaper circulations remaining almost constant throughout the 1964–1972 period, Springfield sellers and newspapers dominated the sample centered around the breaking point determined by the formula derived from Reilly's Law; correspondingly, Columbus merchants and newspapers monopolized the sample surrounding the geographic midpoint.

Results from this research supported

the hypothesis that the type of good or service is a determining factor in the size of a retail trading area. Convenience goods (and services) have the smallest trading areas, followed by shopping and specialty items. In other words, the principle that people will travel greater distances and thereby expend a greater amount of effort for specialty and shopping goods relative to those of a convenience nature is clearly indicated in the results.

Customer patronage patterns did not experience much change over time. The extent of demand for the various products and services remained relatively constant throughout the 1964–1972 period in which the study was conducted, as shown in the data displayed in Tables 1 and 2. Degrees of difference, as determined by the sign test, between Columbus and Springfield patronage for the various goods and services in each of the three surveys were strikingly similar.

Interestingly enough, more non-durable than durable shopping goods were purchased in the two cities.[12] Several reasons can be cited for this, including:

1. Durable goods, particularly automobiles, were often traded or purchased from friends, neighbors, and relatives.
2. Several local dealers in durable goods

offered quicker and more personal service.
3. Respondents felt city dealers of durables (television sets, washers, and cars) were not always worthy of their trust.
4. Hardware stores and car dealers in the area between Columbus and Springfield were very aggressive, as witnessed by the high amount of advertising in city newspapers and on radio and television.

Future Research

Effective trading area determination is both a matter of practical economics and sound business practice. Accurate specification of such areas can result in greater efficiency and, correspondingly, opportunities for cost reduction in sales and distribution operations. And customer service is enhanced.

The value of effective trading area determination has long been established. Yet, questions regarding the best means by which to determine boundaries remain unresolved. Accordingly, further analysis and testing of alternative methods for determining trading areas in locations where they have not previously been applied and for goods and services other than those for which such methods were originally intended is a requirement confronting American business in the 1970s.

---

[12] As the non-durable (v. durable) goods surveyed are generally of lower per unit value and have more frequent replenishment times, it would seem that they should be bought locally and hence have smaller trading areas for merchants in the larger cities.

An Empirical Reappraisal of Behavioristic Assumptions in Trading Area Studies

Joseph Barry Mason and Charles Thomas Moore

Significant amounts of time, money, and energy have been expended in efforts to devise and refine methodologies for defining a trading area and estimating its economic potential. Techniques employed have ranged from gravity models to stochastic processes in a search for the appropriate technique. The results of these studies, in most instances, have been rather disappointing as explanatory devices of factors influencing the shape and outreach of a trading area and its economic potential, even though they have been of some use to retailers.

These studies traditionally have been conducted on a spatially aggregated basis using such proxy socioeconomic variables as average income, average level of education, etc. Even though this simplified approach is conceptually seductive, the use of averages and spatial aggregation has been among the primary criticisms of gravity and other similar models.[1] This approach necessarily assumes: (1) that there are no internal differences of significance

within the area of analysis, and (2) that households with comparable socioeconomic characteristics will depict similar retail center patronage decisions.

The research reported in this article explores two hypotheses: (1) that the use of a spatially disaggregated approach to trading area analysis will reveal significant internal differences within an area that are of value in explaining variations in shopping trip patterns and retail center patronage decisions, and (2) that households comparable in socioeconomic characteristics do not necessarily depict similar retail center patronage decisions.

Methodology

The study is based on survey data obtained from 500 households located in a 340-square mile area north of Birmingham, Alabama. (See Figure 1.) This study area is separated from Birmingham by major terrain, time, and distance barriers. All trips from the

Reprinted from the *Journal of Retailing*, Vol. 46, No. 4, Winter 1970–1971, by permission of the authors and editor.

[1] Charles Thomas Moore and Morris L. Mayer, "Consumer Travel Behavior and the Central City Retail Structure," in Raymond Haas (ed.), *Science, Technology, and Marketing* (Chicago, Ill.: American Marketing Association, 1966), pp. 827–28; and David L. Huff, "A Note on the Limitations of Intra-Urban Gravity Models," *Land Economics* (February 1961), pp. 64–66.

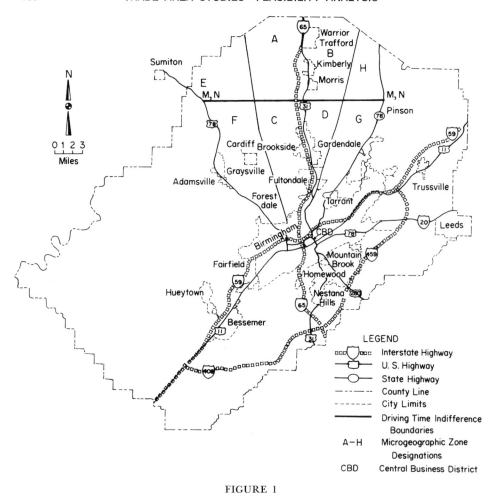

FIGURE 1

Incorporated Areas, Interstate Highway Routes, Primary Federal-Aid Highways,
State Highways, and Driving Time Indifference Zonal Boundaries

study area to Birmingham involve significant expenditures of time and effort.

The study area has a low population density—nineteen households per square mile. It contains nine small incorporated communities with populations ranging from less than 1,000 to 6,000.

The small incorporated communities in this area offer low-order shopping facilities, the largest consisting of 150,000 square feet, to citizens of surrounding areas. The population must go to Birmingham to search for nonconvenience goods. Skilled and semi-skilled blue-collar occupations dominate the labor force living in both the incorporated and the rural portions of the area. The residents now depend on Birmingham almost exclusively as a place of employment.

Average family income in both portions of the area is $5,000, and the average educational level of the household head is eight years.

For purposes of analysis the study area was divided into a series of microgeographic zones based on indifference points in driving time between major highways in the area. This was done to test an initial hypothesis that, based on an analysis of household economic and demographic information,[2] the microgeographic areas are statistically different even though the aggregate area is outwardly homogeneous based on an analysis of census data. The application of discriminant analysis revealed differences significant at the level of .01 between each of the microgeographic areas.[3]

After finding that disaggregation of the total study area yielded statistically significant internal differences between the areas in spite of outward similarity in terms of census data, stepwise multiple regression was utilized to ascertain the variables that were significantly associated with variation in shopping trip patterns depicted by households in the microgeographic areas.[4]

The socioeconomic variables were regressed with the following information for each of the microgeographic areas: number of intrazonal shopping trips; number of interzonal shopping trips originating within the zonal areas and having destinations other than Birmingham; number of Birmingham central business district (CBD) and major retail center shopping trips; and total expenditures made on these trips.

Data Analysis

An examination of Table 1 reveals that the coefficients of multiple determination (R^2) varied widely between the microgeographic areas. For example, the various combinations of the small incorporated communities of Warrior, Morris–Kimberly, Fultondale, and Gardendale, which were examined separately from the nonurban microgeographic areas, yielded R^2s ranging from .34 to .54. A limited number of the R^2 values obtained for the nonurban microgeographic zones were somewhat higher. For example, the R^2 value for Zone B,D as related to the number of Birmingham shopping trips was .66, while for the parallel Zone A,C, all R^2 values were very low relative to those of Zone B,D. Large differences in explanatory success are evident between all the areas even though they are all

[2] The socioeconomic variables analyzed were: number of adults in household, age of respondent, occupation of household head, number of children in household, number of years in present home, number of motor vehicles, number of drivers' licenses, number of years of schooling of the household head, and income level of household. These same variables were utilized in all of the research reported in this article.

[3] The variables that consistently discriminated between the areas were number of adults in household, age of respondent, and occupation of the head of the household.

[4] The approach normally employed in regression analysis is that of all possible regressions. This requires the fitting of every possible regression, which involves X_0 plus any number of variables $X_1, \ldots, X_n$. The stepwise regression procedure begins with a simple correlation matrix and initially inserts into the equation the dependent variable most highly correlated with the independent variable. The partial correlation coefficient is then used as a measure of the importance of variables not yet in the equation. As each additional variable is entered into the equation (the order is determined by the size of the sample correlation coefficient) the partial F-test value for the variable most recently entered, which shows whether the variable has statistically reduced the amount of variation beyond that already removed by variables previously entered into the equation, is computed. When it is found that the amount of variance reduction is not statistically significant, the process is terminated.

TABLE 1

Coefficients of Multiple Determination Depicting the Relationship Between Selected Independent Variables * and the Number of Shopping Trips to the Birmingham Central Business District and Other Birmingham Major Retail Centers, Number of Interzonal Shopping Trips, Number of Intrazonal Shopping Trips, and Total Number of Shopping Trips for Both the Incorporated Communities and the Rural Areas in the Travel Behavior Corridor

Area of Study	Number of Birmingham Shopping Trips †	Number of Interzonal Shopping Trips	Number of Intrazonal Shopping Trips	Total Number of Shopping Trips
Incorporated Communities				
Warrior and Morris–Kimberly	.18	.27	.29	.34
Warrior, Morris–Kimberly, and Fultondale	.30	.27	.34	.54
Gardendale, Morris–Kimberly Warrior, and Fultondale	.05	.07	.10	.11
Rural Areas				
Zone E,F	.34	.27	— ‡	.17
Zone A,C	.16	.30	.28	.14
Zone B,D	.66	.53	.57	.63

* The variables were: number of adults in household; age of respondent; occupation of household head; number of children in household; number of years in present home; number of motor vehicles; number of drivers' licenses; number of years of formal education of household head; and income level of household.
† Included only trips to the Birmingham CBD and other Birmingham major retail centers.
‡ Insufficient data.

outwardly similar in terms of household income, educational level of household head, occupation of household head, and family composition.

Additionally, via the stepwise approach to regression, it was determined that the sets of independent variables were not constant in either level of explanatory success or order of insertion into the regression equation when related to shopping trip patterns. However, in all instances, the first three variables inserted into the regression equation accounted for between 50 and 80 percent of the observable relationship in the data. The variables that appeared most frequently in each set of three included number of adults, number of children, age of respondent, and number of drivers' licenses. Neither occupation of household head, number of years of formal education of household head, nor the income level of the household were found to be of primary importance in relation to variations in shopping trip patterns between the microgeographic zones.

Discussion

Disaggregation of the total study area revealed statistically significant differences between the microgeographic zones even though the total area was outwardly homogeneous based on an analysis of census data. This reveals a limitation of using aggregate data averages in trading area studies because this approach does not reveal possible internal dissimilarities within an area that may be of significance in terms of both marketing policy and investment decisions.

Success was only moderate in the application of stepwise regression analysis even on a disaggregated basis. Levels of explanatory success varied widely between areas—again revealing that spatial aggregation in trading area studies should be employed with extreme caution.

Further, based on this study, one is led to question the validity of the use of traditional socioeconomic variables for purposes of trading area analysis. For, in addition to relatively low levels of explanatory success relative to shopping trips patterns, the variables most heavily relied upon in trading area studies (household income, occupation of household head, and level of education of household head) were not found to be of primary importance in the development of optimal regression equations. Because of the variations in explanatory success between the comparable areas, it can be inferred that households which are comparable in such socioeconomic characteristics as income, occupation, and education (traditional social class variables) do not necessarily depict comparable shopping travel behavior patterns.

Based on this analysis, one must also question the validity of the implicit assumption of many of the trading area models that some form of spatially competitive equilibrium exists and that for a given retail center there are a series of demand gradients in the form of isoprobability contours. Holding population constant, trip patterns varied greatly between the microgeographic areas, a situation which implies spatial disequilibrium. Even if equilibrium exists, the variations in explanatory success forthcoming are so great, even between small areas, as to be of only limited usefulness for purposes of aggregate predictability relative to shopping behavior. This analysis of interarea shopping trips suggests that trading areas are neither regular nor consistent in shape. Consumer perceptions of a retail outlet lead to irregularities in its trading area even in the absence of spatial, temporal, or physical barriers. The above assumptions relative to trading area studies have been criticized by Gunnar Olsson and Stephen Gale as follows:

> Since most spatial theories are extensions of economic theories, traditional work in regional science and theoretical geography has been directed toward the same normative, optimizing constructs as have studies in economics. The modifications of classical economics by Losch, Isard, and others have led to a relaxation of the presumption of a nondimensional economic world but they have not affected any of the normative-behavioristic assumptions.[5]

Certainly, based on this analysis, the implicit assumptions in most trading studies of cost-consciousness and profit maximization on the part of the consumer seem unrealistic, for the consumer is either more than or less than an "economic man." At best, one wonders whether much of the research in the area of location has focused on the

[5] Gunnar Olsson and Stephen Gale, "Spatial Theory and Human Behavior," in Morgan Thomas (ed.), *The Regional Science Association Papers,* Vol. XXI (Philadelphia: University of Pennsylvania, the Regional Science Association, 1968), p. 229.

relevant dimensions of the problem.

Differences were found to exist between the urban and nonurban portions of the total study area in spite of comparable household socioeconomic mixes. This finding tends to refute the contention of many researchers that urban–nonurban area differences have largely disappeared and that differentiation between these types of areas for purposes of market area studies is no longer of primary importance.

Socioeconomic variables do not satisfactorily explain these variations in trip patterns; it may be inferred that psychological or attitudinal differences of the residents may be of greater importance. Certainly primary reliance on the income variable and an assumption of cost-consciousness on the part of the consumer seem to be insufficient for defining a trading area and estimating its economic potential.

LOCATION ANALYSIS

Location study and analysis for retailing functions and activities is essentially a continuous and ongoing process among both existing establishments and potential new entrants. Astute management must constantly reevaluate its locational position in reference to market mix, relative position and scale of competitors, and the reality of the dynamics and changes of the retailing marketplace.

A given location for a retail firm represents a crucial factor input in the total strategy of the firm. Therefore, although a particular firm may be anchored via lease or ownership of the facilities, this in and of itself does not represent an unchanging position, either in terms of the location of doing business and/or the kind, level, and intensity of business conducted within the parameters of the then existing trade area, its composition, and so on.

The dynamics of locational shifts in prime retailing centers attests to the constant reevaluation of relative position, physical facilities, and comparative scale of cost–rental differentials. For example, in some instances a small ready-to-wear firm will relocate half a block toward a principal and high-volume generator of shoppers, perhaps a department store; in other cases, the move may simply be across the street because of apparent affinity of adjacent compatable establishments having a regional or national reputation and corresponding visibility. Assuming that appropriate and suitable facilities will become available, a highly sophisticated in-depth study by management is required, since any change costs money. Aside from physical relocation costs, other costs include building a new identity at the alternative location, generating a continued image for old customer retention, and so on.

135

Likewise, new lease commitments for extended periods of time represent a stress dimension as part of the uncertainties of locational choice. For, as reputable and competitive retailers will attest, a wrong locational choice for a particular line of business may represent an irreversible error that results in loss of market share and at times is a prelude to the demise of the establishment or firm.

Components of Locational Choice

Geographers, marketing specialists, and location analysts (Brian Berry, William Applebaum, Nelson) all generally agree that retailing functions transform into a systematic structure with three distinct locational attributes:

1. Various threshold levels of nucleations as depicted by the central business district, regional, community, neighborhood, and convenience centers. The genesis of each may be through evolution, via population and/or transport networks, and other sectors of commerce, and is essentially unplanned. The counterpart, the regional center, represents a product of research and overt planning to capture markets and market shares in a given urban geographical situation.

2. The linear transport–public right of way development, frequently called a ribbon development. Its emergence and transformation into a solidified and mature market complex can be traced to urban growth sectors and represents a response to an absence of shopping facilities and a presence of adequate population concentrations, with corresponding purchasing power, to support a number of retailing outlets. Cutoff points from a distance consideration (number of linear blocks) evolve in these situations simply because dispersion and the consequent lack of identity prevails. Entry by retailers along lateral streets represents a final filling-in process in an endeavor to get close to the "retailing action area."

3. Specialized areas–concentrations of select and identifiable retailing-service functions. These include furniture marts, medical services, and the like. In the last several decades these have been planned facilities, an endeavor to synergize identity–location vis-à-vis the consumer in the real or potential trade area for the service or particular merchandise line.

The complexities of selecting a retail location include many of these components and other important factors. The final choice depends on the line of business, perception–evaluation of alternative locations, and probable share of markets, which represent just several of the input factors for final selection.

Each situation under consideration reflects a costs of entry, that is, the cost and/or rental for a suitable facility at each identified location. When a solitary location is chosen, the costs of developing the location, which include identity building from the vantage point of consumers, must be underwriten; this, of course, is underscored with uncertainty, the degree depending on the size, scale, and so on, of the venture.

When a location is selected in a well-established retailing center, management is faced with a decision to compete (rentwise) with other firms seeking to enter or enlarge their market position. Consequently, annual rental costs and aggregate costs for the firm period of the lease, plus adaptation costs of the space, must be equated against the realities of competition, potential gross volume of business, and other considerations and factors.

The following is illustrative of the analysis that can be undertaken and represents a segment of the final decision-making process. In the present example, a location has been selected, the rental rate is known, and the proposal to be evaluated is whether to rent or purchase in a commercial condominium arrangement offered by a shopping center. The center has been successful for the last several years. The alternatives are as follows: (1) rent for a 5-year firm lease with a second 5-year firm option, the rent remaining the same for the 10-year period; or (2) buy the facility for $48,300 with a down payment of 25 percent, the balance to be financed with a 25-year loan at 9.5 percent.

The important factors to be considered include the following:

1. Monthly rent: $437.50
2. Rent growth rate: none
3. Purchase price: $48,300
4. Down payment: 25 percent
5. Mortgage interest rate: 9.5 percent
6. Term of mortgage loan: 25 years
7. Resale value increase: none
8. Real estate tax rate: 42¢/$100
9. Equalization rate: 50 percent
10. Buyer's income tax rate: 35 percent
11. Savings interest rate: 6 percent
12. Growth rate of real estate taxes: none
13. Rental area: 2,100 square feet
14. Purchase area: 2,100 square feet
15. Real estate sales commission: 6 percent
16. Special charges: $120 (special charges include condominium

costs for parking area and other public–area maintenance and
reserves for repair–replacement)
17. Special charges growth rate: none

Table 1 represents the proposal–analysis given by the devel-

TABLE 1
Buy–Lease Decision Model

			Monthly Analysis
At End of Year:			
1	*5*	*10*	
32.41	47.32	75.95	Principal payment
284.09	269.18	240.55	Mortgage interest
316.50	316.50	316.50	Mortgage payment
84.52	84.52	84.52	Plus real estate tax
120.00	120.00	120.00	Plus special charges
−129.01	−123.80	−113.78	Less income tax savings at 35%
392.01	397.22	407.24	After-tax cash cost
−32.41	−47.32	−75.95	Less equity accumulation
60.37	60.37	60.37	Plus lost interest on down payment
419.97	410.27	391.66	Effective cost
.00	.00	.00	Less resale value appreciation
419.97	410.27	391.66	Economic cost
437.50	437.50	437.50	Rent
.96	.94	.90	Ratio of cost to rent
199.99	195.37	186.51	Economic cost/1,000 sq. ft.
208.33	208.33	208.33	Rent/1,000 sq. ft.
.96	.94	.90	Ratio of economic cost to rent for equal area

			Cumulative Analysis
Through Year:			
1	*5*	*10*	
1,553.91	7,626.63	14,772.39	Tax savings
372.53	2,270.92	5,915.76	Equity accumulation
.00	.00	.00	Resale appreciation
1,926.44	9,897.55	20,688.15	Total savings
5,050.33	24,986.25	49,079.44	Economic cost
5,250.00	26,250.00	52,500.00	Rent
2,898.00	2,898.00	2,898.00	Real estate commission on sale
2,404.92	11,898.21	23,371.16	Economic cost/1,000 sq. ft.
2,500.00	12,500.00	25,000.00	Rent/1,000 sq. ft.
.96	.95	.93	Ratio of economic cost to rent for equal area

oper–owner to the retail firm. It covers the first, fifth, and tenth years, assuming a firm 5-year lease with an option for an additional 5 years, with no increase in rent. On the monthly and cumulative analysis, the bottom line shows the ratio of economic cost to rent. A ratio of 1 indicates a stand-off, a point of equality if all factors considered perform according to estimates and forecasts. In the subject case, the ratio is .96 (year 1), .94 (year 5), and .90 (year 10). An index of less than 1 indicates a buy situation (an index greater than 1 suggests a rent situation).

On a cumulative basis, at the end of 10 years, the economic cost of owning is calculated at $23,371.16 versus a rental cost of $25,000. The cumulative ratio is higher for the tenth year than that of the monthly analysis because of the selling cost (real estate commission) related to a buy situation.

Suppose the prospective retail tenant firm believes that the assumptions of the analysis are generally plausible except for the monthly special charges, which it believes will increase as the property gets older. Their study, which assumes an additional $30 per month (total of $150) results in the findings in Table 2. As is evident by inspection of Table 2, the analysis suggests a shift from a buy to a rent posture; the ratio now exceeds 1 (economic cost–rent).

Management's further rethinking of the problem suggests an unrealistic assumption at this point; that is, a key input (item 11) assumes value of money via a savings account at 6 percent yield. Since equity capital for them is reasoned to be close to 12 percent, the analysis is further modified at a 12 percent input rate on item 11. The resultant findings, shown in Table 3, clearly suggest, on the assumptions outlined, that management should rent rather than buy, if a firm second 5-year term with no escalation of rent or other provisions is available. This is important since the tenth year (monthly) totals on rent versus buy ($527.76 and $437.50) indicate that an increase of rent of only 1.893 percent (compounded) will equal the break-even point.

The margin is smaller on the cumulative analysis (1.67 percent) to the break-even point because of the sales commission at the end of the contemplated holding period of the investment.

From a very pragmatic viewpoint, one of the most important aspects of location studies is the perceptual ability of the analyst, management, and others. Perception of the competition, the trade area, markets, viability, and long-term outlook for one location vis-à-vis several others, all converge into the synthesis of a finding and viewpoint. This, interfaced with the hard numbers (demographic trends, purchasing power, rental costs, etc.), results in the most plausible decision.

TABLE 2
Buy–Lease Decision Model

			Monthy Analysis
	At End of Year:		
1	*5*	*10*	
32.41	47.32	75.95	Principal payment
284.09	269.18	240.55	Mortgage interest
316.50	316.50	316.50	Mortgage payment
84.52	84.52	84.52	Plus real estate tax
150.00	168.83	195.72	Plus special charges
−129.01	−123.80	−113.78	Less income tax savings at 35%
422.01	446.05	482.96	After-tax cash cost
−32.41	−47.32	−75.95	Less equity accumulation
60.37	60.37	60.37	Plus lost interest on down payment
449.97	459.10	467.38	Effective cost
.00	.00	.00	Less resale value appreciation
449.97	459.11	467.39	Economic cost
437.50	437.50	437.50	Rent
1.03	1.05	1.07	Ratio of cost to rent
214.27	218.62	222.57	Economic cost/1,000 sq. ft.
208.99	208.33	208.33	Rent/1,000 sq. ft.
1.03	1.05	1.07	Ratio of economic cost to rent for equal area

			Cumulative Analysis
	Through Year:		
1	*5*	*10*	
1,553.91	7,626.63	14,772.39	Tax savings
372.53	2,270.92	5,915.76	Equity accumulation
.00	.00	.00	Resale appreciation
1,926.44	9,897.55	20,688.15	Total savings
5,410.33	27,342.69	55,314.43	Economic cost
5,250.00	26,250.00	52,500.00	Rent
2,898.00	2,898.00	2,898.00	Real estate commission on sale
2,576.35	13,020.33	26,340.20	Economic cost/1,000 sq. ft.
2,500.00	12,500.00	25,000.00	Rent/1,000 sq. ft.
1.00	1.04	1,05	Ratio of economic cost to rent for equal area

The essays of John Casparis, Arthur Getis and Judith Getis, Barry Garner, and Brian Berry form an interesting theme. Casparis examines the interrelationship of major retail centers, the central business district, and total retail sales in a spatial context predicated on size of community.

TABLE 3
Buy–Lease Decision Model

	Monthly Analysis		
At End of Year:			
1	5	10	
32.41	47.32	75.95	Principal payment
284.09	269.18	240.55	Mortgage interest
316.50	316.50	316.50	Mortgage payment
84.52	84.52	84.52	Plus real estate tax
150.00	168.83	195.72	Plus special charges
−129.01	−123.80	−113.78	Less income tax savings at 35%
422.01	446.05	482.96	After-tax cash cost
−32.41	−47.32	−75.95	Less equity accumulation
120.75	120.75	120.75	Plus lost interest on down payment
510.35	519.48	527.76	Effective cost
.00	.00	.00	Less resale value appreciation
510.35	519.48	527.76	Economic cost
437.50	437.50	437.50	Rent
1.17	1.19	1.21	Ratio of cost to rent
243.02	247.37	251.32	Economic cost/1,000 sq. ft.
208.33	208.33	208.33	Rent/1,000 sq. ft.
1.17	1.19	1.21	Ratio of economic cost to rent for equal area

	Cumulative Analysis		
Through Year:			
1	5	10	
1,553.91	7,626.63	14,772.39	Tax savings
372.53	2,270.92	5,915.76	Equity accumulation
.00	.00	.00	Resale appreciation
1,926.44	9,897.55	20,688.15	Total savings
6,134.83	30,965.19	62,559.43	Economic cost
5,250.00	26,250.00	52,500.00	Rent
2,898.00	2,898.00	2,898.00	Real estate commission on sale
2,921.35	14,745.33	29,790.20	Economic cost/1,000 sq. ft.
2,500.00	12,500.00	25,000.00	Rent/1,000 sq. ft.
1.17	1.18	1.19	Ratio of economic cost to rent for equal area

The Getis and Garner studies relate to affinity–complementarity of retailing functions. Garner's presentation is quite definitive concerning nucleations for the total market complex of the Chicago area. Berry, in turn, builds on this theme and develops a model for shopping center types, kinds, and locations.

Back in the center-city complex, and particularly related to older or depressed areas, two essays, by George H. Haines, Leonard S. Simon, and Marcus Alexis and William E. Cox, provide the analysis and findings for similar and appropriate location studies.

A simulation model for consumer behavior within a framework of competing retailing establishments is given in the essay by David B. MacKay. The companion study by Peter S. Carusone relates to location in the context of a number of smaller cities in Ohio.

Shopping Center Location and Retail Store Mix in Metropolitan Areas

John Casparis

The shopping trip is second only to the journey to work as a crucial determinant in structuring the pattern of spatial activity of contemporary urbanites. While still dependent on public transport, urbanites were moved *en masse* along axial routes toward a hub of central activity. The dominant position of downtown in our old industrial cities attests to this massing. The growth of urban areas by accretion and the shift to personal transportation by automobile has disrupted the efficiency of the compactly organized, mono-centered city. Such adjustments to the existing structure as limited access highways emptying directly into downtown, parking garages, shopping malls and the like have brought only temporary and partial relief to the congestion and inconvenience of the central business district.

The role of place of work in shaping residence patterns has been discussed by Kain (1962) and Muth (1961) among others. Manufacturers and retailers, as employers, both influence the pattern through their choice of locations. In recent years, enterprising retailers have sought nucleated locations, that is, in a cluster of retail outlets, but not central locations. In this respect they are similar to manufacturers who have sought nucleated but not central locations throughout the standard metropolitan statistical area (SMSA) (Pred, 1964). The shifts in employer location and the residential structure are even more closely intertwined for retailers than for manufacturers, for local residents make up a major share of the "final market" for retailers.

The decline of downtown is a familiar lament and has been documented by this author and others (Casparis, 1967; Sternlieb, 1963). Although shopping has moved closer to its customers, densities high enough for large volume and quick turnover merchandising must still be present. Furthermore, the mix of trade types in shopping centers and retail clusters must reflect the needs and interests of shoppers who had previously patronized downtown. Good case studies of shopping center locations exist; for example, Boston and Detroit have been studied by Cohen and Lewis (1967) and Chicago by Simmons (1964). Whether there are retail location patterns general to all SMSA's has apparently received less study, although an interesting paper along this line has been published by Taeuber (1964). These observations raise the following questions to which this paper is directed:

Reprinted from *Demography*, Vol. 6, No. 2, May 1969, by permission of the author and editor.

where within the SMSA is retailing located, how is the location pattern related to SMSA size, and what is the mix of retail sales in shopping centers?

Data and Method

The dependent variable is retail sales volume in those 116 SMSA's for which the 1963 United States Census of Business published data on sales in central business districts (CBD's) and in major retail centers (MRC's). MRC's are defined by the Census Bureau as

concentrations of retail stores (located inside the standard metropolitan statistical areas in which the CBD cities are located but outside of the CBD's themselves) which include a major general merchandise store —usually a department store. . . . MRC's include not only the planned suburban shopping centers but also the older "string" street and neighborhood developments. . . . (United States Bureau of the Census, 1966, p. V).

A scale map of each SMSA with the political boundary of the central city from which the SMSA takes its name is provided in the reports and on it are indicated the location of the CBD and of every MRC. Using this map, each MRC was assigned to a location either in the central city if it fell inside the political boundary or in the ring if it fell outside.

The sales data were then assigned to either a nucleated or a dispersed location. Nucleated sales include all those transacted in the CBD, the MRC's in the central city and the MRC's in the ring. Dispersed sales include the central city sales (central city minus its CBD and minus its MRC's) and the ring sales (SMSA sales minus its central city and minus its ring MRC's). Based on an average of ten

retail areas, the ratio of sales in one store category to total sales was applied to estimate sales for those cases where the Census had withheld data to avoid disclosure.

Next, the locations of all MRC's were plotted in terms of their straight line distance from the CBD. With the CBD as zero point, as many concentric circles at one mile intervals as were necessary were drawn for each SMSA in such a way that all MRC's could be assigned to a specific concentric mile zone. If an SMSA had more than one CBD or central city, the CBD with the greatest sales volume was treated as the CBD of the SMSA and the lesser CBD(s) was treated as an MRC. MRC's falling outside the scaled maps were pinpointed on a road atlas and the distances to downtown were computed in that way.

Because MRC data are given only by major retail store type, the data for the other areas were combined in the same way. Based on the Standard Industrial Classification Code, the three types are: Convenience Goods Stores which include food stores, eating and drinking places, and drug stores; Shopping Goods Stores which include general merchandise stores, apparel and accessory stores, and furniture stores; and All Other Retail Stores which include lumber and hardware stores, automotive dealers, gas stations, and other retail stores.

The sales data, coded by type, area, and distance zone, were then related to our independent variable: population size of the SMSA as of the 1960 Census.

Findings

At any point in time the morphology of a settlement is closely related to the number of its inhabitants. Through time McKenzie (1925, p. 73) notes that "in the process of community growth there is a development from the simple to the complex, from the general to the specialized; first to increasing centralization and later to a decentralization process." In the 1920's this decentralization process was already being observed in our largest metropolitan communities. With respect to retailing, Burgess (1925, p. 52) found that in Chicago "sub-business centers have grown up in outlying zones." By 1963 the Census counted 972 MRC's spread through 116 SMSA's.

Table 1 shows that as communities grow their retail clusters become more numerous. The mean number of MRC's per SMSA increases from less than two for the smallest SMSA's to almost forty-five for the largest SMSA's. The size of MRC's, as measured by the mean number with a sales volume of at least $50 million and the mean number of stores these contain, also increases with increasing SMSA size. For example, SMSA's with 1.2 to 2.4 million inhabitants average one such mammoth retail cluster with an average of

127 stores per center. Such centers can compete very effectively with the CBD for customers interested in a wide selection, as well as for those buying specialized items. The CBD, however, retains one major competitive asset over the individual MRC: its far larger size allows for a much greater diversification of store types and with it the possibilities for comparison shopping. One measure of this is the mean number of stores per CBD; the CBD's in the smallest SMSA's still have on the average more stores (263) than do the large MRC's of the largest SMSA's (194).

To become large enough to support a major retail development outside the CBD, SMSA's apparently have to grow to between 100,000 and 300,000 inhabitants. An SMSA begins to spin off MRC's at about the point when its CBD has a sales volume of $50 million. In the smallest SMSA's 89 percent of the CBD's have reached this sales volume and each has on the average 1.8 MRC's. The tipping point for the development of very large MRC's seems to begin in the population range

TABLE 1

Sales Volume, in Millions, and Number of Stores in Central Business Districts (CBD's) and Major Retail Centers (MRC's) of 116 Standard Metropolitan Statistical Areas (SMSA's) in 1963, by SMSA Size Class

SMSA Population, 1960 (in thousands)	Number of SMSA's	Percent of SMSA's with CBD Sales of		Mean Number of MRC's per SMSA		Mean Number of Stores per	
		$50 or More	$125 or More	All	Sales $50 or More	MRC with Sales $50 or More	CBD
All SMSA's	116	94.8	33.6	8.38	.64	170	585
100 to 299	37	89.2	2.7	1.84	.03	60	263
300 to 599	33	97.0	12.1	4.24	.03	88	349
600 to 1199	28	96.4	57.1	9.36	.54	138	520
1200 to 2399	11	100.0	100.0	17.18	1.00	127	1056
2400 and over	7	100.0	100.0	44.71	6.57	194	2923

Source: United States Bureau of the Census, 1966, Tables 1, 3, and 8.

of 600,000 to 1.2 million and with a retail volume in the CBD of $125 million or more. Slightly over half of the SMSA's in this size class have MRC's with a sales volume of $50 million and 57 percent of these SMSA's have CBD's doing at least $125 million worth of retailing.

The functional importance of MRC's in the retailing structure of SMSA's is shown in Table 2. Of the 142 billion dollars worth of retailing in these SMSA's the MRC's captured 15 percent and the CBD's 13 percent. As the size of the SMSA increases the importance of retailing in MRC's, or

retail clusters outside the CBD, increases proportionately and at the expense of the CBD. However, the proportion of sales transacted at nucleated locations, in CBD's and MRC's combined, remains constant regardless of SMSA size. Similarly, the proportion of sales at dispersed locations remains constant. For shopping goods it stays around 35 percent and for the other two types around 84 percent.

The ratio of MRC sales to dispersed sales within the city and the ring generally shows that MRC's are relatively more important in the ring than they are in the city. Furthermore, as the size

TABLE 2

Distribution of 1963 Sales in Three Types of Retail Stores Among the Central Business District (CBD), the Major Retail Centers (MRC's), the Central City, and the Ring, by Standard Metropolitan Statistical Area (SMSA) Size Class

SMSA Population, 1960 (thousands) and Retail Type	SMSA Sales (billions)	Percent of SMSA Sales			Ratio of MRC Sales to Dispersed Sales		
		CBD	MRC's	Dispersed	SMSA	City	Ring
Shopping Goods							
All	37.1	30.1	34.6	35.3	.978	.801	1.161
100 to 299	2.7	48.1	19.0	32.9	.580	.719	.290
300 to 599	4.8	39.0	25.1	35.9	.698	.685	.713
600 to 1199	8.4	29.2	35.3	35.5	.997	1.011	.983
1200 to 2399	7.1	28.9	36.3	34.8	1.047	.711	1.346
2400 and over	14.1	24.7	39.4	35.9	1.100	.784	1.423
Convenience Goods							
All	51.8	6.1	10.5	83.4	.125	.103	.148
100 to 299	3.6	8.4	7.6	84.0	.090	.101	.066
300 to 599	6.7	5.7	9.1	85.2	.107	.111	.102
600 to 1199	11.7	5.0	11.6	83.4	.139	.135	.143
1200 to 2399	9.9	5.9	11.7	82.4	.143	.108	.172
2400 and over	19.9	6.5	10.1	83.4	.121	.082	.166
All Other Retail							
All	53.3	8.2	6.8	85.0	.080	.069	.091
100 to 299	4.6	20.9	3.5	75.6	.046	.055	.030
300 to 599	7.7	10.0	5.4	84.6	.064	.058	.072
600 to 1199	13.1	8.5	7.6	83.9	.090	.086	.093
1200 to 2399	9.8	7.0	8.2	84.8	.097	.079	.111
2400 and over	18.1	4.7	6.9	88.4	.078	.060	.093

Source: United States Bureau of the Census, 1966, Tables 1, 2, 3, and 5, and SMSA maps.

of the SMSA increases the functional importance of MRC's in the ring also increases. The ratios in the city either seem not to be related to SMSA size or show little variation by SMSA size. This suggests that the retail structure of the city has reached a certain stability. The density of settlement, the slow rate of population growth and the inflexibility of existing buildings and transportation patterns in the central city may partly account for this stability. In contrast, the availability of open land and the stimulus of a rapidly growing population have contributed to the growth of major retail centers in the ring, and with this a new type of retail structure.

The distribution of sales by type of store reflects the operation of the traditional "laws" of economic location (Hoover, 1963, p. 130). Shopping goods are found in the CBD at points maximally accessible to public transport and foot traffic from places of work, and in city and ring MRC's at transportation breaks suitable for the large scale parking of automobiles. Convenience goods and all other retail stores disperse primarily throughout the SMSA. Secondarily, they attach themselves to shopping goods locations and feed off the retail traffic collected there, both downtown and in MRC's. The sorting of retail functions into either a dispersed or a nucleated location is not affected by the size of the SMSA; the proportions remain constant. However, SMSA size does operate to determine what proportion of sales are to be transacted at the three different nucleated locations (CBD, city MRC, and ring MRC) and at the two dispersed locations in the city and in the ring.

Since the ratio of nucleated to dispersed sales is similar for all SMSA's, we investigated whether the mix of trade types in MRC's is similar to the CBD mix. That is, if similar forces of economic location operate in the MRC as operate in the CBD and the SMSA generally, then the MRC ought to be a miniature version of the CBD's retail structure. Setting the CBD as the norm, the mix of trade types as one moves from the CBD to central and then to peripheral MRC's is shown in Table 3. Shopping Goods Stores are the domi-

TABLE 3

Percentage Distribution of 1963 Sales by Type of Retail Store for the Central Business District (CBD) and Major Retail Centers (MRC's), by Standard Metropolitan Statistical Area (SMSA) Size Class

SMSA Population, 1960 (thousands) and Location of Shopping Center	Retail Type		
	Shop- ping	Conve- nience	All Other
100 to 299			
CBD	51.3	11.7	37.0
MRC's by distance (miles) from CBD			
0– 2	53.4	30.7	15.9
2– 4	54.8	29.0	16.2
4– 6	58.6	26.6	14.8
6– 8	57.3	18.3	24.4
8–10	...	...	...
10–12	33.3	46.7	20.0
12–14	33.3	44.4	22.3
14–16	...	...	...
16–20	...	...	...
20 or more	44.4	33.3	22.3
All MRC's	54.9	28.3	16.8
300 to 599			
CBD	61.8	12.6	25.6
MRC's by distance (miles) from CBD			
0– 2	49.8	28.9	21.3
2– 4	55.6	28.6	15.8
4– 6	59.0	25.6	15.4
6– 8	52.4	28.6	19.0
8–10	38.1	33.3	28.6
10–12	57.3	29.9	12.8
12–14	54.0	14.3	31.7
14–16	45.2	32.2	22.6
16–20	40.6	15.9	43.5
20 or more	40.0	21.4	38.6
All MRC's	53.9	27.2	18.9

TABLE 3—Continued

SMSA Population, 1960 (thousands) and Location of Shopping Center	Retail Type		
	Shopping	Convenience	All Other
600 to 1199			
CBD	59.2	14.0	26.8
MRC's by distance (miles) from CBD			
0– 2	60.7	20.3	19.0
2– 4	54.6	26.5	18.9
4– 6	59.9	25.9	14.2
6– 8	53.8	26.3	19.9
8–10	51.4	32.3	16.3
10–12	60.9	18.6	20.5
12–14	55.9	27.3	16.8
14–16	54.0	18.0	28.0
16–20	62.5	30.4	7.1
20 or more	45.3	22.5	32.2
All MRC's	56.0	25.5	18.5
1200 to 2399			
CBD	61.6	17.6	20.8
MRC's by distance (miles) from CBD			
0– 2	59.2	18.3	22.5
2– 4	61.0	24.6	14.4
4– 6	53.5	26.9	19.6
6– 8	53.4	27.0	19.6
8–10	65.5	24.2	10.3
10–12	46.9	31.0	22.1
12–14	65.9	21.1	13.0
14–16	56.3	26.3	17.4
16–20	65.3	22.6	12.1
20 or more	54.1	26.0	19.9
All MRC's	56.5	25.7	17.8
2400 and over			
CBD	61.7	23.0	15.3
MRC's by distance (miles) from CBD			
0– 2	68.1	24.6	7.3
2– 4	51.3	26.8	21.9
4– 6	52.2	28.5	19.3
6– 8	62.1	23.9	14.0
8–10	69.4	20.5	10.1
10–12	67.5	20.5	12.0
12–14	61.0	24.8	14.2
14–16	63.4	24.9	11.7
16–20	62.6	21.9	15.5
20 or more	64.8	20.3	14.9
All MRC's	63.0	22.8	14.2

. . . No center at location.
Source: See Table 2.

nant retailing function in both CBD's and MRC's; between fifty and sixty percent of total sales are of this type. The difference in retail composition is that in MRC's the Convenience Goods Stores tend to be more important while in CBD's the All Other Retail Stores category tends to be more important. The specialty store, often innovating and taking high risks, still seeks a downtown location where it will be accessible to a metropolitan-wide clientele. Also included in the All Other category are jewelry stores, stationery stores and florists. In the MRC these may more often be included as adjuncts of the convenience goods store, for example books and stationery in a large drug store and flowers in a supermarket, or of the shopping goods store, for example jewelry in a department store. Furthermore, automotive dealers and gas stations are still found in the CBD but they are not generally included in many planned shopping centers. The higher shares of Convenience Goods Stores sales in MRC's is mainly due to the importance of the food supermarket in these retail clusters. Whereas the core of downtown retailing is a number of department stores and women's clothing stores, both shopping goods, in the MRC it is a department store with a food supermarket. Other types of stores will often not risk moving in unless these two types are already there to draw sufficient customers. In the largest SMSA's these differences do not apply. Here the composition of retail trade types in the CBD is reproduced almost identically in the MRC's at every distance zone.

Summary and Conclusion

This paper has described the pattern of retailing of SMSA's and shown how the size of the community influences the location of different types of stores. The decentralization of retailing is directly related to the increasing size of SMSA's. Major Retail Centers spread throughout the SMSA and gain sales in direct proportion to the losses sustained by the CBD. In the city and the ring miniature CBD's, with some modifications, are created which serve both the shopping and convenience goods needs of the SMSA resident. While the retail structure of a community adapts itself to population growth and with this to the changing demands of its customers, the forces which impel stores to seek a nucleated or a dispersed location have remained constant.

In relation to other research, our findings support the observation that as communities grow multiple nuclei of similar functions tend to develop (Harris and Ullman, 1945; Ullman, 1966). However, retailing is a function not only of population size but also of population composition (Hawley, 1941). Residential neighborhoods are stratified according to the socio-economic status of their inhabitants. This sorting may help to explain variations on the general retailing patterns reported in this paper.

REFERENCES

Burgess, Ernest W. 1925. The growth of the city: an introduction to a research project. In Robert E. Park and others, The City. Chicago: University of Chicago Press.

Casparis, John. 1967. Metropolitan retail structure and its relation to population. Land Economics 43: 212–218.

Cohen, Saul B., and George K. Lewis. 1967. Form and function in the geography of retailing. Economic Geography 43: 1–42.

Harris, Chauncy D., and Edward L. Ullman. 1945. The nature of cities. Annals of the American Academy of Political and Social Science 242: 7–17.

Hawley, Amos H. 1941. An ecological study of urban service institutions. American Sociological Review 6: 629–639.

Hoover, Edgar M. 1963. The Location of Economic Activity. New York: McGraw-Hill.

Kain, John F. 1962. The journey to work as a determinant of residential location. Papers and Proceedings of the Regional Science Association 9: 137–160.

McKenzie, Roderick D. 1925. The ecological approach to the study of the human community. In Robert E. Park and others, The City. Chicago: University of Chicago Press.

Muth, Richard F. 1961. The spatial structure of the housing market. Papers and Proceedings of the Regional Science Association 7: 207–220.

Pred, Allen R. 1964. The intrametropolitan location of American manufacturing. Annals of the Association of American Geographers 54: 165–180.

Simmons, James. 1964. The Changing Pattern of Retail Location. University of Chicago Research Paper Number 92, Department of Geography.

Sternlieb, George. 1963. The future of retailing in the downtown core. Journal of the American Institute of Planners 29: 102–112.

Taeuber, Alma F. 1964. Population redistribution and retail changes in the cen-

tral business district. In Ernest W. Burgess and Donald J. Bogue (eds.),
Contributions to Urban Sociology. Chicago: University of Chicago Press.

Ullman, Edward L. 1966. The nature of cities reconsidered. Papers and Proceedings of the Regional Science Association 9: 7–23.

United States Bureau of the Census. 1966. Census of Business, 1963. Vol. 3, Major Retail Center Statistics, Parts I and II, Summary and Akron, Ohio, Youngstown–Warren, Ohio. Washington: Government Printing Office.

Retail Store Spatial Affinities

Arthur Getis and Judith M. Getis

Both geographers and economists have been concerned with the location of economic activities within cities. R. M. Haig, an economist, presented a theory of urban organization in 1927 [1] and the body of theory which has developed is variously termed "urban land use theory" or the "theory of land use and land value." Basically, this theory holds that the utilization of land is determined by the relative efficiencies of various uses in various locations. Efficiency in the utilization of land is measured by the rent-paying ability of firms. The use that can pay the highest rent for a given site will be the successful bidder in a competitive market, and this will result in "an orderly pattern of land use spatially organized to perform most efficiently the economic functions that characterize urban life" [2]. The rent-paying ability of a firm depends on such factors as the firm's space needs, the scale of operation, the degree of mark-up on products, and so on.

In urban land use theory, then, retail firms are distributed about the city as a result of the differential rents which they are capable of paying. Central place theory [3] and the theory of tertiary activity [4] help to identify the hierarchical pattern of shopping centers which develops in urban areas. Christaller substituted transport costs for rent as the mechanism responsible for the subsequent pattern of economic activities, and with the addition of the concept of the range of a good he was able to demonstrate that, under isotropic assumptions, a hierarchical arrangement of centers would develop. In his theory of tertiary activity, Berry has shown how the ideas of Christaller, which deal with relationships between towns, may be applied to intraurban studies. He too identifies a hierarchical arrangement of shopping centers.

Urban land use theory, central place theory, and the theory of tertiary activity are able to tell us a good deal about both the forces operating to shape commercial zones of cities and about the broad spatial patterns which are the result of the interacting economic forces. Nevertheless, the theories are unable to explain or account for the particular location of the individual firm; the precise location of retail stores is indeterminate from the theories just presented. It is suggested in this paper that if groups of stores can be shown to exist in similar forms in urban centers, then retail store spatial affinities

Reprinted from *Urban Studies,* Vol. 5, No. 3, November 1968, by permission of the authors and editor.

must be identified as a factor influencing store location within a specific level of the retail store hierarchy.

There is widespread recognition of the fact that certain types of stores seem to have affinities for other types of stores, and that, as a result of these affinities, such stores are often seen in combination with one another [5]. Garner notes that

Presumably each type [of business] seeks a different set of relationships with other businesses depending upon the "bundle of goods" offered and the buying habits associated with them. In this way, some retail businesses are complementary to each other, whilst others are non-complementary [6].

Yet there has been no attempt to study the arrangement of functions in business centers, to determine whether store affinities operate systematically to form discrete groups of business types [7].

In the study to be described here a new technique of analysis was employed in a search for spatial associations of retail stores within business centers. Because of the newness of the technique, called sequence analysis, and because of the difficulty in handling the data in an optimum way, we must submit the results in a most perfunctory, less-than-satisfying way. That is, the work reported on here is the result of an experiment and it cannot be considered as final at this early date. Our hope is that this report will stimulate others to further explore the subject.

Method

An initial problem was to devise a method by which significant associations among stores could be identified. In effect, what was needed was a test which would isolate those spatially associated store types which occur together more often than chance would dictate. A full explanation of the test is given in an article in the *Transactions* of the Institute of British Geographers [8], and only a brief summary follows.

First the expected mean number of associations of business type B with those of type A is obtained. The expectation is based on a random distribution containing the same number of B and A elements as well as the same number of total elements (N). This is given by the formula

$$\frac{2AB}{N}$$

The variance of the distribution is

$$\frac{2AB[2AB + N(C - 1)]}{N^2(N - 1)}$$

where C is equal to the total number of stores less the number of A's and B's ($C = N - A - B$). Then the expected number of associations must be compared with the observed number. Finally, in most instances it is necessary to employ normal distribution curves for tests of significance. When the expected number of links is large, the normal curve is an appropriate sampling distribution to use. Of course, in that case the following formula would be applied:

$$Z = \frac{\text{Obs} - \text{Exp}}{\sqrt{\sigma^2}}$$

where Z is the standard variate of the normal curve, Obs and Exp are the observed and expected number of links, and $\sqrt{\sigma^2}$ is the square root of the variance. When the expected number of links is small, the Poisson distribution is used for tests.

The Data

In order to determine whether there are spatial associations between retail stores it was of course necessary to record the location of stores relative to other stores. To accomplish this, it was necessary to decide which areas to map. It was decided that if spatial regularities do exist in any level of the retail hierarchy, they will be most apparent in the highest level of the hierarchy, i.e. in the central business district (C.B.D.). It is in the C.B.D. that the greatest number of stores and the greatest range in store types exist. It is in this area that land values are highest and that competition for sites is keenest. Finally, in the C.B.D. several stores of the same type can be found within a relatively small and concentrated shopping area. These facts are significant, for they indicate that stores which commonly seem to cluster can do so most easily and most apparently in the C.B.D.

Data were gathered on the types and locations of retail stores in the C.B.D.'s of thirteen cities [9]. Using a modified standard industrial classification code, business types were plotted on maps of the C.B.D.'s. Two points should be noted about the maps: (1) Only the use(s) occupying the ground floor of a building was considered, and (2) length of store frontage was ignored. Length of frontage was not considered because our concern was with retail establishments and their neighbors, and in the type of analysis employed it is necessary to know only what type of use is on either side of the one in question. There is, however, no doubt that a more refined study would take into account the distance between store entrances.

Heterogeneity: The Example of Philadelphia

Before any analysis of the data was carried out, it was necessary to answer an important question. This was, how many retail establishments in the C.B.D. were we going to consider as constituting our sample in any one city. It is apparent that the size of the sample will affect results when sequence analysis is employed. To take an obvious example, if the whole city were the sample area, we should get clusters labeled residential, industrial, commercial, and so on. The more heterogeneous the data, the more apparent will be clusters of land use types. If only a small portion of a business district constitutes the sample, then, barring any concentration of a specific business type, the results should indicate very few associations which occur more often than chance would have it. However, as the data set is enlarged to contain many shops from the center of the business district all the way to the fringe of the area, the structure of the business district should be more clearly defined. This results from the gradual change in the type of retail establishment found as one leaves the central portion of the business district. One would expect that with a large amount of data a spatial structure containing many significant associations between stores would become evident. The greater the number of significant associations, the easier it is to identify a heterogeneous data set.

However, the number of these associations is really a function not only of the size of the sample but also of the level of taxonomic generalization. At a high level of generalization, for example a classification having two groups— store and not a store, stores may not be shown to be significantly spatially associated unless many non-store elements are contained within the sample. So it would seem that the size of the sample would affect the outcomes in the same way no matter what the level of generalization, but the degree of the effect would probably vary with the fineness of the classification.

To demonstrate these ideas, the data from Philadelphia, the largest city for which data were gathered, were analyzed [10]. First, a small sample containing sixty stores (thirty on either side of Broad Street along the south side of Chestnut Street) was studied. Then 367 stores on both sides of Chestnut Street (from 17th to 5th Street) were analyzed. Figure 1 shows the pattern of retail store spatial affinities found for the two sets of data, and also for two different levels of taxonomic generalization. A line between two business types represents a significant association between them. Regardless of the level of classificatory generalization, it is apparent that there are far more associations for the group of 367 stores than there are for the sample of 60 businesses. Many new store types appear in the larger data set, and these tend to group together on the fringes of the C.B.D. Since the associations shown are those that are statistically significant, it indicates that they occur together more often than chance would have it.

Homogeneity

Because of this effect of sample length on the results of sequence analysis, and because there was a desire to reduce the effect that heterogeneous data would have on meaningful comparisons among the thirteen cities, it was decided to consider only the thirty stores on either side of the highest land value

location in the C.B.D.: the so-called 100 percent spot. Thirty was not an arbitrary number. It resulted from the fact that in the smallest city in the sample, Midland, one could go only this far before reaching the business types on the fringe of the C.B.D.—the store types which when included in the data set were responsible for the obvious results which are characteristic of heterogeneous data. Because this is a pilot study, done as much to test the validity of the technique as to yield results, only one side of the main shopping street was considered for each city [11].

In fact, a rather unexpectedly high degree of homogeneity did result when this selection of sixty stores in each city was made. Table 1 lists the number of stores of each type for each of the cities. A glance at the table shows that the data are remarkably similar from city to city. In other words, in the sample of thirteen cities, regardless of city size and the extent of the C.B.D., taking thirty stores on either side of the 100 percent location gives an apparently characteristic mix of retail store types. The coefficient of variation for all store types having a mean above three was always less than 60 percent. This is a rather low number considering the unrealistically high values one often obtains when means are so low.

Some Characteristic Associations

One of the problems involved in identifying and measuring retail store spatial affinities revolves around the fact that there are not equal numbers of stores of each type in a business center. Stores of certain types are more plentiful than those of others. Table 1 reveals the large number of clothing stores. In fact, they account for ap-

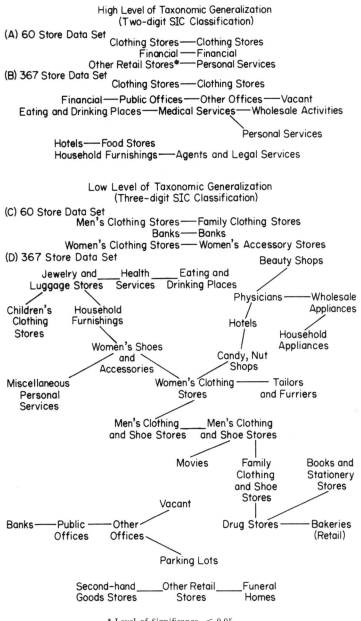

High Level of Taxonomic Generalization
(Two-digit SIC Classification)

(A) 60 Store Data Set

Clothing Stores ——— Clothing Stores
Financial ——— Financial
Other Retail Stores* ——— Personal Services

(B) 367 Store Data Set

Clothing Stores ——— Clothing Stores
Financial — Public Offices — Other Offices — Vacant
Eating and Drinking Places — Medical Services — Wholesale Activities
Personal Services
Hotels —— Food Stores
Household Furnishings —— Agents and Legal Services

Low Level of Taxonomic Generalization
(Three-digit SIC Classification)

(C) 60 Store Data Set

Men's Clothing Stores —— Family Clothing Stores
Banks —— Banks
Women's Clothing Stores —— Women's Accessory Stores

(D) 367 Store Data Set

Beauty Shops

Jewelry and ____ Health ____ Eating and
Luggage Stores   Services   Drinking Places

Physicians ——— Wholesale
Appliances

Children's   Household
Clothing   Furnishings   Hotels
Stores   Household
Women's Shoes   Appliances
and   Candy, Nut
Accessories   Shops

Miscellaneous   Women's Clothing ——— Tailors
Personal   Stores   and Furriers
Services

Men's Clothing ____ Men's Clothing
and Shoe Stores   and Shoe Stores

Movies   Family   Books and
Clothing   Stationery
and Shoe   Stores
Vacant   Stores

Banks —— Public — Other
Offices   Offices   Drug Stores ——— Bakeries
(Retail)

Parking Lots

Second-hand ____ Other Retail ____ Funeral
Goods Stores   Stores   Homes

* Level of Significance ≦ 0.05.

FIGURE 1

Significant Spatial Associations: Philadelphia Central Business District

TABLE 1

Number of Stores by Type for 60–Store Data Set for Sample Cities [1]

Store Type	Midland	Perth Amboy	New Brunswick	Muskegon	Bay City [2]	Saginaw [2]	Trenton	Elizabeth	Lansing	Paterson	Flint	Grand Rapids	Philadelphia
Department stores	1	1	1	5	2	1	2	3	1	2	2	3	1
Variety stores	2	3	5	3	1	2	3	7	4	5	2	4	1
Candy stores	0	1	3	1	1	1	3	2	1	3	0	1	3
Other food stores [3]	1	1	1	0	0	2	0	1	1	0	0	2	1
Men's clothing [4]	5	9	7	2	1	7	2	11	6	6	9	8	9
Women's clothing [4]	8	9	9	6	9	10	4	5	4	8	13	6	5
Women's accessories	1	2	5	4	5	5	7	10	7	11	6	10	9
Family clothing [4]	5	4	3	10	5	6	8	2	5	2	8	1	2
Other clothing [5]	1	2	0	1	1	1	2	2	1	2	0	1	0
Sewing centers	1	1	1	1	0	0	1	0	0	1	1	0	0
Household furnishings [6]	3	1	2	0	2	0	0	1	0	4	0	1	2
Eating and drinking places	3	3	3	5	1	1	7	5	1	2	1	2	4
Drugstores	3	2	3	2	2	1	1	1	7	3	2	2	2
Jewelry and luggage stores	1	3	4	6	6	5	4	4	9	6	8	5	2
Other retail stores [7]	6	8	6	5	6	1	4	2	5	3	2	4	4
Banks [8]	2	0	4	4	4	1	2	4	2	0	2	5	7
Services [9]	4	2	2	2	4	3	3	0	1	1	1	2	4
Vacant stores	5	5	1	1	2	6	5	0	2	1	1	3	0
Other establishments [10]	8	3	0	2	6	4	2	0	3	0	2	0	4

[1] This table has been generalized from the more detailed three-digit SIC code which was used.

[2] Public land ended store sequence before 60 stores were reached.

[3] Includes supermarkets and grocery stores of all kinds.

[4] Includes shoe stores.

[5] Includes fur shops and apparel not classified elsewhere.

[6] Includes furniture, floor covering, appliance and other home furnishing stores.

[7] Includes book stores, florists, music stores, camera stores, gift and novelty shops, optical goods, and miscellaneous retail stores not elsewhere classified.

[8] Includes savings and loan associations as well as banks.

[9] Includes hotels, personal services, parking lots, repair services, theaters, and other service establishments.

[10] These include, among other things, wholesale activities, churches and cemeteries, and other non-retail land uses.

proximately 44 percent of all stores in the sample. A fairly simple method of isolating patterns is to record the next-door neighbors of one of these commonly found businesses, on the theory that the resulting percentages do in fact describe the patterns of store arrangement [12].

Table 2 is an example of this method of procedure. Putting the data from all thirteen cities together, all the next-door neighbors on either side of each women's clothing store were recorded by type. For instance, looking at the table, we note that a women's accessory store was next to a women's clothing store 25 times (there were 96 women's clothing stores in the sample). This means that 14.7 percent of the time a women's clothing store had a women's

TABLE 2

Percentage Distribution of Next-Door Neighbors of Women's Clothing Stores in 13 Sample Cities

Store Type	Number of Times a Next-Door Neighbor (1)	Per Cent (2)	Per Cent of Store Types in 13 Cities Taken Together (3)
Women's accessories	25	14.7	10.5
Other retail stores	20	11.7	7.2
Men's clothing	17	10.0	10.5
Women's clothing	17	10.0	12.3
Jewelry and luggage stores	16	9.5	8.2
Variety stores	15	8.8	5.5
Department stores	9	5.3	3.2
Candy stores	8	4.7	2.6
Family clothing	8	4.7	7.9
Other establishments	7	4.1	4.4
Drugstores	6	3.5	4.0
Vacant stores	6	3.5	4.2
Sewing centers	5	2.9	0.9
Household furnishings	4	2.4	2.3
Banks	4	2.4	4.8
Other food stores	2	1.2	1.3
Services	1	0.6	3.5
Other clothing stores	0	0.0	1.8
Eating and drinking places	0	0.0	4.9
Total	170	100.0%	100.0%

accessory store immediately adjacent to it. If the sample of cities were very large, one could, using this method, issue predictive statements about the likelihood in other cities that store types A and B are associated.

The shortcoming of the method is that it contains no mention of statistical significance. Thus, there is always the possibility that given the large numbers of women's clothing and women's accessory stores found in a C.B.D., we should by chance expect to find them associated 15 percent of the time. Without knowledge of whether the association is in fact statistically significant, it is difficult to show that the two store types do have affinities for one another. It could have happened by chance.

Column 3 of Table 2 gives the percent that the stores of each type constituted of the total sample of stores. Thus, we see that women's accessory stores made up 10.5 percent of all 775 stores in the sample. This indicates that the two types of stores are next door to one another somewhat more often than expected, but it is difficult to say whether or not this is due to chance. It will be noted that in most other cases the discrepancy was not so great. For example, men's clothing stores constituted 10.5 percent of all stores in the sample, and were next door to women's clothing stores 10.0 percent of the time. When the two percentage columns are treated in rank order, a Spearman's test reveals a +0.72 correlation. One might conclude that the patterns of association are similar to what might be expected based on the number of stores in the sample. However, the fact that percentage differences and rank differences show that women's accessory stores, department stores, candy shops, and sewing centers are associated with women's clothing stores more often than might be expected indicates the need for a finer tool of analysis.

Some Significant Associations

The method of sequence analysis outlined was used to analyze the data for each of the thirteen cities. It made it possible to determine in an objective way which business types appeared together more often than chance would have it. The results are presented in Table 3. Only those associations which were (a) significant at less than the 0.01 level and which (b) occurred three or more times have been listed. More associations do occur when the significance level is lowered and when links which occurred one or two times are included, but it is felt that little confidence can be placed in these associations. It should be noted that in five cities no associations met this fairly strict definition of significance. It is

interesting to note that the four cities in which women's clothing stores were significantly associated with other shops were all in Michigan. It is difficult to know what, if any, meaning should be attached to this in view of the relatively small sample of cities studied.

What is interesting about Table 3 is the very small number of significant associations which do appear. This suggests the value of this kind of approach, where a measure of statistical significance is employed, as opposed to the approach where associations were considered by percentage of occurrence. In contrast to some rather elaborate tables of how store types attract and repel other types of stores, then, our conclusion is that in general little can be said about order in the core of the C.B.D. except that there will be a certain typical mix of business types (see Table 1). Some cities may exhibit one or two business types which are associated more often than chance would have it, other cities may reveal no significant linkage at all, but in no city in the sample studies was there a whole host of significant associations.

It can be further postulated that when significant links do occur they are connected with clothing stores.

TABLE 3
Significant Associations for Next-Door Neighbors

Association	City
Women's clothing–Women's clothing	Saginaw
Women's clothing–Department stores	Grand Rapids
Women's clothing–Jewelry stores	Bay City
Women's clothing–Variety stores	Muskegon
Women's accessory stores–Other retail stores *	Trenton
Men's clothing–Jewelry stores	Paterson
Men's clothing–Family clothing stores	Philadelphia
Banks–Banks	Philadelphia
Banks–Variety stores	New Brunswick

* See Table 1, note 7.

Clothing stores seem to attract each other, and other business types are attracted to them. Banks appeared linked to each other only in Philadelphia, where the shopping core cuts across a recognized financial district. There appears to be little in the way of systematic associations, then, and possibly the only meaningful generalization is that when a significant association of business types does occur in a city, it is likely to have a clothing store as one of the partners.

Do these conclusions hold as the level of spatial generalization increases? So far we have considered each store's nearest neighbors—the two stores on either side of it. However, assuming that certain types of stores attract other types of stores, it is logical also to assume that this attraction doesn't dictate that the two types must be immediately adjacent. It may simply be that for one store to be in the general neighborhood of the other is enough. In addition, it is probable that for many store types there are several attractive choices as neighbors. Finally, the process of bidding for land is neither a perfect nor a static one, so that even if the owner of a given store desired to locate immediately next door to another specific one he might not be able to do so. These factors made it desirable to consider more than just first nearest neighbors. Table 4 gives the results of the sequence analysis applied to first, second, and third nearest neighbors of each business.

Once again only those associations which were significant at less than the 0.01 level and which occurred three or more times have been listed. In two of the cities no associations were found. There were a total of thirty associations in all, and once again we note the prominence of clothing stores. Twenty-one out of the thirty links had a clothing store as one of the partners, usually a women's clothing or women's accessory store. In fact, in eight cities out of the eleven that showed some sort of significant associations, women's clothing stores were significantly linked to another business type and sometimes to two types.

Of the nine linkages that did not include a clothing store as one of the partners, seven revolved around either banks or eating and drinking establishments.

At this increased level of spatial generalization, then, more definite patterns become evident but we are still far from accepting the hypothesis that store affinities are numerous and give a great deal of order to the core of the C.B.D. We can identify two separate groups of associations: those in which a clothing store figures as one of the partners in a linkage, and those in which banks and eating and drinking establishments are a partner. It is worth noting that these are separate groups. Clothing stores are not linked to banks or eating and drinking functions.

Significant Associations for the Total Data Set

By treating the cities individually, as we have done to this point, there was the possibility that we were failing to note an underlying unity of the total scheme. It was possible that certain linkage characteristics not statistically significant in any one city might, by a process of accretion, become discernible only when all cities were examined together and treated as one . . . i.e., when patterns from each of the cities were added together, the build-up might be enough that the pattern would in the end become a significant one.

Therefore, tests were performed on

TABLE 4
Significant Associations for First, Second and Third Nearest Neighbors Taken Together

City	Association
Midland	Family clothes–Barber shops
Perth Amboy	Women's clothes–Women's accessories
	Women's clothes–Sewing centers
New Brunswick	None
Muskegon	Women's clothes–Variety stores
	Women's accessories–Public offices
	Children's clothes–Eating and drinking places
	Eating and drinking places–Eating and drinking places
	Eating and drinking places–Candy shops
Bay City	Women's accessories–Women's accessories
	Family clothes–Family clothes
Saginaw	Women's clothes–Women's accessories
	Women's clothes–Variety stores
	Family clothes–Meat and fish markets
	Miscellaneous apparel–Vacant
Trenton	Women's clothes–Women's clothes
	Women's accessories–Other retail stores
Elizabeth	None
Lansing	Women's clothes–Women's accessories
	Women's accessories–Variety stores
Paterson	Sewing centers–Jewelry stores
	Eating and drinking places–Other retail stores
Flint	Women's clothes–Dry goods stores
	Women's clothes–Sewing centers
	Men's clothes–Men's clothes
	Men's clothes–Travel agencies
Grand Rapids	Variety stores–Variety stores
	Banks–Vacant
	Vacant–Vacant
Philadelphia	Women's clothes–Candy shops
	Banks–Retail bakeries
	Banks–Eating and drinking places

the hypothesis of association for the sum of all links for a more generalized category of stores for all thirteen cities. Since the mix of stores was so similar from city to city, it was felt that this provided justification for adding together all the data and, in effect, treating it as one city. A more generalized classification of business types was used to simplify the calculations involved. The only modification involved in the testing procedure was to subtract from each observed frequency 0.5, thus strengthening the test. This correction was deemed important, especially for the smaller numbers, since the integer which can be thought of as standing for a range of values 0.5 less and 0.5 more than itself can imply a range in the observed distribution covering a high percentage of the observed value itself. This is similar to the well-known Yates correction for tests of significance in contingency problems.

Table 5 shows part of the outcome of the tests. The observed numbers of store associations are listed in rank order from 25 to 10. Below 10 only those associations displaying significance at ≤0.05 are listed. Once again

TABLE 5
Observed and Expected Frequencies of Store Associations Using Three-Digit Code

Store Association	Observed	Expected
Women's clothing–Women's accessories	25	20.4
Men's clothing–Jewelry	19	13.4
Men's clothing–Women's clothing	17	20.4
Men's clothing–Family clothing	17	12.9
Women's clothing–Women's clothing	17	11.8
Variety stores–Women's clothing	16	10.4 *
Women's clothing–Jewelry	16	15.6
Women's accessories–Women's accessories	16	8.6 †
Men's clothing–Women's accessories	15	17.4
Women's clothing–Other retail stores	15	10.2
Variety stores–Women's accessories	14	8.9 *
Women's accessories–Jewelry	12	8.7
Women's accessories–Other retail stores	12	12.9
Men's clothing–Men's clothing	11	13.4
Family clothing–Jewelry	11	9.5
Family clothing–Family clothing	10	4.7 *

[Below are listed just those store associations having a
  significance level ≤0.05]

Other establishments–Other establishments	9	1.5 †
Variety stores–Drugstores	8	3.4 †
Variety stores–Banks	8	4.0 *
Vacant–Vacant	7	1.3 †
Eating and drinking places–Vacant	7	3.1 *
Candy stores–Eating and drinking places	5	2.0 *
Women's clothing–Sewing centers	5	1.7 *
Other retail stores–Other establishments	5	1.3 †
Sewing centers–Jewelry	4	1.1 *
Household furnishings–Other establishments	4	1.4 *
Other clothing–Household furnishings	3	0.6 †
Other food stores–Vacant	3	0.8 *

* Represents significance level less than or equal to 0.05 but greater than 0.01.
† Represents significance level less than or equal to 0.01.

we see how very few significant associations there are. Out of a total of some 220 associations which might have been significant, there are only 20 present, and of these only 6 are significant at the ≤0.01 level. In particular, the few significant linkages in the categories with the most number of associations clearly reveal the fallacy in concluding that often observed associations are the result of an affinity of business types for one another. Note, for instance, the high number of associations between women's clothing stores and women's accessory shops, yet this was not a statistically significant link.

What of our hypothesis, that by a process of accretion linkages not significant in any one city might become significant for the total data set? There seems to be justification for accepting it. This becomes more evident if we study Figure 2, which shows the linkages represented in Table 5. Four groups can

be identified. Group A contains those business types we usually associate with the chief shopping aspects of the C.B.D.: the women's clothing and accessory shops, the banks and variety stores. It should be pointed out that in this group only one linkage which was not present when the cities were treated individually (see Tables 3, 4) appears, and this is the drugstore–variety store association. This did not occur often enough to be significant in any single city, but was significant for the total set of observations.

Family clothing stores, represented in Group B, have affinities for one another, but tend to separate themselves from other types of clothing stores. This association is more evidence of a subtle pattern coming to light when the data are grouped. It had not appeared in any one of the cities when first nearest neighbors only were considered (Table 3), although it had

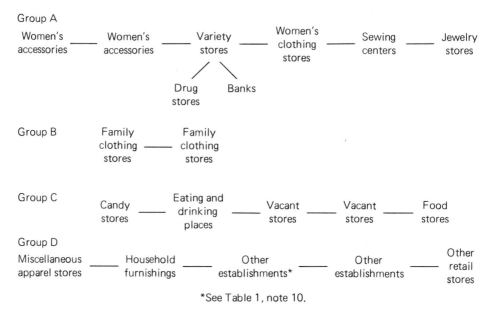

FIGURE 2

Significant Spatial Associations for All Cities Taken Together occurred in one city when first, second, and third nearest neighbors were considered (Table 4).

Groups C and D are made up largely of business types which give the data what heterogeneity they do possess—the business types found on the fringes rather than in the very heart of the C.B.D. Neither of the associations of eating and drinking establishments and of food stores with vacant lots had appeared prior to this analysis, no doubt because of the relative paucity of such establishments in any one city. The same may be said of the business types appearing in Group D, in which, incidentally, all the linkages are new, not being represented in either Table 3 or 4.

As a final point, it might be noted that the business types were grouped into an even broader classification scheme containing only ten categories,

and the method of analysis described earlier was applied to these data. Of 60 possible associations, four appear. They are listed in Table 6 along with non-significant but often observed associations. In fact, none of the most often observed associations are statistically significant, and it is again those business and land use types at the fringes of the C.B.D. which, with very few actual occurrences, appear as significant. Thus, we find non-retail land uses significantly associated with one another, and hotels and eating and drinking establishments linked to land uses in the "other" category.

Conclusions

The core of the C.B.D. is characterized by a certain mix of business types which is similar from city to city.

TABLE 6
Observed and Expected Frequencies of Store Associations Using Two-Digit Code

Store Association	Observed	Expected
Clothing stores–Clothing stores	148	144.7
Clothing stores–Other retail	137	130.0
Department and variety stores–Clothing stores	66	61.5
Food stores–Clothing stores	32	26.0
Other retail stores–Other retail stores	32	28.9
Clothing stores–Non-store uses	26	35.5
Clothing stores–Financial	22	37.2 *
Clothing stores–Household furnishings	21	19.9
Clothing stores–Eating and drinking places	20	32.9 *
[Below are listed just those store associations having a significance level ≦0.05]		
Financial–Financial	10	2.3 †
Non-store land uses–Non-store land uses	10	2.1 †
Services–Other establishments	4	1.0 †
Eating and drinking places–Other establishments	4	1.5 ‡

* If our interest was in store repulsion rather than association, then these "links" represent store types found together less often than chance would have it.
† Represents significance level less than or equal to 0.01.
‡ Represents significance level less than or equal to 0.05 but greater than or equal to 0.01.

Women's clothing stores constitute about 12 percent of the core establishments, while men's clothing and women's accessory shops comprise almost 11 percent each. In the sample of cities studied, jewelry stores were fourth in rank, constituting about 8 percent of the core establishments. The existence of these functions in the C.B.D. can be accounted for by notions from central place theory. However, the positions of the shops relative to one another cannot presently be determined by anything more than reasoning based on intuition, knowledge of grouping characteristics of some retail establishments (e.g., automobile row), differentiation of shoppers' goods from convenience goods stores, the belief that some sort of economies of agglomeration exist between certain kinds of firms, or by some notions derived from empirical evidence of consumer movement. Unfortunately none of the above approaches has produced a model for the spatial structure of business within shopping districts.

The purpose of this study was to test whether retail store spatial affinities could be identified as a factor influencing store location. The findings of the study suggest that there are undoubtedly some significant affinities between business types, but that they are very limited in number and not constant from city to city. Except for a tendency for women's clothing stores, women's accessory shops, and variety stores to be linked, there is very little apparent order.

A second conclusion is based on the fact that more significant associations were identified when three nearest neighbors were studied. This indicates that distance between stores does affect their location patterns even when that distance is small. Since shoppers must be indifferent to the extra effort neces-

sary to walk past three more stores, it is evident that some agglomerative tendencies do exist and that these are more readily discernible among stores selling clothing. However, for any individual city these agglomerative forces are only observable in the most unsystematic way, that is, the same linkages are not noted from city to city.

The final conclusions must, by default, rest with the patterns which emerge when data from a number of cities are grouped together. Here four groups are shown to emerge, the most extensive again displaying a strong bond between women's clothing, women's accessory, and variety stores. Other groups respond to the sorting out effect consistent with heterogeneous data. That is, as more and more of the less frequently occurring stores are added into the sample, they are shown to be significantly grouped if they are located at the ends of the sequence. This being the case, a degree of heterogeneity becomes evident when the data are grouped.

In summary, it has been shown that some retail store spatial affinities exist which are strong enough to create significant associations between business types, although the number of the associations is small. In light of these findings, it is suggested that the theory of urban structure be refined to indicate more clearly what the forces are which bring stores together. Since it is reality which we are trying to explain, some identifiable characteristics of the stores must be included in the theory to give it substance. Further, since the presumption is that store affinities are the result of the entrepreneur's desire to maximize profits, and of his consequent adjustment to certain desires on the part of the consumer, probably one of the most profitable tacks to follow in the development of such a theory would be to combine notions pertaining to the behavior of consumers with those of urban structure and land use already discussed.

REFERENCES

1. R. M. Haig, "Major Economic Factors in Metropolitan Growth and Arrangement," Regional Survey of New York and Its Environs (New York: *Regional Plan of New York and Its Environs,* 1927) pp. 39ff.
2. R. U. Ratcliff, *Urban Land Economics* (New York: McGraw-Hill, 1949), p. 369.
3. Walter Christaller, *Central Places in Southern Germany,* translated by Carlisle W. Baskin (Englewood Cliffs, N.J.: Prentice-Hall, Inc., 1966).
4. Brian J. L. Berry, William L. Garrison, et al., *Studies of Highway Development and Geographic Change* (Seattle: University of Washington, 1959).
5. The most thorough attempt to analyze the degree to which two businesses interchange customers is found in R. L. Nelson's *The Selection of Retail Locations* (New York: F. W. Dodge Corporation, 1958).
6. Barry J. Garner, "The Internal Structure of Retail Nucleations," *Northwestern University Studies in Geography No. 12,* 1966, p. 99.
7. Several researchers have studied the spatial patterns of individual types of businesses. See, for example, R. Artle, *Studies in the Structure of the Stockholm Economy* (Stockholm: Business Research Institute, 1959); B. J. L. Berry, "Ribbon Developments in the Urban Business Pattern," *Annals of the Association of American Geographers,* 49 (1959), pp. 145–55; A. Getis, "The Determination of the Location of Retail Activities with the Use of a Map Transformation," *Economic Geography,* 39 (1963), pp. 14–22; H. R. Parker, "Suburban Shopping Facilities in Liverpool," *Town Planning Review,* 33 (1962), pp. 197–223; A. Rogers, "A Stochastic Analysis of the Spatial Clustering of Retail Establishments," *Journal of the American Statistical Association,* 60 (1965), pp. 1094–1103.
8. A. Getis, "A Method for the Study of Sequences in Geography," *Trans. Institute of British Geographers,* no. 42, December 1967, pp. 87–92.
9. They were Midland, Bay City, Muskegon, Saginaw, Lansing, Flint, and Grand Rapids, all in Michigan; New Brunswick, Perth Amboy, Paterson, Elizabeth and Trenton, in New Jersey; and Philadelphia.
10. For this and all subsequent analyses, use was made of an Elliott 503 computer. The authors appreciate the generous support given by the University of Bristol, England, for the use of their computer facilities. Grateful acknowledgment is given to C. Faithfull of Bristol University for developing the computer program.
11. Preliminary analysis showed that the mix of store types was not significantly different on the other side of the main shopping streets, i.e., the side that is not included in the sample.
12. See H. R. Parker, *op. cit.*

The Hierarchy of Retail Nucleations

Barry Garner

Hierarchies of central places have been most frequently identified from comparative analyses of the functional structure of service centers. A center is accorded an order in the hierarchy depending upon the number and types of goods and services offered to a surrounding and supporting tributary population.[1] In rural areas where such studies have been undertaken, for the most part attention has focused on functional composition for two reasons. Firstly, studies have only dealt with aggregates or total counts of all central functions present in varying sized, discrete settlements that stand apart from their rural surrounds. Secondly, it appears that central functions are distributed among centers at various levels in the hierarchy with a surprising step-like regularity.

In metropolitan areas, however, where these conditions are less true, delimitation of a hierarchy is somewhat more difficult. In the first place, retail nucleations—the counterpart of central places in rural areas—cannot be so readily distinguished from other kinds of business conformations; and sec-ondly, because of the high degree of mobility of urban populations and the resultant interdependence of *all* parts of the urban area, central functions are not distributed among the various business centers with anything like the regularity found in rural areas.

Identification and Delimitation of Centers

Given that retail nucleations are found in association with peakings of land value above the general level in any area, land value data are used for both the initial identification and subsequent delimitation of retail nucleations in the study area.

However, the use of land value data presents difficulties. For example, valuation data for a city may be established on either of two bases: appraisal or assessment. The main difficulty is determining which of these two sources represents most accurately the true market value of retail sites. Appraisal is intended to be a close approximation of the market value of the property, in

Reprinted from *The Internal Structure of Retail Nucleations,* Studies in Geography Number 12, Department of Geography, Northwestern University, 1966.

[1] For an example of this approach, see B. J. L. Berry and W. L. Garrison, "Functional Bases of the Central Place Hierarchy," *op. cit., Economic Geography,* 34 (1958), pp. 145–154, and H. E. Bracey, "Towns as Rural Service Centers," *Transactions and Papers, Institute of British Geographers,* 19 (1953), pp. 95–105.

contrast to assessment, which represents the legal valuation of property for tax purposes.[2] Both types of valuation data are available for the City of Chicago. Appraised values are presented annually in Olcott's Blue Book,[3] and are arrived at from the study of the sale of parcels of land in the urban land market. Assessed values are available from the Cook County Assessor's Office. From a study of the relationship between the two sources of value data, the values presented in Olcott's Blue Book of Chicago were used in this study.

In Chicago, most business land is valued at $150–$200 or more per front foot and is located in association with ridges of higher land value along traffic arteries. Where commercial development is concentrated around major street intersections, values rise above the level of the ridges to reach even higher peaks at the intersections themselves. Moreover, it is readily apparent that the intensity of development increases where peak values reach and are in excess of $750 per front foot.

As an operational definition for this work, all places in the City of Chicago which have land values higher than $750 per front foot in association with commercial land use are considered as forming the basis of a retail nucleation. Using this operational definition, Table 1 lists the sixty-two nucleations

TABLE 1
The Retail Nucleations Included in the Study Area

Center	Peak Land Value ($ per front foot)	Center	Peak Land Value ($ per front foot)
63rd & Halsted	7000	Division & Ashland	1750
Belmont & Ashland	5000	63rd & Cottage Grove	1750
Madison & Pulaski	4000	Roosevelt & Halsted	1700
Irving Park & Cicero	4000	Chicago & Ashland	1600
Diversey & Clark	2750	63rd & Western	1500
47th & Ashland	2500	53rd & Lake Park	1400
Lawrence & Broadway	2500	63rd & Kedzie	1400
79th & Halsted	2500	Devon & Western	1250
111th & Michigan	2500	North & California	1250
Belmont & Central	2000	Madison & Central	1250
Fullerton & Harlem	2000	Madison & Cicero	1250
North & Pulaski	2000	Kinzie & Central	1200
Division & Clark	2000	Madison & Kedzie	1200
Madison & Halsted	2000	North & Milwaukee	1200
71st & Jeffrey	2000	47th & South Parkway	1200
91st & Commercial	1800	Lawrence & Kedzie	1200
Lawrence & Milwaukee	1800	Lawrence & Western	1200
Diversey & Kimball	1750	Howard & Paulina	1200

[2] For a more detailed account of these two evaluation schemes, see R. E. Murphy, J. E. Vance and B. L. Epstein, "Delimiting the C.B.D.," *Economic Geography*, XXX (1954), 197–200, and also B. J. Garner, "Land Values as a Method for Studying the Internal Structure of Central Business Districts" (mimeographed).

[3] C. Olcott, *Olcott's Land Value Blue Book of Chicago and Suburbs* (Chicago: G. C. Olcott Co., 1961).

TABLE 1—Continued

Center	Peak Land Value ($ per front foot)	Center	Peak Land Value ($ per front foot)
79th & Ashland	1200	Madison & Ashland	800
79th & Cottage Grove	1200	Lawrence & Damen	800
26th & Pulaski	1100	Montrose & Broadway	800
Devon & California	1000	Irving Park & Sheridan	800
Bryn Mawr & Broadway	1000	Madison & Western	800
Irving Park & Damen	1000	69th & Halsted	800
63rd & Ashland	1000	Devon & Central	750
67th & Stony Island	1000	Roosevelt & Kedzie	750
Fullerton & Halsted	900	75th & Exchange	750
63rd & Stony Island	900	North & Larrabee	750
75th & Cottage	850	Fullerton & Cicero	750
35th & Halsted	850	Belmont & Clark	750
Belmont & Cicero	850	63rd & Woodlawn	750

Planned Shopping Centers

Lake Meadows
Hyde Park (55th & Lake Park)
Chatham Park
95th & Jeffrey
Scottsdale
South East Village
Howard & Western
Lincoln Village
115th & Michigan

which were identified in the study area with peak values ranging from $750 to $7,000 per front foot. Table 1 also lists a number of planned shopping centers in the city which were used to illustrate some basic structural differences between planned and unplanned retail nucleations in the analyses below.

Commercial developments at and around street intersections can be classified into two groups depending upon the nature of land uses along the projecting arteries. On the one hand, commercial developments give way to non-commercial, usually residential, land uses in all directions. On the other hand, commercial land uses do not stand in isloation, but are contiguous with other business activities extending outward along the projecting arteries. This is especailly true where nucleations have developed at the junction of two or more ribbon developments.

Delimitation of the boundary of a retail nucleation is straightforward in the former case but presents a problem in the latter. Previous researchers have relied heavily upon intuitive notions and extensive field observation in the construction of boundaries under these circumstances. However, for the most part, such highly subjective techniques do not effectively discriminate between nucleated functions and those typically associated with ribbon developments.[4]

In this study, the boundary of a nucleation was drawn at the point of greatest inflection on cross-sectional profiles of land values drawn for both sides of each street leading away from the principal intersection. In the few instances where the point of greatest inflection was not clearly identified, boundaries were located after intensive field investigation of retail land uses at those places.[5]

This method of delimitation is preferred by the author for several reasons. Firstly, it affords a way of standardizing the placing of boundaries and thereby enables comparable delimitations from center to center. Secondly, the technique minimizes the degree of subjectivity in decision making on the part of the researcher and thus leads to relatively more objective boundary determination. Thirdly, the method is based on the underlying premise of land value theory. Competition for locations is more intense at the major intersection, where the peak land value occurs. Outward from the intersection along the major streets there is competition for locations, each kind of business seeking to get as near to the major intersection as its rent-paying ability will allow. The result is a gradual decline in land values with increasing distance from the peak intersection. At the boundaries of the nucleations the values of the land approximate those of the long, commercial ribbons which extend for miles along the major streets. It is at this point that nucleated functions give way to those more commonly associated with ribbon developments.

For each ground floor establishment within the boundaries of a retail nucleation, the following measurements were made: (1) type of business installed; (2) front foot land value; and (3) floor area in square feet. Summations within each retail nucleation yielded aggregate counts of number of establishments, number of business types and total ground floor space in square feet.[6]

[4] For examples of more subjective methods, see M. J. Proudfoot, "The Major Outlying Business Centers of Chicago," unpublished Ph.D. Dissertation. Department of Geography, University of Chicago, 1936. Proundfoot identified seven different boundary types in delimiting retail nucleations. They were named according to the type of land use which was excluded as follows: (a) the neighborhood business boundary; (b) the residential boundary; (c) the vacant property boundary; (d) the wholesale boundary; (e) the congregational boundary; (f) the transportational boundary; (g) the passive boundary. It is interesting to note Proudfoot's comment that, "Boundaries were based entirely on evidence observed in the field. Land values were not used since, for the most part, they bore little relation to specific land use," idem, "The Major Outlying . . . ," op. cit., (private edition circulated by the University of Chicago Libraries, 1938), p. 13. Also see H. M. Mayer, "Generally speaking, boundaries were placed at points where a nucleated, well defined intensive business development gives way to a more dispersed, less intensive ribbon development, to local business use or non-commercial land use such as railroads, institutional, industrial or residential areas, parks or vacant land," "Patterns and Recent Trends in Chicago's Outlying Business Centers," Journal of Land and Public Utility Economies, 18 (1943), pp. 4–16.

[5] The detailed inventory and delimitation by this method of the 62 retail nucleations included in this work are available in B. J. L. Berry and R. J. Tennant, "Chicago Commercial Reference Handbook," (University of Chicago, Department of Geography Research Paper 86, 1963).

[6] The Standard Industrial Classification of the Bureau of the Census was used to classify business types. Land values were obtained from Olcott's Blue Book . . . , op. cit., and floor area was measured from maps in the Sanborn Atlas but should be considered as approximations of the exact floor space only.

Fundamental Empirical Regularities

The theory of tertiary activity states that high order centers are characterized by more business types and establishments, and it might follow, larger floor areas, than lower order centers. Table 2 indicates the validity of this premise in the study area. Log-linear relationships exist between the number of business types in centers and total floor areas on the one hand, and total number of occupied establishments on the other.[7] Furthermore, a log–log relationship exists between total floor area and number of occupied establishments. Relevant pairwise correlations are significant, and are included with their respective regression equations in Table 2. These relationships are illustrated in Figures 1 and 2, respectively. Also included in Table 2 and Figures 1 and 2 are the corresponding data for the sample of planned shopping centers in the City of Chicago.

Interesting differences are found between the fundamental relationships of the planned centers and those of the unplanned nucleations in respect to the criteria shown. Table 2 shows that log-occupied establishments and total number of business types are more highly correlated in the planned centers than in the unplanned nucleations. The coefficient of determination is .92 in the former as opposed to only .84 in the latter.

Conversely, log-floor area and total number of business types show a higher degree of correlation in the unplanned retail nucleations than in the planned shopping centers. The coefficient of determination is .75 in the former, compared to only .65 in the latter. Moreover, the overall degree of correlation is much lower between these two variables than between the log-occupied establishments and number of business types. This is presumably attributed to the much greater variation in the ground floor size of establishments within planned shopping centers as compared

TABLE 2
Selected Size Relationships

| | Correlations (R^2) | | | | | |
| | Unplanned | | | Planned | | |
	(L.F.A.)	(L.E.)	(B.T.)	(L.F.A.)	(L.E.)	(B.T.)
Log floor area (L.F.A.)	X	.85	.75	X	X	.65
Log occupied establishments (L.E.)		X	.84		X	.92
Business types (B.T.)			X			X

| Regression Equations | |
Unplanned	Planned
1. L.F.A. = 0.0208 (BT) + 1.4466	1. L.F.A. = 0.0326 (BT) + 1.294
2. L.E. = 0.0178 (BT) + 1.1860	2. L.E. = 0.0276 (BT) + 0.8016
3. L.F.A. = 1.1451 (LE) + 0.1020	

[7] Occupied establishments are used because of the distorting effects of vacant stores.

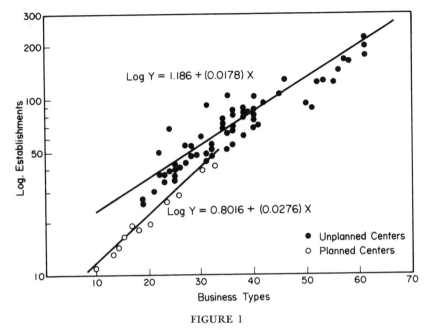

FIGURE 1

Regression of Log. Occupied Establishments on Number of Business Types

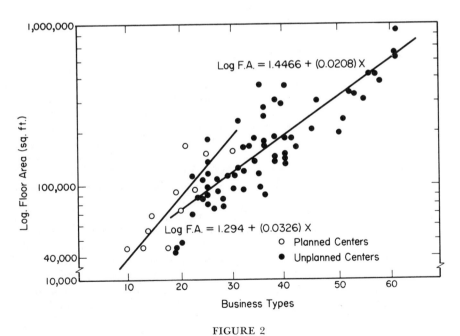

FIGURE 2

Regression of Log. Floor Area on Number of Business Types

to unplanned centers, and greater variability in the size of retail nucleations in general.

Furthermore, it is noted from the scattergrams that planned centers are characterized by markedly different regimes than unplanned centers. The average numbers of business types, numbers of occupied establishments and the average floor areas (sizes) are smaller, as reflected in the lower a values, and the rates of change greater, as reflected in the higher b values, in the regression equations for the planned shopping centers. Thus, in Figure 1, planned shopping centers are characterized by fewer establishments than the unplanned retail nucleations for any given number of business types. This reflects, on the one hand, the greater degree of functional selection, and on the other, the lower degree of duplication of functions in planned shopping centers where only "core" functions are permitted. However, the wide variation in the size of individual planned shopping centers is illustrated by the lower correlation coefficient and the greater degree of scatter about the least squares line in Figure 2. This is explained by the fact that the size of a shopping center is predetermined in the planning process, and the size of its constituent establishments fixed by the level at which the center is to perform.

In both Figures 1 and 2, deviant observations are noticeable in the scatter of unplanned retail nucleations. In other words, there is either a surplus or a deficit of occupied establishments or floor space for the given number of central functions in any given retail nucleation. This is especially noticeable in the relationship between log-floor area and number of business types.

However, it would be too much to expect all observations to fall exactly on the least squares line. The term *deviant* as used here needs further qualification. It is quite conceivable that a certain amount of the observed variability in observations about the least squares line can be explained by chance. To take this into account, it was decided to consider all observations falling within an arbitrarily selected band one standard error of estimate wide, centered about the least squares line, as average for the relationship between the two variables in question. Using this operational definition, only those observations falling outside the one standard error of estimate band are considered deviant cases.[8]

Identification of Two Groups of Retail Nucleations

One interesting point emerges from the discussion of deviant cases. This is that if a particular center is characterized by a larger number of occupied establishments than expected from the number of business types present in the nucleation, it is conceivable to expect it also to deviate with respect to its size. In other words, the nucleation will be larger than expected given the number of business types. Observations of this type were thought to warrant closer inspection.

The spatial distribution of these retail nucleations deviating noticeably in terms of number of occupied establishments *and* floor area is illustrated in Figure 3. Comparison of the distribution of deviant nucleations with indices of social and economic "well-being"

---

[8] For a more refined method of this sort, see E. N. Thomas, "Toward an Expanded Central Place Theory," *Geographical Review*, 51 (1961), pp. 400–411, and D. Snyder, "The Autonomous–Obsequious Hypothesis of Urban Evolution and Its Application to Puerto Rico," (paper presented, A. A. G. meetings, Miami Beach, 1962).

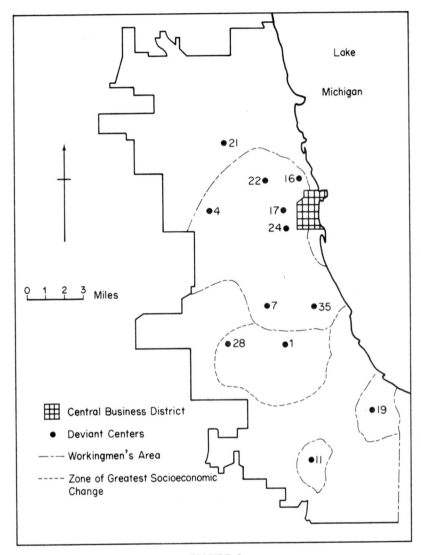

FIGURE 3

Retail Nucleations with More Occupied Establishments and Larger
Floor Area than Expected

within the study area reveals a close correspondence between the deviants and those parts of the city currently experiencing decline and socio-economic change, or with the general area of low income (blue collar) population within the study area.[9]

This preliminary, subjective spatial

[9] These indices were obtained from the Center for Population Research at the University of Chicago. They included data by census tracts for the percentage of houses built before 1918; percent white collar workers; and an accessibility index based on proximity to adjacent industrial areas. Isoline maps were constructed which enabled the determination of homogeneous areas of low socioeconomic status.

correlation suggests that perhaps two statistical populations exist within the overall study area, the one in the relatively "healthy" parts of the city and the other in the low socio-economic areas. In this event, centers in each area would be characterized by a different set of functional relationships between the variables analyzed. The existence of a dual system is not contrary to the underlying premise of the theory of tertiary activity which is fundamentally based on the magnitude of the available purchasing power in a given tributary area. Consequently, . . . there may well be different systems of central places in urban areas. each related to the socio-economic structure of the tributary areas which they serve.

In order to test this hypothesis, the total number of retail nucleations was disaggregated into two groups: the one comprising those nucleations located in an arbitrarily defined low-income area, the other comprising all the remaining centers located in the rest of the city. Tests for differences in the slopes and intercepts of the sub-regression lines using covariance analysis indicate this sub-grouping to be valid. However, there is no significant difference between the slopes of the two regressions, and thus, it cannot be concluded that there are two separate functional relationships in the city. Rather, within the one overall functional relationship, the significant difference in intercepts suggests the existence of two regimes. Each regime comprises a group of nucleations which, in aggregate, differ significantly with respect to mean floor area, mean number of occupied establishments and mean number of business types. The covariance results are shown in Table 3, and the two regimes illustrated in Figures 4 and 5 respectively. Subsequent analysis is based on the existence of these two groups of retail nucleations. For convenience, the group in the low-income area is henceforth referred to as the Workingmen's Centers and the other group, comprising the remainder of the retail nucleations, is referred to as the Rest of the City.

TABLE 3

Covariance Analysis on Elevations of Sub-regression Lines

Log Occupied Establishments on Business Types				
Source	Variation	D.f.	Mean Square	F.
Between	.1719	1	.1719	
Within	.3031	59	.0051	33.7
				(F. $\propto$ .05 = 4.00)

Log Floor Area on Business Types				
Source	Variation	D.f.	Mean Square	F.
Between	.4378	1	.4378	
Within	.7143	59	.0121	36.48 **
				(F. $\propto$ .05 = 4.00)

** Highly significant.

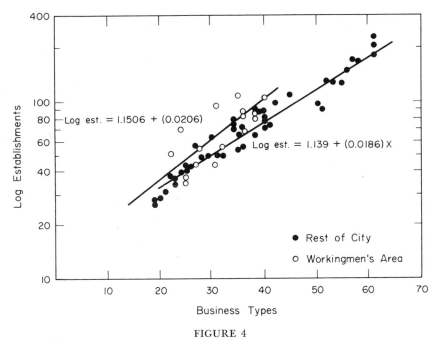

FIGURE 4

Sub-regression of Log. Establishments on Number of Business Types

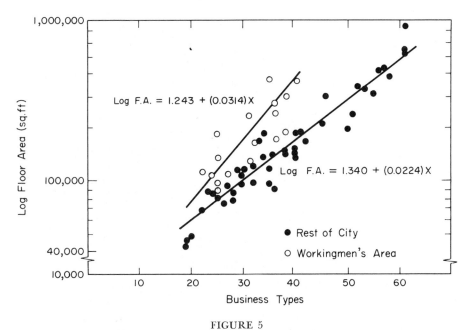

FIGURE 5

Sub-regression of Log. Floor Area on Number of Business Types

Identification of a Hierarchy of Retail Nucleations

The identification of a hierarchy of retail nucleations within the two areas was based upon further analysis of the relationship between the number of occupied establishments and number of business types. This approach was preferred to the use of floor area data for two reasons. Firstly, retail nucleations are characterized by a high degree of variability in aggregate size as a result of initial differences in the size of their component establishments. In part, this may be due to inaccuracies in the initial measurement. Secondly, numbers of occupied establishments and business types seem to offer more information

pertinent to the underlying objective of this work. However, the use of only this particular set of data means that the allocation of a nucleation to a particular level in the hierarchy is based simply upon the number and types of business offered.

The writer does not intend to imply that aggregate store size is an unimportant aspect in the study of service centers. On the contrary, we recognize it to be a very important, but as yet inadequately studied, aspect of retailing activity within the framework of central place theory.[10]

Figure 6 is the scattergram of the relationship between the number of occupied establishments and business types for the retail nucleations in the

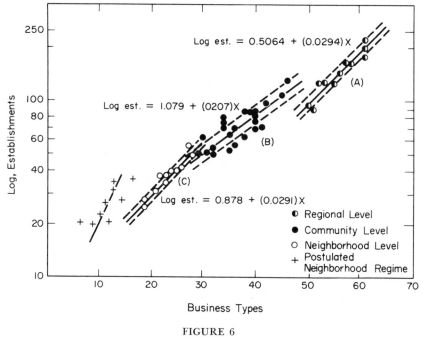

FIGURE 6

Sub-regressions of Log. Establishments on Number of Business Types for Different Level Centers in the Rest of the City

[10] Attention has been called to this problem by B. J. L. Berry, and W. L. Garrison, "Recent Developments in Central Place Theory," *op. cit.*

Rest of the City. Number of business types is plotted on the X-axis, and occupied establishments on the Y-axis. The nucleations have been classified into three groups: A, B and C, which are designated as regional, community and neighborhood centers, respectively. Covariance analysis applied to this sub-grouping indicates significant differences in the elevations of the sub-regression lines, and supports the validity of the threefold classification. The results of the covariance analysis are shown in Table 4. In Figure 6, each group of nucleations is shown with its respective sub-regression line and one standard error confidence band.

The break between the regional and community groups is clearly illustrated by the fact that the confidence bands do not overlap. The distinction between the community and neighborhood groups is, however, not so clear. It becomes increasingly apparent that many small retail nucleations are associated with values less than the $750 cut-off point used in the initial identification of retail nucleations. As a result, these have been omitted from the study. Consequently, the division into groups B and C—community and neighborhood centers—is based primarily on field observations, is thus quite subjective, and must for this reason be considered as arbitrary. For if it should happen that the remaining

neighborhood centers assume the relationship or trend hypothesized in Figure 6, there would be no justification for distinguishing between the two groups in the manner indicated. The assumption made here, therefore, in view of lack of evidence to the contrary, is that the trend line approximates that of the neighborhood centers shown, and of which only the largest are included in the study.

Figure 7(A) contains the basic information concerning the occupied establishments: business types ratios for the nucleations in the Workingmen's Area. Instead of the existence of sub-regimes within the overall relationship, the scattergram reveals a marked tendency for observations to cluster about the general regression line. This tendency is more sharply indicated in Figure 7(B), in which the axes have been scaled to a common unit of measurement, with one standard unit of X representing 37 business types and one standard unit of Y representing 87 occupied establishments. The X and Y axes have also been rotated to an angle phi such that the correlation of X and Y is equal to the cosine of phi ($R_{xy} = \cos \phi$). Since the correlation coefficient is .78, phi is $38°4'$. Scaling and rotation in this manner ensure that direct measurement of distance between points in the graph is an accurate index of the similarity or dissimilarity of nucleations not

TABLE 4

Covariance Analysis on Elevations of Sub-regression Lines for Centers in the Rest of the City

Log Occupied Establishments on Business				
Source	Variation	D.f.	Mean Square	F.
Between	.0362	2	.0181	
Within	.1160	58	.002	9.1 **
			(F. $\propto$ 0.5 $=$ 4.00)	

** Highly significant.

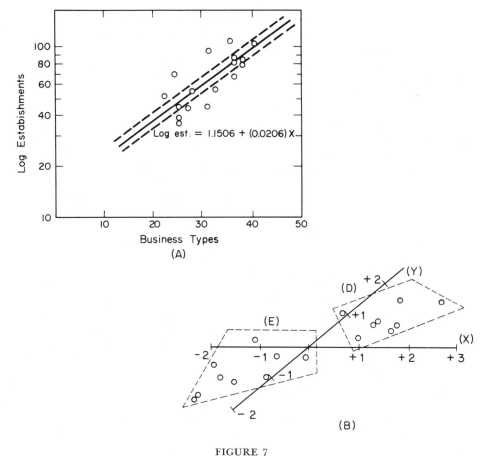

FIGURE 7

The Relationship Between Occupied Establishments and
Number of Business Types at Centers in the
Workingmen's Area

biased by correlation or differing units of measurement between occupied establishments and numbers of business types.[11]

Two groups of centers, D and E, are identified from the application of nearest neighbor techniques to the scattergram.[12] Although each group contains those observations that are closer to another member of the group

---

[11] See C. Radhakrishua Rao, "The Utilization of Multiple Measurements in Problems of Biological Classification," *Journal of the Royal Statistical Society, Series B (Methods),* 10 (1949), pp. 187–188. For an example of the use of the method in a grouping problem, see B. J. L. Berry, "The Impact of Expanding Metropolitan Communities upon the Central Place Hierarchy," *Annals of the Association of American Geographers,* 50 (1960), pp. 112–116.

[12] For a discussion of nearest neighbor techniques, see M. Dacey, "Analysis of Map Distributions by Nearest Neighbor Methods," *Discussion Paper Number 1* (Department of Geography, University of Washington, Seattle, 1958).

than to any other observation, there is considerable within–group distance variation. For convenience at this stage of the analysis, the two groups are called Workmen's Major (D) and Minor (E), respectively. The results of variance analysis shown in Table 5 indicate a significant difference between the mean number of occupied establishments in the two groups. Variance analysis was also used to test the hypothesis that the mean floor area size of the five groups of centers differs significantly, and Table 6 indicates significant between-group differences.

In summary then, five groups of retail nucleations can be identified within the City of Chicago from an analysis of occupied establishment : business type ratios. Three orders of nucleations are typical of the Rest of the City area, compared to only two orders in the Workingmen's Area. The former nucleations are designated regional, community and neighborhood centers and comprise 11, 23 and 11 nucleations respectively. Each order differs significantly in the mean number of establishments, business types and floor area (size). The two orders in the Workingmen's areas are designated major and minor centers respectively. These are also significantly different in their mean numbers of occupied establishments, business types and floor area.

The classification offered here is not the only possible allocation of retail nucleations to various levels or orders in a hierarchy. Rather, it may be considered one of several other systems which are dependent upon the methods of analysis and purpose of study. Thus, for example, the analysis of trade areas associated with each center may well indicate that some nucleations do not warrant the order allocated in the above analysis. However, in view of the fact that each of the five groups

TABLE 5

Variance Analysis Between the Log Occupied Establishments and Number of Business Types for Centers in the Workingmen's Area

Source	Variation	D.f.	Variance Estimate	F.
Between	98,476.485	1	98,476.485	
Within	927.31	15	61.8	159.35 **
Total	107,749.59	16	—	
			(F. $\propto$ 0.5 = 4.54)	

** Highly significant.

TABLE 6

Variance Analysis Between the Mean Floor Area Size of the Five Groups of Retail Nucleations

Source	Variation	D.f.	Variance Estimate	F.
Between	3.3191	4	0.8298	
Within	1.2913	57	0.0227	36.5 **
Total	4.6104	61		
			(F. $\propto$ 0.05 = 2.54)	

** Highly significant.

of retail nucleations is shown to be significantly different from the others, it is deemed acceptable for the purpose of this work.[13]

The Spatial Distribution of the Hierarchies

The spatial distribution of the hierarchy of retail nucleations in the study area is shown in Figure 8, and the ad-

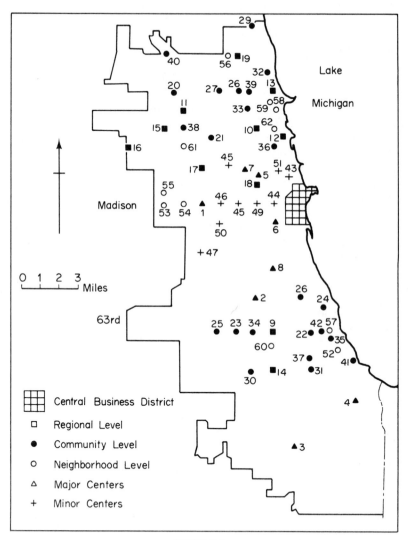

FIGURE 8

The Hierarchy of Retail Nucleations in the City of Chicago, 1961

[13] Thus the classification of centers in B. J. L. Berry et al., *Commercial Structure and Commercial Blight* (Chicago: University of Chicago, Department of Geography, Research Paper 85, 1963) is slightly different from that presented here because of the more powerful grouping technique used.

dress of each center is given in Table 7. Basically, the pattern comprises two distinct clusters, one in the north and the other in the south of the study area. They are separated by a broad band of industrial and transportation land uses. The rectangular grid-iron street pattern has brought about a fairly even spacing of retail nucleations in both areas, with a marked tendency for the

TABLE 7
The Hierarchy of Retail Nucleations in the City of Chicago

Regional					
(1)		*(2)*	*(1)*		*(2)*
		Peak			*Peak*
Number	*Address*	*Value*	*Number*	*Address*	*Value*
9	63rd & Halsted	7000	15	Belmont & Central	2000
10	Belmont & Ashland	5000	16	Fullerton & Harlem	2000
11	Irving Park & Cicero	4000	17	North & Pulaski	2000
12	Diversey & Clark	2750	18	Chicago & Ashland	1600
13	Lawrence & Broadway	2500	19	Devon & Western	1250
14	79th & Halsted	2500			

Community					
(1)		*(2)*	*(1)*		*(2)*
		Peak			*Peak*
Number	*Address*	*Value*	*Number*	*Address*	*Value*
20	Lawrence & Milwaukee	1800	32	Bryn Mawr & Broadway	1000
21	Diversey & Kimball	1750	33	Irving Park & Damen	1000
22	63rd & Cottage	1750	34	63rd & Ashland	1000
23	63rd & Western	1500	35	67th & Stony Island	1000
24	53rd & Lake Park	1400	36	Fullerton & Halsted	900
25	63rd & Kedzie	1400	37	75th & Cottage	850
26	47th & South Parkway	1200	38	Belmont & Cicero	850
27	Lawrence & Kedzie	1200	39	Lawrence & Damen	800
28	Lawrence & Western	1200	40	Devon & Central	750
29	Howard & Paulina	1200	41	75th & Exchange	750
30	79th & Ashland	1200	42	63rd & Woodlawn	750
31	79th & Cottage Grove	1200			

Neighborhood					
(1)		*(2)*	*(1)*		*(2)*
		Peak			*Peak*
Number	*Address*	*Value*	*Number*	*Address*	*Value*
52	71st & Jeffrey	2000	58	Montrose & Broadway	800
53	Madison & Central	1250	59	Irving Park & Sheridan	800
54	Madison & Cicero	1250	60	69th & Halsted	800
55	Kinzie & Central	1200	61	Fullerton & Cicero	750
56	Devon & California	1000	62	Belmont & Clark	750
57	63rd & Stony Island	900			

TABLE 7—Continued

		Workingmen's Major			
(1)		(2)	(1)		(2)
		Peak			Peak
Number	Address	Value	Number	Address	Value
1	Madison & Pulaski	4000	5	Division & Ashland	1750
2	47th & Ashland	2500	6	Roosevelt & Halsted	1700
3	111th & Michigan	2500	7	North & Milwaukee	1200
4	91st & Commercial	1800	8	35th & Halsted	850
		Workingmen's Minor			
(1)		(2)	(1)		(2)
		Peak			Peak
Number	Address	Value	Number	Address	Value
43	Division & Clark	2000	48	Madison & Western	800
44	Madison & Halsted	2000	49	Madison & Ashland	800
45	North & California	1250	50	Roosevelt & Kedzie	750
46	Madison & Kedzie	1200	51	North & Larrabee	750
47	26th & Pulaski	1100			

Notes: (1) Numbers are keyed to Figures 8 and 10.
(2) Peak values are given in dollars per front foot.

nucleations to be located on the mile section-line and half-section streets, which are the principal traffic arteries and which were significant in the initial development of streetcar and bus lines.[14] The importance of Madison and of 63rd streets as major shopping arteries is apparent.

The difference between the number of centers in the northern and southern parts of the city is a direct reflection of the basic pattern of population distribution in the City of Chicago. In the south, where approximately one-third of the city population dwells on two-thirds of the land area, there are only 21 nucleations which are, in general, uniformly spaced. On the other hand, the group in the northern part of the city comprises 41 nucleations which serve the remaining two-thirds of the city population.

In general, nucleations of the same order are not uniformly spaced throughout the study area. This is to be expected from the marked unevenness of the population distribution and purchasing power. Furthermore, because centers with peak values of less than $750 per front foot have been omitted in this work, the pattern shown in Figure 8 cannot be viewed as a complete picture of the distribution of retail nucleations. Nevertheless, several generalizations emerge.

The highest level centers—regional and workingmen's major—are notably dispersed in their respective parts of the city. The community and workingmen's minor centers exhibit a high de-

[14] Mention is made of this in H. M. Mayer, "Patterns and Recent Trends . . . ," *op. cit.,* p. 4.

gree of spatial clustering within which definite linear orientations are apparent. Both types of centers are quite regularly spaced along certain East–West streets, notably 63rd, Madison and Lawrence.

The neighborhood centers, included in the study area, are mostly concentrated in the northern part of the study area and cluster in close proximity to regional centers. In the case of the three centers at the western edge of the city, they are in close proximity to large suburban shopping centers not shown in the map.

It is interesting to note that certain aspects of the spacing of centers in the city are analogous—if even of a somewhat rudimentary level—to findings from studies of the distribution of central places in rural areas. It does raise the possibility that some underlying and fundamental spatial relationship exists in the spacing of different order centers in a hierarchy, regardless of the vast differences in population density and purchasing power between urban and rural areas.

For example, the linear pattern of community and minor centers in the city tends to support Brush's assertion that in rural areas, "lower order centers tend to form rows or belts." Furthermore, the pattern of neighborhood centers appears to support his finding that "low rank centers tend to crowd together in areas farthest away from the largest centers," while regional centers and in part the major centers offer evidence in the city area of "large centers cluster[ing] more closely to one another." [15]

In spite of the incomplete picture of the distribution of retail nucleations within the city, some evidence is also presented in support of the $K = 4$ network found by Berry in Iowa.[16] This is not surprising since the rectangular land survey system is characteristic of both rural and urban Americana. Moreover, the $K = 4$ network was initially postulated by Christaller to result from strong influence of transportation routes on the system.[17] As has already been noted above, public transportation routes played a very important part in the development of the pattern of retail nucleations in the City of Chicago. An ideal $K = 4$ network is postulated for the urban area in Figure 9, and although the actual pattern of retail nucleations deviates considerably from this ideal, close inspection reveals a certain measure of agreement.

Summary of the Hierarchies of Retail Nucleations

The fundamental characteristics in the hierarchies of retail nucleations identified in the City of Chicago are shown in Table 8. Regional order centers are characterized by more than fifty business types, and average 147 occupied establishments. Their average size is approximately 400,000 square feet.

Community order centers have between 29 and 49 business types, but average only 72 occupied establishments. However, the larger community centers may have as many business types as the smaller regional centers. They are considerably smaller than the

15 J. E. Brush, "The Hierarchy of Central Places in Southwestern Wisconsin," *The Geographical Review*, 43 (1953), pp. 380–402.

16 B. J. L. Berry and H. M. Mayer, *Comparative Studies of Central Place Systems*. A report prepared for the U.S. Navy, Office of Naval Research (Project NONR 2121-18; NR 389-126), Department of Geography, University of Chicago, 1962.

17 W. Christaller, Die Zentralen Orke in Suddevtschland. Jena: Gustav Fischer, 1933.

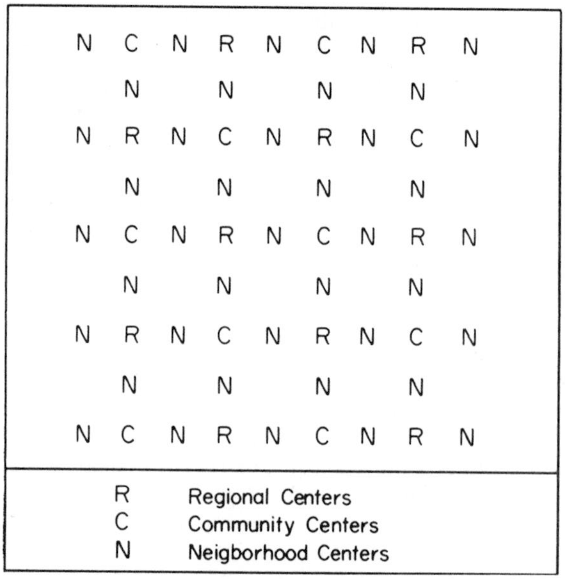

N	C	N	R	N	C	N	R	N
	N		N		N		N	
N	R	N	C	N	R	N	C	N
	N		N		N		N	
N	C	N	R	N	C	N	R	N
	N		N		N		N	
N	R	N	C	N	R	N	C	N
	N		N		N		N	
N	C	N	R	N	C	N	R	N

R	Regional Centers
C	Community Centers
N	Neigborhood Centers

FIGURE 9

An Idealized K-4 System of Retail Nucleations for the
City of Chicago

latter, with 156,015 square feet, and average about two-fifths the size of regional centers.

Neighborhood centers have between 19 and 28 business types, with an average of 23, about half as many as the regional centers. They have roughly one quarter the number of establishments of a regional center. However, within-group variability results in some overlap with smaller community centers. With an average floor area of 80,500 square feet, they are about one-half as large as the community centers. This rather large size is to be expected since only the largest neighborhood centers have been included in the study.

In the Workingmen's Area, the major centers have an average of 36 business types, ranging between 32 and 40.

With 99 occupied establishments they are somewhat smaller than the regional centers in the Rest of the City. Their average size is about 269,000 square feet. On the other hand, minor centers have an average of only 27 business types, and range between 22 and 31. They have approximately half as many occupied establishments, 47, as the major centers. This is a similar proportion shown by that in community to regional centers in the Rest of the City. They are just under half the size of the major centers, with an average area of 113,600 square feet.[18]

It is interesting to compare the centers in the Workingmen's Area with those of the Rest of the City in terms of the basic characteristics so far considered. Firstly, there seems to be a close

[18] It is interesting to note the similarities between these figures and those for planned centers presented by H. Hoyt in, "Classification and Significant Characteristics of Shopping Centers," *Appraisal Journal*, April 1958, pp. 214–222.

TABLE 8
Summary of Fundamental Characteristics of the Hierarchy of Retail Nucleations in the City of Chicago, 1961

Characteristic	Rest of City			Workingmen's Area	
	Regional	Com-munity	Neighbor-hood	Major	Minor
X business type	55.9	36.9	23.4	36.3	26.6
Range in B.T.'s	50+	49–29	28–19	40–32	31–22
X occupied estab.	146.7	72.1	37.5	98.8	47.6
Range occupied estab.	220–89	128–48	54–26	180–68	67–35
X floor area (1)	400,251.8	156,015.0	80,489.0	268,898.7	113,613.3
Range floor area (2)	726.9–195.1	297.2–96.5	182.5–43.5	368.3–172.6	163.2–87.3
X store size (3)	2,674.6	2,158.2	1,888.6	3,083.6	2,450.2
Numbers	11	23	11	8	9

Notes: (1) Floor area measured in square feet.
      (2) In 000's square feet.
      (3) Including only occupied stores, measured in square feet.

correspondence in the relative positions of the community and minor centers to the regional and major centers, respectively. The two lower order centers have about half the number of occupied establishments and floor area of the highest order centers. Secondly, the major and minor centers appear to be similar to the community and neighborhood centers, respectively. This is especially true of the average number of business types. With respect to the number of occupied establishments and floor area, major centers lie somewhere between the regional and community order centers, and in general approximate the largest of the community level group. The minor centers show a similar kind of relationship to the larger neighborhood/smaller community level centers.

The Retail Component of the Urban Model

Brian J. L. Berry

Simple equation systems that describe commercial structure quite exactly have now been developed for many cities and are being used both for analytic purposes and as integral parts of planning models. In this paper I shall review one such equation system developed for Chicago and discuss its applicability as the retail component of an urban model.

Models may be built for a variety of purposes. If they provide accurate descriptions of the phenomena and processes they are supposed to represent, they will be invaluable for basic research even if they do not then find practical application. Sound analytic models will also facilitate analysis of the context of policy, however, by clarifying the arena within which decisions must be made, therefore making possible more pointed criticisms of the postulates on which present policy is based. Moreover, even though they are essentially "passive," good descriptive models can facilitate study of the repercussions of change, whether the change is planned or otherwise.

Passive models may be cross-sectional, describing the state of a system at a point in time, or they may incorporate time as a variable, perhaps as a linear trend term, perhaps in a system of recursive equations, or even in a time-dependent probability process as exemplified by a simulation model.

For a model to assume an "active" or normative role it must incorporate goals and attempt to optimize. The most common example of this kind is the familiar linear programming formulation in which some objective function is maximized or minimized within a set of constraints. Such optimization models may not describe the present state of a system at all, but instead may specify what an efficient system should be like under a given set of assumptions.

The present paper is limited to a discussion of descriptive models which are static and cross-sectional, reporting on the state of a system at a particular point in time. These models have analytic utility and may also be used for short-run adaptive planning in which problems are essentially those of incremental growth and marginal decline. Many examples can be cited in which such models have also been used for long-run planning.[1] I feel, however, that the necessary assumptions are too

Reprinted by permission of the *Journal of the American Institute of Planners,* Volume XXXI, Number 2, May 1965.

[1] For example, Barbara R. Berman, Benjamin Chinitz, and Edgar M. Hoover, *Projection of a Metropolis* (Cambridge: Harvard University Press, 1960).

heroic when one attempts to proceed from short-run cases in which only demand-side changes in numbers and densities of consumers are postulated, to longer-run situations in which both the technology of retailing and consumer behavior may change. Neither is there adequate information to permit "trending" of the parameters in the models—as if trending had any merit when the basic characteristic of retailing today is the technological differential between the older prewar style of unplanned centers and ribbon development and the postwar pattern of planned shopping centers.[2] Recent technological change has not been gradual and trendable, but "lumpy."

The models to be discussed are drawn from two sources. One set was developed for the City of Chicago as part of its Community Renewal Program.[3] The second was prepared for the balance of the six-county metropolitan area for the Northeastern Illinois Planning Commission.[4] The former was supposed to be useful in "laying out the extent, location, nature, and trends of commercial blight and deterioration" in the central city. In contrast, the latter was supposed to help in determining what "pattern of retailing is likely to emerge over the next twenty years" and to facilitate "predicting shopping space requirements."

Approaches to Modeling Retail Systems

The fact that the retail and service trades are consumer-oriented, with spatial patterns that mirror those of population and income, may be taken quite literally in modeling retailing but may often be misleading if care is not taken with the data used. In Chicago in 1958, for example, an equation of the form:

$$(1) \quad E = 899 + 7.344P - 4.414Y$$

closely reproduced the number of retail establishments (E) in "analysis zones" of approximately 300,000 persons each, where the predictor variables were population in thousands (P) and relative income (Y), or income level in relation to a city median set as 100. The coefficient of determination (R^2) is 0.84. The comparable equation for 1948 was:

$$(2) \quad E = 1492 + 10.44P - 13.31Y$$

where E, P and Y are as before and the fit was even better ($R^2 = 0.89$). Note the change in parameters, indicative of the considerable shift in retail relationships already in progress in the 1948–1958 decade, before the full brunt of the newer planned technology was felt on the scale of centers and retail establishments. Much of the 1948–1958 change in Chicago revealed in the differences between equations (1) and (2) can be captured by changes in population and in income levels:

$$(3) \quad C_e = -1.7 + 1.022C_p + 1.248C_y$$

This equation states that the average annual change in retail and selected service establishments (C_e) may be explained by the average annual rates of change in population (C_p) and relative income (C_y). Again the fits are excellent ($R^2 = 0.91$) and again the data com-

---

[2] Brian J. L. Berry, *Commercial Structure and Commercial Blight* (Chicago: University of Chicago, Department of Geography, Research Paper No. 85, 1963).

[3] *Ibid.*

[4] Brian J. L. Berry and Robert J. Tennant, *The Changing Retail Structure of Northeastern Illinois,* Northeastern Illinois Planning Commission, forthcoming.

prise observations for the city's CRP "analysis zones."

One can see the implications of the good fits of these equations for retail modeling. The activity-complex is consumer-oriented. Retail patterns are endogenous, generated by a prior spatial allocation of consumers and their characteristics (even if some important internal feedback is of significance in the areas of employment provided, traffic generated, efforts on population densities, and so on). Hence the high degrees of correlation observed in the simple equations. Changes in numbers of consumers, therefore, lead to retail growth in certain areas, generating new space demands and consequent problems of allocation of this space relative to other uses, and also cause decline in other areas, implying the need for some form of renewal of existing retail facilities.

As Artemus Ward remarked, however: "It ain't what you don't know that's the problem but what you know that ain't so." Simple linear models of the form described above have a serious limitation. They are based on areal observations and the correlations are thus subject to the problem of modifiable units. If the scale of observation is changed, say from large "analysis zones" to small census tracts, the fit becomes much worse. In short, equations of the type given in (1)–(3) are useless with small area data. Why should this be so? Surely, there is nothing wrong with the concept of consumer-orientation? Perhaps, then, areal observations such as analysis zones and census tracts are measuring retail structure the wrong way. Perhaps "anal-

ysis zones" work well because they embrace one or more of the ecological units within which demands and supplies are equilibrated, but small areas such as census tracts work poorly because they cut across such units. If so, sounder models should be constructed using the *correct* ecological units.

Such units are retail business centers and the market areas served by these centers. In both cases there are obvious definitional difficulties, although these are more serious in the instance of market areas than of centers. Simply, the older type of unplanned center may be defined consistently and unambiguously using land value criteria,[5] and of course the more modern planned center is a naively given entity, the unit of development. Experimentation shows the most useful definition of the market area to be that "intensive" area within which a constant rate of accumulation of trips with distance holds.[6]

Armed with such ecological units, the complex interdependencies of centers and market areas and their characteristics may be demonstrated.

Interdependencies and Contrasts

The basic theory of retail structure has been developed by geographers out of an earlier Christaller–Lösch geometric formulation of central place theory.[7] Properties of the theory are well-known. Perhaps the most important for the present discussion is that the retail system approximates an interdependent equilibrium between the

[5] Berry, *op. cit.*, p. 28 ff.

[6] *Ibid.*, p. 61 ff.

[7] *Ibid.*, and Brian J. L. Berry and Allan Pred, *Central Place Studies. A Biobliography of Theory and Applications* (Philadelphia: Regional Science Research Institute, 1961).

numbers and kinds of activities offered by a center on the one hand and the size of the market area served on the other. Symbolically:

$$(4) \qquad B = f[P]$$

$$(5) \qquad D = f[B]$$

where B is the number of kinds of business offered by a center, P is the population served, and D is the maximum distance that consumers will travel to the center.[8] Yet interdependency breeds circularity, for:

$$(6) \qquad P = \pi D^2 d$$

where d is population density. A critical problem therefore exists in choice of model, and it is all the more critical because interdependency expresses itself as multiple collinearity.

A factor analytic framework is useful in clarifying empirically the interdependencies and collinearities among variables indicative of size and functional complexity of business centers and the characteristics of their market areas.[9] Because certain structural interdependencies are thought to have have changed markedly between unplanned and planned centers, however, Tables 1 and 2 report factor analyses

TABLE 1
Unplanned Centers: Normal Varimax Rotated Factor Matrix

Variables	Loadings on Factor [1]				Communality
	1	*2*	*3*	*4*	
Functions	0.925	—	—	—	0.950
Establishments	0.930	—	—	—	0.973
Total center area	0.900	—	—	—	0.978
Shopping center area	0.881	0.417	—	—	0.974
Ground floor area	0.843	0.458	—	—	0.975
Population of trade area	0.555	0.810	—	—	0.996
Area of trade area	0.844	—	−0.438	—	0.978
Median income	—	—	0.848	—	0.835
Social class	—	—	0.941	—	0.940
Family class	—	—	—	0.773	0.719
Total competition	0.438	0.875	—	—	0.969
Planned competition	0.615	—	—	0.445	0.584
Unplanned competition	0.856	—	—	—	0.855
Ribbon competition	—	0.901	—	—	0.959
Discount competition	—	—	−0.693	—	0.612
Population density	—	0.752	—	—	0.974
Eigenvalue	6.729	3.475	2.695	1.372	
Percent of common variance	42.1	63.8	80.6	89.2	

[1] All loadings lying between +0.40 and −0.40 have been omitted to ease reading.

[8] See also W. J. Baumol and E. A. Ide, "Variety in Retailing," *Mathematical Models and Methods in Marketing*, ed. Frank M. Bass et al. (Hammond, Ind.: Richard D. Irwin, 1961), pp. 128–38.

[9] Factor analysis is discussed in detail in Harry Harman, *Modern Factor Analysis* (Chicago: University of Chicago Press, 1960).

TABLE 2
Planned Centers: Normal Varimax Rotated Factor Matrix

Variables	Loadings on Factor [1]				Communality
	1	2	3	4	
Functions	0.612	−0.713	—	—	0.940
Establishments	0.690	−0.547	—	—	0.888
Total center area	0.883	—	—	—	0.961
Shopping center area	0.897	—	—	—	0.955
Ground floor area	0.898	—	—	—	0.966
Population of trade area	0.734	−0.486	—	—	0.827
Area of trade area	0.730	—	—	0.478	0.878
Median income	—	—	0.970	—	0.942
Social class	—	—	0.903	—	0.851
Family class	0.901	—	—	—	0.907
Total competition	0.957	—	—	—	0.971
Planned competition	—	—	—	0.909	0.883
Unplanned competition	0.956	—	—	—	0.942
Ribbon competition	0.943	—	—	—	0.932
Discount competition	—	−0.837	—	—	0.715
Population density	—	—	—	−0.915	0.935
Eigenvalue	7.910	2.377	2.158	2.046	
Percent of common variance	49.4	64.3	77.8	99.6	

[1] All loadings lying between +0.40 and −0.40 have been omitted to ease reading.

for the two types separately. The observations are the business centers of the Northeastern Illinois Metropolitan Area.

In these tables the variables characterizing centers and their market areas are as listed below. In performing the analysis, the common logarithm was taken of all variables except the first. The procedure ensured that the relationships between variables were linear in character, and that the scatters of observations around the best-fitting linear relationships were consistent along the line (that is, the transformations satisfied the conditions of linearity and homoscedasticity).

1. *Functions.* Number of different Standard Industrial Classification four-digit types of business found in the center.

2. *Establishments.* Number of distinct retail establishments (stores) in the center.

3. *Total center area.* Total site area of a planned center; total area within defined land value boundaries for an unplanned center.

4. *Shopping center area.* Total area minus parking for a planned center; total area minus streets and alleys but including off-street parking for unplanned centers.

5. *Ground floor area.* Ground floor area of business establishments in center.

6. *Population of trade area.* Total population residing within the intensive trade area of the center.

7. *Area of trade area.* Intensive trade area in square miles.

8. *Median income.* Median income level of the market area as reported in 1960 census.

9. *Social class.* Factor score for the market area on the first dimension of a factor

analysis of census-reported socio-economic data for the market area.[10]

10. *Family class.* Factor scores on a second dimension of social and economic structure.[11]

11. *Total competition.* Total number of establishments located in the market area, excluding the center itself.

12. *Planned competition.* That part of 11 located in planned centers.

13. *Unplanned competition.* Likewise, in unplanned centers.

14. *Ribbon competition.* Likewise, ribbon retail development.

15. *Discount competition.* Likewise, discount shopping centers.

16. *Population density.* $d = [6/7]$.

Underlying Patterns: Unplanned Centers

Table 1 provides the factor analytic results for unplanned centers. A four-factor solution representing independent, additive components of the variance embraced 90 percent of the common variance.

Factor 1 in Table 1 is clearly a statement of size differences among centers: numbers of functions, of establishments, space consumption, and size of center are collinear. Moreover, the larger the center, the larger is the area of its trade area, the greater the population resident in the area, and the greater the total center competition, both planned and unplanned. The statements are consistent with the theory that postulates a hierarchy of unplanned business centers within the city.[12] Because of the collinearity, it is possible to construct nomographs such as Figure 1 expressing the commonality of the scales.[13]

Factor 2 relates unplanned centers to the population geography of the metropolis. As densities increase, so does the population of the trade area served and the space requirements of the center. Also, total competition is greater at higher densities, largely because of increased business activity in the ribbons.

Factor 3 says that as socio-economic class increases (that is, in higher-income communities), the area of the trade area diminishes and there is little discounting competition; conversely, discounting competition increases, the lower the income level of the communities served.

Factor 4 relates planned center competition to family structure. In communities characterized by larger families, single family homes, relatively little participation of females in the labor force, etc.—that is, in the newer suburbs —planned center competition is less than in areas with older, smaller families. This is apparently at variance with our ideas of planned centers in the suburbs and results from the star-shaped pattern of the built-up area of Metropolitan Chicago. The new, large, planned centers are located as close as possible to the city center, in the interstices between the older railroad-oriented fingers of development. From these locations they not only serve the interstices themselves, but large markets

---

10 Factor analysis of the many census variables recorded for census tracts within cities shows that these variables consistently degenerate to just three basic dimensions of variation, called social rank, family structure, and segregation. See Berry and Tennant, *op. cit.,* Appendix A. Social rank is composed of a highly correlated cluster of variables describing incomes, education, occupation, value of housing, etc. It has also been called "economic attainment."

11 Family structure is a dimension based on family size and age structure, participation of women in the labor force, and the like. It has also been called the "familism–urbanism" scale.

12 Berry, *op. cit.*

13 Figure 1 is drawn from Berry, *op. cit.*

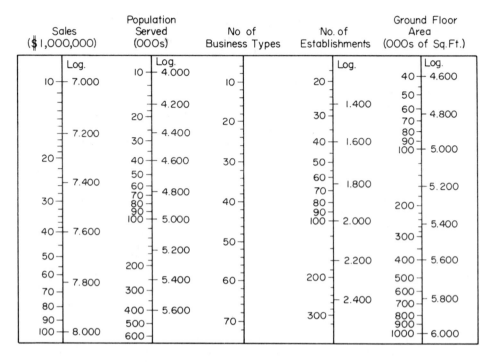

Centers Serving Higher Income Communities. Nomograph illustrating the interdependency of variables descriptive of unplanned business centers serving the higher income communities of the City of Chicago. To use, place a straight edge horizontally across the page and read the expected sales (1958 dollars), population of market area, number of different kinds of business provided, number of establishments, and ground floor area for any desired size of center.

in the older, innermost parts of adjacent pairs of radiating railroad axes.

Underlying Patterns: Planned Centers

Factor 1 in Table 2 also indexes the hierarchy of centers. However, consistently with factors 2 and 4 of Table 1, it says not only that larger planned centers have more functions and establishments, greater space requirements, and serve greater numbers of people in larger trade areas in which there is substantial competition; but also that the market areas are larger where families are older and smaller and where ribbon competition is greater in the

inner radial axes. Note also that competition from other centers comes only from the unplanned, which contrasts with the competition confronting the unplanned centers themselves. This again results from the star-shaped geography of the metropolitan area, for interstitial location protects the planned centers from each other. Their only competition is from unplanned centers in the older radials. However, unplanned centers compete not only with other unplanned centers in their radial sectors, but with planned centers in the interstices on either side.

The other three factors in Table 2 are less interesting. Factor 2 picks out a special relationship of the size of center to discounting competition, caused by the fact that discounters have not yet entered the market areas of all centers. Factor 3 simply restates the relationship of social class to income levels. Finally, factor 4 isolates the few instances where planned centers face competition from other planned centers—in the areas of lowest population density, at the periphery of the metropolitan area.

Contrasts

Apart from differences in location of planned and unplanned centers relative to the socio-economic geography of the metropolitan area, the factor structures are the same. In both cases the most critical dimension of differentiation of centers is that of size (that is, of position in the hierarchy of centers) and this may be indexed by any one of a battery of collinear variables characterizing either the center's size, the numbers and kinds of functions it performs, or the size of the market area it serves. However, although the factor structures are the same, the levels and slopes of relations among the variables differ markedly between planned and unplanned centers. Let the 16 variables listed above be represented by the following letters: F, E, T, S, G, P, A, Y, C_S, C_F, I, J, K, L, d. Then for unplanned centers:

$$E = 1.154 + 0.016F \qquad r^2 = 0.96 \qquad (7)$$

$$T = 3.946 + 0.855E \qquad r^2 = 0.91 \qquad (8)$$

$$S = 3.619 + 0.922E \qquad r^2 = 0.88 \qquad (9)$$

$$G = 3.374 + 0.968E \qquad r^2 = 0.87 \qquad (10)$$

and for planned centers:

$$E = 0.800 + 0.028F \qquad r^2 = 0.82 \qquad (11)$$

$$T = 4.385 + 1.027E \qquad r^2 = 0.79 \qquad (12)$$

$$S = 4.287 + 0.836E \qquad r^2 = 0.67 \qquad (13)$$

$$G = 4.025 + 0.823E \qquad r^2 = 0.69 \qquad (14)$$

Apparently the fits were closer when the individual decision-making unit was the small businessman and centers were made up of many such units in summation [equations (7)–(10)]. Increasing scale has meant a retreat from, or an additional source of variance grafted upon, the more traditional competitive equilibrium [equations (11)–(14)]. Note how the differences in parameters in the two sets of equations are consistent with the known scale shift and the reduction of intra-center competition in the planned case.[14] Use of the ecological units rather than areal observations is thus a step which enables reproduction of known properties of centers. Moreover, in contrast to areal units, the expressions may be transferred from one area to another, for the results appear to have some generality. For example, for the few planned centers within the City of Chicago:

$$E = 0.843 + 0.026F \qquad r^2 = 0.90 \qquad (15)$$

which does not differ significantly from equation (11), even though it covers only a small portion of size range of centers covered by equations (11)–(15).

Calibration of the Model

The object of the models being used for illustrative purposes in this paper is

---

[14] James W. Simmons, *The Changing Pattern of Retail Location* (Chicago: University of Chicago, Department of Geography, Research Paper No. 96, 1964).

either to facilitate renewal treatment of commercial blight or to aid in anticipating the space demands accompanying new retail growth. Model construction was based fundamentally on the concept of consumer-orientation and avoided problems of modifiable units by using centers and market areas as the units of observation. Hence, retail changes were to be determined by prior changes in population distribution and characteristics. Factor analysis suggested that functions of centers and space demands were collinear with size and population of market area served, and hence with position of centers in the hierarchy (factor 1 in both Tables 1 and 2). In the case of unplanned centers, space demands showed an additional independent pattern of covariance with population densities (factor 2, Table 1). Also, for unplanned centers the size of market area varies with socioeconomic class (factor 3, Table 1), whereas planned centers show space demands correlated with family structure (factor 1, Table 2). Thus the basic model fitted each of a series of dependent variables as a function of the following market area characteristics: population of market area P; population density d; social class C_S; and family class C_F. All of these variables were not expected to be significant in every case, but they spanned the important independent factors revealed by the prior use of factor analysis. Least squares fits using multiple regression analysis produced the parameters outlined in Table 3 for the metropolitan area of Northeastern Illinois. Separate estimates of parameters were made for the unplanned and for the planned centers not only because of the technological differences between them, but also because the set of equations for unplanned centers was needed for use in predicting reductions in the space demands in older communities in the metropolitan area, whereas equations for planned centers were essential under conditions of growth as the metropolis continues to expand.

To use the models requires that population predictions be available on a small area basis, and that some estimates of market areas have been made. Presumably, in dealing with incremental growth and marginal decline, the latter are based upon modifications of the present market area map (a complete map is available for the City of Chicago and Northeastern Illinois). Entry of population, density, etc., into the relevant model will then provide an estimate of the desired property—for example, space demands. Comparison of this figure with present capacity indicates growth requirements or potential decline.

TABLE 3
Parameters of Models Describing Retail Relationships for Centers in Northeastern Illinois

Dependent Variable	Independent Variables Regression Coefficient and Errors for				Intercept	R^2	Type of Center
	P	d	C_S	C_F			
Establishments	0.655 (0.074)	−0.600 (0.089)	0.185 (0.046)	0.093 (0.040)	1.107	.93	Unplanned
Establishments	1.083 (0.239)	−0.303 (0.238)	0.113 (0.082)	−0.025 (0.095)	−2.657	.74	Planned
Total area	0.645 (0.075)	−0.418 (0.091)	0.086 (0.046)	0.068 (0.040)	4.130	.90	Unplanned
Total area	1.000 (0.223)	−0.584 (0.223)	0.127 (0.077)	0.154 (0.089)	3.265	.83	Planned
Shopping center area	0.728 (0.081)	−0.421 (0.097)	0.068 (0.043)	0.071 (0.050)	3.574	.91	Unplanned
Shopping center area	0.777 (0.204)	−0.436 (0.203)	0.058 (0.070)	0.184 (0.081)	3.406	.82	Planned
Ground floor area	0.734 (0.072)	−0.379 (0.087)	0.100 (0.044)	0.040 (0.038)	3.238	.83	Unplanned
Ground floor area	0.745 (0.192)	−0.378 (0.191)	0.077 (0.066)	0.193 (0.076)	3.094	.83	Planned
Total establishments in market area	1.294 (0.111)	0.193 (0.135)	−0.048 (0.069)	0.035 (0.060)	−3.981	.96	Unplanned
Total establishments in market area	0.922 (0.114)	−0.291 (0.114)	0.005 (0.039)	0.235 (0.045)	−0.424	.96	Planned

The Dynamics of Commercial Structure in Central City Areas

George H. Haines, Jr., Leonard S. Simon, and Marcus Alexis

The problem of "adequate" retail shopping alternatives for residents of inner cities has been a major topic in the literature.[1] The term "adequate" is open to subjective interpretation because one would consider not only the physical presence of stores, but also their cleanliness, merchandise assortments, personnel, and so on. It would, therefore, be very difficult to attempt to study all aspects of "adequate" for all types of stores in an inner city environment.

Researchers have reported that many consumers do their principal shopping well outside their neighborhoods. Such out-of-neighborhood shopping requires a particular outlook on the part of the individual and the means (method of transportation) to travel to the out-of-neighborhood shopping areas. Studies have shown that fewer inner city families own cars than those residing in other areas. For example, Alexis, Simon, and Smith found that only 43% of the families with incomes under $5,000 owned automobiles as contrasted to 95.6% for those with incomes over $5,000.[2] Thus, an inner city resident appears to be more confined to shopping in his own neighborhood than an individual living in the suburbs. Therefore, the alternative choices, or the store mix, confronting the consumer in a neighborhood becomes an important vehicle for assessing his ability to satisfy his shopping needs in the given area. If certain types of stores are not available, then no neighborhood shopping satisfaction can be achieved; similarly, the implications on shopping efficiency of a very limited number of alternatives or of unusual birth or death rates for particular types of stores are substantial. To illustrate, a highly dynamic commercial structure imposes a greater cost on the consumer in terms of information collection and evaluation. This study examines four central city neighborhoods and evaluates whether

Reprinted from the *Journal of Marketing*, Vol. 35, April 1971, published by the American Marketing Association, by permission of the authors and editor.

1 William E. Cox, Jr., "Business Opportunities in the Inner City," paper presented at the American Marketing Association Conference on Inner City Marketing, Buffalo, N.Y., June, 1970.

2 Marcus Alexis, Leonard S. Simon, and Kenneth M. Smith, "Some Determinants of Food Buying Behavior," *Empirical Foundations of Marketing: Research Findings in the Behavioral and Applied Sciences,* Marcus Alexis, Robert J. Holloway, and Robert S. Hancock (eds.) (Chicago: Markham, 1969).

the inner city consumer must select from a different store mix than other city residents.

Research Design

Data for this study were collected in Rochester, New York. The reason for selecting this city was convenience. In addition, two of the present authors had previously examined the question of price levels in inner city stores as contrasted to other outlets throughout the Rochester metropolitan area.[3] Some of the special characteristics which made this area an especially interesting laboratory were cited in that earlier work. Thus, by using Rochester again, the advantage of knowing much about the research area permitted some definite improvements in the experimental design.

Two inner city neighborhoods and two others referred to as central city neighborhoods were chosen for purposes of comparison in the present analysis. Cox describes a neighborhood as being a section of an urban area that is predominantly residential in terms of land use and located between the central business district and surrounding suburban communities.[4] For the objectives of this study inner city neighborhoods can be distinguished from central city neighborhoods on several dimensions. Inner city neighborhoods are characterized by lower quality housing, higher density units, and a lower incidence of home owner-ship. They exhibit a lower reported median income and have relatively higher unemployment rate. Additionally, residents of inner city neighborhoods have a higher proportion of lower social class occupations. The following four neighborhoods located within the city limits of Rochester were used for the study:

Maplewood—Almost completely white; many single and two-family dwellings; lower-middle few families with children; predominantly single and two-family dwellings; lower-middle class outlook.

19th Ward—Very mixed; black home-owning families penetrating one border; almost all families, many with grown children; economically solid middle class. Single and two-family houses.

Third Ward—About 60% black and definitely in transition; mostly families but some singles; primarily one, two, and three story housing; economically, lower middle and upper lower class; definitely a slight step up from the worst ghettos in the city.

West Half of Model Cities—Named for urban renewal project; heaviest concentration of blacks in city; traditional ghetto for all types of backgrounds; deteriorated housing; economically, contains many of the very poor and those on relief; many multi-unit dwellings and some high rises; mixture of families and single persons. This area includes the section of Joseph Avenue which was severely damaged in the riots in Rochester in 1964.[5]

---

3 Results of this earlier study are reported in Marcus Alexis and Leonard S. Simon, "The Food Marketing Commission and Prices Paid by Income Groups," *Journal of Farm Economics*, Vol. 49 (May, 1967), pp. 436–446, and in Alexis, Simon and Smith, same reference as footnote 2.

4 William E. Cox, Jr., "A Commercial Structure Model for Depressed Neighborhoods," *Journal of Marketing*, Vol. 33 (July, 1969), pp. 1–9.

5 This area was one of seven studied by Rosenthall in 1967; Richard Rosenthall, "After the Riots—A Position Paper for Retailing," *Stores* (December, 1967), pp. 11–20.

The last two areas are inner city neighborhoods, while Maplewood and 19th Ward are considered central city neighborhoods; they were selected for purposes of contrast. The Third and Nineteenth Wards share a major shopping artery. The stores on this common street were included in the commercial structure for both areas since a consumer residing in either area would view these stores as realistic alternatives available in his own neighborhood.

A census of all retail stores and service facilities (except gasoline stations) was taken in each area. In addition, a 1967 study of land and building use by the Planning Bureau of the City of Rochester was also available. Thus, store turnover by type during this two-year period (1967–1969) could be identified by noting the stores which had either ceased to exist or had been newly opened.

Because of the difficulties of collecting data in inner city neighborhoods, a new approach to obtaining data was developed. In conjunction with the Urban League of Rochester, a team of black high school students, interested in a summer learning and work experience, was formed in the spring of 1969. This team collected the census data during the spring of 1969. The problems and benefits of using this particular approach to data collection are discussed elsewhere.[6]

Every block of every street in the four neighborhoods was canvassed. Student interviewers were instructed to record the names, addresses, and types of business at every retail store location. If doubts arose in regard to the type of enterprise, the interviewers were asked to record as much information as possible about the nature of the operation, so that a subsequent judgment could be made; for example, a problem such as this might occur when an establishment sold at both wholesale and retail. In cases where the 1967 City Planning Bureau study showed the existence of an establishment, but none could be located, the data were double-checked by sending a supervisor to inspect the site. Reported changes in the type of retail enterprise were accepted at face value after a random spot check if completed interview records found no errors in the recording of these data.

Commercial structures are defined as the retail and service stores of a neighborhood.[7] The categorization system for retail and service stores used by Cox is also used in this article to permit comparison of data. In this system, for example, "Total Service Stores" include auto repair, parking, washing, furniture and upholstery repair stores, electrical repair, and so on, as opposed to barber and beauty shops, dry cleaning establishments, and shoe repair type "Service Stores."

Questions to Be Studied

The following principal questions were investigated with the collected data:

1. How different, if at all, is the commercial structure of inner city neighborhoods from that of the control neighborhoods?
2. Have there been significant changes in makeup within any one of the four neighborhoods from 1967 to 1969?
3. Which types of retail enterprises appear to be the most stable and which the least?

[6] Marcus Alexis, George H. Haines, Jr., and Leonard S. Simon, "Collecting Market Research Data in the Inner City Environment," working paper, University of Rochester, College of Business Administration, Rochester, N.Y.
[7] Same reference as footnote 4.

4. How do the inner city neighborhoods studied compare with the reported structure of other inner city marketplaces in the United States?

The fourth question required the availability of other data similar to the authors'. Fortunately, such data were available from the works of Cox and Andreasen.[8]

Methodology

The basic tool employed in answering the above questions is a test for a significant difference between or among multinomial distributions. Each of the general categories of store types is considered as one outcome on a multinomial distribution, and comparisons are then made through time or across neighborhoods or cities.[9] The test procedure gives a Chi-square value, along with the degrees of freedom associated with Chi-square, which is used to test the null hypothesis of no significant differences between the observed multinomial distributions. This test procedure can be used for quite small samples giving a distinct advantage over a contingency table Chi-square test in a situation containing "cell" sizes of less than five. However, this test cannot be used if the estimate of the overall proportion in a category is zero, which is the case if all observations across samples in a category are zero or one.[10] A BASIC program to perform the computations is available from the authors upon request.

The Data

Tables 1 through 4 present the relevant data for each of the four neighborhoods. The first column in each table records stores by type which existed according to the 1967 City Planning Bureau study, but which could not be found in 1969. The second column shows stores which were found in the 1969 study, but which were not reported in the 1967 study. The third column gives stores which appeared in both studies. If the type of store at a particular site changed, it would show up in both the first and second columns, but if the type remained the same and ownership or management changed, the store would appear in the third column only. The fourth column provides the proportion of all stores present in either 1967 or 1969 which appeared in both 1967 and 1969. Neither the 1967 study nor the present one collected adequate information on ownership or management to identify turnover on these factors. The fifth column is the sum of columns 1 and 3, and the sixth column is the sum of columns 2 and 3. The fifth and sixth columns represent the overall store composition of each neighborhood at two different periods in time.

Results

The first test compared the commerical structure of the four areas at the two different points in time—1967 and 1969. Using the multinomial test for

8 Same reference as footnote 4 and Alan R. Andreasen, "A Study of Inner City Business in Buffalo, New York," working paper, School of Management, State University of New York at Buffalo, N.Y., January, 1970.

9 Harold Freeman, *Introduction to Statistical Inference* (Reading, Mass.: Addison-Wesley, 1963), Ch. 14.

10 Richard F. Potthoff and Maurice Whittinghill, "Testing for Homogeneity: I. The Binomial and Multinomial Distributions," *Biometrika,* Vol. 53 (1966), pp. 167–182.

TABLE 1
Commercial Structure of Maplewood

Store Type	Stores Existing in 1967 but Not 1969	Stores Existing in 1969 but Not 1967	Stores Appearing in Both 1967 and 1969	Proportion of Stores Appearing in Both 1967 and 1969	1967 Commercial Structure	1969 Commercial Structure
Food stores	11	7	30	62.5%	41	37
Eating and drinking establishments	7	22	35	54.7	42	57
Prescription drug and proprietary stores	1	1	7	77.8	8	8
Automobile group stores—dealers, parts stores, etc.	0	3	5	62.5	5	8
Lumber, building materials, hardware stores	5	8	9	40.9	14	17
Service stores—barber and beauty shops, dry cleaning, shoe repair, etc.	21	38	49	45.2	70	87
General merchandise stores	2	1	1	25.0	3	2
Apparel group stores	5	11	3	15.8	8	14
Furniture and appliance stores	4	10	8	36.4	12	18
Secondhand stores	0	0	1	100.0	1	1
Other retail stores	16	19	13	27.1	29	32
Total service stores—auto repair, parking, electrical repair, etc.	4	5	5	35.7	9	10
Total stores	76	125	166	—	242	291

TABLE 2
Commercial Structure of 19th Ward

Store Type	Stores Existing in 1967 but Not 1969	Stores Existing in 1969 but Not 1967	Stores Appearing in Both 1967 and 1969	Proportion of Stores Appearing in Both 1967 and 1969	1967 Commercial Structure	1969 Commercial Structure
Food stores	9	6	30	66.7%	39	36
Eating and drinking establishments	7	9	32	66.7	39	41
Prescription drug and proprietary stores	1	2	6	66.7	7	8
Automobile group stores—dealers, parts stores, etc.	2	2	0	0.0	2	2
Lumber, building materials, hardware stores	1	5	3	33.3	4	8
Service stores—barber and beauty shops, dry cleaning, shoe repair, etc.	22	27	44	47.3	66	71
General merchandise stores	0	1	2	66.7	2	3
Apparel group stores	2	2	7	63.6	9	9
Furniture and appliance stores	1	1	8	80.0	9	9
Secondhand stores	2	1	0	0.0	2	1
Other retail stores	3	10	13	50.0	16	23
Total service stores—auto repair, parking, electrical repair, etc.	4	1	2	28.6	6	3
Total stores	54	67	147	—	201	214

TABLE 3
Commercial Structure of 3rd Ward

Store Type	Stores Existing in 1967 but Not 1969	Stores Existing in 1969 but Not 1967	Stores Appearing in Both 1967 and 1969	Proportion of Stores Appearing in Both 1967 and 1969	1967 Commercial Structure	1969 Commercial Structure
Food stores	18	7	43	63.2%	61	50
Eating and drinking establishments	14	23	48	56.5	62	71
Prescription drug and proprietary stores	0	0	6	100.0	6	6
Automobile group stores—dealers, parts stores, etc.	1	6	0	0.0	1	6
Lumber, building materials, hardware stores	3	3	6	50.0	9	9
Service stores—barber and beauty shops, dry cleaning, shoe repair, etc.	39	19	38	39.6	77	57
General merchandise stores	0	1	4	80.0	4	5
Apparel group stores	3	4	5	41.7	8	9
Furniture and appliance stores	4	4	4	33.3	8	8
Secondhand stores	5	1	1	14.3	6	2
Other retail stores	6	10	14	46.7	20	24
Total service stores—auto repair, parking, electrical repair, etc.	6	7	2	13.3	8	9
Total stores	99	85	171	—	270	256

TABLE 4
Commercial Structure of Model Cities

Store Type	Stores Existing in 1967 but Not 1969	Stores Existing in 1969 but Not 1967	Stores Appearing in Both 1967 and 1969	Proportion of Stores Appearing in Both 1967 and 1969	1967 Commercial Structure	1969 Commercial Structure
Food stores	25	20	47	51.1%	72	67
Eating and drinking establishments	22	21	37	46.3	59	58
Prescription drug and proprietary stores	0	0	6	100.0	6	6
Automobile group stores—dealers, parts stores, etc.	0	0	6	100.0	6	6
Lumber, building materials, hardware stores	7	6	10	43.5	17	16
Service stores—barber and beauty shops, dry cleaning, shoe repair, etc.	31	9	28	41.2	59	37
General merchandise stores	3	1	2	33.3	5	3
Apparel group stores	11	3	11	44.0	22	14
Furniture and appliance stores	3	4	11	61.1	14	15
Secondhand stores	7	1	3	27.3	10	4
Other retail stores	15	2	15	46.9	30	17
Total service stores—auto repair, parking, electrical repair, etc.	8	0	10	55.6	18	10
Total stores	132	67	186	—	318	253

homogeneity described above, it was found that the null hypothesis of homogeneity could not be rejected (at α = .05) in 1967. However, this was not the case for 1969; here the null hypothesis of homogeneity was rejected (at α = .05). The test results are: 1967 — χ^2 = 42.5283, 36.97 degrees of freedom; 1969 — χ^2 = 52.9949, 37.5863 degrees of freedom. Thus, the answer to the first question is that in 1967 there was no difference in the commercial structure of the four neighborhoods, but in 1969 significant differences in commercial structure did appear.

One way to identify the factors which might have produced this result is to examine the estimated probability of a store of a specific kind occuring in any one of the four areas. This overall probability can be compared to the pro-portion of stores of a given type found in each neighborhood. The estimated probability of each existence of a specific type of store over all neighborhoods is given in column 1 of Table 5. These estimates are derived on the minimum Chi-squared parameter estimation procedure and are computed as part of the homogeneity testing procedure.[11] The actual proportions for each neighborhood are found in columns 2 through 5 of Table 5. When the estimated probabilities of existence are compared to the observed proportions in each neighborhood it can be seen that the major discrepancies occur in food and service stores. In the case of food stores, Maplewood has 12.7% food stores and Model Cities 26.5% as compared to an expected proportion of 19.0%. For service stores, Maplewood

TABLE 5
Estimated Probability of the Existence of a Specific Store in Any Neighborhood Compared to Actual Proportions in 1969

Store Type	Estimated Probability of Existence in Any Neighborhood	Proportion in Maplewood	Proportion in 19th Ward	Proportion in Third Ward	Proportion in Model Cities
Food	.190	12.7	16.8	19.5	26.5
Eating and drinking	.223	19.6	19.1	27.8	22.9
Prescription drug and proprietary	.025	2.7	3.7	2.3	2.4
Automobile group	.021	2.7	0.9	2.3	2.4
Lumber, building materials, hardware	.049	5.8	3.7	3.5	6.3
Service	.254	30.0	33.2	22.2	14.6
General merchandise	.011	0.7	1.4	2.0	1.2
Apparel group	.044	4.8	4.2	3.1	5.5
Furniture and appliance	.049	6.2	4.2	3.1	5.9
Secondhand	.007	0.3	0.5	0.8	1.6
Other retail	.094	11.0	10.7	9.4	6.7
Total service	.031	3.4	1.4	3.5	3.9

[11] Same reference as footnote 10.

has 30.0%, 19th Ward 33.2%, and Model Cities 14.6%, compared to an expected proportion of 25.4%. Possible causes for these differences are discussed below.

A second approach is to test if there are significant differences in the commercial structures within each of the four neighborhoods between 1967 and 1969. In these separate examinations, there was not one instance of a significant difference between the 1967 and 1969 commercial structures using an alpha level of .05. Thus, no significant changes were found in the overall commercial structure within any of the four neighborhoods from 1967 to 1969.

How can this result be reconciled with the preceding one which showed that by 1969 the neighborhood commercial structure could no longer be considered homogeneous across neighborhoods? The answer to this question should lie in an examination of the births and deaths of establishments in the areas, as well as the structure of those stable stores which existed in both 1967 and 1969. These are the three factors which determine the 1969 commercial structure from that which existed in 1967. Although any one neighborhood did not change sufficiently to cause a statistically significant difference in structure for the neighborhood over time, systematic changes within all neighborhoods compared to each other were sufficient to cause a significant difference between the neighborhoods in 1969.

The distribution of stable stores across the four areas was tested, and the null hypothesis of homogeneity could not be rejected using an alpha level of .05. This finding was expected given the preceding finding of no significant differences in overall commercial structure of the four neighborhoods. Next, the distribution of births by store type for all four neighborhoods was compared, and a similar comparison was made of deaths. Births are stores found in 1969 which were missing from 1967 data, and deaths are the opposite. The null hypothesis of homogeneity was not rejected in the case of deaths, but was rejected in the case of births. Based on an alpha level of .05 the test results are: Deaths — $\chi^2 = 23.1995$, 24.06 degrees of freedom; births — $\chi^2 = 46.8822$, 22.886 degrees of freedom. The death test was based on 11 categories because the overall probability of death of a drug and proprietary store was zero. The birth test was based on 10 categories because the overall probability of birth of a second-hand or general merchandise store was zero. Thus, the results indicate the proximate cause of the lack of homogeneity in the commercial structures of the four neighborhoods was a lack of homogeneity in entry (by store category) of new stores in the four areas. The estimated probabilities of finding a new store entrant of a particular type in each of the four neighborhoods, if entry likelihood was homogeneous, are compared to the actual proportions of entry in Table 6.

There was no entry at all in the prescription drug and proprietary store category in either of the inner city areas. Similarly, both these areas had a lower than expected proportion of entry in the service category. In contrast, both these areas had a higher proportion of entry in the eating and drinking establishment category. The poorer of the two inner city areas, Model Cities, had a much higher entry in food stores, and also in lumber, building materials, hardware, and a much lower entry in other retail stores and total service stores. Nineteenth Ward and Maplewood had a much higher than expected proportion of entry in service stores; in fact, the con-

TABLE 6
Store Births 1967–1969

Store Type	Expected Proportion of All Neighborhoods	Maple-wood	Nine-teenth Ward	Third Ward	Model Cities
Food	12.2	5.6	9.0	8.2	29.8
Eating and drinking	21.0	17.6	13.4	27.1	31.4
Prescription drug and proprietary	0.7	0.8	3.0	0.0	0.0
Automobile group	3.3	2.4	3.0	7.1	0.0
Lumber, building materials, hardware	5.8	6.4	7.5	3.5	9.0
Service	27.6	30.4	40.4	22.4	13.5
General merchandise	0.0	0.8	1.5	1.2	1.5
Apparel group	6.3	8.8	3.0	4.7	4.5
Furniture and appliance	5.9	8.0	1.5	4.7	6.0
Secondhand	0.0	0.0	1.5	1.2	1.5
Other retail	12.6	15.2	14.9	12.0	3.0
Total service	4.3	4.0	1.5	8.2	0.0

centration of entry in the Nineteenth Ward in the service-store category is a remarkable 40.4%!

Which types of retail enterprises appear to be the most stable? This question can be answered by the data in Tables 1 through 4 and by comparing the overall expected proportion of deaths given in Table 7 with the overall birth proportion data in Table 6.

Utilizing these data, the stability question can be addressed in two ways: (1) Stability over time within a store category, and (2) stability in terms of entry and exit of stores from a neighborhood commercial structure as measured by columns 1 and 2 of Tables 1 through 4. The two are not always the same, although they can be. Prescription drug and proprietary stores are clearly very stable on both measures. However, food stores are quite stable in terms of over time within a category measure (this is the figure in column 4 of Tables 1 through 4), but yet represent a store category with the second

TABLE 7
Store Deaths 1967–1969
Expected Proportion Over All Neighborhoods

Store Type	Overall Expected Proportion
Food	17.6
Eating and drinking	14.4
Prescription drug and proprietary	0.0
Automobile group	.8
Lumber, building materials, hardware	4.4
Service	30.6
General merchandise	1.5
Apparel group	6.3
Furniture and appliance	2.9
Secondhand	4.6
Other retail	11.8
Total service	5.6

highest death proportion and a very high entry proportion at least in the poorest neighborhood. On the other end of the scale, other retail and service stores not only have a relatively high birth and death proportion figure, but also a relatively high turnover figure, while total service stores have a high turnover figure but a low birth and death rate as a proportion of all stores.

Data from two other inner city areas were used to compare structure across cities. The Cox data for the Hough area of Cleveland were compared with each of the inner city neighborhoods in the present study.[12] However, gasoline stations were deleted from the Cox data before testing for homogeneity, as the data herein excluded gasoline stations. Since the Cox data were collected in 1968, it was not possible to make precise comparisons from a time standpoint. Therefore, the Cox data were tested against each of the present inner city neighborhood data for both 1967 and 1969. In all four comparisons the null hypothesis of no difference could not be rejected at the .05 level.

The test results were:

$$\chi^2 = 5.4551, 13.16 \text{ degrees of freedom,} \\ 1969 \text{ Third Ward}$$

$$\chi^2 = 3.1500, 12.01 \text{ degrees of freedom,} \\ 1967 \text{ Third Ward}$$

$$\chi^2 = 9.1779, 13.47 \text{ degrees of freedom,} \\ 1969 \text{ Model Cities}$$

$$\chi^2 = 5.4551, 13.16 \text{ degrees of freedom,} \\ 1967 \text{ Model Cities}$$

The 1967 Third Ward comparison is based on 11 categories, as in this case an expected overall zero proportion of automobile group stores occurs.

Andreasen's data on the inner city of Buffalo were collected in 1969 so that a comparison of Model Cities and Third Ward individually for 1969 only is made to Buffalo.[13] The Buffalo comparisons were for only 11 categories, since the number of gasoline stations

could not be separated out of one of Andreasen's classifications to make all 12 categories directly comparable with the Rochester area. Again, the null hypothesis of no difference could not be rejected at the .05 level. The results are:

$$\chi^2 = 15.8465, 11.01 \text{ degrees of freedom,} \\ \text{Model Cities and}$$

$$\chi^2 = 16.533, 11.08 \text{ degrees of freedom,} \\ \text{Third Ward.}$$

Since the assumption of homogeneity for Model Cities and Third Ward was rejected in 1969, Buffalo's store mix must lie somewhere between these two. Finally, Buffalo was compared to Hough, and again the null hypothesis could not be rejected. Interestingly, an empirical χ^2 equal to zero was obtained; i.e., there was absolutely no observable difference between the commercial structure in the two cities (the data include all 12 categories of stores).

These findings lend support to the hypothesis that the retail store structure for people purchasing in inner city neighborhoods is about the same despite differences which might arise from city to city due to economic climate, cultural outlook, and racial mix.

Discussion and Conclusions

The commercial structure of a neighborhood was found to be an appropriate means of evaluating the alternative shopping choices available to the consumer, especially to those living in the inner city. A method of analyzing and comparing the commercial structure of central city neighborhoods was developed and applied to four neighbor-

---

12 Same reference as footnote 4.
13 Andreasen, same reference as footnote 8.

hoods in the Rochester metropolitan area—Maplewood, 19th Ward, Third Ward, and Model Cities. The results of this analysis indicate that the commercial structure of inner city neighborhoods is changing relative to that of other city neighborhoods due to the differential entry in store categories. Several hypotheses which have significant policy implications for inner city shopping alternatives may be drawn from these differences.

First, the higher birth rate of food stores in Model Cities may reflect entrepreneurial beliefs that the needs of this commodity are not being adequately met within the existing commercial structure. This perceived need could result from the lack of large supermarkets in Model Cities relative to the Third Ward,[14] yet small grocery stores are hardly an adequate substitute if this is the case. There are several supermarkets a few blocks outside the Model Cities neighborhood accessible only to a very limited number of Model Cities residents without cars. These are not included in the analysis. Or, alternatively, the higher birth rate could be due to the lower entry costs (e.g., inventory) of getting into food retailing. For example, it is a practice of many wholesalers to finance a significant portion of the inventory after the initial stocking is completed. A combination of the two effects may exist since the birth rate of service stores in the 19th Ward is high (and service stores also require less capital), perhaps reflecting a different set of entrepreneurial perceptions.

Second, the probability of a store in the drug and proprietary class opening in either Model Cities or the Third Ward is zero. This is a particularly

interesting finding because there is concern about the limited number of food store chains in the inner city. Yet no one has examined the same question with respect to drug and proprietary chains. If there are increasing numbers of poor whose health needs are now being better met by Medicare and similar programs, there may be a market opportunity here. On the other hand, the expected death rate in this group is also zero so that the number of alternatives available to the consumer has not diminished either.

Third, neighborhoods appear to change so gradually that more than two years are needed to establish trends in store composition; recall that in comparing 1967 commercial structure with 1969 in each of the four neighborhoods a significant difference could not be established. Such gradual changes make the job of planning for revitalization of inner city neighborhoods more difficult.

Fourth, there is a marked similarity in the commercial structure of inner city neighborhoods across three major cities despite their apparently different economic and cultural environments. Therefore, policy questions focusing on improvement of the inner city commercial structure could be studied at wider levels than city or county government and applied more broadly.

The number of stores is only a partial indicator of the range and quality of retail services available in any given district. Size, illumination, cleanliness, use of special displays, store hours, racial character of operating personnel, and other operating characteristics are also relevant factors, but a discussion of such additional factors in-

[14] Marcus Alexis, George H. Haines, Jr., and Leonard S. Simon, "The Character of Food Stores in Four Central City Neighborhoods," working paper #7013, Graduate School of Management, University of Rochester, Rochester, N.Y.

fluencing store choice is beyond the scope of this article. These other factors, moreover, are conditional upon the group of stores from which the consumer can choose. The type of analysis presented above is a prerequisite to the effect of these other factors.

A Commercial Structure Model for Depressed Neighborhoods

William E. Cox, Jr.

A large body of theory and empirical evidence demonstrates that a spatially distributed population has predictable requirements for consumer goods and services, resulting in a systematic distribution of retail and service establishments to serve the population.[1] In this paper, existing theory and empirical data are employed to develop a model for determining buying power and commercial structure in the depressed neighborhoods of urban areas.

Many marketing academicians and practitioners have been searching for ways in which they can employ their professional skill to help the urban poor, to assist the "black capitalism" movement, and to reconstruct the depressed neighborhoods of our cities. A commercial structure model provides a basis for assistance in urban problems that are dependent upon marketing expertise. The model has been developed as a result of more than three years of work with several neighborhood development organizations in Cleveland, Ohio. It is designed to encompass published information about Cleveland and other cities of 50,000

population or more, but readily lends itself to the substitution of survey data for published information and to adaptation to reflect neighborhood differences. The model is valid for the Cleveland neighborhoods in which it has been tested, in spite of its relatively crude and simple character. More sophisticated versions of the model have been and will continue to be tested, but the results to date suggest that the model presented here is preferred on a comparative cost/benefit basis.

Four neighborhoods were selected in Cleveland as areas for study. Two of the neighborhoods (Hough and Cedar–Central) are severely depressed; a third neighborhood (Glenville) is moderately depressed and showing signs of becoming severely so; the fourth neighborhood (Mt. Pleasant) is beginning to decline and might be termed slightly depressed. Neighborhoods are considered to be those sections of urban areas that are predominantly residential in terms of land use and are located between the central business district and surrounding suburban communities. These neighborhoods are characterized

Reprinted from the *Journal of Marketing*, Vol. 33, July 1969, published by the American Marketing Association, by permission of the author and editor.

[1] For an introduction to this evidence, see: Brian J. L. Berry, *Geography of Market Centers and Retail Distribution* (Englewood Cliffs, N.J.: Prentice-Hall, Inc., 1967).

as depressed in that they have (1) relatively low family incomes, (2) high unemployment rates, and (3) high vacancy rates for the commercial structure of the area.

In the development of the commercial structure model, primary emphasis was placed on the need to evaluate the existing commercial structure of the four neighborhoods and to produce recommendations for modifications of the structure where required. Commercial structure is defined in this paper as the retail and services stores of a neighborhood, although in a broader context non-store retail and service businesses, manufacturers and wholesalers could be considered part of the commercial structure.[2] The commercial structure of Cleveland and the four neighborhoods, measured by the number of retail and service establishments, is shown in Table 1 for the years 1950, 1960, and 1965.

The four neighborhoods are divided into a total of 26 market areas, with the market area serving as the basic unit for analysis of commercial structure. There are 52 census tracts within these four neighborhoods, with one to four census tracts in each market area. It was found that a minimum population of 10,000 persons was necessary to produce a statistically significant relationship between the population and the commercial structure of a market area. For census tracts with less than 10,000 population, adjacent tracts were combined to obtain the minimum population required for a market area. Natural boundaries and shopping survey data were used as a basis for assignment decisions. Market Area 13, located in the Hough neighborhood and consisting of three census tracts, has been selected as the example for this paper.

Table 2 shows that the total population of Market Area 13 peaked in 1960. Then from 1960 to 1965 the total population declined, while the percentage of Negro residents continued to rise. Median income followed the same pattern as total population, so that total income in the market area dropped very sharply between 1960 and 1965, creating severe pressures within

TABLE 1
Commercial Structure of Cleveland and Four Neighborhoods, 1950–1965

	Number of Retail and Service Establishments			Change 1950–1965	
	1950	*1960*	*1965*	*Number of Establishments*	*Percent Change*
City of Cleveland	18,295	14,818	13,242	−5,053	−27.6%
Hough	1,047	887	728	− 319	−30.5
Cedar–Central	2,004	1,538	1,250	− 754	−37.6
Glenville	1,564	1,306	1,082	− 482	−30.8
Mt. Pleasant	627	497	452	− 175	−27.9

Source: Real Property Inventory of Metropolitan Cleveland, *Retail Stores and Shopping Areas,* 1950 Edition, Part I of Report 27 (Cleveland: Real Property Inventory, 1950). Real Property Inventory of Metropolitan Cleveland, *Retail Stores and Shopping Areas,* 1960 Edition, Part II of Report 37 (Cleveland: Real Property Inventory, 1960). Real Property Inventory of Metropolitan Cleveland, *Retail Stores and Shopping Areas,* 1965 Edition, Part II of Report 42 (Cleveland: Real Property Inventory, 1965).

[2] Brian J. L. Berry, *Commercial Structure and Commercial Blight,* Department of Geography Research Paper No. 85 (Chicago, Ill.: University of Chicago, 1963).

TABLE 2
Population and Income Changes, Market Area 13 (Hough) 1950, 1960, 1965

	1950	1960	1965
Total population	17,049	19,334	16,402
Negro population	1,086	15,892	14,984
Percent negro	6.4%	82.2%	91.4%
Median family income [a]			
(before taxes)			
(Current $)	$2,833	$4,598	$4.050
(1958 $)	$3,419	$4,470	$3,719

a Median income data are for Hough area, which includes Market Area 13 and seven additional census tracts. The median income figure of $3,315 for 1965 that is used in the paper is for Market Area 13 *only* and refers to families *plus* unrelated individuals—comparative figures are not available for 1950 and 1960.

Sources: U.S. Bureau of the Census. *U.S. Census of Population: 1950, Vol. III, Census Tract Statistics, Chapter 12.* U.S. Government Printing Office, 1952. U.S. Department of Commerce, Bureau of the Census. *U.S. Censuses of Population and Housing: 1960, Census Tracts.* Final Report PHC (1)-28. Washington: U.S. Government Printing Office, 1962. U.S. Department of Commerce, Bureau of the Census, *Current Population Reports.* Series P-23, No. 21, "Characteristics of Selected Neighborhoods in Cleveland, Ohio: April, 1965." Washington: U.S. Government Printing Office, 1967. U.S. Department of Commerce, Bureau of the Census. *Current Population Reports.* Series P-28, No. 1390, "Special Census of Cleveland, Ohio: April 1, 1965." Washington: U.S. Government Printing Office, 1965.

the declining commercial structure. This pattern is not unique to Market Area 13, Hough, or Cleveland—it is typical of most depressed neighborhoods.

In order to evaluate the commercial structure of these neighborhoods, it is necessary to determine the potential demand for retail and service establishments by line of trade. The potential demand, in turn, is primarily determined by the buying power and shopping behavior of the residents of the neighborhoods. The proposed model for evaluating the commercial structure of a depressed neighborhood is, therefore, based on buying power

and shopping behavior, with the special feature of providing the recommended number of retail and service establishments for each line of trade.

The Commercial Structure Model

The commercial structure model for a depressed neighborhood is based on three equations. In the first equation (1), the total Expenditures for Current Consumption by neighborhood residents is determined:

$$E = (C)(I)(a)(b) \qquad (1)$$

where E = Expenditures for Current Consumption

C = Consumer units (families and unrelated individuals)

I = Median family income (before taxes)

a = Tax ratio

b = Expenditures ratio

The second equation allocates the total Expenditures for Current Consumption on the basis of shopping behavior data, and provides the estimated annual expenditures in retail and service establishments in the market area:

$$T = (d)(E)(e)(f) \qquad (2)$$

where T = Expenditures in retail and service establishments in the market area

d = Percentage allocation of Expenditures for Current Consumption (E) by type of store

e = Shopping pattern ratio

f = Trade flow ratio

The recommended number of establishments for each line of retail and service trade is then determined in equation (3):

$$S = \frac{T}{gh} \qquad (3)$$

where S = Recommended number of establishments for each line of retail and service trade

g = Dollar sales per square foot for each line of trade

h = Recommended average establishment size in square feet for each line of trade

Commercial Structure in Market Area 13

Determination of the recommended commercial structure for Market Area 13 begins with the calculation of the total Expenditures for Current Consumption by the residents of the area. Equation (1) indicates that total annual Expenditures (E) are $17,669,000:

$$E = (C)(I)(a)(b) \qquad (1)$$

$$E = (5,712)(\$3,315)(.935)(.998)$$

$$E = \$17,669,000$$

Data on consumer units and median family income were derived from a special census conducted in 1965 by the Bureau of Census. Appropriate tax and expenditures ratios were drawn from Table 3, using the median family income (before taxes) figure for Market Area 13 of $3,315. The tax ratio adjusts median income from a before-tax to an after-tax figure. Median family income (after taxes) is then adjusted to an expenditure base by the use of the expenditure ratio.

An alternative approach to the use of a single median income figure for the market area would be to take the full distribution of consumer units by income classes, thereby applying the relevant tax and expenditure ratios to the consumer units within each income class. This approach involves a substantial increase in the amount of data

TABLE 3
Tax and Expenditure Ratios

Family Income (Before Taxes)	Tax Ratio	Expenditure Ratio
Under $1,000	100.0%	295.1%
$ 1,000–1,999	100.0	140.6
2,000–2,999	98.7	108.8
3,000–3,999	93.5	99.8
4,000–4,999	92.2	98.3
5,000–5,999	90.4	89.8
6,000–7,499	89.3	89.4
7,500–9,999	88.8	87.6
10,000–14,999	86.3	81.5
15,000 and over	79.7	61.0

Source: Adapted from: "Consumer Expenditures and Income, Cleveland, Ohio," *BLS Report No. 237-71, Table 1-A.* Washington: U.S. Department of Labor, 1964.

and number of calcualtions required. In addition, it may be necessary to estimate the number of consumer units within any particular income class as a result of conflicting class limits in the source data. It is customary to assume a rectangular or uniform distribution of consumer units around the mid-point of each income class.

Both approaches, therefore, require assumptions about the distribution of income, and it is clear that the model is very sensitive to these assumptions. The use of the full distribution generally produces higher estimates than the single median income figure approach, but in depressed neighborhoods the typical secular decline in total income suggests that the more conservative single median income figure approach is more realistic. For economically stable or growing neighborhoods the full distribution approach would be more appropriate.

Approximately 66% of the total Expenditures for Current Consumption (E) will be spent in retail and service establishments as shown in Tables 4 and 5.

TABLE 4

Percentage Allocations of Expenditures for Current Consumption in Convenience Store Types

Store Types	Percentage Allocation (d)	$ Sales per Square Foot of Floor Space (g)	Average Store Size in Square Feet (h)
Food group stores	24.070%		
Grocery and delicatessen stores	19.659	$100	2,000
Meat and fish stores	1.172	60	1,200
Fruit and vegetable stores	0.087	25	1,200
Candy, nut, confectionery stores	0.176	20	1,200
Dairy products stores	2.022	60	1,200
Bakery stores	0.716	25	1,800
Eggs and poultry stores	0.195	60	1,200
All other food stores	0.043	25	1,200
Eating and drinking establishments	2.338	40	1,500
Drug and proprietary stores	3.627	70	1,500
Automotive group stores			
Tires, battery, accessory stores	0.270	15	4,000
Lumber, building materials, hardware stores			
Paint, glass, wallpaper stores	0.026	25	1,500
Heating and plumbing stores	0.082	25	3,000
Electrical supply stores	0.043	25	1,200
Hardware stores	0.397	25	1,800
Service stores			
Barber and beauty shops	1.591	25	900
Cleaning and pressing stores	0.970	40	800
Shoe repair, hat cleaning stores	0.164	40	900
Laundry stores	0.435	20	1,400
Miscellaneous personal service stores	0.508	40	1,000
Total	34.521%		

Sources: Values for *(g)* and *(h)* were derived from:
  (1) Field Surveys, Bureau of Business Research, Western Reserve University, 1965–1968.
  (2) Files, County Commissioner's Office, Cuyahoga County, Ohio.
  (3) Regional Planning Commission, *Suburban Shopping Centers: Technical Supplement* (Cleveland: Regional Planning Commission, 1961), Tables S-4, S-19.

TABLE 5

Percentage Allocation of Expenditures for Current Consumption in All Other Store Types

Store Types	Percentage Allocation (d)	$ Sales per Square Foot of Floor Space (g)	Average Store Size in Square Feet (h)
General merchandise stores	12.348%		
Department stores	9.997	$50	16,000
Dry goods, general stores	1.281	40	2,000
Variety stores	1.070	60	5,000
Apparel group stores	3.465		
Men's and boys' clothing stores	1.044	55	1,500

TABLE 5—Continued

Store Types	Percentage Allocation (d)	$ Sales per Square Foot of Floor Space (g)	Average Store Size in Square Feet (h)
Women's and girls' clothing stores	1.271	60	1,500
Family clothing stores	0.413	50	1,500
Shoe stores	0.657	55	1,350
Child and infant clothing stores	0.077	50	1,600
Miscellaneous apparel stores	0.003	50	1,200
Furniture and appliance stores	3.262		
Furniture stores	1.633	25	4,000
Floor covering stores	0.263	30	3,000
Drapery, curtain, upholstery stores	0.065	30	1,600
China, glass, metalware stores	0.009	30	1,700
Music stores	0.310	30	1,400
Other home furnishing stores	0.024	30	1,500
Household appliance stores	0.628	40	2,000
Radio and TV stores	0.330	40	1,600
Automotive group stores			
New and used car dealers	3.545	30	10,000
Used car dealers	0.238	20	10,000
All other auto stores	0.177	20	1,500
Gasoline stations	2.750	10	4,000
Lumber, building materials, hardware stores			
Lumberyards	0.524	25	4,000
Building materials stores	0.183	25	3,000
Beverage stores	1.156	60	1,850
Secondhand stores	0.011	40	1,200
Other retail stores	2.160		
Fuel, ice dealers	0.059	40	2,000
Feed, farm, garden stores	0.027	25	1,200
Jewelry stores	0.191	40	1,200
Book, stationery stores	0.099	40	1,200
Sporting goods stores	0.108	40	1,500
Florist shops	0.185	30	1,200
Cigar stores	0.276	40	1,000
Camera, photographic supply stores	0.072	40	1,200
All other stores	1.143	40	1,300
Total service stores			
Funeral home service	0.100	40	1,800
Auto repair, washing, parking	0.707	40	1,200
Electrical repair stores	0.121	30	1,200
Furniture and upholstery repair stores	0.099	30	1,200
Other repair stores	0.486	30	1,200
Total	31.332%		

Sources: Values for *(g)* and *(h)* were derived from:
(1) Field Surveys, Bureau of Business Research, Western Reserve University, 1965–1968.
(2) Files, County Commissioner's Office, Cuyahoga County, Ohio.
(3) Regional Planning Commission, *Suburban Shopping Centers: Technical Supplement* (Cleveland: Regional Planning Commission, 1961), Tables S-? S-19.

These establishments have been classified into convenience stores and all
other stores, with convenience stores
listed in Table 4 and all other stores
in Table 5. Convenience stores are those
patronized on the basis of their convenient location; while all other stores,
including shopping and specialty stores,
are those patronized on the basis of
their assortments or strong customer
loyalty.[3] For each store type, the allocation of the total Expenditures for Current Consumption (E) is shown as a
percentage allocation (d) in Tables 4
and 5. Derivation of the percentages is
based on linkages between U.S. government data on consumer expenditures
and retail sales. The basic source of
these data is the merchandise line sales
statistics of the 1963 Census of Business
adjusted to represent patronage patterns within depressed neighborhoods.[4]
The linkages and adjustments involved
extensive calculations and cannot be
included in this paper but are explained in a technical supplement available from the author.

Drug and Proprietary Store as an Example

In order to illustrate the application of
the commercial structure model to a
specific type of store, drug and proprietary stores have been selected as an
example. Table 4 indicates that the

percentage allocation (d) for drug and
proprietary stores is 3.627%. Substituting this figure into equation (2) and
multiplying it by (E) gives $636,000 as
the amount of money that residents of
Market Area 13 will spend annually in
all drug and proprietary stores, regardless of location.

After determining the expenditures
in all drug and proprietary stores by
the residents of Market Area 13, it is
necessary to estimate how much of the
total will be spent in drug and proprietary stores located in Market Area
13. Two components of shopping behavior are employed in this decision—
one related to the type of store (shopping pattern ratio) and the other to the
character of the market area (trade flow
ratio). Drug and proprietary stores are
classified as convenience stores, since
most of their trade is based on convenient location.[5] Based on studies in
Cleveland and other metropolitan
areas, it is assumed that 90% of all
expenditures in convenience stores
would be made in stores within one
mile of the family residence.[6] The
shopping patern ratio (e) for drug and
proprietary stores is therefore .90, and
this figure is substituted for (e) in equation (2).

For all other stores, it is assumed that
only 50% of all expenditures will be
made within one mile of the family
residence, thereby reflecting the ten-

[3] E. J. McCarthy, *Basic Marketing,* Third Edition (Homewood, Ill.: Richard D. Irwin, Inc., 1968), p. 341.

[4] U.S. Bureau of the Census, *U.S. Census of Business: 1963, Merchandise Line Sales,* BC 63-RS-7, East North Central Region (Washington, D.C.: U.S. Government Printing Office, 1965).

[5] For a summary of many studies dealing with the classification of stores, see W. L. Garrison, et al., *Studies of Highway Development and Geographic Change* (Seattle, Wash.: University of Washington Press, 1959).

[6] Regional Planning Commission, *Suburban Shopping Centers: Technical Supplement* (Cleveland, Ohio: Regional Planning Commission, 1961), Table S-5; Bernard LaLonde, *Differentials in Supermarket Drawing Power* (East Lansing, Mich.: Bureau of Business and Economic Research, Michigan State University, 1962), pp. 59–69.

dency to search and travel over a larger area for these types of stores.[7] The shopping pattern ratio (e) for all other stores is consequently .50 and this value should be substituted in equation (2) for studies concerned with the stores listed in Table 5.

The assumed values for the shopping pattern ratio (e) are based on limited evidence. For particular types of stores, the assumed value may not be the true value, yet the limited evidence suggests that it is useful as an initial estimate. If greater precision is desirable, and a sensitivity analysis can test this, survey data may be substituted for any or all types of stores.

The character of the market area may be expressed in the form of the trade flow ratio (f) which has the primary role of adjusting the shopping pattern ratio (e) to the characteristics of individual market areas. The shopping pattern ratio presents a distance model of shopping behavior; but since market areas do not conform to the one mile boundary specified by the distance model, it is necessary to adjust the shopping pattern ratio. The average trade flow for depressed neighborhoods in Cleveland has been calculated by the author to be 70%, so that the total expenditures in the stores located in the market area amount to 70% of the expenditures level of the residents of the market area. The 70% figure, therefore, reflects both the export expenditure of the residents and the import expenditures of nonresidents in the

stores in a given market area, so that the actual expenditures in stores in a market area will be:

Total Expenditures in stores in a Market Area = Total Residents' Expenditures

\+ Nonresident's Expenditures in Market Area − Resident's Expenditures Outside Market Area

Trade flow estimates were calculated for each market area by adjusting the distance model of shopping behavior using maps and concentric circle techniques.[8] A probability model such as the one developed by Huff could be substituted for the distance model, although considerable modification in his model would be required.[9] Thompson has argued that survey data on consumer attitudes should provide the basis for shopping behavior models and that both the distance and probabilistic models have been deficient.[10] There are, therefore, a number of alternative bases for developing the shopping model and the researcher must select the one that most closely meets his objectives. In this study, the need to base the commercial structure model entirely on previously published data dictated the choice of the distance model of shopping behavior.

The distance model of shopping behavior assumes that the most important factor in determining *where* consumer expenditures take place is the distance

[7] Same reference as footnote 6; David Caplovitz, *The Poor Pay More* (New York: The Free Press, 1967), pp. 49–57.

[8] For a discussion of distance models and measurement techniques, see Richard L. Nelson, *The Selection of Retail Locations* (New York: F. W. Dodge Corporation, 1958).

[9] David L. Huff, "Defining and Estimating a Trading Area," *Journal of Marketing*, Vol. 28 (July 1964), pp. 34–38.

[10] Donald L. Thompson, "Future Directions in Retail Area Research," *Economic Geography*, Vol. 42 (January 1966), pp. 1–18.

from the place of residence to the commercial structure of a market area. It assumes also that the initial distance boundary is one mile and then adjusts the boundary to fit each market area. The assumptions are developed for depressed urban neighborhoods with their high densities of population and commercial structure; it is unlikely that such assumptions are appropriate for other neighborhoods. There are, obviously, a number of additional factors that may influence where expenditures are made such as store size, merchandise variety, credit availability, and parking facilities. Data for these factors, however, must generally be collected specifically for each market area and line of trade and, therefore, could not be included in a model based on previously published information.

Using a distance model of shopping behavior for Market Area 13 results in an estimated trade flow figure of 66%, reflecting an above-average export of expenditures by residents of the area. This figure when expressed as a ratio using the Cleveland neighborhood average of 70%, gives a trade flow ratio of .943 (66/70) for Market Area 13 which is substituted for (*f*) in equation (2). The determination of the trade flow figure for Market Area 13 is presented in the Appendix to this paper.

Total annual expenditures in drug and proprietary stores located in Market Area 13 are estimated to be $544,000, as shown in equation (2):

$$T = d(E)(e)(f) \qquad (2)$$
$$T = (.03627)(\$17,669,000)(.90)$$
$$(.943)$$
$$T = \$544,000$$

Given the total annual expenditures in drug and proprietary stores located in Market Area 13, the recommended number of stores may be determined.

Tables 4 and 5 provide estimates of the two factors (*g*) and (*h*) shown in equation (3), with the factors for drug and proprietary stores drawn from Table 4:

$$S = \frac{T}{gh} \qquad (3)$$
$$S = \frac{\$544,000}{(\$70)(1,500)}$$
$$S = 5 \text{ stores}$$

Five drug and proprietary stores are recommended for Market Area 13, based on the average factor values for (*g*) and (*h*) displayed in Table 4 and equation (3). These average factor values have been developed specifically for depressed neighborhoods in Cleveland, but available information for other urban areas suggests that the same or similar values may be appropriate for depressed neighborhoods in those areas. It should also be noted that the average values do not imply a uniform distribution of retail productivity and store size; a range of values for both (*g*) and (*h*) would be both expected and desirable for any market area. As an example, one alternative would be to have the total recommended space of 7,500 square feet for drug and proprietary stores in Market Area 13 divided into one store with 3,500 square feet and four stores with 1,000 square feet each.

It has been suggested that the model should omit (*h*), the recommended average establishment size in square feet for each line of trade, from equation (3). The model would then estimate the square footage of floor space recommended for each line of trade in a market area. This approach would avoid the question of whether the recommended store space should be divided into few or many, small or large stores, and would also be consistent with previous studies in this area.[11] The model presented in this article emphasizes the number of stores rather than the store area (in square feet) for two reasons. (1) Published data on the number of stores were available, and there were no published data on store area by line of trade for each market area. (2) The question of the distribution of store sizes must ultimately be resolved by someone, and the inclusion of (h) in the model forces the explicit acknowledgment of this responsibility. There are admittedly many factors that influence the recommended distribution of store sizes for each line of trade in a market area but recommendations must nevertheless be made.

If the average factor values for (g) and (h) in equation (3) are multiplied, the average annual gross sales volume for each of the five drug and proprietary stores would be $105,000. Taking published operating ratios for drug stores, a gross volume of $105,000 would produce a pre-tax profit of $13,000, including the owner's wages. With an alternative space distribution of one store with 3,500 square feet and four stores with 1,000 square feet, the expected gross volumes would be $245,-000 for the large store and an average of $70,000 for each of the smaller stores. The pre-tax profits (including the owner's wages) would be about $24,500 for the large store and $10,500 for the smaller stores.

Additional combinations of alternative factor values for (g) and (h) can be explored from the standpoint of pre-tax profit distributions—or from other criteria if desired. An important feature of the model is that it lends itself to a program of sensitivity testing in which a number of values of (g) and (h) can be evaluated in terms of their effect on

S, the recommended number of establishments for each line of trade in the market area.

The latest edition of the *Real Property Inventory* of Cleveland indicates that there are three drug and proprietary stores in Market Area 13. Comparing the actual number of stores with the recommended number suggests that there is an opportunity for two additional drug and proprietary stores in Market Area 13. This finding is not typical for most types of stores in Market Area 13, as shown in Table 6, in which the total excess number of stores is 29. Among the most serious cases of excess capacity in Market Area 13 are eating and drinking establishments (excess of 16), grocery and delicatessen stores (excess of 4), and barber and beauty shops (excess of 4). The best opportunity in Market Area 13 is in the dairy store category, in which the potential demand will support four additional establishments.

Application of the commercial structure model to the 26 market areas indicates that there is a general condition of over-capacity in the commercial structure of Cleveland's four depressed neighborhoods. Basically, the problem may not be one of too much total square footage but of poor distribution of the existing space; there may be too many small stores and too few large stores in the depressed neighborhoods.

Implications

If excess capacity in the commercial structure of America's depressed neighborhoods is common (this writer suspects that it is), then many of the currently popular government and private enterprise programs to stimulate small

[11] Same reference as footnote 6, Tables S-2, 3, 16, 17, and 21.

TABLE 6
Recommended and Actual Commercial Structure for Market Area 13

Store Type	Recommended Number of stores	Actual Number of Stores
Total Retail Stores	55	68
Total food group stores	24	25
Grocery and delicatessen stores	15	19
Meat and fish stores	2	2
Fruit and vegetable stores	0	0
Candy, nut, confectionery stores	1	0
Dairy product stores	4	0
Eggs and poultry stores	0	1
Bakery stores	2	2
All other food stores	0	0
Eating and drinking establishments	6	22
General merchandise stores	2	1
Department stores	1	0
Dry goods, general stores	1	1
Variety stores	0	0
Apparel group stores	3	2
Men's and boys' clothing stores	1	0
Women's and girls' clothing stores	1	0
Family clothing stores	0	1
Shoe stores	1	0
Child and infant clothing stores	0	0
Misc. apparel stores	0	1
Furniture and appliance stores	3	3
Furniture stores	1	0
Floor covering stores	0	0
Draperies, curtains, upholstery stores	0	0
China, glass, metalware stores	0	0
Music stores	1	2
Other home furnishing stores	0	0
Household appliance stores	1	1
Radio and TV stores	0	0
Automotive group stores	1	1
New and used car dealers	1	0
Used car dealers	0	0
Tires, batteries, accessory stores	0	1
All other automotive stores	0	0
Gasoline stations	6	5
Lumber, building materials, hardware stores	1	4
Lumberyards	0	0
Building materials stores	0	0
Paint, glass, wallpaper stores	0	0
Heating and plumbing stores	0	0
Electrical supply stores	0	0
Hardware stores	1	4
Drug and proprietary stores	5	3
Beverage stores	1	0

TABLE 6—Continued

Store Type	Recommended Number of stores	Actual Number of Stores
Secondhand stores	0	2
Other retail stores	3	0
Fuel, ice dealers	0	0
Feed, farm, garden stores	0	0
Jewelry stores	0	0
Book, stationery stores	0	0
Sporting goods stores	0	0
Florist shops	0	0
Cigar stores	0	0
Cameras, photo supply stores	0	0
All other stores	3	0
Total Service Stores	23	39
Barber and beauty shops	11	15
Cleaning and pressing stores	5	8
Shoe repair, hat cleaning stores	1	4
Laundry stores	2	3
Funeral service	0	1
Misc. personal service stores	2	1
Auto repair, parking, washing	1	6
Electrical repair stores	0	1
Furniture and upholstery repair stores	0	0
Other repair stores	1	0
Total Retail and Service Stores	78	107

Sources: Actual number of stores: Real Property Inventory of Metropolitan Cleveland, *Retail Stores and Shopping Areas,* 1968 Edition, Part II of Report 45 (Cleveland: Real Property Inventory, 1968).

business in the "ghetto" may be misdirected. Encouraging more small merchants may be the worst possible strategy where excess capacity exists; it would be far more productive to encourage the development of larger stores by either expanding the existing stores or attracting new large stores to the depressed areas. The development of larger stores will, of course, also add to the capacity and force out many smaller stores, but this is the price that must be paid for efficient retailing in depressed neighborhoods.

The development of larger retail and service stores in depressed neighborhoods must reflect the potential demand for such stores by line of trade, in both the short and long run. By substituting population and income forecasts in equation (1) for current data, the required future commercial structure may be estimated. The future, however, should not be a carbon copy of the past commercial structure; one of the major advantages of the model presented in this paper is that it lends itself to simulations of consumer response to new retail and service stores and of changing patterns of consumer shopping behavior.

In view of the massive investments that are required in the depressed neighborhoods of America's cities, it is important to direct these investments on the basis of the best available information. The commercial structure model presented herein provides a means of combining published information, together with survey data (when available), for the purpose of evaluating existing commercial structures and planning programs for the development of strong, attractive commercial structures in the depressed neighborhoods of America.

APPENDIX

Determination of the Trade Flow Ratio

Total Expenditures for Current Consumption in Convenience and All Other Stores in Market Area 13 amount to $7,705,000, while the total Expenditures for Current Consumption by the residents of Market Area 13 in all such stores without regard to location is $11,638,000. These figures provide the basis for the Market Area 13 trade flow figure:

$$\frac{\$\ 7,705,000}{\$11,638,000} = .66 = 66\%$$

The development of this and related figures is shown in the following table:

Trade Flow Estimate for Market Area 13

Expenditures for Current Consumption Within Stores Located at Market Area 13	Location of Expenditures for Current Consumption by Residents of Market Area 13		
Residents of Market Area 13	Market Area 13	Other Areas	Total
Convenience stores	$2,465,000	$3,636,000	$ 6,101,000
All other stores	897,000	4,640,000	5,537,000
Total	$3,362,000	$8,276,000	$11,638,000
Residents of Other Areas			
Convenience stores	$2,653,000		
All other stores	1,690,000		
Total	$4,343,000		
Total expenditures by residents and non-residents	$7,705,000		

A Microanalytic Approach to Store Location Analysis

David B. MacKay

Introduction

Store location methods and store choice models examine the consumer–retailer relationship from polar perspectives. A significant body of literature has appeared on store location methods, and the literature on the store choice process is starting to grow. Paradoxically, neither approach has tried to incorporate work done by the other, or even evaluate its significance.

Store location methods, which include gravity models [14, 23], analog methods [5, 19], and map transformation methods [12, 18], are spatially defined but implicitly contain unrealistic assumptions about consumer behavior. All the store location methodologies are highly aggregative and assume that differences between consumers, such as the number of stops made on shopping trips, are unimportant or else negate each other. Such differences are usually overcome by assuming that all consumers make single-stop shopping trips; the complication introduced by studying multistop trips and the empirical fallacy of the single-stop assumption have been mentioned [3, 15, 17].

To say that consumers engage only in single-stop shopping implies that their store choice decisions are not affected by the presence of neighboring establishments. The importance of this assumption is illustrated in the figure, in which it is assumed that the utility of travel to the consumer is a direct linear function of distance. In the figure are four retail stores that sell product Type 1, at Locations A, B, C, and D. Two other stores, which sell Types 2 and 3, are at Locations E and F. Under the assumption that shopping trips are single-stop, a consumer at Origin O would never shop at Location D if behavior is governed by the utility function posited above. If, however, the consumer makes multiple-stop shopping trips, then stops would be made at Location D when Types 1 and 2, Types 1 and 3, or Types 1, 2, and 3 were needed simultaneously.

Given the unrealistic assumptions of the spatial models, the behavioral models of store choice seem to present an attractive alternative. Several behavioral models have been suggested for portraying the consumer's selection of retail stores, including a patronage model [2], a decision model [7], and the models which portray store choice as an extension of brand choice [1, 22]; see [10] for a review of related work on the store choice process. Unfortunately, most of the behavioral models

Reprinted from the *Journal of Marketing Research,* published by the American Marketing Association, Vol. IX, May 1972, by permission of the author and editor.

(except for [7]) are aspatial. Their scope, therefore, is severely restricted.

Research Design

A spatially defined model of store selection that accounts for multistop shopping trips can be defined by means of discriminant analysis and Monte Carlo simulation.[1] The framework for the model portrays consumers as going through a three-stage, sequential process of store selection: (1) the decision to go shopping or not to, (2) the decision of how many stops to make, and (3) the decision of which establishment to visit on each stop.

This decision sequence is, admittedly, artificial. One might argue, for example, that consumers' decision processes are holistic. However, sequential processes have been suggested previously [24] and the use of Markov chains to model store selection—e.g., [17, 20]—also implies a sequential decision procedure. Evidence is presented later that the sequential process describes consumer behavior better than the holistic approach, although the evidence is not conclusive.

Two sets of discriminant functions can be used to determine the probability of alternative events occurring for the first two decision stages of the sequential decision process. Unless one is concerned with a very simple situation, the third decision stage must be subdivided before it can be portrayed mathematically; the shopping trip is modeled in two phases, trip generation and trip structure.[2]

Trip Generation

Trip generation refers to the consumer's itinerary of store types to visit on individual shopping trips. The third stage of the decision process is replaced by a set of discriminant functions, which is used to compute the probabilities of stops at alternative types of businesses. An itinerary can be simulated for a consumer at any given point in time by sequentially sampling from the discriminant functions of the three decision stages wtih a Monte Carlo process.

Given an appropriate set of inputs, posterior probabilities are generated by the discriminant functions for each alternative at each stage in the decision process. As an example, the probability of Mrs. Smith's going on a shopping trip or staying home on Monday morning is determined by the two discriminant functions which model the first stage of the decision process. These define a discrete probability distribution which can be sampled by a Monte Carlo process. If the event sampled indicates that no trip is to be made, the simulation proceeds to the next point in time, say Tuesday, and again determines the probability of a shopping trip. The probability for Tuesday differs from that for Monday, because the result of Monday's decision is included in the inputs for Tuesday's discriminant functions. If Mrs. Smith goes shopping on Tuesday, a second set of discriminant functions is used to determine the probability of Mrs. Smith's making stops $(1, \ldots, n)$ on the shopping trip. A Monte Carlo sampling procedure is again used.

---

[1] The use of discriminant procedures for computing probabilities is a simple procedure; see [9, 13]. In functionally defining a simulation, it causes some complications, but these are minor [16].

[2] This artificial dichotomy has been used in the regional science and urban geography literature to describe individual movement [8]. In reality, the concepts are not independent, but are considered so here as a first approximation.

The third stage in trip generation is to determine which types of stores are visited at each stop. The probabilities of choosing each stop are computed as functions of the discriminant scores, and then Monte Carlo sampling is used to select the event chosen. This event becomes input for another set of discriminant functions which determines the probabilities of different establishment types being chosen, and so on for the second stop, until the number of stops determined by the second stage is set. After completing Mrs. Smith's itinerary for Tuesday, the simulation constructs her itineraries for the rest of the simulated periods. Then itineraries of other consumers are simulated.

Three major sets of discriminant functions have been described in constructing the framework for the itinerary generation phase. The independent variables which provide input for these discriminant functions are:

1. *Household characteristics:* demographic and socioeconomic variables such as family size, age group, education level, employment status, income, and number of drivers' licenses per household.

2. *Attitude toward stores:* an index of attitude toward the primary supermarkets in the trading area, the product of beliefs about supermarket characteristics and perceived importance of these beliefs.

3. *Shopping trip variables:* household shopping habits, including measures of mode of travel, accompaniment to store, distance from store to home and from last store frequented, establishments visited previously, and timing of shopping trips.

The variables eligible to enter the different sets of discriminant functions are in Table 1. The functional relationship of these variables to a set of discriminant functions may be illustrated by considering the set of discriminant functions last mentioned, those which determine the type of establishment to be frequented on a stop of the shopping trip:

$$E_j(1, \dots, i, \dots, e) = f(H, A, S);$$
$$j = 1, \dots, s, A = g(P, V)$$

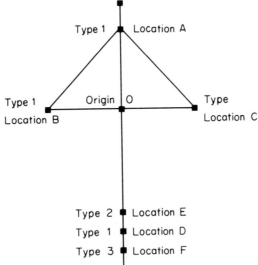

The Effect of Multistop Shopping

where $E_j(1, \ldots, i, \ldots, e) =$

$$\begin{cases} 1 = \text{establishment type } i \text{ visited} \\ \quad \text{on stop } j \\ 0 = \text{establishment type } i \text{ not} \\ \quad \text{visited on stop } j \end{cases}$$

$H = $ consumer's household characteristics

$S = $ characteristics of the consumer's shopping trip

$A = $ consumer's attitude toward principal stores

$P = $ consumer's perception of principal store stimuli

$V = $ consumer's evaluation of the perceived stimuli

$e = $ the number of establishment types considered

$s = $ the number of stops to be made on a shopping trip

Trip Structure

Trip structure requires that the establishment types be replaced by specific

TABLE 1
Variable Sets Used for Different Discriminant Functions

| Variable Set | Discriminant Functions [a] | | |
	To Shop or Not Shop	Number of Stops	Establishment Selection [b]
Household characteristics	×	×	×
Attitude toward stores	×	×	×
Shopping trip variables			
Timing	×	×	×
Mode		×	×
Accompaniment		×	×
Distance			×
Establishment			×

[a] The variable set is an input for the related discriminant function.
[b] The establishment selection functions which determine the order of the first supermarket stop do not employ distance or establishment variables.

stores. This is accomplished by movement heuristics, which provide "rules" for the simulated consumers to follow in selecting stores.

Three of the heuristics used for movement are:

1. *Single-stop distance minimization:* the consumer forms a list of stops which he plans to make but determines the establishments by picking those closest to his trip origin, in this case, home.
2. *Modified sequential distance minimization:* the consumer minimizes the total distance traveled for small trips but on larger trips reverts to a sequential distance minimization technique as the distance from home increases.
3. *Discriminant heuristic:* same as the modified sequential distance minimization heuristic, except that when the consumer's itinerary indicates that a stop is about to be made at a principal establishment (for which location analysis is being conducted), a discriminant function is used to determine which establishment is selected.

Each heuristic can be simulated, and comparing the simulated and actual data gives an indication of the heuristic's validity.

The rationale for the modified sequential distance minimization heuristic is that as consumers move further from home while shopping, the quality of their information set decreases and they are less able to minimize the total distance traveled (distance need not be measured in terms of mileage, but can include time and account for barriers, etc.). On stops farthest from home, the consumer thus selects stores on a sequential distance minimization basis. For stops near home, where the information set is more complete, distances between multiples of stops are minimized.

In the empirical study described in the next section, the principal establishments of the discriminant heuristic were supermarkets. On long shopping trips, consumers often stop at distant supermarkets, designated "other" because the frequency of stops there is very slight. If the Monte Carlo sampling procedure indicates that an "other" category is to be visited, the supermarket is selected from those in the area around the stop last made. Selection is determined by distance minimization. For shopping trips which have proceeded a significant distance from home, the supermarket chosen is that nearest to the last stop, thereby minimizing sequential distance. If the consumer is on a trip near home, an establishment is chosen to minimize total trip distance.

Input and Output

Inputs for the discriminant heuristic include the household characteristics, shopping trip variables, and attitudinal variables (Table 1). The attitudinal index toward the three major supermarkets is defined as a product of perceived stimuli and the importance attached to them. Stimuli are characteristics of establishments, such as price level, decor, etc., and are defined in a matrix $(m \times n)$, where m is the number of stimuli and n is the number of principal stores. The matrix is premultiplied by a vector $(l \times m)$ which records the importance placed on stimuli by the consumer to derive the attudinal vector toward the principal stores. This attitude measure [11] has been used as a measure of brand preference [6].

Output is derived from the simulation at several points. When trip structuring has been completed, the number of stops made at different establishments is computed. For some establishments, such as nonprofit institutions, the computation of stop frequencies by establishment may be sufficient. Most firms, though, are concerned with profits and sales, so a regression analysis is used to translate each consumer stop at a supermarket into the amount spent at the store.

The simulation can also be used to predict sales for stores that are not yet built. To evaluate potential sites for a new store location, a pair of spatial coordinates for the new store must be added to the list of supermarkets at which simulated consumers can shop. The vector of attitudes toward principal stores must also be redefined to include the new store by positing a vector of perceived stimuli for the new store. If the store is part of a chain established in the area, the attitudinal index may be estimated from reactions of consumers who live in the trading areas of similar stores. A final consideration in using the simulation in prediction is that the discriminant heuristic cannot be used because it is impossible to define a discriminant heuristic for consumer movement when one of the principal stores is not yet in operation.

Data

Supermarkets were chosen for this study primarily because consumers stop at supermarkets more than at other stores. Also, the managerial decision of where to locate a new supermarket is a frequent one and requires a significant investment. Finally, supermarket location analysis has been the primary thrust of most retail location studies, so it affords a good basis of comparison with other studies. The research design used here can be applied to studying other types of establishments, although some, such as ethnic restaurants, would be more suited for other methods.

Financial limitations required that the site chosen for empirical study have: (1) a modest size, (2) a degree of self-containment, and (3) a grid network of roads. These requirements limited the complexity of the situation being studied.

The site chosen was Tinley Park, Illinois, one of the most rapidly developing communities in the greater Chicago area, with a preliminary 1970 census estimate of 12,253 persons. Several shopping centers have been built in recent years, and a new one is under development. The town is in a rural–suburban area between Chicago and Joliet and is in transition from being a self-contained community to becoming a part of suburban Chicago.

Completed travel diary information was received from a sample of 302 Tinley Park residents, a response rate of slightly over 50%. Responses were received from mail questionnaires, which also requested information on the demographic and socioeconomic characteristics of the households sampled and attitudes toward selected supermarket characteristics.

Information was collected in the late spring and early summer of 1970. Tests were made for respondent bias and fatigue. The questionnaire proved to be a satisfactory and effective instrument.

Results

Travel diary data were collected only for shopping trips on which supermarkets were visited. Before the simulation was validated, a simple examination of the travel diary data showed that the assumption of single-stop shopping is not valid, since on the average, 2.7 stops were made on shopping trips that included supermarkets. A break-

down of stops by establishment type is in Table 2.

TABLE 2
Mean Number of Stops [a]

Establishment Type	Number of Stops
Variety store	24.4
Drugstore	21.8
Supermarket [b]	16.2
Gasoline station	16.2
Friend's home	14.2
Financial institution	12.7
Other food store	12.2
Cleaning and laundry	11.2
Post office	5.9
Other	38.6
Total	173.4

[a] Made at 10 establishment types for every 100 shopping trips.
[b] Supermarkets that were visited on trips where the consumer had previously stopped at another supermarket. The total number of stops per 100 trips is therefore 273.4.

The simulation underwent several validation tests, ranging from sensitivity to different random number seeds and initialization periods to tests of internal, functional, cell, and population level validation (see [4] for procedures and [15] for details). The simulation performed well. None of the distributions, such as trip length, distance from home to supermarket, etc., were significantly different from those of the sample population. A split sample was used for testing both the discriminant functions and the simulation itself. All of the discriminant and regression functions were fitted to the data from approximately 200 respondents, and the simulation was then run with data from the remaining 100. All tests of the individual functions and the simulation reported how well the actions of this group of 100 were predicted.

Functional Level Validation

Discriminant functions were evaluated on the basis of the number of correct classifications, and were considered acceptable if the number of correct classifications was better than that expected by chance (at the .05 level).[3]

Sixteen sets of discriminant functions were used in the simulation, seven to determine the days of the week, one to determine the number of stops, one to select specific supermarkets, and the seven remaining to determine the establishment types visited on different stops of a trip.

Shopping trips of up to four stops (not including home) were considered, because less than 15% of all trips included more than four stops, and the data base was insufficient to estimate these relatively rare occurrences. To ensure that every shopping trip generated by the simulation contained a supermarket stop, three discriminant function sets were defined which predicted the first stop on which a supermarket stop would occur for trips of two, three, or four stops. The remaining four discriminant function sets predicted the type of establishment visited on the first, second, third, or fourth stop. Although a supermarket had already been visited, it was possible to stop at another in completing the shopping trip. As Table 2 shows, this was actually a common occurrence.

Two of the 16 discriminant functions were marginally insignificant; these determined the number of stops to be made and the order of the supermarket on a two-stop trip. Later work suggests that this problem may have been caused by the manner in which the sample was split. It is, of course, possible that the decisions modeled by these two discriminant function sets are best represented as random processes, in which case the discriminant functions would not be statistically significant. Other possibilities include the omission of significant variables or the choice of an inappropriate construct for modeling store selection. Despite this disappointment, the discriminant functions were retained to complete the simulation.

Consistency

The discriminant functions showed a high degree of internal consistency. For example, the variables which determined if a shopping trip was to be made on a Monday were generally the same as those that determined if a trip was to be made on other days of the week, although the relative contribution of the different variables changed from day to day.

Examination of the store type selection and supermarket selection discriminant functions supported the initial contention that valuable information is destroyed in aggregation. Attitudinal, distance, establishment, and timing variables were the most significant contributors to these functions. These variables would all be destroyed in an aggregative analysis. (A modified BMD 07M stepwise discriminant program was used for computation, and only variables over a .05 significance level were permitted to enter.)

Entering discriminant function variables upheld the assertion that multistop trips should be explicitly considered in location methods. Two types of variables, those that measured distance from the consumer's last stop and

---

[3] Discriminant function evaluation methods were slightly different from those reported in most marketing studies; see [16].

those that recorded the type of establishment visited on the last stop, were important contributors to the discriminant functions which determined the type of establishment to be visited next. Neither type would be present in a single-stop model of consumer behavior.

Results of the simulation were also consistent with those obtained in other studies. The distribution of simulated stops at different stores, for example, displayed the extreme skewness that has been found in almost all origin–destination studies. Tests were also made on the spectral properties of consumers' shopping patterns. Consumers with different demographic and socioeconomic characteristics displayed different spectra; these differences were highly significant statistically, and these results correspond to expectations [21].

Descriptive Results

Of the three movement heuristics, the discriminant heuristic came the closest to describing actual consumer behavior. A comparison of the percentage of consumer stops generated by the simulation for the four supermarkets with that recorded by the 100 respondents in the evaluation sample is given in Table 3.

Two naive models were used to aid in evaluating two constructs of the simulation, the multistop heuristic and the three-stage decision process. The first naive model entailed the use of the single-stop heuristic in the trip structure phase; the resulting distributions of the multistop and single-stop heuristics are in Table 3. A Kolmogorov–Smirnov test was used to compare the actual distribution of stops with those generated by the two heuristics. Test results showed that the multistop distribution was in agreement with the actual distribution at a 0.66 level of significance. This agreement was

TABLE 3

Percentage of Consumer Stops by Store

	Actual Distribution	Simulated Distributions		Single-Stage Distribution [a]
		Multi-stop	Single-stop	
Store A	31.6	34.1	46.1	39.0
Store B	21.9	15.5	16.9	17.9
Store C	32.6	37.5	34.7	28.0
Store D [b]	13.9	12.9	2.3	15.1
Significance		0.66	0.54	0.001

[a] Derived from an expected value classification matrix of discriminant functions which predicted store choice.
[b] Included all supermarkets other than A, B, or C.

much better than that between the single-stop distribution and the actual distribution (significantly different at the 0.001 level).

The second naive model was constructed by computing the column sums of an expected value classification matrix. The matrix was derived from a single set of discriminant functions which classified respondents by which supermarket they visited. An expected value classification matrix, **C**, was used because it reflected the sampling properties of the Monte Carlo process [16]. By taking column sums of the c_{ij} elements (the expected number of observations in group i classified in group j), a rough estimate of the results of a holistic, single-stage decision process was provided. Results of the second naive model are also in Table 3. This naive model was much closer to the actual distribution than was the single-stop heuristic with a significance level of 0.54, but it was still short of the results obtained using the multistage decision heuristic.

The simulation also described sales at each supermarket in Tinley Park. Since sales figures were not available, the figures could not be verified; but simulated aggregate Tinley Park sales could be compared to an aggregate food expenditure projection based upon the 1967 Census of Business. Those data projected annual food expenditures of $8,357,700; the simulation's estimate was $8,160,765. Considering the chances for error in projection and the fact that the simulation data were completely independent of census data, this comparison was thought to be very good.

Predictive Results

In addition to describing the existing situation in Tinley Park, the simulation was used to predict sales levels for hypothetical stores at various locations. There was no way, however, of testing the accuracy of these predictions. Testing will have to wait until supermarkets currently being constructed in the area are completed.

Even though the dollar value of sales estimates for hypothetical stores cannot be evaluated, it is possible to say something about the advantage of using multistop heuristics for prediction. Using the figure as an illustration, suppose that supermarkets already exist at Locations D and F, and a new supermarket is constructed at E. The single-stop assumption implies that if the stores were similar, a person living close to E, on the road between E and O, would go to E. The sales of the supermarket at D would be diminished, but the sales of the supermarket at F would be unaffected. This phenomenon is not observed in the real world, and it was not observed with the multistop heuristics in the simulation, either.

Implications

Microanalytic simulation provides a powerful tool for both managerial and research-oriented interests. While the method is considerably more complex than those employed by most businesses, its outputs are of more value, since it provides an explicit estimate of the impact of existing stores on proposed stores. Management has tried to subjectively modify sales estimates by evaluating the impact of competitive and sister stores on a new store, but other questions—such as the influence of a variety store or even a bank as a generator of customer traffic—have not arisen. Microanalytic simulation provides the means of directly evaluating the impact of these factors.

Management may also use such a system to evaluate the effect of environmental changes, such as the change of a two-way street to a one-way street or the construction of a bypass around the business district. The application to city and regional planning is also obvious.

Though not fully explored in this study, the application of microanalytic methods to studying different physical and spatial combinations of retail offerings may prove to be its most significant advantage over contemporary methods. The retailer does not seek just to maximize earnings from one type of store, but to find the most profitable combination of store styles and spatial locations. This combination cannot be found with methods that do not consider multipurpose, multistop trips, nor with models that use highly aggregated data.

Validated simulations also provide a way for researchers to explore consumers' decision-making processes. A comparison of the store choices predicted by the simulation with those predicted by a single set of discriminant functions indicated that the simulation was a better predictor of store choice. This result supports the hypothesis that a sequential decision process may be more common than a holistic decision process. Other decision heuristics could also be tested; the simulation could, for example, admit heuristics similar to those posited by a decision model [7].

Output generated by the simulation can be used to examine facets of shopping behavior that cannot be evaluated from the raw input data. For example, the output could be used to measure and detect differences in shopping patterns between consumer groups. Such analyses require extensive inputs, often beyond the boundaries of the original data set.

An interesting extension of the model would be to other establishment types—including, perhaps, such non-business institutions as health and welfare facilities—and to more complex environments—such as the inner city of a large metropolitan area. Much has been hypothesized but little is known about the ways in which urban transportation systems, physical and sociological barriers to movement, and the like affect individuals' choices of retail outlets. The simulation of consumer movement under such conditions would require the development of movement heuristics which take such factors into account, but would provide insight into how an urban retail environment affects store choices.

REFERENCES

1. Aaker, David A., and J. Morgan Jones. "Modeling Store Choice Behavior," *Journal of Marketing Research,* 8 (February 1971), 38–42.
2. Allvine, Fred C. "The Patronage Decision-Making Process," unpublished doctoral dissertation, Indiana University, 1966.
3. Ambrose, P. J. "An Analysis of Intra-Urban Shopping Patterns," *Town Planning Review,* 38 (January 1968), 327–34.
4. Amstutz, Arnold E. *Computer Simulation of Competitive Market Response.* Cambridge, Mass.: The M.I.T. Press, 1967.
5. Applebaum, William. "The Analog Method for Estimating Potential Store Sales," in Curt Kornblau, ed., *Guide to Store Location Research, with Emphasis on Supermarkets.* Reading, Mass.: Addison-Wesley, 1968, 232–43.
6. Bass, Frank M., Edgar A. Pessemier, Richard D. Teach, and W. Wayne Talarzyk. "Preference Measurement in Consumer Market Research," Paper No. 257, Herman C. Krannert Graduate School of Industrial Administration, Purdue University, September 1969.
7. Baumol, William, and I. T. Ide. "Variety in Retailing," *Management Science,* 3 (October 1956), 93–101.
8. Berry, Brian J. L. *Geographic Perspectives on the Urban Systems.* Englewood Cliffs, N. J.: Prentice-Hall, 1970.
9. Dixon, W. J., ed. *Biomedical Computer Programs.* Berkeley: University of California Press, 1970.
10. Engel, James F., David T. Kollat, and Roger D. Blackwell. *Consumer Behavior.* New York: Holt, Rinehart and Winston, 1968.
11. Fishbein, Martin. "A Behavior Theory Approach to the Relations Between Beliefs About an Object and the Attitude Toward the Object," in Martin

Fishbein, ed., *Readings in Attitude Theory and Measurement*. New York: John Wiley & Sons ,1967, 389–400.

12. Getis, Arthur. "The Determination of Location of Retail Activities with the Use of a Map Transformation," *Economic Geography*, 43 (January 1963), 14–22.

13. Hodges, Joseph L., Jr. *Discriminatory Analysis*. Randolph Air Force Base, Texas: Air University School of Aviation Medicine, United States Air Force, 1955.

14. Huff, David L., and Larry Blue. *A Programmed Solution for Estimating Retail Sales Potentials*. Lawrence: Center for Regional Studies, University of Kansas, 1966.

15. MacKay, David B. "Consumer Movement and Store Location Analysis," unpublished doctoral dissertation, Northwestern University, 1970.

16. ———. "Discriminant Inputs for Monte Carlo Simulations," *Combined Proceedings*. Spring and Fall Conferences, American Marketing Association, 1971, 513–7.

17. Marble, Duane F. "A Simple Markovian Model of Trip Structures in a Metropolitan Region," *Proceedings*. Regional Science Association, Western Sections, 1964, 150–6.

18. McGarrity, Richard. "An Application of Space Transformation in Evaluating the Urban Location Pattern of Multi-Unit Retail Firms," unpublished doctoral dissertation, Northwestern University, 1969.

19. Nelson, Richard L. *The Selection of Retail Locations*. New York: McGraw-Hill, 1966.

20. Nystuen, John D. "A Theory and Simulation of Urban Travel," *Studies in Geography, No. 13*. Evanston, Ill.: Northwestern University Press, 1967, 54–83.

21. Oi, Walter Y., and Paul W. Shuldiner. *An Analysis of Urban Travel Demands*. Evanston, Ill.: Northwestern University Press, 1962.

22. Rao, Tanniru R. "Consumer's Purchase Decision Process: Stochastic Models," *Journal of Marketing Research*, 6 (August 1969), 321–9.

23. Reilly, William J. *The Law of Retail Gravitation*. New York: Reilly, 1931.

24. Simon, Herbert A. "A Behavioral Model of Rational Choice," in Herbert Simon, ed., *Models of Man*. New York: John Wiley & Sons, 1956, 241–60.

Institutional Change and Adaptive Behavior In Small-City Retailing

Peter S. Carusone

A study of retailing in nonmetropolitan cities was undertaken in 1968. The problem the research focused upon was the lack of empirical data relating to the nature, extent, and impact of retail trade decentralization in such cities. Since the U.S. Census of Retailing does not report central business district (CBD) data for cities of less than 100,000 population, the prevailing state of knowledge on the subject has been characterized by divergent views generally unsupported by empirical research.

Richard Nelson, writing in 1958, claimed that the downtowns suffering most from shopping center competition are those in cities of 25,000 to 250,000 population.[1] Herbert Landsman, in 1964, described small cities as having few new retail developments and no shopping centers of any consequence.[2] Ronald Boyce, in 1963, descried the lack of attention to small-city problems and pointed out that small communities are witnessing far more change, relatively, than the large metros.[3] Homer Hoyt, in 1966, claimed that the central areas still retain their dominance in smaller cities where there are not enough residents in any one section of the metro area to support a regional center.[4]

To shed some light on the extent to which the process of decentralization has affected the retail trade structure of the small city, an exploratory study of the GAF market[5] in ten nonmetropolitan cities in Ohio was conducted. The results of the research show that the small city is experiencing substantial upgrading, decentralization and expansion of retail trade facilities[6]; that it is possible to explain the growing relative importance of small-city retailing by analyzing the small urban

---

Reprinted from the *Marquette Business Review*, Vol. XVIII, No. 2, Summer 1974, by permission of the author and editor.

[1] Richard L. Nelson, *The Selection of Retail Locations.* New York, F. W. Dodge Corp., 1958, p. 34.

[2] Herbert S. Landsman, "Spatial Aspects of Retail Competition," in Stephen A. Greyser (ed.), *Toward Scientific Marketing.* Chicago, American Marketing Association, 1964, p. 475.

[3] Ronald R. Boyce, "Commercial and Industrial Development in Smaller Cities," *Public Management* (August, 1963), pp. 174–178.

[4] Homer Hoyt, "Trends in CBD Shopping Goods Sales," *Urban Land* (July–August, 1966), p. 8.

[5] General merchandise, apparel, furniture, home furnishings and equipment stores.

[6] See Peter S. Carusone, "The Shake-Out in Small-City Retailing," *Bulletin of Business Research* (Columbus: The Ohio State University, Center for Business and Economic Research, June, 1970), pp. 1–3, 6–8.

retailing system within an ecological framework [7]; and that the shift in point of patronage resulting from this decentralization process has important policy and strategy implications throughout the channel of distribution.[8] Subsequent analysis of data from the study has provided additional insights into the performance patterns of independent merchants, their propensity to respond to a changing competitive environment and their rationale for seeking to maintain the status quo.

Purpose

The main purpose of this paper is to evaluate the adaptive behavior of independent merchants in relation to the opportunities which institutional change in the small city has produced. What changes in store policies, merchandising or promotional strategies or effort have downtown merchants implemented in response to emerging suburban competition? What kinds of cooperative programs have been adopted to stimulate downtown shopping in the face of an expanded, upgraded, and decentralized retail structure? Why have downtown merchants chosen to stay downtown rather than move to the suburbs? How do these tendencies compare with the opportunities for adaptive behavior in small-city retailing?

The Research

To minimize the possible influence of factors arising from regional differences, the scope of inquiry was limited to a single geographic area—central Ohio. Criteria were developed to guide the initial stages of investigation with respect to defining the concept of "small city" and selecting cities to survey.

1. The city should represent the dominant trade center for GAF merchandise in its respective county.
2. The city should be large enough so that the emergence of suburban shopping facilities is a distinct possibility.
3. The city should be small enough so as to retain substantial homogeneity in terms of overall retail structure with the smallest cities which qualify under point 2.
4. The city should contain some degree of social and economic separation from larger neighboring cities.

In addition to an intensive review of the relevant literature and secondary sources of statistical information, the preliminary investigation included correspondence and personal interviews with numerous retailing executives, field inspections of six cities and a pilot study of one city.

The result of the preliminary analysis was to select the cities for the study according to the following operational definition: *Small city*—the largest urban place in a nonmetropolitan county where the city has a population in excess of 10,000 and where the county contains a total population in excess of 25,000. Selected population and income data for each of the ten survey cities are shown in Table 1.

---

[7] See Peter S. Carusone, "The Growing Strength of Small-City Retailing," *Journal of Retailing* (Winter, 1970–71), pp. 50–57, 76.

[8] See Peter S. Carusone, "A Shift in the Point of Patronage," *MSU Business Topics* (Autumn, 1970), pp. 61–69.

TABLE 1

Selected Population and Income Characteristics: Small Cities in Central Ohio and State of Ohio

City	County	Population 1967 (000)	Population 1960–67 Percent Change	Income per Capita 1967
Bellefontaine		12.2	7.0%	
	Logan	36.3	4.3	$2,338
Coshocton		14.5	10.7	
	Coshocton	33.2	3.1	2,226
Mount Vernon		13.8	3.8	
	Knox	40.4	4.1	2,360
Urbana		11.1	5.7	
	Champaign	31.2	5.1	2,232
Washington CH		13.5	8.9	
	Fayette	26.0	4.8	2,086
Subtotal		65.1	7.2	
Subtotal		167.1	4.2	2,262
Chillicothe		28.1	12.3	
	Ross	65.4	6.9	2.272
Lancaster		34.4	15.1	
	Fairfield	72.3	13.1	2,451
Marion		39.3	5.9	
	Marion	66.8	11.0	2,652
Newark		46.5	11.2	
	Licking	105.6	17.1	2,527
Zanesville		38.9	—0.5	
	Muskingum	81.1	2.4	2,315
Subtotal		187.2	8.3	
Subtotal		391.2	10.3	2,448
Total		252.3	8.0	
Total		558.3	8.4	2,392
State of Ohio		10,749.2	10.7	2,736

Source: U.S. Bureau of the Census; Development Department, State of Ohio; "Survey of Buying Power," *Sales Management,* June 10, 1968.

Design of Study

The major objective of the study was to provide a comprehensive description and analysis of the extent to which the process of decentralization has affected the retail trade structure for GAF stores in the small city. To guide the research, a series of operational objectives was set forth:

1. to determine the division of retail trade among GAF stores, in 1958, 1963 and 1967, between downtown and suburbs
2. to determine the division of retail trade among GAF stores by line-of-business, ownership, and size-of-store
3. to determine the rationale for development of suburban retail centers in the small city
4. to determine the rationale for decisions

of downtown merchants to remain downtown
5. to identify shifts in the geographical distribution of downtown GAF store locations.

Because the study was exploratory in nature and was the first of its kind, a research plan using the case study method was developed. To satisfy the multifaceted data requirements, a variety of data-gathering techniques was utilized.

The major part of the research project involved an intensive effort to reconstruct data from the *Census of Business* by obtaining realistic approximations of sales for each city's GAF stores, according to the various classifications (location, line-of-business, ownership, etc.). The resulting breakdowns, it should be noted, represent direct estimates of parameters rather than sampling estimations of a larger population.

The Field Survey

Secondary sources were searched before, during and after each field survey. Personal observation of all GAF retailing facilities was carried out to obtain information on store locations, store sizes (measurement by pacing), variety of merchandise carried and other operating characteristics.

Personal interviews were conducted with 71 retail store owners and managers and with 18 chamber of commerce and retail merchants' association officials, bankers, and other persons believed to have information of value to the study. Since the main purpose of the interviews was to secure information on specific past events, most of the merchants contacted were persons known to have a good knowledge of the local

retailing situation. Others were selected from among store groups thought to be important to the study.

Computation Procedures

A combination of techniques was used in the computation of sales volume estimates by the various store groupings. Standard space–productivity ratios by line-of-business were applied to the square footage of floor space in each line of business category with adjustments according to each city's deviation from the norm. Actual and estimated sales figures for individual stores, when available from the field survey or from secondary sources, were also used. Where knowledge concerning qualitative performance of individual stores dictated, the standard space–productivity ratios were further modified.

The upper limit for each city's total GAF sales was imposed by *Census of Business* data for each of the three census years. The fact that GAF stores in small cities are highly visible and relatively few in number made the task of obtaining a reasonable degree of sales proportionality among groups of stores quite manageable.

Institutional Change

The major findings of the study, as reported elsewhere, show that the small city is experiencing substantial expansion, upgrading and decentralization of retail trade facilities. As shown in Table 2, decentralization in the cities surveyed effected a decline in the share of GAF store sales concentrated in the CBD from 88 percent in 1958 to 49 percent in 1967. The growth in total GAF store sales, in fact, exceeded the growth in total personal income (80

TABLE 2
Estimated GAF Store Sales by Location: Small Cities in Central Ohio

City	Year	Downtown ($mills.)	Suburban ($mills.)	Total City ($mills.)	Downtown Percent to Total
Bellefontaine	1958	$ 5.7	$ 0.1	$ 5.8	99%
	1967	8.9	0.1	9.0	99
Coshocton	1958	5.8	0.2	6.0	96
	1967	6.9	2.1	9.0	77
Mt. Vernon	1958	7.0	0.2	7.2	97
	1967	7.7	4.2	11.9	65
Urbana	1958	2.5	0.2	2.7	92
	1967	2.8	1.6	4.4	64
Washington CH	1958	4.8	0.8	5.6	86
	1967	5.0	1.8	6.8	74
Subtotal	1958	25.8	1.5	27.3	95
	1967	31.3	9.8	41.1	76
Chillicothe	1958	7.5	1.6	9.1	82
	1967	5.8	16.8	22.6	26
Lancaster	1958	8.9	1.8	10.7	83
	1967	7.2	11.6	18.8	38
Marion	1958	13.1	1.3	14.4	91
	1967	14.0	12.5	26.5	53
Newark	1958	12.1	2.1	14.2	85
	1967	9.8	21.8	31.6	31
Zanesville	1958	13.4	2.8	16.2	83
	1967	12.7	11.7	24.4	52
Subtotal	1958	55.0	9.6	64.6	85
	1967	49.5	74.4	123.9	40
Total	1958	80.8	11.1	91.9	88
	1967	80.8	84.2	165.0	49

percent to 66 percent, respectively) over the nine year period.

The development of suburban shopping centers and discount houses in the small city has transformed a traditionally low-capacity retailing system into a higher-capacity, consumer-oriented one. Expansion of temporal, spatial and service dimensions of competition is evident from the introduction of larger scale operations, longer store hours, improved accessibility, convenient parking facilities, one-stop shopping, and modern, attractive surroundings.

Retailing in the small city has matured quickly—from a system which seemed to be in the extinction mode in 1958 to one which is capable of both retaining a larger proportion of local consumer expenditures and exerting a stronger pull on outlying towns and rural areas.

Decline of the Independent Sector

The major change in the institutional structure of small-city retailing stems from the emergence of relatively large-scale retail establishments, especially those which emphasize mass merchandising techniques such as "discounting" and self-service. The number of discount houses in the ten cities combined increased from three in 1958 to 22 in 1967. The number of planned shopping centers containing GAF stores increased from three in 1958 to 15 in 1967. In 1958 the largest stores ranged in size from 25,000 to 40,000 square feet of floor space, but by 1967 they ranged from 40,000 to 100,00 square feet. As shown in Table 3, the aggregate scale of new commercial developments has been substantial, both in absolute terms and in relation to population.

As might be expected, regional and national chains accounted for most of the new large-scale developments and, consequently, for the largest share of the increase in sales over the nine-year period. Chain stores had an estimated 63 percent share-of-market in 1967 compared with only 49 percent in 1958.

Table 4 shows a breakdown of sales according to ownership (chain versus independent) and tenure (new versus established store). The term "new" refers to stores completely new to their respective cities since 1958, and does not include stores relocated from within the same city. "Established" refers to stores which were doing business in their respective cities both in 1958 and 1967, plus those in operation during 1958 but not at the end of year 1967.

As shown in Table 4, established chains account for the single largest share (46.3%) of the total nine-year increase in sales. Two-thirds of this amount, in turn, represents business done by national department store chains, namely, Sears, Ward's and Penney's.

TABLE 3
Selected Measures of Change in Size of GAF Stores

	1958	1967
Number of stores 25,000 square feet and over	23	49
Average size of store (sq. ft.)	6,100	9,300
Total floor space (000 sq. ft.)	2,979	4,447
Floor space per capita	3.6	5.0

TABLE 4
Sales Trends by Ownership and Tenure

	GAF Sales $mill.			Percent of Total Change
	1958	1967	Change 1958–67	
Established independents	$46.9	$ 47.5	$ 0.6	0.8%
Established chains	45.0	78.8	33.8	46.3
New independents	—	12.8	12.8	17.5
New chains	—	25.9	25.9	35.4
Total	$91.9	$165.0	$73.1	100.0%

New chain stores account for the second largest share (35.4%) of the total 1958–67 increase in sales. Discount houses account for the major part (three-fifths) of this amount.

Independent stores (both new and established) account for less than 19 percent of the total increase in sales.

Opportunities for Adaptive Behavior

One of the prerequisites for survival of retail stores is the capacity to adapt to changing market conditions. The opportunity for adaptive behavior carries with it the responsibility to pursue a strategy that corresponds to consumer needs under current conditions. The relatively poor overall performance of independent merchants in the cities studied would seem to be indicative of a lack of adaptive behavior.

Traditionally, small-city retailing has been characterized as a low-capacity system of small, less specialized stores which, due to a limited market, had to appeal to a cross-section of many income and occupational groups. The need to meet a heterogeneous market demand out of a relatively small physical plant meant that each merchant was trying to satisfy mass merchandising needs from limited merchandise assortments.

As the institutional structure has changed, however, it would seem that the conditions that once precluded specialization have tended to dissipate. If the decentralization has served to expand the size of the local market and if mass merchandisers are now satisfying mass merchandising needs, the most logical opportunity for the independent merchant, it would seem, would be to orient his strategy toward a single market segment through specialization. There were only a few changes reported which tended in this direction.

Competitive Response of CBD Stores

One of every six downtown stores reportedly made some major or minor change in store policies, merchandising or promotional strategy or effort as a direct response to new suburban competition. As shown in Table 5, about half of these changes simply involved increasing advertising or remodeling. About one-fourth involved expansion of floor space and/or changes in merchandise variety or assortments. Most of these merchandise changes, incidentally, tended toward expansion of line rather than contraction. Nearly one of every five changes involved increased emphasis on lower price-lines, conversion to self-service, extension of store hours or other measures seemingly designed to compete directly with discount houses and shopping centers.

One incidence of competitive response is noteworthy in that it was the only change of its kind encountered, and reportedly had met with considerable success. It involves the expansion, remodeling, and reorganization of the S & L store in Marion, Ohio.

S & L is an independently owned departmentized specialty store consisting of an apparel shop, a gift shop, a leased shoe department and a leased men's department. In 1958 the store sold only clothing and contained about 7,000 square feet. By expanding into adjacent properties as vacated by other stores, the S & L amalgamation of some 20,000 square feet of floor space gradually emerged. With a new, modern facade across the Center Street entrances the store makes an attractive addition to downtown Marion.

TABLE 5
Downtown Store Changes in Response to Suburban Competition 1958–1967

	Number of Stores Reporting Change
Increase in advertising	14
Remodeling of facilities	13
Increased floor space and/or change in merchandise variety or assortments	13
Lowered price lines, conversion to self-service, extension of store hours, provision of off-street parking	11
Liberalized credit terms, greater emphasis on personalized service, added style shows	5
Total incidents of change	56
Total—Stores making changes	51
Downtown stores making no change	265
Total—Downtown stores (1967)	316

Cooperative Programs

Cooperative programs for the purpose of stimulating downtown shopping were limited mainly to provision of joint parking facilities (sometimes in conjunction with the city) and cooperative advertising. A distinct lack of solidarity among downtown merchants tended to limit the extent of cooperation in almost any other kind of program. Two incidents of cooperative effort are noteworthy.

Merchants in downtown Chillicothe installed a temporary mall for six months in 1967 which was discontinued when City Council determined that "the street was needed to handle through traffic." The project was constructed on a volunteer basis with trees, flowers and sod arranged in concrete blocks laid on the street. Streets north and south of the mall block were used for diagonal curb parking with a one-way traffic pattern on streets bordering the mall. Some blamed the mall's failure on the fact that the installation was not permanent. Others blamed the

general economy or local political problems.

Merchants in Marion, through the Chamber of Commerce, incorporated a series of off-street, metered parking lots in 1961. The lots are situated to the rear of the stores which face the main street. Many of these stores have since remodeled and have built rear entrances facing the lots. This effort reportedly has been quite successful in stimulating downtown shopping, and even instrumental in delaying the eventual development of the city's major suburban shopping center.

Why CBD Merchants Remain Downtown

Relocation is a strategic aspect of adaptive behavior which some downtown, independent merchants pursued, but most did not. While a number of reasons were reported as to why downtown retailers chose to remain downtown, the most important one according to the merchants of every city was that "performance is satisfactory." Of course, precisely what constitutes satisfactory performance for any given merchant involves elements of subjective reasoning not reflected in sales or profit figures.

Despite the overall decline in relative importance of the small-city CBD, many of the surviving downtown stores have continued to increase sales in the face of suburban competition. It is possible that a contraction in the "supply" of downtown GAF facilities since 1958 has served to correct, at least partially, the demand–supply imbalance effected by the initial impact of decentralization. A related factor is the shift in floor space usage within the CBD, from higher to lower productivity lines of business.

Other reasons cited for the decision to remain downtown include: rent differential with suburban locations, apathy to change, merchant owns his own building, overall strength of the downtown, lack of suitable suburban sites and fear of remoteness or other uncertainties.

Rationale for Maintaining Status Quo

The declining relative importance of the independent sector is a classic example of failure to respond to changes in the market environment. In the first instance, prior to the entry of new chain stores and the expansion of established ones, there is a failure to anticipate and provide for an orderly transition to a higher-capacity, decentralized retailing system. In the second instance, after the major impact of institutional change, there is a failure to take advantage of what seem to be the most promising opportunities for adaptive behavior—i.e., those that lean toward specialization. Moreover, there is a general unwillingness to participate in cooperative ventures which could help to

overcome diseconomies of scale and other limitations.

The fact that independents on the whole have demonstrated a lack of adaptive behavior does not, of course, justify concluding that the majority of them are insensitive to the needs of their customers. A special cross-tabulation of the data was run in order to pinpoint subgroups of independent stores for which sales performance might warrant use of the term "satisfactory." The results of this analysis, summarized in Table 6, indicate that it is quite possible that substantial numbers of independents in operation during 1967 could be doing an adequate job of serving some segment of the market.

As shown in Table 6, while total sales of all independents in the apparel line-of-business increased only 15 percent from 1958 to 1967, most of this relatively poor performance is attributable to the loss of sales by stores which went out of business prior to 1967. Comparing the increase in sales of new apparel independents with the loss of sales of discontinued operations accounts for a net loss of $1.9 million, or minus 44 percent. Much of this loss can be traced to attrition among men's and boys' wear establishments. The apparel independents which were open for business both in 1958 and in 1967, on the other hand, showed an increase in sales of about 45 percent.

In the general merchandise store category, the reverse situation seems to be the case. The performance of stores which were operating throughout the survey period was rather lackluster (26 percent increase in sales) while the net gain of new stores over discontinued operations amounted to $3.5 million, or plus 250 percent. Much of this net increase can be traced to the opening of

TABLE 6

Estimated Sales by Line of Business and Ownership New Stores, Out-Of-Business Stores, and Stores in Continuing Operation From 1958 to 1967

	1958		1967		Percent Change in Sales
	No./ Stores	Sales $000	No./ Stores	Sales $000	
Total, all stores	487	$91.9	479	$165.0	80%
Chain stores	161	$45.0	179	$104.7	133%
Independents	326	46.9	300	60.3	29
Independents only					
General merchandise stores	23	$14.2	25	$ 21.0	48%
Apparel stores	148	12.8	113	$ 14.7	15
Furn. and home furn. stores	155	19.9	162	$ 24.6	24
General merchandise stores					
Continuing stores (1958 and 1967)	17	$12.8	17	$ 16.1	26%
Out-of-bus. stores (1958 only)	6	1.4	—	—	—
New stores (1967 only)	—	—	8	4.9	250 *
Apparel stores					
Continuing stores (1958 and 1967)	89	$ 8.5	89	$ 12.3	45%
Out-of-bus. stores (1958 only)	59	4.3	—	—	—
New stores (1967 only)	—	—	24	2.4	—44 *
Furn. and home furn. stores					
Continuing stores (1958 and 1967)	101	$13.7	101	$ 17.8	30%
Out-of-bus. stores (1958 only)	54	6.2	—-	—	—
New stores (1967 only)	—	—	61	6.8	10 *

* Percentage change, new store sales compared with out-of-business store sales.

several discount houses and the closing of several variety stores and dry goods stores.

Conclusions

The adaptive behavior of independent merchants has been evaluated in relation to the opportunities which institutional change in the small city has produced. As such, some additional light is shed on the performance patterns of independent merchants, their propensity to respond to a changing competitive environment, and their rationale for seeking to maintain the status quo.

While the major findings of the study reported here have broad implications for firms throughout the channel of distribution, and for urban planners and geographers, attention in this paper has been focused on the demonstrated performance and behavior of the "small-town merchant" and his ability to survive in a more highly competitive and geographically differentiated market situation.

Need for Further Research

The research is believed to be the first comprehensive study of retail trade decentralization in the small city. As such, it was designed to be sufficiently broad and exploratory so as to encompass as many aspects of the potential problem area as practicable. It represents an attempt to identify problems rather than to find a solution for specific problems already known to exist. Thus, the analysis presented in this paper should serve to evoke a number of specific questions the resolution of which could be constructively pursued in future research.

First, there is a need to determine what particular market segments are being served by independent merchants in a post-decentralization situation. Are the residents of the local community continuing to patronize central business district stores while the major drawing power of the new suburban centers is more toward outlying communities and rural areas? What are the strategy implications of this situation for the independent merchant whose clientele remains essentially the same despite substantial changes in the overall institutional structure?

Second, there is a need for an attitudinal study of independent merchants in the small city, to determine their awareness of the dimensions of the decentralization problem, their inclination toward truly adaptive behavior and the extent to which they may be willing to subordinate some of their independence to others in a trade-off for improved survival and growth prospects.

Third, a study of small-city consumer buying habits should be undertaken to determine precisely what changes in shopping patterns occur as the result of substantial retail decentralization. Such a study would serve to pinpoint the specific merchandise lines and patronage appeals responsible for the shift away from out-of-city and catalogue shopping, and for the shift from downtown to suburban shopping. A before-and-after methodology could be employed to measure expenditure and shopping patterns both prior to and after the development of a major small-city shopping center.

Finally, a compartive study of small cities in some other region of the country should contribute materially to the body of knowledge concerning retail trade flows and retail trade decentralization. Any attempt to project the results of the present study to another region, say, the Southwest, might not be valid because of differences in the characteristics of trading areas, population densities and retail trade structures from those which are typical of the Midwest.

CONSUMER BEHAVIOR, PROFILES, AND PREFERENCES

Mapping a market is a continuous inventory process used by market researchers to monitor changes of market segments and their respective quality. A number of dimensions are utilized for this purpose:

1. Age
2. Income
3. Family life cycle
4. Education
5. Home ownership
6. Ethnicity
7. Socioeconomic status
8. Motivations, values, interests
9. Place of residence
10. Residence identity–image
11. Freqeuncy–location of convenience goods purchase
12. Frequency–location of shopper goods purchase

Refinement of market segments in a trade area can permit an analyst greater latitude in outlining potential tenancies, say, for a required shopping center, as opposed to mere aggregate data on consumers. This kind of micro-consumer analysis can be further extended through questionnaire data, assuming that time and costs permit.

Recent developments in sampling theory and practice along with advances in multidimensional scaling techniques provide insights heretofore absent in market research. The latter in particular generates findings along attitudinal–lifestyle measures that can signal specialized but profitable retailing opportunities. Further advances in theory and application suggest powerful means for measures of store image, management–service satisfactions, and the like.

Motivation and mobility is the central theme of a study by John R. Thompson of a university town, Athens, Georgia.

In two companion studies on shopping center preference, James A. Brunner and John L. Mason report on Toledo while William E. Cox and Ernest F. Cooke are concerned with Cleveland. Both are definitive studies within the data-assumption matrix utilized.

Social class structure vis-à-vis the purchase of a new television set provides the research design by Grady D. Bruce and William P. Dommermuth. Predictors of consumer behavior are formulated with implications for retail shopping activities.

W. Bruce Weale discusses matters of identity and image, which represent one of several intangible dimensions of retail firm assets and corresponding viability. Patrons of a discount store are the subject of an analysis in a college town by Dardis and Sandler.

In a study of the retailing base of Barberton, Ohio, several years ago, the author found another, less researched dimension of consumers, home-town loyalty, which transcends store loyalty or brand preferences. The notion of buying and spending in the place of residence pervades the typical shopper for convenience goods, which is most likely, and for shopper goods. Manifestly, in this kind of situation, home-town loyalty becomes an important, although random, variable in any gravity model of retail attraction, massing and concentration of retailing facilities, and so on.

Shopper Mobility

John R. Thompson

That consumers frequently trade outside their local trade center is a continuing problem for retailers, particularly for those located in small towns. However, the phenomenon of consumer out-shopping has seldom been reported in the literature of marketing.[1]

The study reported in this article investigated the factors which affect shopping outside local retail trade areas by permanent residents. Shopping behavior and the personal characteristics which facilitated or impeded out-of-town shopping were examined. Such characteristics include: family size, income, age, education, race, presence of credit cards, and so forth.

The study also examined the attitudes of respondents toward local shopping conditions in order to determine some of the reasons for out-of-town shopping. Primarily, this information includes responses concerning shopping difficulties experienced by the respondents, such as limited selections of merchandise, inconveniences, high prices, and so forth. Lastly, the study attempted to determine why the respondent shopped out of town. Significant relationships between characteristics of the respondent and out-shopping were examined.

Basis for Study

The data were provided by permanent full-time residents of the city of Athens, a university town, located about 70 miles from Atlanta. An area sampling procedure was employed in such a manner that cross representation was obtained of the permanent full-time residents of the city. The data were collected by personal interview from 340 respondents, primarily housewives.

Of the total of 340 respondents, 61% had shopped out-of-town at some time within the six months prior to the interview. In this study, an out-shopper is defined as a consumer who has made at least one purchase out of town in the previous six months. The median number of such shopping trips was three. The frequency of out-of-town shopping trips was high, with over 17% of the respondents indicating that they had shopped out of town more than six times within the previous six months.

Atlanta was the overwhelming choice

Reprinted from the *Atlanta Economic Review*, January 1971, by permission of the author and publisher.

1 An exception to this statement is Robert O. Herrman and Leland L. Beik, "Shoppers' Movements Outside Their Local Retail Area," *Journal of Marketing*, October 1968, pp. 45–51.

as the site of the out-shopping trip, with over 75% of respondents reporting that the destination of their last trip for shopping purposes was Atlanta.

Purchase Categories

Table 1 shows the types of purchases which were made out of town. Generally speaking, these products were most frequently either very large ticket items or had some elements of fashion or status. This finding is consistent with information contained elsewhere.[2] For example, over 36% of the people reporting purchases of automobiles said they had made their last purchase out of town; similarly, approximately 34% said they had made their last purchase of a man's suit out of town. On the other hand, items such as children's clothes, which apparently do not carry the same connotations in the minds of

the consumer, and housewares were purchased out-of-town by only 9% and 12% of the respondents respectively.

In addition to out-of-town shopping in person, out-shopping is also accomplished by mail. In certain categories of products, the mail-order system is relatively important and compounds the problem for local retailers. As with personal out-shopping, catalog purchases were also higher among high-income groups.

Personal Characteristics

Table 2 indicates characteristics of the respondent families. Consistent with previous reports, as income increased, the amount of out-shopping also increased.[3] This was true in every income category. Low-income families apparently then become a part of the captive market for retailers in a given

TABLE 1
Out-of-Town Purchases

Purchase Category	Number Reporting Purchases	Percent Purchased out of Town	Percent Purchased by Mail
Automobile	312	36.2	—
Mens suit	287	34.1	—
Ladies coat	298	30.8	—
Rugs or carpeting	255	29.0	3.5
Furniture	285	27.4	.7
Ladies dress	309	26.5	.6
Sporting goods	242	19.4	3.3
Curtains, drapes	284	18.6	3.2
Jewelry	252	15.9	.8
Appliances	285	12.6	1.4
Housewares	291	12.4	2.1
Childrens clothes	268	9.3	2.2

[2] Brian J. L. Berry, *Geography of Market Centers and Retail Distribution* (Englewood Cliffs, N.J.: Prentice-Hall, Inc., 1967), p. 24 ff.

[3] Stuart U. Rich, *Shopping Behavior of Department Store Customers* (Boston, Graduate School of Business Administration, Harvard University, 1963), p. 141.

TABLE 2
Out-of-Town Shopping and Personal Characteristics

Characteristic	Percent of Out-Shoppers	Percent of In-Shoppers	Total Shoppers
A. Income			
Under $5,000	43.2	56.8	44
5,000–9,999	42.3	57.7	97
10,000–14,999	74.1	26.9	93
15,000–19,999	77.4	22.6	53
Over 20,000	84.4	15.6	32
Did not answer			21
$\chi^2 = 40.57, p < .001$			
B. Occupation of Head of Household			
University faculty, secondary teachers	81.8	18.2	77
Other professional	76.2	23.8	42
Manager, proprietor	72.2	27.8	54
Clerical, sales	58.8	41.2	51
Laborer	40.7	59.3	59
Student	53.8	46.2	13
Retired	40.0	60.0	30
Unemployed		100.0	3
Did not answer			11
$\chi^2 = 50.51, p < .001$			
C. Education of Head of Household			
No school		100.0	1
Grade school	26.3	73.7	38
High school	45.1	54.9	91
College	74.7	25.3	99
Graduate school	76.1	23.9	109
Did not answer			2
$\chi^2 = 51.28, p < .001$			
D. Age of Head of Household			
Under 30	74.4	25.6	43
31–40	69.8	30.2	106
41–50	60.0	40.0	80
51–59	55.7	44.3	61
60 and over	40.4	59.6	47
Did not answer			3
$\chi^2 = 15.90, p < .02$			
E. Presence of Children			
0 Children	60.3	39.7	53
1 Child	63.9	36.1	65
2	66.3	34.7	86
3	61.0	39.0	77
4	59.9	41.1	39
5	25.0	75.0	16
6	100.0	0.0	3
More than 6	0.0	100.0	1
Total			340
$\chi^2 = 14.04, p < .05$			

TABLE 2—Continued

Characteristic	Percent of Out-Shoppers	Percent of In-Shoppers	Total Shoppers
F. Age of Youngest Child			
Under 2	76.1	23.9	21
2	75.0	29.0	16
3	58.8	41.1	17
4	80.9	19.1	21
5	56.3	43.7	16
Over 5	58.4	41.6	190
Total			281
$X^2 = 8.04, p < .40$			
G. Local Credit Cards or Charge Accounts			
With local credit	65.4	34.6	280
Without local credit	43.1	57.9	57
Did not answer			33
Total			370
$X^2 = 12.37, p < .005$			
H. Out-of-Town Credit Cards or Charge Accounts			
With credit	71.7	28.3	240
Without credit	37.1	62.9	97
Did not answer			3
Total			340
$X^2 = 35.84, p < .001$			

area. This finding is supported by other studies which the author has conducted and which are reported in *Georgia Business*.[4] One of the significant facilitating factors determining willingness to shop out of town is the level of income in the family.

A significant relationship is also shown between the occupation of the household head and the amount of out-shopping. For example, nearly 82% of university faculty and secondary teachers had shopped out of town.

Education and out-shopping show a significant correlation. That is, the more highly educated persons shopped out of town. There is less significant relationship between the age of the head of the household and out-shopping.

Out-shopping is more prevalent among holders of out-of-town credit cards. Table 2 shows this relationship as well as an indication of the effects of local credit accounts on out-shopping.

Local Drawbacks

Out-shopping was significantly greater among persons who reported having had some difficulty in shopping locally. This information is shown in Table 3. The most frequently mentioned reasons for shopping out-of-town were that too small a selection is found locally and prices in the local market are too high, or that parking problems had been experienced. Again, these reasons

[4] John R. Thompson, "Out-of-Town Shopping in the CSRA," *Georgia Business*, March 1970.

TABLE 3
Shoppers and Difficulty in Local Shopping

Experienced Difficulties in Shopping in Athens	Percent of Out-Shoppers	Percent of In-Shoppers	Total Shoppers
Yes	65.6	34.4	293
No	35.7	64.3	42
No answer			5
Total			340

$\chi^2 = 14.77, p < .001$

may not be the specific factors accounting for the out-shopping. They were mentioned as being more important to the shopper than any of the others—such as unpleasant store appearance and inconvenient store hours.

Conclusions and Comparisons

Of the respondents, 61% shopped out of town at some time in the last six months, and the frequency of their trips was high. The median number of such out-of-town purchases was three, but a substantial proportion of the respondents indicated more than six. By far the most important destination of the out-shopping trip was Atlanta—the dominant city in the Athens area. Some 62% of the respondents said that the purpose of the trip during which the purchase was made was shopping. Apparently consumers are willing to undergo the secondary costs necessary to purchase out of town. Out-shopping is most prevalent among high-income groups, highly educated groups, and younger families. It is also greater among families holding out-of-town charge accounts. The most commonly given reasons for failing to shop at

home are poor selection, high price, and local parking problems.

Herrman and Beik concluded that their findings could be construed as "representative of similar groups in other towns and cities away from metropolitan centers." [5] This study supports the propriety of that belief.

Implication

These studies suggest that high-income, well-educated consumers cannot be restricted to the offerings in the local market area. This is consistent with previous findings regarding shopper movement and level of income. Studies show that high-income shoppers have the mobility to cope with frustrations of shopping as they are perceived.[6]

What this suggests is the nature of the market for the small-town retailer. Is it one consisting of the low-income group, the elderly, and the underemployed with large families? These studies do not purport to identify these as market elements. For one thing, the usual manner of categorizing income is insufficent to make that determination, but it may be inferred. It is possible that the question of high prices in

[5] Herrman and Beik, op. cit., p. 46.
[6] For example, Charles J. Collazo, Jr., "Effects of Income Upon Shopping Attitudes and Frustrations," *Journal of Retailing*, Spring 1966, pp. 1–7.

poverty areas should be directed to less densely populated areas. The lower income shopper is confined to the local area. Is the low-income consumer a captive of the local market whether the market consists of the big-city ghetto or a small-town location?

The Influence of Driving Time upon Shopping Center Preference

James A. Brunner and John L. Mason

In the existing body of literature dealing with determination of planned shopping center trade areas, considerable attention has been devoted to discussing or recommending the consideration of such variables as population density, purchasing power or income distribution, driving time or distance, market penetration, natural barriers, and locational interdependence or competition. These topics would appear to lend themselves to many types of quantitative treatments which would not only support the authors' judgments and hypotheses but would also be in harmony with the current trend toward more scientific investigations in marketing. Unfortunately, numerical information pertaining to shopping center trade areas has been notably lacking.

Although it may be assumed that developers, managers, and consultants in the shopping center field have undertaken quantitative studies on the shopping habits of consumers, these generally have not been reported and are not available in sufficient quantity for the formulation of generalizations. An especially important void in this regard lies in the statistical measurement of the spatial dimension of the trade areas relevant to shopping centers, which is a precondition to most further analysis of customer preferences and habits for such retail centers. Therefore, the purpose of this study was to measure the influence of driving time upon customer preference for specific shopping centers and the significance of driving time in estimating the trade area of a center. Driving time, rather than distance, was used as the most meaningful measurement tool in the determination of trade area, as the effort required to reach a center is not necessarily correlated with the distance involved. In a non-quantitative way, most of the recent discussions of shopping centers have recommended this approach.

Previous Studies

Considerable attention has been devoted to the analysis of the retail sales of specific communities in order to ascertain their suitability as locations for retail establishments. Some of the earliest research on trading areas pertained to the influence of the major demand variables that affect retail po-

Reprinted from the *Journal of Marketing*, Vol. 32, April 1968, published by the American Marketing Association, by permission of the authors and editor.

tential,[1] but these studies have pertained primarily to trading areas of individual stores or cities.

In those studies that are available, estimates of retail areas have been based upon population characteristics, purchasing power, the location of other retail establishments, and other significant factors. Some researchers have used a quantitative approach with the objective of developing laws or theories of retail attraction, while others have relied upon consumer buying habit surveys as they pertain to convenience shopping goods in order to determine the behavioral patterns of average or typical consumers. The ultimate objective of these studies has been to determine whether any systematic relationships exist among these variables which are relevant for the development of a theory of retail shopping.

Studies on the relationships between purchasing power and retail sales are to be found in the literature as early as 1923 by Lawrence F. Mann, and more recently by Vera Russell in 1957.[2] In 1958, Robert Ferber related retail sales as a dependent variable to several factors such as the income of a city, the distance from the community under investigation to the nearest larger city, and the ratio of the number of retail establishments in the city to the number of the next largest community.[3]

Closely allied to the influence of driving time upon shopping center preference is the relationship between retail potential and distance. The early pioneers in this area were primarily concerned with determining the trading areas surrounding cities in order to define the outer limits of these areas. In 1925, Copeland maintained that a positive relationship could be demonstrated between his classification of consumer goods and the trading area of a community.[4] Later, considerable interest was aroused by William J. Reilly's study of the relationship between distance and retail trade, which was based upon a three-year study of trade patterns. From this was developed what is known today as Reilly's law of retail gravitation in which the factors of population and distance between communities are incorporated. This law was subjected to many tests over the years by Reilly and Converse and by others who were interested in developing a theory of retail gravitation and are adequately described elsewhere.[5]

However, in these investigations, the research was not on planned shopping centers; in addition, the spatial factor was considered in terms of distance rather than travel time involved. The objective of this study has been to measure the spatial factor in temporal terms and to formulate some conclusion on this basis.

Setting of the Study

The City of Toledo is located in Northwestern Ohio at the western extremity of Lake Erie. In the three-county stan-

---

[1] An excellent review of the literature on these topics is presented in Donald L. Thompson, *Analysis of Retailing Potential in Metropolitan Areas* (Berkeley, California: Institute of Business and Economic Research, University of California, 1964).

[2] Vera K. Russell, "The Relationship Between Income and Retail Sales in Local Areas," *Journal of Marketing*, Vol. XXI (January, 1957), p. 330.

[3] Robert Ferber, "Variations in Retail Sales Between Cities," *Journal of Marketing*, Vol. XXII (January, 1958), pp. 295–303.

[4] Melvin T. Copeland, *Principles of Merchandising* (Chicago and New York: A. W. Shaw Co., 1925), p. 69.

[5] Same reference as footnote 1, pp. 30–36.

dard metropolitan statistical area consisting of two counties in the State of Ohio and one in Southeastern Michigan, there are 195,540 occupied households and a population of approximately 659,000 persons. The effective buying income per family is $8,006, the second highest of the major Ohio markets. In addition, Toledo is third in Ohio in retail sales per capita; and total retail sales in 1964 were $852 million. Because it is a relatively isolated market, Toledo is frequently used as a test market by manufacturers.

In addition to the central business district, which suffered a diminution in sales from 1958 to 1963 from $113 million to $88 million, there are five major planned shopping centers. Data are presented for these centers in Table 1. It may be observed that sales volume of the largest center was approximately two and one-half times that of the second largest center, and six times as large as the sales of the smallest center in the Toledo area. In terms of establishment mix, the largest center had

three department stores as compared to two in the second largest center, and one each in the three smaller centers.

Information for this study was obtained from automobile licenses and was gathered in the period between Thanksgiving and Christmas of 1965. Five probability samples of approximately the same size and totaling 2,036 license numbers were systematically drawn from each of the shopping center parking lots throughout the shopping days and hours of this four-week period. The domiciles of the shoppers were then determined from automobile registration records, plotted on a map, and classified by census tracts. Utilizing driving time data determined in a previous study,[6] it was then possible to approximate the driving times for these households to the centers at which they had shopped at the time of this study. The trading area patterns of the shopping centers are not circular as is occasionally depicted, but in isochrons or amoeba-like patterns.[7] Further, as is shown on the map (Figure 1), there is

TABLE 1
Selected Characteristics of the Five Principal Planned Shopping Centers in Toledo, Ohio, 1963

Characteristic	Shopping Center				
	A	B	C	D	E
Retail sales (in millions of dollars)	47,214	18,821	17,858	12,256	6,895
Retail stores (total)	53	38	39	30	17
Convenience goods stores	8	9	11	9	4
Shopping goods stores	34	17	18	13	11
All other stores	11	12	10	8	2

Source: Retail Sales—U.S. Bureau of the Census, Census of Business, 1963 *Retail Trade: Major Retail Centers, Toledo, Ohio–Michigan, SMSA,* BC63-MRC-103, U.S. Government Printing Office, Washington, D.C. 1965, pp. 103–9, 103–12.

[6] The driving time data were obtained in conjunction with another, unrelated study of the shopping centers in July, 1965.

[7] Hawley suggested that such areas were ". . . star-shaped rather than circular in appearance, the number of points varying with the number of radiating thoroughfares." Amos Hawley, *Human Ecology* (New York: Ronald Press Company, 1950), p. 246.

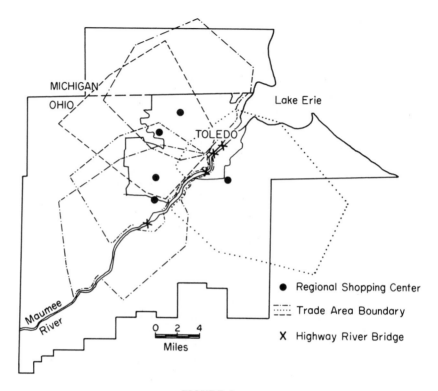

FIGURE 1

Trade Areas of Shopping Centers—Greater Toledo

considerable overlapping of the trading areas of the various centers.

Influence of Driving Time on Shopping Center Preference

Previous studies have suggested that consumers are reluctant to drive more than 20 minutes to patronize a shopping center, although empirical evidence is not presented to support this assertion.[8] However, it is clearly evident from this investigation that a shopping center's trading area is limited by the factor of driving time and that the most

significant driving time dimension for trade area analysis is 15 minutes. Between 70% and 76% of each center's patrons reside within 15 minutes driving distance of the center (see Table 2) and, although a substantial proportion of each center's customers is obtained from driving time increments of less than 15 minutes, relatively few patrons reside within time increments beyond 15 minutes (see Table 3). Moreover, Center A, which had three department stores, attracted 76% of its shoppers from an area within 15 minutes driving time, thereby suggesting that even the powerful drawing power of these

[8] Richard L. Nelson, *The Selection of Retail Locations* (New York: F. W. Dodge Corporation, 1958), pp. 209–210.

TABLE 2

Cumulative Percentage of Customers of Shopping Centers by Driving Time Required to Reach Shopping Center Patronized, Toledo, Ohio, 1956

Shopping Center	Driving Time in Minutes			
	0–5	0–10	0–15	0–20
	Percent of Customers			
A	17.7	48.9	76.4	81.7
B	31.3	53.0	76.5	87.2
C	31.7	54.1	72.5	84.6
D	27.5	58.5	72.7	85.8
E	37.5	59.4	70.1	81.6

TABLE 3

Percentage of Customers of Shopping Centers by Driving Time Required to Reach Shopping Center Patronized, Toledo, Ohio, 1965

Shopping Center	Driving Time in Minutes				
	0–5	6–10	11–15	16–20	21 or Over
	Percent of Customers				
A	17.7	31.2	27.5	5.3	18.3
B	31.3	21.7	23.5	10.7	12.8
C	31.7	22.4	18.4	12.1	15.4
D	27.5	31.0	14.2	13.1	14.2
E	37.5	21.9	10.7	11.5	18.4

department stores was insufficient to overcome this pattern of consumer driving reluctance. Shopping centers C and E, which are located on the fringes of the urban areas and dependent to a lesser degree upon the urban shoppers, attracted slightly more customers from rural areas at a driving distance of greater than 15 minutes. Nevertheless, all five centers attracted more than 81% of their customers from trading areas within 20 minutes or less driving distance of the respective centers.

A pattern also existed between the percentage of a center's customers who

resided within ten minutes driving time and its sales. As may be noted in Table 3, approximately 49% of Center A's customers resided within 10 minutes driving time as compared to approximately 59% of those of the smallest center, Center E. This suggests the hypothesis that, with a ten-minute driving time limitation, the smaller the center in terms of sales, the more dependent it is upon patrons who reside close to the center. However, beyond this driving distance, the same pattern did not prevail. A possible explanation is that the smallest centers do not offer as wide a variety or assortment of goods and stores as the larger competitors and, therefore, they are more dependent upon those who reside within a relatively short driving distance. Thus, one may conclude that the propensity to shop at a center is inversely associated with the driving time to reach the center, and that a time limitation of 15 minutes would be applicable for approximately three-fourths of the center's patrons.

Characteristics of the Trade Areas

Selected economic and demographic factors such as population, number of households, number of families, and family incomes, which are frequently used to determine market areas, are presented on a percentage basis for the trading areas within 15 minutes driving time of each center in Table 4. In order to compute these percentages, it was necessary to total each characteristic for each center's 15-minute driving time trade area. The data for the five shopping centers were then totaled, and percentages to indicate the relative economic and demographic size of each center's trade area were computed. Be-

TABLE 4

Comparison of the Relative Size of Selected Demographic and Income Characteristics in the 15 Minute Trade Areas of the Five Major Shopping Centers in the Toledo, Ohio Area

	Shopping Center					
	A	B	C	D	E	Total
Characteristic	Percent of Total Characteristic For Each Shopping Center [a]					
Population	28.8	23.6	18.1	17.3	12.2	100.0
Households	28.6	24.0	18.2	17.7	11.5	100.0
Families	28.8	24.0	17.5	17.7	12.0	100.0
Family Income	29.8	25.0	14.9	18.8	11.5	100.0

Source: Based on *Census of Population* data.
[a] Because the 15-minute driving time trade areas for each shopping center overlap with the trade areas of other centers, data associated with the overlapping areas were included more than once in computing the total. A more detailed explanation and illustration of this point is included in the paper.

cause the trade areas overlapped (see Figure 1), the income and demographic data in the overlapping sectors were included more than once in computing the total. For example, a household located in the overlapping trade areas of both Center A and Center B was included twice in computing the grand total of households for all centers.

As may be noted in Table 4, the socio-economic characteristics of the trade areas represented a cross-section of the urban area; and the population, households, families, and total family income percentages for each center were approximately the same. For example, about 29% of each of these factors were associated with Shopping Center A, and similar patterns existed for the other four shopping centers, with a few minor variations.

Thus a comparison of the socio-economic characteristics of the population in 15-minute trade areas of the five, suburban shopping centers reveals nothing of a unique nature which might affect the driving time preferences and limitations of the centers' patrons. As might be expected, the socio-economic comparison does indicate that the larger shopping centers will be found in trade areas with the greatest population.

Summary

The objective of this study has been to investigate the importance of driving time upon the preferences of consumers for regional shopping centers. Although it is recognized that population, purchasing power, population density, newspaper circulation, and other factors are influential in determining the shopping habits of consumers, a factor which is generally overlooked is the driving time required to reach the center. In this study it was demonstrated that the driving time required to reach a center is highly influential in determining consumer shopping center preferences. The most consistent and significant driving time dimension in delineating shopping center trade areas was found at the 15-minute driving points, as three-fourths of each center's shoppers resided within this range. However, additional research is needed to ascertain the degree to which these observations are generally true for other shopping centers in other communities and to determine the effect of expressways on shopping patterns, as a fully developed expressway complex did not exist in Toledo at the time of the study.

Other Dimensions Involved in Shopping Center Preference

William E. Cox, Jr.
Ernest F. Cooke

Several authors have commented on the significance of driving time in determining customer preference for alternative shopping facilities.[1] A quantitative study of shopping center driving time in Toledo, Ohio was reported by Professors Brunner and Mason in the April, 1968 issue of the *Journal of Marketing*.[2]

This article responds to Brunner and Mason's call for "additional research . . . to ascertain the degree to which [their] observations are generally true for other shopping centers in other communities." [3] A 1967 license plate survey of 93,500 passenger cars in 18 Greater Cleveland shopping centers was utilized in a driving time study to provide the required data to respond to the call for additional research.[4]

The Brunner and Mason Study

The Brunner and Mason article is a further contribution to the extensive body of literature on retail trade areas which has developed since the formulation of "Reilly's Law." [5] The objective,

Reprinted from the *Journal of Marketing*, Vol. 34, October 1970, published by the American Marketing Association, by permission of the authors and editor.

[1] Eli P. Cox and Leo G. Erickson, *Retail Decentralization* (East Lansing, Michigan: Bureau of Business and Economic Research, Michigan State University, 1967), p. 52; E. Jerome McCarthy, *Basic Marketing*, Revised Edition (Homewood, Illinois: Richard D. Irwin, Inc., 1964), p. 577; Richard L. Nelson, *The Selection of Retail Locations* (New York: F. W. Dodge Corp., 1958), p. 149; and Brian J. L. Berry, *Geography of Market Centers and Retail Distribution* (Englewood Cliffs, New Jersey: Prentice-Hall, Inc., 1967).

[2] James A. Brunner and John L. Mason, "The Influence of Driving Time upon Shopping Center Preferences," *Journal of Marketing*, Vol. 32 (April, 1968), pp. 57–61.

[3] Same reference as footnote 2, p. 61.

[4] *The Mobile Shopper in Greater Cleveland* (Cleveland: The Plain Dealer Marketing and Research Department, 1967); Malcolm Gienke, Julian Schneider, James Shalaty, Suzanne Simmons Palmer, and Bruce Tomcik, *A Study of the Influence of Driving Time upon Shopping Center Preference*, unpublished term paper, School of Management, Case Western Reserve University, 1969.

[5] William J. Reilly, *The Law of Retail Gravitation* (New York: The Knickerbocker Press, 1931); Paul D. Converse, *A Study of Retail Trade Areas in East Central Illinois*, Business Studies Number 2 (Urbana, Ill.: The University of Illinois, 1943); Cox and Erickson, same reference as footnote 1; James E. Suelflow, *Market Potential—Its Theory and Application* (Madison, Wisc.: The University of Wisconsin, Bureau of Business Research and Service, 1967), pp. 1–9; and Donald L. Thompson, *Analysis of Retailing Potential in Metropolitan Areas* (Berkeley, California: Institute of Business and Economic Research, University of California, 1964), pp. 29–39.

259

results, and possible limitations of the Brunner and Mason study are best expressed by their "Summary":

The objective of this study has been to investigate the importance of driving time upon the preferences of consumers for *regional* shopping centers. (Emphasis added.) Although it is recognized that population, purchasing power, population density, newspaper circulation, and other factors are influential in determining the shopping habits of consumers, a factor which is generally overlooked is the driving time required to reach the center. In this study it was demonstrated that the driving time required to reach a center is highly influential in determining consumer shopping center preferences. The most consistent and significant driving time dimension in delineating shopping center trade areas was found at the 15-minute driving points, as three-fourths of each center's shoppers resided within this range.[6]

The basic results of the Brunner and Mason study, shown in Table 1, are remarkably consistent especially at the 15-minute and 20-minute driving points. Brunner and Mason place their emphasis on the 15-minute driving point, calling it, "the most significant driving dimension for trade area analysis." [7]

Cleveland Compared to Toledo

Cleveland provides sufficient contrast to Toledo to justify using it for additional research. As shown in Table 2, Cleveland is more than three times as large as Toledo in terms of population, number of households and retail sales, and has a 16% higher effective buying income per household than Toledo. Cleveland ranks 11th in the United States among at S.M.S.A.'s in population, number of households, and retail sales, while Toledo ranks 50th in population and 49th in number of households and retail sales.

The Cleveland Study

Table 3 summarizes the results of a driving-time study for the seven *major regional* shopping centers in Cuyahoga County, Ohio (which includes Cleve-

TABLE 1

Selected Characteristics of the Five Principal Planned Toledo Shopping Centers 1963, and Cumulative Percentage of Their Customers by Driving Time, Toledo, Ohio, 1965

Shopping Center	Retail Sales (in millions of dollars)	Total Number of Retail Stores	Driving Time in Minutes			
			0–5	0–10	0–15	0–20
A	47	53	17.7	48.9	76.4	81.7
B	19	38	31.3	53.0	76.5	87.2
C	18	39	31.7	54.1	72.5	84.6
D	12	30	27.5	58.5	72.7	85.8
E	7	17	37.5	59.4	70.1	81.6

Source: James A. Brunner and John L. Mason, "The Influence of Driving Time upon Shopping Center Preferences," *Journal of Marketing,* Vol. 32 (April, 1968), pp. 58–59.

[6] Same reference as footnote 2, p. 61.

[7] Same reference as footnote 2, p. 59.

TABLE 2

Comparison of Cleveland and Toledo S.M.S.A., 1966

	Cleveland		Toledo	
Population	2,078,800	(11) [a]	670,000	(50) [a]
Households	620,300	(11)	202,400	(49)
Effective buying income per household	$10,096	(25)	$8,725	(116)
Retail sales ($1,000 of $'s)	$3,358,321	(11)	$1,023,120	(49)

Source: Sales Management Survey of Buying Power (June 10, 1969).

[a] The S.M.S.A.'s rank among all S.M.S.A.'s is shown in parentheses.

TABLE 3

Selected Characteristics of Eight Regional Planned Shopping Centers and Cumulative Percentage of Their Customers by Driving Time, Cleveland, Ohio, 1967

Shopping Center Number	Total Store Space (thousand square feet) [a]	Total Number of Stores [a]	Driving Time in Minutes [b]			
			0–5	0–10	0–15	0–20
3	518	53	39.8	56.4	68.1	72.3
5	712	53	40.9	64.1	73.9	79.3
17	635	69	42.4	54.0	69.5	77.2
28	1,350	103	27.3	36.1	55.5	68.4
38	900	73	34.3	51.9	64.5	78.0
49	407	63	63.7	79.3	83.7	86.3
59	1,000	63	28.6	55.5	64.0	83.1

[a] *The Mobile Shopper in Greater Cleveland* (Cleveland: The Plain Dealer Marketing and Research Department, 1967).

[b] Malcolm Gienke, Julian Schneider, James Shalaty, Suzanne Simmons Palmer, and Bruce Tomcik, *A Study of the Influence of Driving Time upon Shopping Center Preference,* unpublished term paper, School of Management, Case Western Reserve University, 1969.

land and is part of the Cleveland S.M.S.A.). The other 11 shopping centers which were part of the license plate survey were not included in the driving-time study because of smaller size, limited number of parking spaces, and/or location outside of Cuyahoga County. Table 3 indicates that the results for Cleveland are not as consistent as the results for Toledo. Among the five centers included in the Toledo study, the percentage of customers living within 15 minutes driving time ranged from 70.1% to 76.5%, a spread of only 6.4%. In Cleveland, however, the percentages for seven centers ranged

from 55.5% to 83.7%, a spread of 28.2%. This sharp difference in results is actually further magnified because the seven centers in the Cleveland study are closer in size than the five centers in the Toledo study. As shown in Table 1, the smallest center in Toledo has 17 stores and the largest has 53 stores, a range of over three to one. The smallest center in Cleveland · has 53 stores and the largest center has 103 stores, or a range of less than two to one. In Toledo, 1963 retail sales ranged from $7 million for the smallest center to $47 million for the largest center, or a range of almost seven to one. Comparable retail sales data are not available for Cleveland because one center (No. 59) did not open until 1966 and another (No. 38) opened in 1963. The other five centers had 1963 retail sales which ranged from $23 million (Center 3) to $65 million (Center 28), a range of less than three to one.[8] Also, Toledo did not have an expressway system at the time of the studies while Cleveland had one which was partially completed.

Significance of Driving Time

The consistency of the data in the Toledo study apparently led Professors Brunner and Mason to conclude that "driving time . . . is highly influential in determining consumer shopping center preferences." [9] The Cleveland data, however, show much greater variability in driving time at every driving point (5, 10, 15, and 20 minutes) and suggest the possibility that willingness to drive to a shopping center is determined more by other factors than by driving time. If this suggestion is valid, the willingness to drive might be considered to be a measure of the relative "drawing power" of a shopping center.

As an example of how willingness to drive might be used to measure the relative "drawing power" of a shopping center, Center 28 in the Cleveland study has 44.5% of its customers living more than 15 minutes away while Center 49 has 16.3% living more than 15 minutes from the center. Thus, Center 28 draws many more of its customers from be-

yond the 15-minute driving point than Center 49 and will be considered as having more relative "drawing power" than Center 49. This same measure can be used for the five Toledo shopping centers. For example, Center E has the greatest "drawing power" with 29.9% of its customers from beyond 15 minutes driving time, and Center B has the lowest drawing power with 23.5% of its customers from beyond 15 minutes driving time.

Reilly's Law

In using the willingness to drive to measure the relative "drawing power" of a shopping center, some of the factors other than driving time that may be associated with shopping center preferences are examined. Gravitational models of retail shopping behavior such as Reilly's Law have long been employed in similar situations. The idea behind gravitational models is that there are attractions which draw customers to a shopping facility, and there is a friction or inertia which the customer must overcome in order to shop at a given facility.[10] A number of factors may be used to represent the relative attractiveness of a shopping facility, such as the number of parking spaces, the size of the center, and the types of stores in the center. The friction or inertia to be overcome by the customer is usually measured in terms of distance or driving time, although perceived driving time has been suggested as an alternative measure.[11] Since driving time is incorporated in the willingness-

[8] *1963 Census of Business, Major Retail Centers, Cleveland, Ohio, S.M.S.A.* (Washington, D.C.: Bureau of Census, 1965), pp. 22-14 to 22-18.

[9] Same reference as footnote 2, p. 61.

[10] Cox and Erickson, same reference as footnote 1, p. 3, and Thompson, same reference as footnote 5, p. 38.

[11] Donald L. Thompson, "New Concept: Subjective Distance or Store Impressions Affect Estimates of Travel Time," *Journal of Retailing*, Vol. 39 (Spring, 1963), pp. 1–6.

to-drive measure used in this study, other locational factors will be examined for their association with variations in the willingness to drive.

If the differences in driving time for the Cleveland shopping centers studied indicate differences in customers' willingness to drive to a given shopping center, then a possible explanation may lie in the relative location and attractiveness of each center. The next step is to explain these differences in driving time by the location of the shopping centers and their relative attractiveness.

Location

Two factors are considered in location: (1) proximity of the center to other major shopping centers, and (2) distance from the center to major natural barriers. These figures are tabulated for the seven Cleveland shopping centers in Table 4.

As noted in Table 4, Center 28 is the most distance from any other major center and has the best "drawing power" (44.5%). Center 49 is close to Lake Erie, which forms the entire northern boundary of the Cleveland S.M.S.A., and thus limits all of this center's

"drawing power" (16.3%) to an almost semi-circular rather than circular form. To a lesser extent this is also true of Center 5, which is six minutes driving time from Lake Erie and which has the second lowest "drawing power" (26.1%). Since the area of a circle varies with the square of the radius, this "truncating" effect causes disproportionate changes in the area enclosed within each driving-time boundary.

Attractiveness

Several measures of each center's attractiveness are tabulated in Table 5. The total store area is a measure of the size of the shopping center as is the number of parking spaces. The number of department stores was considered to be a measure of the center's ability to "draw" customers living more than 15 minutes away, while the number of supermarkets was considered as a measure of the center's ability to draw customers who lived within 15 minutes of the center.

Analysis of these data in Table 5 shows high correlations of the percentage of shoppers living more than 15 minutes driving time from the center

TABLE 4
Relative Location of Seven Major Cleveland Shopping Centers, 1967

Shopping Center	28	59	38	3	17	5	49
% Customer living within 15-minute driving time	55.5	64.0	64.5	68.1	69.5	73.9	83.7
% Customer living over 15-minute driving time	44.5	36.0	35.5	31.9	30.5	26.1	16.3
Driving time to nearest major shopping center in minutes	22	9	11	12.5	8	12.5	15
Driving time to lake in minutes	Over 20	Over 20	Over 20	15	Over 20	6	1

Source: Malcolm Gienke, Julian Schneider, James Shalaty, Suzanne Simmons Palmer, and Bruce Tomcik, *A Study of the Influence of Driving Time upon Shopping Center Preference,* unpublished term paper, School of Management, Case Western Reserve University, 1969.

TABLE 5

Measures of the Relative Attractiveness of Seven Major Cleveland Shopping Centers, 1967

Shopping Center	% Customers over 15 Minutes Driving Time [a]	Total Store Space (thousand square feet) [b]	Total Department Store Space (thousand square feet) [c]	Total Supermarket Space (thousand square feet) [c]	Parking Spaces [b]	Enclosed Mall [b]
28	44.5	1,350	570	84	6,600	no
59	36.0	1,000	520	25	6,000	yes
38	35.5	900	427	36	5,000	yes
3	31.9	518	276	49	5,000	no
17	30.5	635	299	76	4,100	no
5	26.1	712	417	69	4,000	no
49	16.3	407	102	81	4,500	no

[a] Malcolm Gienke, Julian Schneider, James Shalaty, Suzanne Simmons Palmer, and Bruce Tomcik, *A Study of the influence of Driving Time upon Shopping Center Preference,* unpublished term paper, School of Management, Case Western Reserve University, 1969.

[b] *The Mobile Shopper in Greater Cleveland* (Cleveland: The Plain Dealer Marketing and Research Department, 1967).

[c] Interviews with officials of shopping centers and department stores in Cleveland, Ohio, August, 1969.

with (1) total store space (correlation coefficient, $r = 0.88$); (2) total department store space ($r = 0.87$); and (3) total parking spaces ($r = 0.77$) in a given center. Centers 5 and 49 were shown to have lowered these correlations. It should be noted that because of their proximity to the lake, a lower percentage of shoppers living more than 15 minutes away is logical; however, as a result, these centers increase the unexplained variance. There is an intuitive appeal to the idea that a shopping center with an enclosed mall has more "drawing power," all other factors equal, than a center without an enclosed mall. Some variation is also explained by the distance to the nearest major shopping center and by the presence or absence of supermarkets, which are assumed to draw primarily from within 15 minutes driving time.

It should be noted that this study (like Brunner and Mason's) emphasizes measures of attractiveness on the supply side (traffic-generating characteristics of the shopping centers), rather than the demand side (patronage decisions and consumer characteristics). Some of the demand-side analyses previously published in the *Journal of Marketing* include articles by Kelley, Cox, Bucklin, and Moore and Mason.[12]

A Driving Time Model

Based on the preceding analysis, the following tentative model uses seven factors to predict the percentage of

[12] Eugene J. Kelley, "The Importance of Convenience in Consumer Purchasing," *Journal of Marketing,* Vol. 23 (July, 1958), pp. 32–38; Reavis Cox, "Consumer Convenience and the Retail Structure of Cities," *Journal of Marketing,* Vol. 23 (April, 1959), pp. 355–362; Louis P. Bucklin, "The Concept of Mass in Intra-urban Shopping," *Journal of Marketing,* Vol. 31 (October, 1967), pp. 37–42; Charles T. Moore and Joseph B. Mason, "A Research Note on Major Retail Center Patronage," *Journal of Marketing,* Vol. 33 (July, 1969), pp. 61–63.

shoppers living more than 15 minutes driving time from the center:

$$M = k_1B + k_2D - k_3S + k_4P + k_5T - k_6L + k_7E + K_8$$

where M = Measure of "drawing power" expressed as percent of customers who live more than 15 minutes driving time from the center

B = Total center store space in square feet

D = Total department store space in square feet

S = Total supermarket space in square feet

P = Total number of parking spaces

T = Driving time in minutes to nearest major center

L = Dummy variable equal to 1 for Centers 49 and 5, and zero for all other centers to account for the truncating effect of Lake Erie on the center's market area

E = Dummy variable equal to 1 for Centers 59 and 38, and zero for all other centers to account for the effect on "drawing power" of an enclosed mall

k_1 to k_8 are equation constants

The hypothesis to be tested is that the "drawing power" of a shopping center is highly associated with its location and attractiveness. Further, "drawing power," as measured by the willingness to drive more than 15 minutes to the center, varies widely between shopping centers. The variations in drawing power, however, are closely related to the location and attractiveness of the centers.

Analysis of the Model

This model was analyzed using a stepwise linear multiple regression program which rejected all independent variables except the total store space B and the dummy variable L, which accounted for the truncating effect of Lake Erie. The equation with these two independent variables is:

$$M = 20.2 + (17.6 \times 10^{-6})B - 8.8L$$

The multiple correlation coefficient is 0.977, the index of determination is 0.955, the F-ratio is 42.5 (the F-ratio for 1% significance level would be 18.0), and the T-statistics both exceeded the 1% (two-tail) limits. From this equation it appears that the independent variables B and L explain over 95% of the variation in M, with less than one chance in a hundred (based on the F-ratio test) that this conclusion is incorrect.

According to this analysis, the percentage of customers who live more than 15 minutes driving time from these seven Cleveland shopping centers [M] is almost completely explained by (1) the size of the shopping center store area in square feet [B], and (2) the limiting effect of natural barriers on some shopping centers [L].

Limitations of the Study

It should be emphasized that this study is limited by the relatively small number of shopping centers available for use in the analysis, and caution should be used in applying the findings to other shopping center populations. In applying the original seven independent variable models to another city it should be recognized that the inability to obtain a large sample of shopping centers will limit the number of variables that can be used in a statistically significant manner. For example, with seven observations and two independent variables a multiple correlation coefficient of .945 is required for significance at the 1% level. Also, this model is obviously highly collinear among some of the independent variables. The reason for suggesting a model with so many variables is that the statistically significant variables for another shopping center population might differ from those found in this study. For example, in another city total department store space [D] and total supermarket space [S] might be significant factors in explaining differences in shopping center preferences as measured by the over 15-minute driving-time percentage. The purpose of the model has been to provide a conceptual framework for further empirical research on driving time.

Another limitation of this study is the implicit assumption that for a given city the density and location structure of population (customers) and other smaller shopping centers (competition) relative to each shopping center are uniform. That these factors might not be uniform between different cities is obvious and may explain some differences in results between cities. In the Toledo study, the 15-minute driving-time boundary of all five shopping centers overlapped; in the Cleveland study, no more than three of the seven shopping centers had overlapping 15-minute boundaries (3, 5, and 17; 38, 49, and 59; and 28, 38, and 59). Nevertheless, these studies have assumed that the factors of population (customers) and supermarkets (competition) are of essentially uniform density within a given city.

13 Same reference as footnote 2.
14 Same reference as footnote 2, p. 61.

Conclusions

The objective of this study has been to determine if the consistent results obtained by Professors Brunner and Mason in their study of driving time for five Toledo shopping centers would hold for a larger, more complex trading area such as Cleveland, Ohio.[13] The results show that driving times varied much more for Cleveland than for Toledo.

A number of factors were tested to explain the variations in driving time for Cleveland shopping centers. Two factors—center store space, and location of the center relative to natural barriers—were isolated in a step-wise multiple regression analysis. The first factor increases a center's "drawing power" as measured by the percentage of people who lived more than 15 minutes from the center; the second factor decreases a center's "drawing power."

Distance (as measured by driving time) is obviously important and is associated with consumer shopping preferences for shopping centers. Tables 1 and 3 clearly show a positive relationship between shopping preferences (as measured by the cumulative percentages of customers residing in successive driving-time zones) and driving times. The question arises as to whether this is sufficient to support the claim of Professors Brunner and Mason that "the driving time required to reach a center is highly influential in determining consumer shopping center preferences."[14] It might be stated that driving time is the determining factor if all other factors are equal. If all other factors are not equal, it is difficult to separate the determining factor without access to data on the shopping choices of individuals relative to both distance factors and shopping center characteristics.

The authors' contention is that consumer shopping center preferences, as viewed from the supply side, are influenced by both (1) driving time, and (2) the location and attractiveness of shopping centers. It has been determined that the "willingness to drive" more than 15 minutes to a shopping center varied widely between Cleveland centers with the variations almost completely explained by the location and attractiveness of the centers. Therefore, the authors conclude that location and attractiveness are important determinants of consumer shopping center preferences and suggest that these factors may also determine driving time as measured by the willingness to drive more than 15 minutes to a shopping center. The causality suggested in the latter instance from these findings and methods has not been demonstrated. It seems just as logical to suggest, however, that location and attractiveness determine driving time as vice versa, particularly in view of the objective measures of location and attractiveness used in this study.

Further Research

It would be interesting to see if the suggested model could be used to ex-

plain the small difference in drawing power among the five Toledo shopping centers, especially since the Toledo centers vary so much more in relative size than the Cleveland centers. Certainly, further study is indicated and Chicago is suggested as another area where a similar analysis could be carried out. The *Chicago Tribune* has been conducting license plate studies of Chicago shopping centers since 1957, so the basic data are available. Testing this model for both Toledo and Chicago would not only help verify or disprove it, but it would also give some indication as to the importance of the density and location structure of population (customers) and other smaller shopping centers (competition), which might vary more from city to city than between different areas of the same city.

The data in this study could also be compared to the retail sales reported for these centers when the 1967 Census of Business figures become available. Although these data have the limitations of including sales of retail establishments located next to a shopping center, this distortion is usually small. These additional data might help to demonstrate the feasibility of building a model that would predict total retail sales for proposed shopping centers in any urban area.[15]

[15] Nelson, same reference as footnote 1, p. 209.

Social Class Differences in Shopping Activities

Grady D. Bruce
William P. Dommermuth

That social class differences may be used to explain some differences in consumer behavior is generally accepted.[1] However, precise statements on the nature of these differences are few [4].

This paper reports the results of an investigation of social class differences in shopping activity. Considerable marketing effort (by manufacturers and retailers) consists of attempts to influence shopping activity. Some of the more direct means of influence include advertising, product differentiation, and price competition. Less direct means include exclusive and selective distribution. If differences in shopping activity exist between social classes, the discovery of the nature of these differences should aid in the formulation of productive marketing strategies.

Research Design

The Universe and Sample

The Universe included all the telephone households in a Southwestern city in which a new television set had been purchased in the two-year period preceding the study. A systematic random sample (n = 891) was drawn from the city directory in the section listing telephone numbers in numerical sequence.

Interview Procedure

Interviewers asked for the husband, wife, or other adult head of household. Three filter questions were asked of individuals contacted in order to qualify them as respondents: "Did you buy a TV set in the last two years?" "Was it purchased in the city?" "Was it new or used?" Affirmative answers to the first two questions and a "new" answer to the third were required for the interview to continue.

Shopping activity was measured by asking the respondent for the name of the store in which the set had been purchased. Then, the respondent was asked for the names of other stores that had been visited while looking for a set. Similarly, respondents were asked for the brand of set purchased, as well as for other brands examined.

Reprinted from *Marquette Business Review*, Vol. XII, No. 1, 1968, by permission of the editor.

[1] Published studies of the relationship between the value systems of different social classes and consumption behavior include [2, 7, 8, 9, 10].

Organization of Data

The data were organized according to the shopping matrix concept previously suggested for displaying the manner in which purchasers are divided with respect to their degree of search activity among retailers in relation to their search activity among brands [3].

Three social classes were operationally defined as follows:

1. Lower class: households located in the area of the city in which census tract median household incomes ranged from $2,009 to $4,436. Negroes made up 34 per cent of the area's population; Latin Americans made up another 34 per cent.
2. Working class: households located in the area of the city in which census tract median household incomes ranged from $4,299 to $5,941. Negroes made up 9 per cent of the population; Latin Americans made up another 5 per cent.
3. Middle class: households located in the area of the city in which census tract median incomes ranged from $5,009 to $9,081. Negroes and Latin Americans combined made up 8 per cent of the area's population.

Shopping matrices were developed for the lower class (Figure 1), the working class (Figure 2), the middle class (Figure 3), and the total sample (Figure 4).

The cells in each matrix show the percentage of respondents with the specified brand-store shopping activity patterns.

Findings

Fifty-five per cent of all respondents visited only one store and examined only one brand before making a purchase. This shopping activity pattern for television sets is consistent with the findings in two other studies of different universes [3, 6]. Using the one-store, one-brand cell as a measure of relative shopping *inactivity,* the least shopping activity is found in the lower class. Here 70 per cent of the respondents made a purchase after shopping in one store and looking at one brand. The most shopping activity took place in the working class, with 45 per cent of these respondents making a purchase after visiting one store and looking at one brand.[2] Shopping activity in the middle-class was intermediate of shopping activity in the working class and lower class.

As the three social-class matrices indicate, there were respondents in each class who were active in the comparison of stores and/or brands. The degree

FIGURE 1

The Shopping Matrix, Lower Class ($n = 136$)

		Stores				
		1	2	3	4	5 or more
Brands	5 or more	0	1	0	1	0
	4	0	0	1	1	0
	3	1	0	2	0	0
	2	5	8	0	0	0
	1	70	1	0	0	0

[2] Percentages for the lower class and working class are significantly different from the total sample at better than the .01 probability level.

FIGURE 2
The Shopping Matrix, Working Class ($n = 191$)

		Stores				
		1	2	3	4	5 or more
Brands	5 or more	0	0	0	1	4
	4	1	2	3	2	1
	3	1	2	7	0	0
	2	7	8	2	0	0
	1	45	4	1	0	0

FIGURE 3
The Shopping Matrix, Middle Class ($n = 564$)

		Stores				
		1	2	3	4	5 or more
Brands	5 or more	0	0	1	1	2
	4	0	0	2	1	0
	3	3	3	5	1	0
	2	6	6	2	0	0
	1	56	6	1	0	0

FIGURE 4
The Shopping Matrix, All Social Classes

		Stores				
		1	2	3	4	5 or more
Brands	5 or more	0	0	0	1	2
	4	0	0	2	1	0
	3	2	2	5	1	0
	2	5	6	2	0	0
	1	55	6	1	0	0

of the relationship between store shopping activity and brand shopping activity was discovered through the computation of coefficients of correlation for each social class and for the total sample. That shopping activity does tend to be generalized to stores and to brands is shown in Table 1. The association is weakest ($r = .44$) for lower-class respondents and strongest ($r = .74$) for working-class respondents.

Two distinct categories of shopping activity remain to be examined for social class differences: (1) activity in which respondents visited only one store but examined more than one brand, and (2) activity in which more than one store was visited, but the

TABLE 1
Association of Store Activity with Brand Activity

	Coefficient of Correlation [a]
Lower class	.44
Working class	.74
Middle class	.48
All	.58

[a] Each coefficient significantly different from zero at the .01 probability level or better.

same brand examined in each store. These two activity patterns represent, respectively, situations in which there was pre-purchase "store determination," independent of "brand determination" and pre-purchase "brand determination," independent of "store determination."

Chi-square was computed across social classes for each of the activity patterns. Actual frequencies did not differ from expected frequencies for either pattern.[3] However, significantly *fewer* lower-class respondents than all respondents visited more than one store while examining the same brand.[4]

In general, the findings show considerable shopping activity among working-class respondents. A relatively low proportion (45 per cent) of the working class was willing to visit only one store and to examine only one brand before making a purchase. The remaining 55 per cent tended to compare *both* stores and brands with greater frequency than respondents in the lower class or middle class.

A relatively high proportion (70 per cent) of the lower class made a purchase after visiting only one store and examining only one brand. The remaining 30 per cent tended to compare *both* stores and brands with much less fre-

quency than respondents in the working class.

Interpretation

The findings indicate association between social class and shopping activity rather than causation. However, they are consistent with the varying value systems of the different classes.

Lower-class persons, found to exhibit the least shopping activity, generally perceive a narrow range of alternatives for the improvement of their position; they are characteristically apathetic. As one author states:

The lower-class persons themselves react to their economic situation and to their degradation in the eyes of respectable people by becoming fatalistic; they feel that they are down and out, and that there is no point in trying to improve, for the odds are all against them. They may have some desires to better their position, but cannot see how it can be done [5, p. 211].

Or:

The central assumption of the lower-class value system is that the situation is hopeless. Because he has to struggle merely to stay alive, because he knows that re-

[3] Activity pattern (1): $x_2 = 5.02$, d.f. $= 3$; $p > .10$.
  Activity pattern (2): $x_2 = 7.5$, d.f. $= 3$; $.05 < p < .10$.
[4] Exact $p = .02$.

spectable people sneer at him as "no-good," because he lacks the technical and social skills necessary for success, the lower-class person gives up [5, p. 213].

Working-class persons, found to exhibit the greatest shopping activity, typically have lower mobility perceptions and mobility expectations than middle-class persons [1]. But there are other methods for improving one's life situation, as indicated in this profile of the working-class person:

His work has little intrinsic interest; he learns to adjust, to lower his aspirations, to become adroit at working without thinking and without dreaming of future advancement. As he retreats from work as a thing of inner importance, he turns to his family and to consumption pleasures. He cannot live extravagantly, but in our productive economy he can live comfortably and can expect his home slowly to add one gadget to another. He takes pride in this method of "getting ahead" [5, p. 210].

Given the nature of the working-class value system, it would appear reasonable to expect these individuals to approach a purchase situation with a relatively high interest in the gains (monetary or otherwise) that could potentially result from a comparison of stores and brands. If consumption expertise is the primary means whereby the working-class person may "get ahead," then shopping activity is logical. On the other hand, lower-class persons, who also have low mobility perceptions and mobility expectations, can see no way to "get ahead." The lower-class person may be expected to view shopping activity as producing little, if any, potential gain.

Implications

The findings are suggestive for both manufacturer–retailer relations and re-

tailer–consumer relations. The implications derive from a consideration of community social class structure as one of the predictors of the *potential* for brand competition and store competition in the community. In other words, differences in shopping activity among social classes appear to be reflective of differences in effort likely to be expended by persons within a social class in the purchase of a product.

From a manufacturer's viewpoint, a comparison of the social class structure in different cities would appear to be most useful in decisions on distribution intensity and promotion. Although income, size of the market, and a number of other factors, of course, would be involved ultimately in the adoption of an intensive distribution policy, the initial indication is that such a policy would be most logical where the lower class predominates and least logical where the working class predominates.

Intensive cooperative advertising would seem to be more feasible for retailers with a predominance of lower class over middle class or middle class over working class customers. For stores whose customers are predominantly working class, the manufacturer may well want to concentrate a disproportionate share of his promotion dollars on in-store promotions and the training of sales personnel, such training directed toward holding customers once they visit the store.

From a retailer's point of view, convenience of location has traditionally been considered crucial in the sale of convenience goods, but of relatively less importance for shopping goods. These findings suggest that convenience of location may, in fact, be crucial for a substantial part of the total market for at least one "shopping good"—and have differential importance among social classes, depending upon the social-class distribution of the retailer's customers. That is, it appears that retailers concentrating on this product and others for which there are similar shopping activity patterns may utilize information on social class structure in making location decisions, as well as in the choice of advertising media, in sales training, and in in-store display.

Conclusion

Although social class is undoubtedly only one of many factors influencing shopping activity, this research indicates that the social class structure (a marketing *uncontrollable*) in a community may play a crucial role in the determination of brand and store competition in the community. As a consequence, manufacturers and retailers, whether they are already in a market or are considering entry, may use information on social class structure as one of the predictors of the *potential* for competition—and thereby improve decisions on marketing controllables.

REFERENCES

1. Charles M. Bonjean, Grady D. Bruce, and J. Allen Williams, Jr., "Social Mobility and Job Satisfaction: A Replication and Extension," *Social Forces,* 45 (June, 1967), pp. 492–501.
2. Richard P. Coleman, "The Significance of Social Stratification in Selling," in Martin L. Bell (ed.), *Proceedings of the 43rd National Conference of the American Marketing Association,* Chicago, American Marketing Association, 1960, pp. 171–184.
3. William P. Dommermuth, "The Shopping Matrix and Marketing Strategy," *Journal of Marketing Research,* 2 (May, 1965), pp. 128–132.
4. John A. Howard, *Marketing Theory.* Boston, Allyn and Bacon, 1965.
5. Joseph A. Kahl, *The American Class Structure.* New York, Holt, Rinehart and Winston, 1965.
6. George Katona and Eva Mueller, *The Dynamics of Consumer Reaction.* New York, New York University Press.
7. Charles W. King, "Fashion Adoption: A Rebuttal to the 'Trickle Down' Theory," in Stephen A. Greyser (ed.), *Toward Scientific Marketing.* Chicago, American Marketing Association, 1964.
8. Pierre Martineau, "The Personality of the Retail Store." *Harvard Business Review,* 1 (January–February, 1958), pp. 47–55.
9. Pierre Martineau, "Social Classes and Spending Behavior." *Journal of Marketing,* 23 (October, 1958), pp. 122–130.
10. Lee Rainwater, Richard P. Coleman, and Gerald Handel, *Workingman's Wife.* New York, Oceana Publications, Inc., 1959.

Measuring the Customer's Image
of a Department Store

W. Bruce Weale

It is a retailing truism that 80 per cent of many stores' sales represents repeat business. Precisely correct or not, the fact remains that a store's future business with the same customers depends largely on how well it has met the aspirational level of the consumer's image of satisfactory price, quality, and service. It is within this framework that the consumer evaluates her concept of the store's image. This matrix operates within a broader setting, however, than do these factors by themselves. The way in which the consumer relates these to herself depends on her degree of identification with the over-all store's image. This involves reconciling the self image to the store image if the former is different from the latter. To do so requires a plausible reason on her part. She must either up-trade or down-trade in a store where she feels her prestige status rating does not match that of the stores involved.

It is easier for the customer to upgrade her self image by trading at a higher ranking store. However, only strong inducements such as price, convenience, or necessity, etc., will justify her down-trading.

Pierre Martineau suggests that a shopper asks herself such questions as [1]:

1. Who are the other shoppers?
2. How will the clerks treat me?
3. What are the price ranges?
4. Do I fit in that store?

The answers to these questions partially determine the image of the store in its relation to the customer's self status level.

Other factors being equal, consumers will seek out those stores whose image most closely correlates with the self status image. For it is in such stores that she is most at home, will find merchandise suitable to her tastes, and will see and be seen by those people with whom she wants to be associated.

Studies of income as a determinant of consumption often prove misleading as *Life* magazine's study shows.[2] Occupation and station in life are perhaps more causal in this regard. Consumers often buy out of their class

Reprinted from the *Journal of Retailing*, Summer 1961, by permission of the author and editor.

[1] Pierre Martineau, "The Public Image-Motivational Analysis for Long-Range Merchandising Strategy," *The Frontiers of Marketing Thought and Science*, A.M.A., 1957.
[2] *Life Study of Consumer Expenditures*, Vol. 1 (New York: Time, Inc., 1957).

TABLE 1
Data on Respondents

Age
(Per Cent)

1.20	Below 20
24.70	20–29
37.60	30–39
23.00	40–49
7.30	50–59
6.20	60–over
100.00	Total

Education
(Per Cent)

.56	Some grammar
2.80	Completed grammar
3.93	Some high school
30.30	Completed high school
28.00	Some college
23.00	Completed college
9.00	Graduate education
2.41	No answer
100.00	Total

Economic Group
(Per Cent)

4.44	0–3,000
7.30	3,001–4,000
14.00	4,001–5,000
31.40	5,001–7,500
25.80	7,500–10,000
12.30	10,000–over
4.76	No answer
100.00	Total

Social Class Distribution

25.8%	of respondents—wives of professionals (college professors, M.D.'s, accountants, architects, engineers, etc.)
33.7%	of respondents—wives of managers, proprietors, supervisors, and business executives
40.5%	of respondents—wives of clerks, sales and office employees
100.0%	Total

market and compensate by under-consuming in another commodity. The Ford income consumer may buy a Cadillac by virtue of lower food or clothing expenditures than are normal for his income level. This spending pattern often occurs when the buyer's prestige status level is below his aspirational status level. By buying the status symbol of a higher level, he reconciles his self status to its rightful place in the hierarchy of prestige level of status.

It is of great importance, then, for a store to know its over-all image as well as its various merchandise category images. Only then can it fully satisfy the potential markets that it purports to serve. The closer management's image of its organization is to that held by potential customers, the more effective will be the store's communication through advertising and public relations. This sense of identity will affect the buying, pricing, and service functions of the store. It would be a mistake for management to try to implement such policies without a knowledge of the consumer image of the store. Errors in direction by management cannot be compensated for by sharpness of techniques in operation. It behooves management to measure its store image periodically to determine the framework within which it should operate.

The following experiment was used to delineate the store images for four competitive establishments in Tallahassee, Florida. The principles and techniques used could be applicable, with given modifications, to fit other individual situations.

SIZE OF SAMPLE. One hundred and seventy-eight white respondents were interviewed from fifteen suburban residential developments in and around Tallahassee to determine where certain customer prototypes were most likely (and least likely) to shop.

To delineate the image of the four department stores, some twenty-one social stereotypes or customer prototypes were used. These stereotypes were selected, not as definitive connotations or rigid representativeness of the city's population, but because each of the types could be found in certain segments of the buying population. Also, they did connote a rough range of social strata, discernible. enough in the minds of the respondents to enable them to project a personal image of each prototype.

No attempt was made to correlate the projected image with the empirical facts the study would produce.[3] These twenty-one stereotypes may have suggested slightly different kinds of women to different respondents, but they were definite enough to suggest certain social classes. The stated preferences of these twenty-one prototypes as to where they would be most likely, and least likely, to shop were sufficient to delineate a profile of the social class overtones for each store. Thus, within the limitations of this framework, a rather sharp differentiation of the image of each store emerged.

While this distribution is not truly representative of all occupational levels in Tallahassee, it constitutes the basis of the hierarchy of customers for the merchants in town.

The presence in Tallahassee of the Florida State University and the state government offices sets a relatively high level status of employment. Tallahassee has few in the skilled and unskilled labor classes, or what might correspond to either the lower-lower class or the upper-lower classes using Lloyd Warner's [4] categorizations. It was decided, therefore, to confine the survey to the upper-lower, and middle-upper and the middle-lower classes. This, to all intents and purposes, represents the bulk of the department stores' customers in our city and the group to which the stores have geared their merchandising policies.

Methods of Interviewing

By using IBM facilities, the respondents' occupational status was compared with the status of the twenty-one prototypes of wives attributed to most likely, and least likely, shop in the four stores. From the total distribution, an image for each of the stores was delineated and compared with those of its competitors. The four stores compared were of the department store category and are considered among the key retail houses of the city. While certain higher status specialty stores exist, this survey was designed to delineate the store images of these competing stores. They are designated as Stores A, B, C, and D.

From total respondents' choices, store D was most often selected as the place where twenty-one categories would be most likely to shop. In order of preference selection the stores ranked D, C, B, and A.

In ranking by "least likely to shop," stores A, D, B, and C were chosen. (See Table 2.)

[3] H. G. Gough suggests an interesting technique of validating a social stereotype with actual criteria by the use of An Adjective Check List—the University of California, Institute of Personality Assessment.

[4] W. Lloyd Warner and Paul Lunt, *The Social Life of a Modern Community* (New Haven, Conn.: Yale University Press, 1950).

TABLE 2
Total Choices of 178 Respondents for 21 Prototypes

Store	Most Likely to Shop	Least Likely to Shop
A	570	1,247
B	836	840
C	1,009	341
D	1,296	1,185
	3,711	3,613

Least Likely to Shop in Store A in Rank Order

1. Wife of lawyer	101
2. Fashion model	99
3. Wife of F.S.U. professor	94
4. Business executive	91
5. Actress	88
6. Society woman	88
7. Professional woman	86
8. Public school teacher	78

Store A was rated at the bottom of the "most likely" list by the total respondents and was least likely to be shopped by the greatest number of prototypes.

The following prototypes were most likely to shop in store A.

Category	Number of Choices *
1. Negro maid	80
2. Waitress in a grille	74
3. Seamstress	69
4. Salesgirl	55
5. High school student	47
6. Housewife	42
7. Wife of A & M professor †	32
8. Farmer's wife	32
9. State office worker	21

* The ranking was limited to only the eight or ten prototypes with sufficient frequency of choice.
† Florida Agricultural and Mechanical University (Negro University).

It is obvious that the prototypes attributed most likely to shop in store A are generally found in the lower social status.

Since the respondents themselves were largely upper status prototypes (59.8 percent) they did not expect to see themselves shop in this store whose image they delineated as being below their own status group.

An unfair fact in this comparison, however, is the newness of the operation of store D in town, as compared with the other three competitors who have been in Tallahassee many years. However the store is part of a national chain that is well known throughout the country.

The total over-all image of store A was over twice as negative (L.L.) to be shopped as it was positive (M.L.) to be shopped by the respondents.

Store B had an almost equally divided reaction. Almost as many like (M.L.), as dislike (L.L.), to shop there. The prototypes (M.L.) to shop there are listed in order of attributed choices.

Most Likely to Shop	Total Choices
1. Farmer's wife	140
2. Negro maid	90
3. Waitress in grille	84
4. Housewife	79
5. Wife of F.S.U. student	71
6. Salesgirl	69
7. Wife of F.S.U. professor	64
8. Seamstress	47
9. High school student	47

With the exception of the wife of an F.S.U. professor, these status types are not usually attributed to the highest social order. The farmer's wife identification as first choice types this store in a rural image in the minds of respondents.

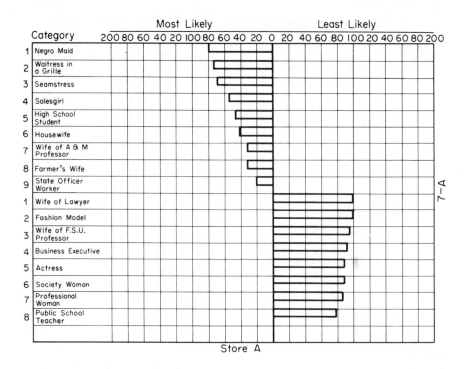

Most Likely | Least Likely

Category

200 80 60 40 20 100 80 60 40 20 0 20 40 60 80 100 20 40 60 80 200

1 Negro Maid
2 Waitress in a Grille
3 Seamstress
4 Salesgirl
5 High School Student
6 Housewife
7 Wife of A & M Professor
8 Farmer's Wife
9 State Officer Worker
1 Wife of Lawyer
2 Fashion Model
3 Wife of F.S.U. Professor
4 Business Executive
5 Actress
6 Society Woman
7 Professional Woman
8 Public School Teacher

7-A

Store A

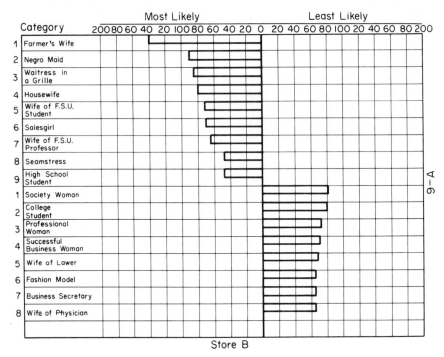

Most Likely | Least Likely

Category

200 80 60 40 20 100 80 60 40 20 0 20 40 60 80 100 20 40 60 80 200

1 Farmer's Wife
2 Negro Maid
3 Waitress in a Grille
4 Housewife
5 Wife of F.S.U. Student
6 Salesgirl
7 Wife of F.S.U. Professor
8 Seamstress
9 High School Student
1 Society Woman
2 College Student
3 Professional Woman
4 Successful Business Woman
5 Wife of Lawer
6 Fashion Model
7 Business Secretary
8 Wife of Physician

9-A

Store B

278

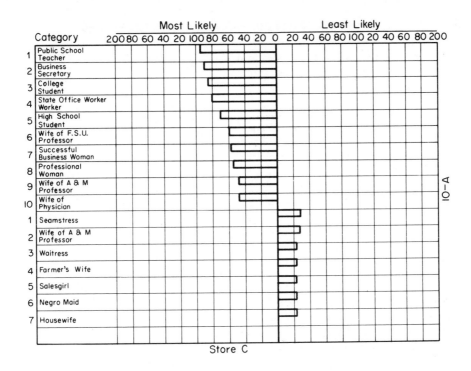

Store C

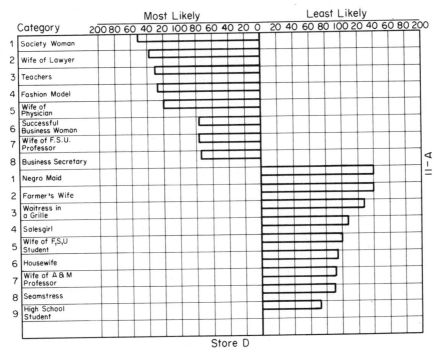

Store D

279

Listed in order of L.L. to shop in store B were also the higher status customers.

Least Likely to Shop	Total Choices
1. Society woman	81
2. College student	80
3. Professional woman	72
4. Successful business woman	71
5. Wife of lawyer	68
6. Fashion model	66
7. Business secretary	65
8. Wife of physician	65

Store B, then, also has a sharp image for certain occupational status groups, and is about equally negative for other groups to be found least likely to shop there.

Store C has a stronger positive image than any in terms of the ratio of M.L. to L.L.; some 1,900 to only 341 L.L. Its image is delineated more to the middle status group than it is to either the lower or upper class groups.

Most Likely to Shop in Store C	Total Choices
1. Public school teacher	92
2. Business secretary	87
3. College student	83
4. State office worker	81
5. High school student	68
6. Wife of F.S.U. professor	59
7. Successful business woman	56
8. Professional woman	53
9. Wife of A & M professor	47
10. Wife of physician	46

Because of store C's middle status position, it is not too far removed from lower status groups to find only small numbers of the L.L. to shop there.

Least Likely to Shop in Store C	Total Choices
1. Seamstress	31
2. Wife of A & M professor	31
3. Waitress	27
4. Farmer's wife	25
5. Salesgirl	24
6. Negro maid	24
7. Housewife	23

Store D has the highest positive image of the four stores and is the place where the highest status groups are most likely to shop according to the respondents. The preference of these prototypes is strongly expressed as follows:

Most Likely to Shop in Store D	Total Choices
1. Society woman	152
2. Wife of lawyer	138
3. Teacher	131
4. Fashion model	128
5. Wife of physician	120
6. Successful business woman	77
7. Wife of F.S.U. professor	77
8. Business secretary	75

The image was strongly against the following types shopping in store D.

Least Likely to Shop in Store D	Total Choices
1. Negro maid	141
2. Farmer's wife	140
3. Waitress in grille	127
4. Salesgirl	107
5. Wife of F.S.U. student	99
6. Housewife	93
7. Wife of A & M professor	92
8. Seamstress	90
9. High school student	72

While the higher and stronger status was attributed to store D, its image has the advantage of age to its credit. It is the oldest established store in town and has had many years of good will to accumulate to its credit. Whether this high status is justified by the merchandising facts and policies is open to question. The fact remains, however, that in the minds of the respondents such an image exists.

Capitalizing on Store Image

The delineation of the four store images does not explain how these images were formed. That was not the purpose of this research. However, heritage by virtue of age, location, degree of services offered, prices, and quality of merchandise are only a few of the variables that help determine the aura each store develops.

That each store develops its own particular image is a refutation of the merchandising policy of trying to be all things to all people. This is not consistent with the way consumers evaluate management's attempts. What tends to appeal to one status level is not likely to be as appealing to another level. Consequently the consumer types the store's image to fit her scheme of status values, irrespective of what the store purports its merchandising specialties and services to be.

It would necessarily follow, then, that whatever image exists for each store should be examined in several respects.

Strategic Image Decisions

1. Does the store image, as delineated, register with the same image as the management and promotion divisions have envisioned and are now operating on?
2. Is net profit maximized most by better tailoring the store image to fit the image customers already have, or is it better to go after those market segments that are not now shopping in the store?
3. If the image can be changed, how can it be accomplished, and how permanent will the changes be?

Intelligent future policy for each store will depend on how wisely management interprets the answers to these questions. Today Caveat Emptor is not really the determining philosophy of the store, but Caveat Venditor—let the seller beware—beware of not being that personality the public wants and expects it to be.

Limitations of Study

It is recognized that in any attempt to study the image or personality of any given store, many variables enter into the picture; the type of its advertising, the quality of its stocks, its prices, the attitude of its employees to the public, the displays, the physical plant, to name just a few. Further, many separate images within one store appear to different classes of people. One department may enjoy a high quality image while another may represent the opposite concept.

Obviously store personality or image is not the sole determinant of patronage. There are many other cogent reasons for such choice as: location, traffic and parking conditions, service facilities, prices, etc. But when these factors are somewhat equalized, then store image has a decided role to play in preselecting customer types.

Within these limitations, the above

study enabled the stores to verify what they had somewhat suspected—that certain occupational–status types tended to regard their store as the best place for their shopping.

Following this initial research, more refined methods are indicated to measure the actual clientele in terms of whether it represents the market seg-ment desired. Another factor that needs exploration is whether the store is capitalizing on its strongest points of differentiation, in catering to the desired market segment. Still another is whether a proposed program can be implemented in terms of adoption, promotion, and public relations.

Shopping Behavior of Discount Store Customers in a Small City

Rachel Dardis
Marie Sandler

Discount stores have been part of the retailing scene for more than fifty years. Early stores were usually small, located in low-rent areas, and patronized only by card-holding members.[1] Although these stores still exist today, the modern discount store originated in the early fifties.[2] This store has been defined as a "departmentalized retail establishment utilizing many self-service techniques to sell hard goods, health and beauty aids, apparel and other soft goods, and other general merchandise."[3] The lower-than-average markup employed by the discount store and the resulting emphasis on competitive pricing was a major attraction for customers.[4]

Although discount stores have been studied in several metropolitan areas, more research is necessary if we are to understand their growth in the past decade. In particular, information concerning the type of customer patronizing discount stores, reasons for patronage, and the share of total buying which regular customers are willing to give to discount stores is of real interest in determining the implications of this retailing trend.[5]

The present study was concerned with shopping behavior patterns and socioeconomic characteristics of customers of a particular discount store. This store, which was established in 1963, was the only one of its type in a New York state college town with limited shopping facilities. Unlike many other discount stores it was located in a shopping center that contained a wide variety of retail outlets including supermarkets, apparel stores, and drugstores.

Reprinted from the *Journal of Retailing*, Vol. 47, No. 2, Summer, 1971, by permission of the authors and editor.

[1] Alfred L. Seelye, ed., *Marketing in Transition* (New York, Harper and Brothers, 1958).

[2] Stuart U. Rich and Bernard Portis, "Clues for Action from Shopper Preferences," *Harvard Business Review*, 41 (March/April 1963), 132–49.

[3] "The True Look of the Discount Industry," *The Discount Merchandiser*, 7 (July 1967), 4-TL.

[4] Tom Mahoney and Leonard Sloane, *The Great Merchants* (New York: Harper and Row Publishers, 1966); Rich and Portis, *Clues for Action;* David Rachman and Linda Kemp, "Profile of the Boston Discount House Customer," *Journal of Retailing*, xxxix (Summer 1963), pp. 1-8.

[5] Gerald B. Tallman and Bruce Blomstrom, "Retail Innovations Challenge Manufacturers," *Harvard Business Review*, 40 (September/October 1962), 130–41.

Procedure

Discount Store A shoppers were interviewed during the week of July 10 to 15, 1967, using a systematic sampling procedure. The twelve hour shopping day (10 A.M. to 10 P.M.) was stratified into for periods of three hours each, and sampling was limited to two hours in each three-hour period. Sampling was performed each day in the six-day shopping week in order to obtain a representative sample of customers. Every fifteenth store entrant was selected, and all shoppers eighteen years of age and over were interviewed. The questionnaire took approximately three minutes to administer, a factor that may have been responsible for the relatively low refusal rate of 11 percent.

Store Entrants[6]

The composition of discount store entrants for the week of the survey is given in Table I. The majority of entrants were adults, while children outnumbered teenagers by two to one. The proportion of adults shopping each day

varied from 13 percent on Wednesday to 24 percent on Saturday. Saturday also accounted for a considerable proportion of teen-age shoppers (23 percent) and children (29 percent). As might be expected, the final shopping period in the day accounted for the greatest number of adult shoppers (30 percent) while children were more heavily represented in the morning and early afternoon periods. Most of the teenagers (49 percent) were shopping with their parents or other family members, although a sizable proportion were with friends (34 percent) or alone (17 percent).

The adults constituted the target population under investigation in this study. Eighty-six percent of the adults were interviewed; 11 percent refused while 3 percent were excluded as not being in the population (interviewed before, could not speak English, entered when the interviewers were busy).

Characteristics of Respondents

Eighty-seven percent of the respondents were permanent year-round residents of

TABLE I
Discount Store Entrants

		Sex	
Entrants	*Total* *(n = 1,131)* *(percent)*	*Male* *(n = 500)* *(percent)*	*Female* *(n = 631)* *(percent)*
Adults (18 and over)	67	62	71
Teenagers (13 to 18)	10	10	10
Children (under 13)	20	23	17
Employees, Service personnel	3	5	2

[6] If we wish to obtain an estimate of the total number of store entrants the sample size of 1,131 must be multiplied by 15 and increased by 50 percent because sampling was limited to two hours in each three-hour period. This gives a total number of 24,570 store entrants if we exclude employees and other service personnel.

the county in which Store A was located or neighboring counties while 11 percent were visitors or summer residents. Permanent residents who had patronized the store for at least six months and who shopped there every few months or more were defined as regular customers and accounted for 78 percent of all shoppers.

Socioeconomic characteristics for all respondents and regular customers are given in Tables II, III, IV, V, and VI.[7] The median age for respondents was 36 years old with the 65 and over age group accounting for only 5 percent of the respondents. This confirms the appeal of discount stores to the younger age groups.

The educational level of the respondents was above average with 85 percent having at least a high school education. The fact that 47 percent had attended college reflects the location of the store in a college town and indicates the extent to which college educated persons are willing to patronize discount stores.

Respondents' occupations were

TABLE II
Distribution By Age

Age	All Respondents (n = 644) (percent)	Regular Customers (n = 511) (percent)
18–25 years	21	23
25–35 years	27	27
35–45 years	21	22
45–55 years	16	15
55–65 years	10	8
65 years and over	5	4

TABLE III
Distribution By Education

Education	All Respondents (n = 652) (percent)	Regular Customers (n = 511) (percent)
Less than seventh grade	1	1
Junior high school	5	4
Partial senior high school	9	9
High school graduation	38	41
Partial college training	16	16
College graduation	17	17
Graduate professional degree	14	12

7 Although socioeconomic characteristics for both groups appear similar, chi-square analysis indicated a significant difference in age and education between regular customers and other respondents at the 0.01 level of significance. Regular customers were younger and while they had a greater proportion of high school graduates they also accounted for a smaller proportion of persons holding advanced degree.

TABLE IV
Distribution By Occupation

Occupation	All Respondents (n = 650) (percent)	Regular Customers (n = 511) (percent)
I. Higher executives, major professionals	7	7
II. Business managers, lesser professionals	12	10
III. Administrative personnel, minor professionals	8	8
IV. Clerical and sales workers, technicians	14	13
V. Skilled manual employees	10	12
VI. Machine operators and semiskilled employees	8	8
VII. Unskilled employees	3	4
VIII.* Homemakers	27	27
IX.* Undergraduate and graduate students	10	11

* Categories not included in the Hollingshead Scale.

TABLE V
Distribution By Income

Income	All Respondents (n = 609) (percent)	Regular Customers (n = 479) (percent)
$0–3,000	10	11
$3,000–5,000	10	10
$5,000–7,500	25	25
$7,500–10,000	18	19
$10,000–15,000	23	23
$15,000 and over	14	12

TABLE VI
Distribution By Socioeconomic Status

Socioeconomic Status	All Respondents (n = 530) (percent)	Regular Customers (n = 407) (percent)
Class I	19	17
Class II	14	12
Class III	23	24
Class IV	35	36
Class V	9	10

grouped according to the Hollingshead Occupational Scale [8] with two addi- tional classifications for homemakers and full-time college students. All oc-

[8] August B. Hollingshead, *Two Factor Index of Social Position* (New Haven, Conn.: 1957).

cupational groups were well represented with unskilled employees accounting for the smallest proportion. The results for income were consistent with the educational and occupational data. The lowest income groups were least well represented while more than one-third of the respondents earned $10,000 or more annually.

The socioeconomic status of shoppers was established using the Hollingshead *Two Factor Index of Social Position*,[9] which is based on occupation and education of the head of the household. The two lower or working classes accounted for the majority of the shoppers, a finding which is in agreement with a recent study published in *Discount Merchandiser*.[10] However, it is interesting to note that one-third of the sample were in the professionally oriented two higher classes.

Over three-fourths of the shoppers were married, and in general family sizes were small. Thirty percent of the families were childless, and for families with children the mean number of children was 2.3. Two percent of the respondents were Negro, a finding which was in agreement with current census data for County A.

Shopping Behavior

Forty-eight percent of the respondents were shopping in family groups, while 27 percent were alone. More than half the customers interviewed had come to the shopping center just to shop at the discount stores, while 19 percent were combining grocery shopping and general shopping. As might be expected, the proportion of "discount store only"

shoppers varied by day and time period. If ranged from a low of 34 percent (Saturday: 1:30 to 3:30 P.M.) to a high of 85 percent (Saturday: 7 to 9 P.M.). Only four of the eighteen stores in the shopping center were open during the latter period.

Nine percent of the shoppers interviewed were visiting Store A for the first time, but 56 percent had been shopping there since the store opened in 1963. The majority of the respondents (56 percent) and regular customers (65 percent) shopped at Store A at least several times a month. As might be expected, frequency of discount store patronage was inversely related to travel time. Median travel time was approximately fourteen minutes for both respondents and regular customers.

Respondents were asked about general shopping behavior as well as about shopping behavior in discount stores. More than three-quarters of the shoppers claimed that they compared merchandise and prices in different stores. While frequency of comparison shopping was independent of the shopper's age, it was related to education and occupation. The least educated shopper was less likely to compare prices than was the college graduate.

Respondents were also queried concerning purchase plans, and a surprisingly large percentage (38 percent) had traveled to the discount store without a definite purchase in mind. For the 61 percent who planned to purchase merchandise, the average number of items was 1.3.

Rank based on purchase plans and rank based on total sales in discount stores for twelve merchandise categories is given in Table VII. Major ap-

[9] *Ibid.*

[10] "How to Do Right by Working Class Shoppers," *The Discount Merchandiser*, 8 (December 1968), 53–57.

TABLE VII
Purchase Plans By Merchandise Category

Category	Purchase Plans	Rank Based on Purchase Plans *	Rank Based on Sales †
Hardware, auto accessories, paints	90	1	3
Linens and domestics	59	2	8
Toys and sporting goods	55	3	5
Housewares and traffic appliances	50	4	6
Drugs and toiletries	49	5	7
Men's and boys' clothing	38	6	2
Women's and girls' clothing	34	7	1
Children's and infants' clothing	31	8	4
Shoes	25	9	9
Stationery, greeting cards, books, and magazines	19	10	10.5
Cameras and photo supplies	16	11	12
Garden supplies	13	12	10.5
Other	38	—	—

* Number of items that 394 respondents planned to purchase.
† Total sales in discount stores in 1967 excluding major appliances and furniture. *Discount Merchandiser* (June 1968), p. 14–TL.

pliances (not stocked in Store A) and furniture were excluded from discount store sales. There is considerable divergence between the first eight ranks, resulting in a negative rank correlation coefficient of 0.429. It must be remembered, however, that these purchase plans refer to a particular week only and that price of item was not taken into consideration. The relatively low rank accorded to children's and infants' clothing might have been expected in view of the small family size of the respondents. A positive rank correlation of 0.603 was obtained when all twelve categories were used.

Travel time was inversely related to purchase plans at the 0.01 level of significance—a finding which is somewhat surprising. It suggests that the "amusement" or leisure activity component of shopping is relatively important. It also points out the need for in-store display and promotion to stimulate sales.

Shopping Behavior (Regular Customers)

The length of time regular customers had patronized Store A ranged from less than one year (13 percent) to two years and over (78 percent). Sixty-five percent had patronized the store since it was first opened.

In order to find out the reasons for discount store patronage, regular customers were queried concerning major reasons for store patronage and the availability of price discounts. Lower prices, convenient hours, and parking were the main reasons for patronizing Store A (Table VIII). Those customers who indicated lower prices as a reason for store patronage were also given a list containing eight major categories of merchandise and asked to select those categories for which Store A had the same quality for lower prices. It is interesting to note that hard goods were considered to be "good buys" by nearly

TABLE VIII
Reasons for Patronizing Discount Store

Reasons	Regular Customers (n = 511) (percent)
Lower prices	58
Convenient hours and parking	54
Large selection of merchandise	24
Location near residence	15
Other	11

half the respondents while the proportion was much lower in the case of soft goods (Table IX).

Regular customers were also asked what proportion of total buying they did at Store A. The results are given in Table X. More than half the customers purchased items in each of the eight major categories with the exception of children's and infants' wear where family size undoubtedly exercised a deterrent effect.

The amount purchased in each category (none, some or little, around half, all or most) was also analyzed with respect to socioeconomic and shopping behavior characteristics.

For all categories belief in lower prices had a significant influence on the amount purchased. A positive significant relationship also existed between amount purchased and socioeconomic characteristics for some hard goods such as toys and sporting goods and housewares and traffic appliances. The results for soft goods are of particular interest. In nearly all instances, the higher the particular socioeconomic characteristics the smaller the amount purchased. In general this relationship was significant at the 0.01 level. The results are summarized in Table XI.[11]

The ranks of the various merchandise categories by belief in lower prices,

TABLE IX
Belief in Lower Prices By Merchandise Category

Category	Regular Customers (n = 299) (percent)
Drugs and toiletries	58
Hardware and auto accessories	50
Toys and sporting goods	49
Housewares and traffic appliances	46
Linens and domestics	29
Women's and girls' clothing	27
Men's and boys' clothing	24
Children's and infants' clothing	22

11 When chi-square analysis was run with purchase or nonpurchase in place of amount of each category purchased the results were very similar.

TABLE X

Relative Importance of Store A Purchases By Merchandise Category *(n = 511)*

Category	Don't Know (percent)	Buy All or Most (percent)	Buy Around Half (percent)	Buy Some or Little (percent)	Buy (column 2–4) (percent)	Don't Buy (percent)
Men's and boys' clothing	—	7	9	42	58	42
Women's and girls' clothing	1	9	10	44	63	37
Children's and infants' clothing	—	7	7	26	40	60
Linens and domestics	1	9	10	35	54	46
Drugs and toiletries	—	14	16	42	72	28
Hardware, auto accessories	—	10	14	45	69	30
Toys and sporting goods	—	18	15	35	68	32
Housewares and traffic appliances	—	9	13	39	61	39

TABLE XI

Relationship Between Amount Purchased and Selected Socioeconomic and Shopping Behavior Characteristics *

Category	Education (n = 511)	Income † (n = 479)	Socioeconomic Status (n = 407)	Price Belief (n = 299)	Shopping Frequency (n = 511)
Men's and boys' clothing	0.01	0.01	0.01	0.01	0.01
Women's and girls' clothing	0.01	0.01	0.01	0.01	0.01
Children's and infants' clothing	0.01	0.01	0.01	0.01	0.05
Linens and domestics	0.01	—	0.05	0.01	0.01
Drugs and toiletries	—	—	—	0.01	0.01
Hardware and auto accessories	—	—	—	0.01	0.01
Toys and sporting goods	0.01	0.01	—	0.01	0.01
Housewares and traffic appliances	—	—	0.01	0.01	0.01

* Chi-square tests indicated significant relationships at the levels shown.
† Income groups were low, medium, and high.

proportion purchased, and purchase plans were also compared (Table XII). In this table ranks in the second column were based on the number of customers who purchased a particular category of merchandise while the third column ranks were obtained by assigning weights to the amount purchased. "All or most" was given a weighting of three; "around half" a weighting of two; and "some or little," a weighting of one. The final column gives the rank based on the number of items regular customers planned to buy on the day of the interview.

All of the rank correlation coefficients between price belief and purchase behavior are significant. This confirms the lower price appeal of discount stores, at least as far as this particular discount store is concerned.

Regular customers also patronized other types of stores for items similar to those they purchased in Store A. National chain department stores were the most popular and were patronized by three-fourths of the shoppers. Independent department stores (58 percent), variety stores (50 percent), specialty stores (47 percent), and other discount stores (47 percent) were also mentioned. This result indicates that Store A has succeeded in attracting customers from traditional retail outlets since its opening in 1963.

Conclusion

This study was concerned with socioeconomic characteristics and shopping behavior of discount store customers.

TABLE XII

Rank Comparisons Based on Percentage of Regular Customers in Each Category

	Rank			
Category	Price Belief (n = 299)	Purchase (n = 511)	Weighted Purchase (n = 511)	Purchase Plans (n = 259) *
Men's and boys' clothing	7	6	5	7
Women's and girls' clothing	6	4	7	5.5
Children's and infants' clothing	8	8	8	8
Linens and domestics	5	7	6	5.5
Drugs and toiletries	1	1	2	3
Hardware and auto accessories	2	2	4	1
Toys and sporting goods	3	3	3	2
Housewares and traffic appliances	4	5	1	4
Rank correlation coefficient	1.00	0.88 †	0.76 †	0.92 †

* Rank based on number of items in each category that the 259 regular customers planned to purchase.
† Significant at the 0.01 level.

Unlike most other discount store studies, its scope was limited to a single discount store in a shopping center in a restricted market area. The competitive potential of the discount store was evaluated in terms of reasons for patronage and the share of total buying which regular customers did at this store. It was felt that such information would contribute to an understanding of the reasons for customer patronage of discount stores.

The sampling design yielded a sample size of 1,131 store entrants, including 760 adult shoppers. Of these, 86 percent responded to the questionnaire for a sample size of 652 persons in the target population.

Comparative shopping was characteristic of these discount store shoppers. More than three-fourths said they compared merchandise and prices in different stores. Thus it was not surprising to find that price was a major reason for discount store patronage. Convenient hours and parking were other most frequently cited reasons. These findings support the results of several other studies.

When regular customers who gave lower prices as a reason for store patronage were queried concerning availability of price discount by merchandise category, hard goods emerged as "better buys" than soft goods. Interestingly enough, belief in lower prices was significantly correlated with purchase plans of regular customers on the particular day of the interview. It was also correlated with the share of total buying regular customers did at Store A. These results suggest the importance of price and in particular belief in "price discounts" as a major factor in discount store patronage.

The amount purchased was also significantly related to socioeconomic characteristics for clothing and household textiles, and in general the relationship was negative. The opposite was true for those hard goods where a significant relationship existed while in other cases socioeconomic characteristics had no influence on the amount purchased. While opinions concerning the availability of "price discounts" in discount stores differ there seems little doubt that comparison shopping is more difficult for soft goods due to lack of standardization.[12] If hard goods rather than soft goods afford the greatest price saving (and price-conscious shoppers in this study indicated a belief in this) then it appears that the wealthy, well-educated shopper is concentrating his purchases where the potential saving is greatest—at least, in the particular store studied.

Finally the fact that 65 percent of the regular customers had patronized the store since its opening in 1963 suggests that store loyalty exists. The success of the store in attracting and retaining customers testifies to its ability to compete with other traditional retail outlets. The results of this study also indicate that the appeal of discount stores is by no means confined to a particular market segment but rather that different merchandise categories may attract different classes of customers.

12 Louise Skow and Rachel Dardis, "Price Variations for Soft Goods in Discount and Department Stores," *Journal of Marketing,* 33 (April 1969), 45–50.

RETAIL
LAND VALUES

Land suitable and appropriate for retailing activities has value
because of its scarcity in a physical and locational context. Scarcity
of retail land can be viewed from several vantage points. Each
aspect relates to a proposed use or group of uses within the reality
of markets–trade areas and the physical attributes and configuration of a parcel of land.

These parameters then serve the interfacing of the individual
firm with the establishments' image, potential share of markets,
and other important factors equated to the bid and purchase price
paid for a site at a given location. Relative expectation concerning individual merchandise lines of the several firms competing
for a site and location usually provides the margin of difference
between the purchaser and the remainder of the interested buyers.

Manifestly, the level of land value prevailing at several urban
locations reflects and is a translation of the comparative productivity of a site for retail establishments. Starting with the best
retail site in a community, a scaling down of values to less desirable locations is basically an index of the relative quality and
implied productivity of land suitable for retailing functions.

Physical size and other constraints (shallow depth, minimum
frontage, etc.) contribute to less than optimum value because of
limited utility vis-à-vis the potential market represented by new
market entrants or local expanding retailing situations. Accordingly, in a given market context, the assembly of land, thereby
maximizing the use-potential of the combined parcels, results in
imputed incremental value gains to the new assemblage. Important concerns, however, in this regard are the realities of the
supply–demand matrix, the indicated growth of the retailing base
in general, and, more specifically, the demand aspects of a given

location. For it is evident that assemblage per se does not generate increments in land value.

The general level of land values for retail use, and any specific values attaching to a given site, are market translations (by buyers, sellers, mortgagees, etc.) of the present qualities and future continued expectations within the general sphere of the economics of locations. Important indexes for forecasting the anticipated quality of retail locations include the crucial matters of markets (in an aggregate sense), locational share or potential of markets based on merchandise line, the environment, including stability and compatability of adjacent land uses, and the competitive frame of reference to other locations.

Urban Land Value Parameters

Both the resource nature and competitive aspect of urban land interact in a manner to generate clusters of land values within an urban system; the boundaries usually represent the dominance and influence of the urbanized area. Therefore, where there has been a significant increase in land values, care must be taken to identify and separate the component of increase which is due to inflation and the remaining part, due to urbanization.

As an example, where price is a controlling factor in a land purchase decision, the proximity and/or accessibility elements become more random in the ultimate selection. Conversely, constrain the choice to one of several points that represent premium locations and physical development potentials, and the price, whether unit or aggregate, escalates tremendously. Furthermore, where a site has unique locational attributes, for example, high-intensity pedestrian traffic, certain retailing functions respond to monopoly land values, all other retailing functions being non-competitive. This gives rise to the notion of 100 percent retail locations.

In a study completed several years ago by the author, an analysis of land values in 66 SMSA's revealed a distinct clustering and value affinity. A factor analysis identified the following seven factors:

1. Factor A—affluence
2. Factor B—income–living costs
3. Factor C—land values
4. Factor D—commuter access
5. Factor E—trade area dominance
6. Factor F—commercial complexity
7. Factor H—highway access

As noted in Table 1, factor C (land values) is comprised of the following variables:

Variable 22—Number of establishments in the central business district
Variable 23—Number of radio stations
Variable 29—Number of freight–barge–passenger steamship lines
Variable 34—Highest value commercial land per square foot
Variable 35—Highest value residential (single family) land per square foot
Variable 38—Highest value warehouse land per square foot

Land values per se, as noted in Table 2, do not influence other urban dimensions significantly. As tabulated on a multifactor basis related to the variables included in this study, factor C (land values) relates to four variables, the highest area of accounting concerning the number of establishments in the central business district. Even this contribution is not too significant.

Two essays in this section provide an appreciation of land value structures for retail–commercial use. Barry Garner's exhaustive and scholarly analysis of land value patterns within retail nucleations in the greater Chicago market lends further credence to anchor uses, compatibility, and complementarity of retail functions. It represents one of the few definitive studies on the internal aspects of essentially organized shopping centers of the last two decades. The study by Paul B. Downing formulates a theory of center-city commercial land value. Milwaukee serves as a testing ground for the notion of the centrality of land values, markets, and land use.

Studies of land values for retail functions will always have limitations. This is because of the product–resource, which is highly localized and differentiated with respect to both the interrelationships of the community and its location and physical size attributes. The market in land does not reflect free entry in the sense that a firm can pick and choose the right location and the proper size, setting, and configuration of a site. This is aside from matters of hold-up prices, inability to purchase adequate land for optimum planning of a facility, and so on. Therefore, the level, trend, and matrix of retail land values represents only a rough proxy of locational preferences and resultant retailing developments. The constriction on regional and national firms is quite evident; that is, they locate either in a regional or community center or the central business district. The rent they pay, which in turn is translated into related land values, represents a limited market entry cost. Consequently, the imputed land values at these locations must of necessity be viewed as containing bias and distortion.

TABLE 1
Normal Varimax Rotated Factor Matrix

Variables									
	A	*B*	*C*	*D*	*E*	*F*	*G*	*H*	h^2 *
14	97								1.02
17	97								1.02
1	96								1.02
4	96								1.02
20	96								1.02
26	96								1.00
16	94								1.01
7	93								1.01
28	92								96
13	88					36			1.02
15	88								1.01
6	86					30			93
25	86			31					1.00
8	85								91
30	77								84
22	60		38			57			93
23	59		32					37	81
24	53						31	32	56
29	40		31			55			66
2	31	66							65
11		89							95
12		—84							88
9		84			35				94
10		75					37		75
33		75							73
21		69			64				1.01
40		59						37	58
3		—37		—41	41				55
18		36			75				76
34			80						75
35			69						63
38			32					75	86
31				72					61
27				66			35		63
19					88				.90
39						55			35
32							60		55
36							42		25
5							39		42
37								58	71
Common variance	.364	.511	.563	.610	.669	.713	.751	.791	

Source: Edwin M. Rams, *Means of Access and the Socio-Economic Structure of Urban Areas in the United States*, Academy Publishing Co., 1965.
* h^2 is the communality coefficient; 19 of the total of 40 variables (47.5%) had 90–99% of their variance explained by the factors; 28 or 70% had over 70% of their variance explained by the factors; 37 or 92.5% of the variables had over 50% of their variance explained by the eight factors.

TABLE 2
Urban Dimensions with Multi-factor Attributes

---

(2) Population Density
        9.6% accounted for by factor A (affluence)
        43.5% accounted for by factor B (income–living costs)
(3) Percent Migrants from Different County
        16.8% accounted for by factor E (trade area dominance)
  (—) 13.7% accounted for by factor B (income–living costs)
  (—) 16.8% accounted for by factor D (commuter access)
(9) Per Capita Income
        70.6% accounted for by factor B (income–living costs)
        22.3% accounted for by factor E (trade area dominance)
(10) Per Household Income
        56%   accounted for by factor B (income–living costs)
        13.7% accounted for by factor G (highway access)
(18) Per Household Sales
        13%   accounted for by factor B (income–living costs)
        56%   accounted for by factor E (trade area dominance)
(21) Quality Index
        47.6% accounted for by factor B (income–living costs)
        40.9% accounted for by factor E (trade area dominance)
(22) No. Establishments in the Central Business District
        36%   accounted for by factor A (affluence)
        14.4% accounted for by factor C (land vaules)
        32.5% accounted for by factor F (commercial complexity)
(23) No. Radio Stations
        34.8% accounted for by factor A (affluence)
        10.2% accounted for by factor C (land values)
        13.7% accounted for by factor H (industrial diversification)
(24) No. TV Stations
        28%   accounted for by factor A (affluence)
        9.6% accounted for by factor G (highway access)
        10.2% accounted for by factor H (industrial diversification)
(25) Daily Newspaper Circulation
        74%   accounted for by factor A (affluence)
        9.6% accounted for by factor D (commuter access)
(27) No. Rail Carriers
        43.5% accounted for by factor D (commuter access)
        12%   accounted for by factor G (highway access)
(29) No. Freight–Barge–Passenger Steamship Lines
        16%   accounted for by factor A (affluence)
        9.6% accounted for by factor C (land values)
        30%   accounted for by factor F (commercial complexity)
(38) Highest Value Per Sq. Ft., Warehouse Land
        10.2% accounted for by factor C (land values)
        56%   accounted for by factor H (industrial diversification)
(40) Rental Rate Per Sq. Ft. of Warehouse Building
        34.8% accounted for by factor B (income–living costs)
        13.7% accounted for by factor H (industrial diversification)

Source: Edwin M. Rams, *Means of Access and the Socio-Economic Structure of Urban Areas in the United States,* Academy Publishing Co., 1965.

The Relationship Between Land Value and Land Use Within Retail Nucleations

Barry Garner

In this chapter, we turn to an analysis of the ground-floor arrangement of functions within the sample retail nucleations. The objective is to determine whether the hypothesized structure of business centers presented in the models is an adequate representation of the real world situation.

The Representation of Land Values

Evidence presented above suggests that the general level of land values at retail nucleations is in accord with their level in the hierarchy. Land values were also found to vary considerably within and between centers at different levels in the hierarchy. In general, high order centers are associated with high peak land values. Because of such variability, problems in the use of land values arise. When comparing values between centers at the same level in the hierarchy, there is no problem. However, serious distortions are introduced when cross-comparisons between centers at alternative levels are attempted.

Direct comparison of absolute land values is consequently unsatisfactory. However, since values within nucleations reflect distance as a function of decreasing accessibility away from the peak intersection, they can be considered as relative to the peak lot value. Thus, each value can be represented as a percentage value of the peak lot. In this indexed form, values may be compared between centers at the same and at alternative levels in the hierarchy. Land values in this indexed form are used as the basis for the following discussion.[1]

The Representation of Threshold

Identification of the range in threshold values for each business type is not possible from the data available to the author. Moreover, it is even difficult to measure the value of the mean threshold for each individual business type. The methods used by Berry and Garrison to rank functions by absolute threshold size in Snohomish County,

Reprinted from *The Internal Structure of Retail Nucleations,* Studies in Geography Number 12, Department of Geography, Northwestern University, 1966.

[1] For a more detailed explanation of this method, and an example of its use in analyzing internal structure, see B. J. Garner, "Land Values as a Basis for the Analysis of Functional Differentiation within the Central Business District" (mimeographed).

Washington, cannot be applied to similar studies in large urban areas because there is no such thing as a population: establishment ratio for retail nucleations.[2]

The use of a proxy variable to rank functions is, however, suggested from the relationships presented [earlier]. Since the number of establishments of each business type decreases as threshold size increases, the lowest threshold type will at the same time be the most ubiquitous in the urban area. Therefore, a ranking of central functions by total number of establishments in the urban area should approximate their ranking by threshold size.

In this study, however, only the total number of establishments occurring at each of the sixty-two retail nucleations is known. Moreover, the study is restricted to consideration of nucleated functions. Many of these appear to be highly concentrated only at higher order nucleations, although in actual number of establishments, they may be equal to other types which are more widely dispersed between centers. To overcome this, functions have been ranked by their frequency of occurrence at retail nucleations. This ranking is shown in Table 1.

A note should be added about the ranking of functions in the table. Firstly, functions are ranked according to their occurrence at all sixty-two nucleations. Separate rankings are not identified for centers in the Rest of the City and in the Workingmen's Areas, respectively. Although this would perhaps be a desirable breakdown, preliminary investigation showed that disaggregation of the data resulted in an excessive number of tied ranks. Because of this, it was difficult to discriminate effectively between the order of functions.

Secondly, the high ranking of certain functions is not believed to be an accurate representation of threshold size. This arises for either of two reasons: (1) Upper-floor functions are underestimated; for instance, photographic studios are predominantly in upper-floors at high order centers and should perhaps be associated with a lower threshold than is indicated by the frequency ranking; (2) Certain functions, such as fish markets or fruit and vegetable stores, are only marginal in retail nucleations and probably have a lower threshold than indicated on account of their more frequent occurrence in (a) ribbon developments, and (b) the smaller neighborhood centers omitted from the study. Thus, the rank order of individual functions is not believed to be identical to a ranking based upon exact threshold sizes. However, evidence presented [elsewhere] suggests that the ranking by frequency of occurrence at centers is a viable approximation of the ranking by mean threshold size.

The hypothesized internal structure of retail nucleations expressed in the simple model is based upon the arrangement of functions by mean threshold value. We must, therefore, relate these to the mean of the range in land values for each individual function. The mean land value is not, however, calculated for individual functions at each sample center. Rather, centers sampled from each order or level in the hierarchy have been grouped. The grand mean land value for each function for the group of centers as a whole has been calculated. Empirical verification of the hypothesis is, therefore, based upon the

2 B. J. L. Berry and W. L. Garrison, "Functional Bases of the Central Place Hierarchy," *Economic Geography*, 34 (1958), pp. 145–54.

TABLE 1

Central Functions Ranked by Frequency of Occurrence at Retail Nucleations in the City of Chicago

(1)	(2)	Description	(1)	(2)	Description
4	5715	China and glasswear	31	5311	Department stores
5	5664	Children's shoes	33	5251	Hardware
6	5681	Furriers	33	5733	Music stores
6	5942	Book shops	33	7251	Shoe repairs
7	5699	Miscellaneous apparel	35	5422	Meat markets
7	7631	Watch repairs	35	5641	Children's wear
9	5423	Fish markets	35	5999	Miscellaneous retail
10	5431	Fruit and vegetables	35	6159	Personal loans
12	5633	Hosiery	36	7215	Laundromats
13	5634	Apparel accessories	37	783	Movie theaters
15	5719	Miscellaneous furniture	38	5732	Radio and television
16	5632	Lingerie	39	5411	Groceries
16	5996	Camera shops	41	60	Banks
16	7949	Sports promoter	42	5997	Gift and novelty
17	5713	Floor covering	43	'10	Supermarkets
17	5943	Stationers	44	5462	Bakeries
17	64	Insurance agents	44	8099	Optometrists
18	7221	Photographer	45	5441	Candy stores
19	5499	Delicatessen	48	5921	Liquor
20	5952	Sporting goods	49	5665	Family shoes
21	5631	Millinery	49	5712	Furniture
21	5651	Family clothes	49	5971	Jewelers
21	5993	Cigar stands	49	605	Currency exchange
22	5231	Paint and glass	50	7231	Beauty shops
22	5714	Drapery	51	5331	Variety
23	5392	Army and Navy stores	53	5621	Women's clothes
24	5722	Appliances	53	7211	Dry cleaners
27	5663	Women's shoes	54	5612	Men's clothes
28	5662	Men's shoes	58	5813	Bars
28	5992	Florists	61	5912	Drugstores
30	801	Medical services	62	5812	Eating places

Notes: (1) Number of centers at which function occurs.
(2) S.I.C. identification code.
'10 University of Chicago code numbering.

analysis of the relationship between mean threshold size and mean land value for each function by *level of center*. In this way, the generalizations presented relate to what is believed to be the structure of the *average* center at each level in the hierarchy.

The Change in Mean Land Value for Functions at Different Level Centers

It was hypothesized above that lower level functions will occur on lower level values at higher order centers because they are displaced outwards from the core area. The mean percent values for individual functions at different level centers in the Rest of the City and in the Workingmen's Area are shown in Table 2.

Superficially, it seems the data tend to support the validity of the hypothesis. Low order functions are shown, in

TABLE 2
Mean Percent Land Values for Functions by Level of Center

	Level of Center				
S.I.C. Code	R	C	N	Major	Minor
5231 R	17.5	34.8	39.9	41.0	—
5251 N	23.5	45.4	36.3	34.4	11.3
5311 C	48.7	50.2	—	91.3	—
5331 C	41.3	60.5	60.1	46.6	48.0
5392 C	21.5	48.2	—	46.9	28.0
5411 N	22.8	58.6	46.7	31.8	43.7
10 N	19.0	38.7	45.3	—	39.0
5422 N	22.2	34.1	54.3	21.4	37.5
5423 N	14.2	—	—	11.8	30.0
5431 C	—	31.4	—	22.1	11.3
5441 C	49.1	54.2	54.2	63.3	25.6
5462 N	31.8	34.2	46.7	36.9	38.0
5499 C	28.8	58.5	—	—	22.0
5612 C	38.4	54.2	41.7	48.2	47.1
5621 C	41.3	50.4	37.5	50.4	28.0
5631 R	25.3	75.0	—	44.4	43.8
5632 R	32.5	—	46.7	49.9	—
5633 R	53.7	—	—	56.3	—
5634 R	56.2	37.5	—	56.3	—
5641 C	32.7	61.1	—	48.5	36.0
5651 C	44.1	44.5	—	26.9	44.3
5662 R	49.0	45.7	—	56.5	32.4
5663 R	43.7	72.4	—	51.5	43.8
6664 R	41.7	—	—	—	—
5665 C	39.3	54.5	—	49.5	52.3
5671 R	19.2	58.8	—	17.7	—
5699 R	32.0	32.9	—	—	—
5712 C	23.4	41.2	—	31.1	32.8
5713 R	22.4	51.3	—	28.0	—
5714 R	19.8	27.3	—	26.9	30.0
5715 R	15.1	19.6	—	—	—
5719 R	14.5	21.1	—	31.6	—
5722 R	31.8	49.7	—	38.9	—
5732 C	26.2	49.7	40.6	29.4	32.8
5733 C	19.6	35.4	—	44.1	43.8
5812 N	28.0	45.5	43.6	30.6	35.7
5813 N	19.6	45.3	43.4	17.9	47.2

TABLE 2—Continued

S.I.C. Code		Level of Center				
	R	C	N	Major	Minor
5912 N	40.8	58.2	93.5	46.6	69.2
5921 C	22.1	51.0	45.1	20.6	32.2
5942 R	—	75.0	—	—	—
5943 C	18.3	41.7	—	26.0	—
5952 R	21.9	33.4	—	38.3	—
5971 C	35.3	47.0	46.7	42.8	25.6
5992 C	13.9	56.5	41.7	—	—
5993 R	—	100.0	—	59.5	100.0
5996 R	25.1	46.9	—	—	—
5997 C	24.5	40.2	30.7	36.3	28.0
5999 R	27.5	33.7	—	47.9	11.3
60 C	27.6	49.9	24.9	63.4	59.4
605 N	30.9	41.9	48.6	—	28.8
6159 C	25.8	44.6	55.8	23.4	37.5
64 R	24.1	23.2	—	—	—
65 N	20.1	39.8	38.9	—	28.8
7211 N	18.9	44.7	46.3	23.0	29.3
7215 N	17.7	41.1	42.7	—	23.2
7221 R	20.5	35.3	—	34.0	—
7231 N	19.3	44.5	38.6	17.5	—
7241 N	18.3	31.2	45.4	12.1	22.1
7251 N	14.7	41.8	26.1	—	35.0
7631 C	24.0	—	41.2	—	37.5
783 C	30.5	53.7	43.8	32.3	31.0
7949 R	28.2	—	—	—	—
801 N+	22.1	45.9	35.8	15.0	11.3
8099 N+	25.1	37.4	43.7	28.4	36.0
Vacant	21.7	43.2	71.4	32.1	37.3

Notes: R, C and N indicate regional, community and neighborhood level function and center, respectively.
N+ typical of the neighborhood level and all higher levels in the hierarchy.

most cases, to be displaced onto lower value land as order in the hierarchy increases. However, this is not entirely true. For it is apparent that there is a marked down-shift in the general level of percent values at the regional centers. This arises on account of the disproportionately high peak values at the high order regional centers. Because of this, neighborhood and community functions always appear to be on lower value land when they occur at these centers. Similarly, when regional level functions occur at centers below that level, they always occur on higher value land. It is not, therefore, completely valid to discuss the values associated with neighborhood and community level functions when they occur at the regional centers. However, because there is no marked difference in value levels between the other centers, comparisons can be made about them without reservation.

Centers in the Rest of the City

In general, neighborhood functions are displaced onto lower value land when they occur at community centers. This is consistent with expectation. Bakeries illustrate this nicely. They are found on land valued at 46.7 percent of the peak at the neighborhood centers in which they are typical. They are displaced onto land valued at only 34.2 percent at the higher level community centers.

This is not, however, true for all neighborhood functions and it is perhaps more instructive to look at the deviant cases than those behaving as expected. Several neighborhood functions occur on higher value land when they occur at the community centers. They are namely: hardware, grocery, eating places, bars, real estate agents, beauty shops and shoe repairs. In the case of eating places and bars, deviation is probably the direct result of product differentiation at the higher level center. However, the same argument does not apply to the other business types. No immediate explanation is available for the higher values associated with hardware, grocery stores, beauty shops and shoe repairs. Real estate agents reflect, perhaps, the greater importance of the higher order centers in the provision of business services and suggest that they are perhaps only marginal functions at the neighborhood level.

Centers in the Workingmen's Area

There is less evidence of this regularity at the major and minor centers. In part, this can be attributed to disturbances in land values at these centers

associated with decline of trade areas, and in part, it is related to the lower level of demand serviced. For example, the level of demand necessary to support a function at the community level in the rest of the city may only be available at locations in the equivalent of regional (i.e., major) centers in this part of the city. Error in classification may, therefore, cause disturbance of the regularity.

This would appear to be the case for women's clothes, jewelers, banks, motion picture theaters and Army and Navy stores. These are all considered to be typical of the community level in the Rest of the City. But, they are all found on higher value land at major centers—the equivalent of regional centers in the workingmen's area—than at minor centers.

On the other hand, this is probably not the explanation for the deviation of hardware stores in this part of the city. Although they are classified as neighborhood functions, they also occur on higher value land at major centers. Hardware stores were also noted to deviate at centers in the Rest of the City where they occurred on higher value land at the community level centers.

One explanation for this consistent deviation is suggested. Presumably, hardware stores are less important as independent suppliers of hardware goods at higher order centers where they are in competition with a variety of alternative suppliers. Variety stores, department stores and even supermarkets offer a wide range of similar goods. If it can be assumed that hardware stores become more specialized to counteract this increased competition, it is conceivable that their rent-paying ability is increased, thereby enabling them to occupy higher value sites at higher order centers.

In general, lower order functions are displaced onto lower value land at higher order centers. However, it is difficult to say whether the hypothesis is supported at the regional level centers because of the down-shift in level of percent values. In spite of this, enough evidence is presented to lend general support to the hypothesis at the other centers.

Rank Order of Functions by Level of Center

It is perhaps more meaningful to generalize about relative changes in values for functions at higher order centers than to make statements about the absolute changes evident in Table 2. This is best done from the analysis of differences in the rank order of functions at each level of center. By doing this, comparisons can be made about location of lower order functions at higher order centers despite any changes in general level of percent values.

Thus, although percent values are generally lower at the regional centers, lower order functions should exhibit a similar ranking at this and lower level centers. Moreover, the analysis of changes in rank order enables verification of the hypothesis that functions typical of any given level are ordered among themselves according to threshold size.

In addition to merely ranking functions by percent value at each level in the hierarchy, functions have also been grouped on the basis of similarity of land values. Similarity in value between different functions is measured by the

difference in land values between each function and all others in the array. The smaller the difference in value between any two functions, the greater their land value similarity, or the greater their affinity for similar locations within retail nucleations. A matrix of value differences is formed, and functions are classified by the application of linkage analysis into groups comprising those activities showing the greatest similarity in land values.[3] In this way, not only can differences in the rank order of functions between alternative levels be investigated but at the same time it is possible to see any significant changes in the zonal arrangement of functions at the different level centers.

The rank order of functions is not expected to be identical for any two levels in the hierarchy. Sampling variability alone precludes this. However, significant differences in the ranking of functions can be detected by using Spearman rank correlation coefficients. Although minor changes may occur in the rank order of individual business types, these are not considered important *unless* they result in a significant difference in overall ranking when measured by rank correlation coefficients. Thus, a non-significant rank correlation is taken as an indication of dissimilarity between rankings.

Table 3 shows the ranking and zonal arrangement of neighborhood functions at the different levels of center. There does not appear to be a consistent pattern in arrangement from center to center. The changes in rank order of the neighborhood functions at the different centers can be summarized as follows:

---

[3] A more detailed discussion of this method and its application is found in B. J. Garner, "Notes on the Application of Nearest Neighbor Linkage Analysis" (mimeographed).

TABLE 3
Clustering of Neighborhood Level Functions

	Level of Center					% Peak Value
Zone	Neighborhood	Community	Regional	Major	Minor	
I	Drugs				Drugs	60%
II	Meat market	Grocery Drugs				50%
III	Currency X Bakery Grocer Supermarket Barber Dry cleaner	Medical Eating place Bars Hardware		Drugs	Bars	45%
IV	Opticians Eating place Laundromats Bars	Dry cleaning Beauty shop Currency X Shoe repairs Laundromats	Drugs		Grocer	40%
V	Real estate Beauty shop	Real estate Supermarket Opticians		Eating place	Supermarket Bakers Meat market	37%
VI	Hardware Medical	Bakery Meat market Barbers	Bakery Currency X	Bakery Hardware Grocery	Optician Eating place Shoe repair	30%
VII	Shoe repair		Eating place Opticians Hardware Grocer Meat market Medical	Opticians Dry cleaner Meat market	Dry cleaner Real estate Currency X Laundromat Barbers	20%
VIII			Bars Beauty shop Supermarket Dry cleaner Barbers Laundromats	Barbers Bars Beauty shop Medical		15%
IX			Shoe repairs Fish market	Fish market	Hardware Medical	

1. There is no significant difference between the overall ranking of functions at the neighborhood, regional, major and minor centers. However, the ranking of neighborhood level functions at the community centers is significantly different from that at all others.
2. Although neighborhood functions as a group are concentrated in approximately the same value zones at neighborhood and community centers, they are displaced onto lower value zones at the regional level. In the Workingmen's centers, they are found on land intermediate in value to that at regional and community centers.

3. The significant difference in rank order of neighborhood functions at the community level results from: (a) the higher ranking of hardware stores, groceries, eating places, bars, real estate offices and shoe repairs; and (b) the lower rank order of bakeries, barbershops, meat markets, currency exchanges and optometrists.

4. Certain of these functions show consistent changes in rank order at other centers. Hardware stores rank much higher at regional and major centers, but rank much lower at minor centers. Real estate agents and shoe repairs also rank high at minor centers. Conversely, barbershops rank lower at regional centers, and meat markets much lower at major centers.

5. Drugstores are outstanding in their consistently high rank order in all centers.

The rank order and zonal arrangement of community level functions are shown in Table 4. The more complex arrangement typical of higher order centers is immediately apparent. Notable differences in the arrangement of community level functions shown in the table can be summarized as follows:

1. There is less regularity in zonal arrangement between different centers. At the regional level, functions are concentrated in the lower value zones, but are more dispersed at both the major and minor centers.

2. The clustering of community functions into value zones is less consistent between centers than is the case of the neighborhood level functions. In major centers, a completely different set of land value zones is evident.

3. In spite of changes in zonal arrangement, community functions are ranked in essentially the same order at community, regional and major centers. The ranking at minor centers is, however, significantly different from that at all others.

4. The difference in rank order at minor centers is due to changes in four func-

tions: (a) family clothes and music stores which rank much higher, and (b) candy stores and delicatessens which rank much lower.

5. Certain functions rank consistently higher or lower at centers other than the community level. These are: (a) banks, gift and novelty stores and members of the furniture group—radio and television stores, music stores and general furniture stores—which rank higher at all other centers, and (b) children's clothes stores, delicatessens, motion picture theaters and liquor stores which rank lower at all other centers.

6. Certain other functions are characterized by a marked change in rank only at one other center. Thus, jewelers and family clothes stores rank higher at regional centers, and variety stores rank much lower at major centers. The extremely low rank order of florists at the regional level centers is presumed to be the result of sampling error.

Table 5 shows the ranking and zonal arrangement of regional level functions at the highest order centers. The basic difference in pattern is the change in zonal concentration at major centers where functions are clustered in higher value zones. However, in spite of this difference, there is a highly significant correlation between the two ranks. The distinction between an inner area of clothing functions and an outer area of furniture and other functions is clearly apparent at this level.

It is shown, therefore, that three basic differences exist in the rank order of each set of functions between alternative centers. These are: (1) the ordering of neighborhood functions at the community level is significantly different from the ranking at all other centers; (2) the ordering of community level functions at minor centers is significantly different from the ranking at all others; and (3) the ranking of neighborhood and community level func-

TABLE 4
Clustering of Community Level Functions

Zone	Community	Regional	Major	Minor	% Peak Value
			Level of Center		
I	Children's wear Variety		Dept. store Banks Candy		60%
II	Delicatessen Florist Family shoes Candy Men's clothes Movie theater			Bank Family shoes	52%
III	Liquor Dept. store Women's clothes		Women's clothes		50%
IV	Banks Radio–TV	Candy	Family shoes		49%
V	Army and navy Jewelers	Dept. store	Children's wear Men's clothes Army and navy	Variety Men's clothes	45%
VI	Loans Family clothes	Family clothes	Music Jewelers	Family clothes Music	42%
VII	Stationery Furniture Gifts	Women's clothes Variety	Variety		40%
VIII		Family shoes Men's clothes	Gifts	Loans Children's wear	36%
IX	Music Paint and Glass	Jewelers Children's wear Movie theater Delicatessen Banks	Movie theater Furniture Radio–TV	Furniture Radio–TV Liquor Movie theater Army and navy Women's clothes Gifts	27%
X		Radio–TV Loans	Family clothes Stationery	Candy Jewelers	25%
XI		Gifts Furniture	Loans Fruit and veg.	Delicatessen	22%
XII		Liquor Army and navy	Liquor		20%
XIII		Music Stationery Paint and glass Florist			15%

TABLE 5
Clustering of Regional Level Functions

Zone	Regional	Major	% Peak Value
I	Apparel accessories	Cigar stand	
		Men's shoes	
		Hosiery	
		Apparel accessories	56%
	Hosiery		
	Men's shoes	Women's shoes	50%
II		Corsets and lingerie	
		Children's shoes	48%
	Women's shoes	Millinery	
	Children's shoes	China and glass	40%
III		Household appliances	
		Sports goods	35%
IV	Corsets and lingerie		
	Misc. apparel	Photographers	
	Household appliances	Misc. furnishings	30%
V		Floor covering	
	Sports promoters	Drapery	27%
	Millinery		
	Cameras		
	Insurance		23%
VI	Floor covering		
	Sports goods		
	Photographers		
	Drapery		20%
VII	China and glass		
	Misc. furnishings		10%

tions is significantly different between major and minor centers.

Are Functions Ranked by Threshold?

Functions typical of each level in the hierarchy show, in general, similar rank order at the different centers. But, are they ranked by threshold size? In order to verify the hypothesis that high value functions are at the same time high threshold functions, rank correlations of the value and ubiquity scales were calculated for the set of neighborhood, community and regional level functions respectively at each center.

When all functions in any given ar-

ray (e.g., all the neighborhood level functions at regional centers, or all the community level functions at major centers, etc.) are included in the calculation of the correlation coefficients, a significant correlation between value and threshold is found only at the neighborhood level. At these centers neighborhood functions are ranked according to expectation; high value neighborhood functions are high threshold functions.

At other centers, it becomes increasingly obvious that the measure of threshold used in this work is inadequate. Comparisons of the ranking by percent value and mean threshold size indicate that large differences in rank order occur for certain functions.

These functions are listed in Table 6. Two interesting generalizations can be made about them. Firstly, certain functions show large differences in rank order repeatedly at several centers. Secondly, some functions are unique in that they deviate only at one center. With the exception of paint and glass stores, functions deviating at more than one center are characterized by a high mean value but a low threshold index. They include eating places, bars, drug, variety and army and navy stores, men's and women's clothes and shoe stores.

The consistent deviation of these types at more than one center presumably results from shortcomings in the measurement of mean threshold rather than from sampling error in mean land value.

Measuring thresholds by frequency of occurrence at retail nucleations does not take into account shifts in scale of operation or product differentiation of functions when they occur at higher level centers. Thus, for example, many drugstores clearly change function at higher levels in the hierarchy. They are usually larger scale operations providing a greater "bundle of goods" to

TABLE 6
Functions with Large Rank Differences

Community Centers	Regional Centers	Major Centers	Minor Centers
	Neighborhood Functions		
(b) Meat markets	(a) Hardware		
(a) Eating places	Eating places		Eating places
(a) Bars		Bars	
(a) Drugstores	Drugstores	Drugstores	Drugstores
(a) Currency exchange			
(a) Dry cleaners			
	(a) Laundromats		
(a) Beauty shops			
			(b) Medical services
	Community Functions		
(b) Paint and glass	Paint and glass		
(a) Variety stores	Variety stores		Variety stores
(a) Army and navy	Army and navy		Army and navy
			(b) Delicatessens
(a) Men's clothes	Men's clothes	Men's clothes	Men's clothes
	(a) Women's clothes	Women's clothes	
(b) Family clothes			
(a) Family shoes			
	Regional Functions		
	(a) Men's shoes	Men's shoes	
	(a) Women's shoes	Women's shoes	
	(b) China and glassware		
	(b) Miscellaneous furnishings		

Notes: (a) Functions with high mean value and low mean threshold.
(b) Functions with low mean value and high mean threshold.

the consumer, which in turn increases their latitude of product differentiation. However, this is not revealed by the S.I.C. classification nor by the index of threshold used in this work. Thus although drugstores are ubiquitous in the urban area, there is presumably a marked upward shift in the range of thresholds resulting in the ability to occupy higher value land. Similar arguments can be extended to the other functions in this group.

In the case of paint and glass stores, the low frequency of occurrence would seem to be an overestimation of threshold size. This activity is not a true central function since it occurs more frequently in ribbons. Thus, the few establishments included by the method of delimiting retail nucleations in this work is not an accurate index of their degree of ubiquity in the urban area.

The remaining functions deviate at only one level. They include functions similar to those above with high mean value and low threshold index, such as laundromats, dry cleaners, currency exchanges and family stores, and conversely, functions with low mean value but a high threshold index, such as meat markets, hardware and family clothes stores. Deviation in the former case is presumed to be related to sampling error in mean land values.

Many of these functions were noted to have changed rank considerably in the above analysis of rank orders. In the latter group, it would seem that threshold is overestimated.

Two high threshold furniture functions should be included in this list. China and glassware and miscellaneous furniture stores rank on low value land at the regional center although they are associated with a high threshold index. In this case, the difference in rank order is probably not related to error in sampling. Rather, it suggests the subtle difference between inter- and intra-center location. These functions need the centrality offered by high order centers—although this may be an intuitive conception. However, because of their large space needs and association with comparative shopping habits, they are unable to compete successfully for high value inner locations. Consequently, they are situated toward the periphery of high order centers where they are interspersed with lower order functions.

It is interesting to note that if, on the grounds of measurement error, these deviant cases are removed from the arrays, significant correlations are obtained. These are listed in Table 7. However, it is to be noted that even after removing deviant community level functions from the ranking at regional

TABLE 7
Significant Rank Correlations Between Land Value and Threshold Size

	Level of Center				
	N	C	R	Major	Minor
Neighborhood functions	.45	.81	.60	.55	.63
Community functions	—	.52	X	.52	X
Regional functions	—	—	.71	.50	—

Notes: All correlations are significant at the five percent level.
　　　　X represents the lack of significant correlation.
　　　　— indicates that functions are not considered at that level.

and minor centers, the two variables are still not significantly correlated.

Summary

The rank order of functions at the different centers can be summarized as follows:

1. Apart from only one or two exceptions, functions typical of any given level in the hierarchy (i.e., neighborhood level functions, etc.) appear to be arranged in similar rank order when they occur at higher order centers. Furthermore, lower order functions are generally found on lower value land at higher order centers.
2. Certain functions are associated with minor changes in rank order at different centers. Since these changes do not destory the overall ranking, they are presumed to be due to sampling error.
3. When allowance is made for shortcomings in the threshold index used in this work and sampling variation in land values, evidence suggests that functions trend toward a ranking by mean threshold size. Thus, in most cases, those functions which have a high mean threshold also tend to be associated with a high mean land value.
4. Shortcomings in the threshold estimation

and in sampling error, as reflected in the mean value, combine in such a way as to destroy the hypothesized relationship in the case of community level functions at regional and minor centers.

The Internal Structure of Nucleations

So far we have been dealing with the ranking of functions separately at different level centers. We now combine the rankings in order to test whether the pattern of internal arrangement hypothesized in the sample model is a valid representation of the real world nucleation. Generalizations about the internal structure of retail nucleations are made at two levels of data aggregation: firstly, the aggregate structure by S.I.C. major groups, and secondly, internal structure based on individual functions.

NEIGHBORHOOD CENTERS. The average structure of neighborhood centers based on S.I.C. major groups is shown in Table 8. The variety group and personal loan offices rank first and second on land valued at 60.0 and 56.0 percent

TABLE 8
The Internal Structure of Neighborhood Centers by S.I.C. Groups

S. I. C. Group	Description	Percent Value
53	Variety	60.1
6159	Loans	55.8
59	Miscellaneous	51.5
54	Food	49.4
605	Currency exchange	48.6
783	Motion picture theaters	43.8
58	Eating and drinking	43.5
56	Apparel	40.8
57	Furniture	40.6
72	Personal service	39.8
80	Medical services	39.8
65	Real estate agents	38.9
52	Hardware	38.1

of the peak, respectively. These groups are not, however, typical of the neighborhood level, but are included to show that when higher order functions occur at lower order centers, they sometimes occupy higher value land than functions typical of that level. The high ranking of the groups comprising essentially neighborhood level functions —the food, miscellaneous and eating and drinking groups—is consistent with expectation. Personal services and hardware stores and medical services tend to be characteristic of the lower value peripheral part of neighborhood nucleations.

The arrangement of individual functions within the neighborhood level centers is shown in Table 9. Drugstores are located on the highest value land at 93.5 percent of the peak value. This is expected since they are peak lot uses at this level. The predominant convenience nature of the neighborhood center is reflected in the location of food functions on sites above 45.0 percent of the peak. Hardware stores, personal services, with the exception of dry cleaners and barbers, medical services and real estate agents are found at the periphery on low value land.

The predictions of the model are verified at the neighborhood level where neighborhood functions occupy the core area of the nucleation.[4] The ranking of functions by land value is significantly correlated with the ranking by threshold size ($R_S = .45$). The rather low coefficient is accounted for by the anomalous occurrence of meat

TABLE 9
The Internal Structure of Neighborhood Centers

S. I. C. Code	Description	Percent Value	
5912	Drugstores	93.5	90.0%
5422	Meat markets	54.3	50.0%
605	Currency exchange	48.6	
5462	Bakeries	46.7	
5411	Grocers	46.6	
7211	Dry cleaners	46.3	
7241	Barbers	45.4	
10	Supermarkets	45.3	
8099	Optometrists	43.7	
5812	Eating places	43.6	
5813	Bars	43.4	
7215	Laundromats	42.7	40.0%
65	Real estate agents	38.9	
7231	Beauty shops	38.6	
5251	Hardware	36.3	
801	Medical services	35.8	30.0%
7251	Shoe repairs	26.1	

[4] In this and all other discussion of internal structure, high order functions are omitted from discussion when they occur at lower order centers. Thus here mention is made only of the neighborhood functions. Analysis indicates that when higher order functions appear at lower order centers, there is no significant correlation between their threshold size and land value location.

markets on higher value land than is expected from threshold size, and to the low threshold index associated with eating places and bars.

COMMUNITY CENTERS. The structure of community level centers by S.I.C. major groups is shown in Table 10. Motion picture theaters and the apparel and variety groups are found on the highest value land. The food group is notably displaced onto lower value land at this level, where it is found in association with the personal service and hardware groups on land valued at approximately 40.0 percent of the peak. Banks and medical services are found between 45.0 percent and 50.0 percent of the peak, while the furniture group is located at the periphery on land at 36.9 percent of the peak value.

The arrangement of individual functions at community centers is shown in Table 11. According to the hypothesis, community level functions should occupy the high value inner core area, and should be surrounded by lower value land by the neighborhood level functions. The empirical evidence is quite convincing. With the exception of drugstores and groceries, which are interspersed among the higher value community level functions, neighborhood functions are notably concentrated toward the periphery of the nucleation on the lower value land. It is not surprising to find drugstores on high value land at this level, but there is no immediate explanation, apart from sampling error, for the high value location of grocery stores at this level.

Conversely, community level functions are not all clustered in the core area; certain of them are located amongst the neighborhood functions on low value peripheral sites. In order of decreasing value, these are loan offices, family clothing stores, stationers, furniture, gift and novelty, and men's shoe stores. Loan offices are found more frequently on upper floors in the core area suggesting that they are perhaps unable to afford the higher value ground-floor core sites. Comparable

TABLE 10
The Internal Structure of Community Centers by S. I. C. Groups

S. I. C. Group	Description	Percent Value
783	Motion picture theaters	53.7
56	Apparel	53.2
53	Variety	53.0
59	Miscellaneous	51.1
60	Banks	49.9
801	Medical services	46.0
58	Eating and drinking	45.4
6159	Loans	44.7
54	Food	44.3
605	Currency exchange	41.9
72	Personal services	40.9
52	Hardware	40.1
65	Real estate	39.8
8099	Optometrists	37.4
57	Furniture	36.9

TABLE 11
The Internal Structure of Community Centers

S. I. C. Code	Description	Percent Value	
C 5641	Children's clothes	61.1	
C 5331	Variety stores	60.5	
			60.0%
N 5411	Grocers	58.6	
C 5499	Delicatessen	58.5	
C 5992	Florists	56.5	
C 5665	Family shoes	54.5	
C 5441	Candy	54.2	
N 5912	Drugstores	54.2	
C 5612	Men's clothes	54.2	
C 783	Motion picture theaters	53.7	
C 5921	Liquor stores	51.0	
C 5311	Department stores	50.0	
C 5621	Women's clothes	50.0	
			50.0%
C 60	Banks	49.9	
C 5732	Radio and television	49.7	
C 5392	Army and navy stores	48.2	
C 5871	Jewelers	47.0	
N 801	Medical services	46.0	
N 5812	Eating places	45.5	
N 5251	Hardware	45.4	
N 5813	Bars	45.3	
N 7211	Dry cleaners	44.7	
C 6159	Loan offices	44.5	
N 7231	Beauty shops	44.5	
C 5651	Family clothes	44.5	
N 605	Currency exchanges	41.9	
N 7251	Shoe repairs	41.8	
C 5943	Stationery stores	41.7	
C 5712	Furniture	41.2	
N 7215	Laundromats	41.1	
C 5997	Gift and novelty stores	40.1	
			40.0%
N 65	Real estate agents	39.8	
N 10	Supermarkets	38.9	
N 8099	Optometrists	37.4	
C 5733	Music stores	35.4	
C 5231	Paints and glass	34.8	
N 5462	Bakeries	34.2	
N 5422	Meat markets	34.1	
N 7241	Barber shops	31.2	
			30.0%

Note: N and C represent neighborhood and community level functions, respectively.

rents are found only at some spots removed from the peak at the ground-floor level. There is no logical explanation for the occurrence of family clothing and stationery stores on low value land.

However, it is understandable why furniture stores should be found on low value locations. Because of their heavy reliance upon comparative purchasing, sales of furniture are not directly related to concentrations of buyers at the more central locations. This, together with their need for larger sites, forces furniture stores to locate at low rent peripheral sites.

Although the empirical evidence generally supports the predicted pattern of internal structure, it is not verified statistically. The lack of a significant correlation between values and thresholds can, however, be attributed to the disproportionately large difference in rank of a very small number of the thirty-six functions included in the initial correlation. If these are omitted from the calculation, a significant rank correlation of .34 is obtained.

Ten functions account for this difference. Five of these are functions for which it is believed thresholds are underestimated—namely, eating places, bars, drugstores, variety, men's and women's clothing stores. The other five would seem to be related to error from overlap in land values and include meat markets, candy stores, stationers, florists, and paint and glass stores.

These functions apart, the structure of community level centers is in general accordance with the hypothesis

that the community functions are located in the high value core area, and are surrounded at the periphery by lower order neighborhood functions.

REGIONAL CENTERS. The structure of the regional level centers based on S.I.C. major groups is shown in Table 12. Apart from the lower level of values, the pattern is not radically different from the aggregate structure of the community centers.[5]

The clothing and variety groups and motion picture theaters again rank on the highest value land. However, they are joined at this level by currency exchanges, which ranked somewhat lower at the community level. The most noticeable difference in arrangement at this level is the location on lower value sites of the personal service and miscellaneous groups. Medical services are also found on low value ground-floor sites at regional centers. At this level, they are more commonly found at centrally located upper floors, where they constitute older, upper-floor medical complexes.

Table 13 shows the relative location of individual functions in regional centers. The arrangement is much more complex than the geometry hypothesized in the simple model. Regional, community and neighborhood functions are not concentrated in discrete zones of decreasing value land. Rather, evidence suggests that functions typical of each level are interspersed with each other to form zones of overlapping land use according to the more complex model.

---

[5] This is an interesting finding since B. J. L. Berry states, "Functions performed (at regional centers) differ from community centers not so much in types included, as in their number and variety." See B. J. L. Berry and R. M. Lillibridge, "Guides for the Provision of Shopping and Allied Service Districts in Residential Communities," Community Renewal Program, Chicago, 1962 (mimeographed).

TABLE 12
The Internal Structure of Regional Centers by S.I.C. Groups

S.I.C. Group	Description	Percent Value
56	Apparel	39.2
53(1)	Variety	37.1
605	Currency exchange	30.9
783	Motion picture theaters	30.5
54	Food	28.3
60	Banks	27.6
6159	Loans	25.8
8099	Optometrists	25.1
64	Insurance	24.1
58	Eating and drinking	23.8
801	Medical services	22.1
57	Furniture	21.6
59	Miscellaneous	21.5
52	Hardware	20.5
65	Real estate agents	20.1
72	Personal services	18.2

Note: (1) This includes 5392 (army and navy stores). When this is omitted, the 53 group ranks first with a value of 44.9 percent.

TABLE 13
The Internal Structure of Regional Centers

S.I.C. Code		Description	Percent Value	
R	5634	Apparel accessory	56.2	
R	5633	Hosiery stores	53.7	50.0%
C	5441	Candy	49.1	
R	5662	Men's shoes	49.0	
C	5311	Department stores	48.7	
C	5651	Family clothes	44.1	
R	5663	Women's shoes	43.7	
R	5664	Children's shoes	41.7	
C	5621	Women's clothes	41.3	
C	5331	Variety stores	41.3	
N	5912	Drugstores	40.8	40.0%
C	5665	Family shoes	39.3	
C	5612	Men's clothes	38.4	
C	5971	Jewelers	35.3	
R	5641	Children's clothes	32.7	
R	5632	Corset and lingerie	32.5	
R	5699	Miscellaneous clothing	32.0	
R	5722	Household appliances	31.8	
N	5462	Bakeries	31.8	
N	605	Currency exchanges	30.9	
C	783	Motion picture theaters	30.5	30.0%
C	5499	Delicatessen	28.8	

TABLE 13—Continued

S.I.C. Code	Description	Percent Value	
R 7949	Sports promoters	28.2	
N 5812	Eating places	28.0	
C 60	Banks	27.6	
C 5732	Radio and television	26.2	
C 6159	Loan offices	25.8	
R 5631	Millinery stores	25.3	
N 8099	Optometrists	25.1	
R 5996	Camera stores	25.1	
C 5997	Gift and novelty	24.5	
R 64	Insurance	24.1	
C 7631	Watch repairs	24.0	
N 5251	Hardware	23.5	
C 5712	Furniture	23.4	
N 5411	Grocers	22.8	
R 5713	China and glassware	22.4	
N 5422	Meat markets	22.2	
C 5921	Liquor stores	22.1	
N 801	Medical services	22.1	
R 5952	Sporting goods stores	21.9	
C 5392	Army and navy stores	21.5	
R 7221	Photographers	20.5	
N 65	Real estate agents	20.1	20.0%
R 5714	Drapery stores	19.8	
C 5733	Music stores	19.6	
N 5813	Bars	19.6	
N 7231	Beauty shops	19.3	
N 10	Supermarkets	19.0	
N 7211	Dry cleaners	18.9	
N 7241	Barbers	18.3	
C 5943	Stationery stores	18.3	
N 7215	Laundromats	17.7	
C 5231	Paint and glass stores	17.7	
R 5715	Floor covering	15.1	
N 7251	Shoe repairs	14.7	
R 5719	Miscellaneous furnishing	14.5	
N 5423	Fish and sea foods	14.2	
C 5992	Florists	13.9	

Note: R, C and N indicate regional, community and neighborhood level functions, respectively.

Neighborhood functions are, generally speaking, clustered toward the periphery, although perhaps not as noticeably as at the community level center. Notable exceptions are drugstores, bakeries, eating places and optometrists. These are interspersed with high order functions in the core area. Community level functions are highly scattered throughout the center. Some of them are interspersed with the regional functions on high value land. Notable among these are candy stores, department and variety stores and jewelers.

Only the regional level clothing functions are concentrated in the core area. Some are found at the periphery in association with neighborhood level functions. This is especially true of photographic studios, sports goods stores, and members of the furniture group, including floor covering, drapery stores, china and glassware and miscellaneous furniture stores. Field investigation suggests that photographic studios, like medical services and personal loan offices, are more commonly found on upper floors in the core area. In order to locate on comparable value sites at the ground-floor level, they must move outwards toward the periphery. If it can be assumed that comparative shopping habits are associated with the purchase of sports goods as well as furniture items, the peripheral location of these functions can also be explained in terms of buying habits.

The most notable features in the arrangement of functions within regional centers can be summarized as follows:

1. There is a marked concentration of clothing functions in the high value core area. This not only comprises the more specialized regional level but also the more general community level types.
2. Peripheral sites are occupied by personal services and food functions together with certain members of the regional level furniture group.
3. Between these extremes, the body of the center is characterized by a complex mix of community and regional level functions in which the miscellaneous group and financial services are significant.

The more complex arrangement of functions within the center is reflected by the lack of a significant rank correlation between value and threshold. When all functions are included, the coefficient is only .19. However, as was the case at the community level, this low coefficient is due, in large part, to large differences in rank order for one or two individual types. If these are omitted from the calculation, a significant correlation of .63 is obtained.

The observations exerting a distorting effect on the hypothesized relationship fall into two groups. Firstly, candy stores, women's clothes, variety, drugstores and men's clothes stores deviate because of underestimated threshold size. Presumably, scale shifts resulting in steep rent-bid curves enable them to compete for high value core locations in spite of their high degree of ubiquity in the urban area. Secondly, there is a group of functions for which it seems that the mean land value is under- or overestimated. This includes watch repairs, paint stores, china and glass stores, miscellaneous home furnishings, florists and fish markets.

Deviation in the case of watch repairers and miscellaneous furnishings may, however, be related to shortcomings in the S.I.C. classification rather than to error in the mean value. Most jewelers offer watch repair services to their customers. However, classification by dominant line of business identifies these as jewelers and not as watch repairers. Establishments whose sole function is the repair of watches occur infrequently in the urban area. Hence, occurring at few nucleations, they are recorded as high threshold functions using the method adopted in this work. Similarly, miscellaneous furniture stores comprise establishments which do not have any dominant line of business. Since these are also few in number, they too appear as high threshold functions because of their low frequency of occurrence at centers.

Apart from the distorting effects that these functions have on the ranking by value and threshold, the pattern of arrangement of functions at the regional level is in general accord with the hypothesized arrangement. However, considerable overlap between different level functions is apparent. This is presumably a reflection of product differentiation and its effect upon the mean land value for individual functions.

WORKINGMEN'S CENTERS. The internal structure of major and minor centers by S.I.C. major groups is shown in Tables 14 and 15, respectively. The patterns are basically similar. The variety group and banks are found on the highest value land, and personal services and medical services are found on the low-

TABLE 14

The Internal Structure of Minor Centers by S.I.C. Groups

S.I.C. Group	Description	Percent Value
60	Banks	59.4
53(1)	Variety	48.0
59	Miscellaneous	41.6
58	Eating and drinking	41.4
56	Apparel	40.9
6159	Loans	37.5
8099	Optometrists	36.0
57	Furniture	34.8
783	Motion picture theaters	31.0
54	Food	30.9
72	Personal services	29.4
65	Real estate agents	28.8
605	Currency exchange	28.8
52	Hardware	11.3
801	Medical services	11.3

Note: (1) 5932 (Army and navy stores) excluded.

TABLE 15

The Internal Structure of Major Centers by S.I.C. Groups

S.I.C. Group	Description	Percent Value
60	Banks	63.4
53(1)	Variety	59.7
56	Apparel	46.4
59	Miscellaneous	38.0
52	Hardware	37.7
57	Furniture	33.0
783	Motion picture theaters	32.3
54	Food	31.2
8099	Optometrists	28.4
58	Eating and drinking	27.8
6159	Loans	23.4
72	Personal services	21.7
801	Medical services	15.0

Note: (1) 5932 (Army and navy stores) excluded.

est value land at both centers. The food group is also typical of low value locations.

Two notable differences exist. The eating and drinking group ranks high in value at minor centers. As was pointed out above, there is an exceptional concentration of eating places and bars at minor centers, and it is significant that they appear on high value land. Conversely, hardware stores rank much higher in value at major centers.

The arrangement of individual functions within minor centers is shown in Table 16. Although some neighborhood functions cluster on low value land, they are generally more dispersed among the community level functions on higher value land. There is little evidence of community level functions occupying the high value core of the nucleation. Although the few regional level functions appearing at minor centers do not cluster as a group in the innermost part of the nucleation, they nevertheless tend to occupy higher value sites.

Cigar stores and drugstores occupy the highest value sites. Bars are located on high value inner locations in the same way as at the neighborhood centers. The food group also ranks high at this center, especially groceries, supermarkets, bakeries and meat markets. These are only found at locations of comparable value at neighborhood centers in the Rest of the City.

High value community level functions include banks and representatives of the clothing functions—family shoes, men's and family clothing stores. Furniture stores appear on relatively high value land at these centers. This is in direct contrast to their location at the community level to which the minor center is assumed to be functionally equivalent.

The arrangement of individual functions at major centers is shown in Table 17. A more complex pattern is immediately evident. Its most significant feature is the dispersed location of the regional level functions. Apart from the clustering of clothing functions on the innermost high value sites, the rest are scattered on lower value land toward the periphery, where they are interspersed with neighborhood and community functions.

The highest value land is occupied by department stores, banks, candy stores and cigar stands. Following these there is a notable concentration of clothing functions, comprising the more specialized regional level types—men's shoes, hosiery, apparel accessory, women's shoes, infants' wear, and the more general community level men's and women's clothes stores. Family clothes stores are; however, not included in this group, but are found toward the periphery on lower value land. Drug and variety stores are also displaced onto relatively lower value land at these centers. In general, furniture functions are found on low value sites, although this is not true of music stores and household appliances. These are both found on higher value land in the middle parts of the nucleation. At the periphery, low value sites are occupied by representatives of the personal services and food group of functions.

The empirical evidence does not support the hypothesized pattern. High order functions neither cluster in the inner high value sites, nor are they surrounded by lower order functions on lower value land. The pattern is considerably more complex; functions typical of each level are markedly dispersed throughout centers.

A suggested reason for the considerable overlap in arrangement is the

TABLE 16
The Internal Structure of Minor Centers

S.I.C. Code		Description	Percent	Value
R	5993	Cigar stands	100.0	
N	5912	Drugstores	69.2	60.0%
C	60	Banks	59.4	
C	5665	Family shoes	52.3	50.0%
C	5331	Variety stores	48.0	
N	5813	Bars	47.2	
C	5612	Men's clothes	47.1	
C	5651	Family clothes	44.3	
R	5663	Women's shoes	43.8	
R	5631	Millinery	43.8	
N	5411	Grocers	43.7	
C	5733	Music stores	43.7	40.0%
N	10	Supermarkets	39.0	
N	5462	Bakeries	38.0	
N	5422	Meat markets	37.5	
C	7631	Watch repairs	37.5	
C	6159	Loans	37.5	
N	8099	Optometrists	36.0	
C	5641	Children's clothes	36.0	
N	5812	Eating places	35.7	
N	7251	Shoe repairs	35.0	
C	5712	Furniture	32.8	
C	5732	Radio and television	32.8	
R	5662	Men's shoes	32.4	
C	5921	Liquor stores	32.2	
–	5934	Secondhand furniture	31.3	
C	783	Motion picture theaters	31.0	
N	5423	Fish markets	30.0	
R	5714	Drapery stores	30.0	30.0%
N	7211	Dry cleaners	29.3	
–	5939	Secondhand stores	29.2	
N	65	Real estate agents	28.8	
N	605	Currency exchange	28.8	
C	5392	Army and navy stores	28.0	
C	5621	Women's clothes	28.0	
C	5997	Gift shops	28.0	
C	5441	Candy	25.6	
C	5971	Jewelers	25.6	
N	7215	Laundromats	23.2	
N	7241	Barbers	22.1	
C	5499	Delicatessen	22.0	20.0%
N	5251	Hardware	11.3	
N	801	Medical services	11.3	
C	5431	Fruit and vegetable stores	11.3	

Note: R, C and N indicate regional, community and neighborhood level functions, respectively.

TABLE 17
The Internal Structure of Major Centers

S.I.C. Code		Description	Percent Value	
C	5311	Department stores	91.3	90.0%
C	60	Banks	63.7	
C	5441	Candy	63.3	60.0%
R	5993	Cigar stands	59.5	
R	5662	Men's shoes	56.5	
R	5633	Hosiery	56.3	
R	5634	Apparel accessory	56.3	
R	5663	Women's shoes	51.5	
C	5621	Women's clothes	50.4	
R	5632	Corset and lingerie	50.0	50.0%
C	5665	Family shoes	49.5	
C	5641	Children's clothes	48.5	
C	5612	Men's clothes	48.2	
C	5392	Army and navy stores	46.9	
C	5331	Variety stores	46.6	
N	5912	Drugstores	46.4	
R	5631	Millinery	44.4	
C	5733	Music stores	44.1	
C	5971	Jewelers	42.8	
R	5231	Paint and glass stores	41.0	40.0%
N	5462	Bakeries	36.9	
R	5722	Appliances	39.8	
R	5952	Sports goods stores	38.3	
C	5997	Gift and novelty	36.3	
N	5251	Hardware	34.4	
R	7221	Photographers	34.0	
C	783	Motion picture theaters	32.3	
N	5411	Grocers	31.8	
R	5719	Miscellaneous furniture	31.6	
C	5712	Furniture	31.1	
N	5812	Eating places	30.6	30.0%
C	5732	Radio and television	29.4	
N	8099	Optometrists	28.4	
R	5713	Floor covering stores	28.0	
R	5714	Drapery stores	27.0	
C	5651	Family clothes	27.0	
C	5943	Stationers	26.0	
C	6159	Loan offices	23.4	
N	7211	Dry cleaners	23.0	
N	5431	Fruit and vegetables	22.1	
N	5422	Meat markets	21.4	
C	5921	Liquor stores	20.6	20.0%
N	5813	Bars	17.9	
N	7231	Beauty shops	17.5	
N	801	Medical services	15.0	
N	7241	Barbers	12.1	
N	5423	Fish markets	11.8	

Note: R, C and N indicate regional, community and neighborhood level functions, respectively.

poverty of the S.I.C. classification. Functions have probably been misclassified by level at Workingmen's centers owing to the reduced level of demand serviced. For instance, although a function may be classified as typical of a community center in the Rest of the City, it may not be typical of the equivalent level center in the Workingmen's area. Hence, taxonomic error would easily destroy regularity in functional arrangement.

The lack of visual regularity in the tables is also reflected in a lack of a significant statistical correlation between land values and thresholds at major and minor centers. However, if certain deviating functions are omitted from the calculation at minor centers, a significant coefficient of .46 is obtained. Functions for which there is a large difference in rank order are hardware, variety and fruit stores, delicatessens, men's clothes, family shoes and drugstores, bars, banks and medical services. Similarly, a significant rank correlation of .51 is found at major centers if deviating functions are removed. These include department stores, fish markets, candy, men's, women's and family clothes stores, floor covering and miscellaneous furniture stores, gift shops and banks.

Five of these functions were listed above as having an underestimated threshold value. The rest appear to deviate more because of irregularities of mean value than of threshold. It is likely that these are the functions which have been misclassified since they assume a different level in the Workingmen's area on account of the lower level of demand serviced. For instance, banks have large differences in rank order at both major and minor centers because of their high value. Presumably, they become high-rent-paying functions in place of the more specialized activities which are not present at

these centers. Family clothes and family shoe stores are other types for which a similar argument seems to apply. However, more detailed analyses of the shift in level of functions associated with areal differences in socio-economic characteristics are needed before valid generalizations of this sort can be meaningfully proposed.

Therefore, there is less empirical evidence to support the hypothesized geometrical arrangement at these centers than at those in the Rest of the City. This is presumed to arise from shortcomings in classification. Consequently, there is no statistical verification of the hypotheses at major and minor centers.

Similarities in Internal Structure Between Centers in the Rest of the City and Workingmen's Area

In spite of shortcomings in the data, some statements can be made about the similarities in internal structure of major and minor centers with those in the Rest of the City. It was shown that minor centers tend to be most like community centers, and major centers most like regional centers in functional structure. The same analogy exists with respect to their internal structure, although, perhaps, a little less clearly. Nevertheless, in both minor and community level centers, neighborhood functions tend to cluster on low value land at the periphery. This is, however, more apparent at community than at minor centers. In the latter, neighborhood functions are found in some cases on inner, high value sites.

The major difference between the two patterns is in the location of the food group of functions which are more clustered on higher value land at minor than at the community centers. This presumably reflects the more important role of convenience functions at minor centers. Apart from bars, which enjoy a rather anomalous position on high value land at minor centers, similar functions occupy high value sites in both centers. In other respects the two types of center show a high degree of similarity in internal structure.

There is more similarity between the major centers and the regional centers. In both, the high value core sites are occupied by the general and more specialized clothing functions, department stores, candy, variety and drugstores. The same kinds of functions are also typical of low value locations at both centers and include a variety of personal services and food functions. One notable difference is in the location of furniture stores. These are peripheral uses at regional centers, but are notably concentrated at sites intermediate to the high and low values at major centers.

Summary

At each of the five centers studied, the empirical evidence presented tends to support the hypothesized internal structure of retail nucleations. Allowing for shortcomings in the classification of functions, the effect of sampling error on land values, and the under- and over-estimation of thresholds by the proxy variable used in this study, mean land values and mean threshold size tend to be significantly correlated at each center. It must be concluded, therefore, that there is some general underlying order to the arrangement of retail activities within retail nucleations. This order is founded on the premise that high mean threshold functions are at the same time high-rent-paying functions, and therefore are found in association with high mean

land values. Thus, generally speaking, high order functions occupy the innermost, high value part of the nucleation at any level in the hierarchy, and are surrounded concentrically by the sets of functions typical of each preceding lower level. The occurrence of lower order functions on high value land is accounted for by increased rent-paying ability at higher order centers arising from scale shifts and product differentiation.

Range in Land Values of Functions

All establishments of a given type are not concentrated at the same location within retail nucleations. They are dispersed in varying degrees throughout them. The extent of dispersion varies directly with the degree of product differentiation between establishments. Because of this, each establishment has its own individual and unique threshold size, and a range of thresholds is created for each business type. Lower order functions are thereby enabled to compete with higher order functions for locations whenever their threshold ranges overlap. Thus, the apparently complex internal structure of retail nucleations can be rationalized.

Translated into land value terms, the range in thresholds is presumably reflected in the dispersion of land values about the mean values used in the above analysis. Although data are not available to determine the threshold range of each function, the range in land values for each function can be empirically determined. Since there is, in general, a direct relationship between mean thresholds and mean land values, the range in value can be substituted as a proxy variable for the threshold range. Using this information, the fundamentals of the pattern of functional dispersion, and the extent to which different functions overlap as postulated in the more complex model, can be appreciated.

Absolute Variability in Land Values

Figures 1, 2, and 3 show the absolute range in land values for functions at neighborhood, community and regional level centers respectively. In the figures, functions are arrayed horizontally from left to right in order of decreasing mean land value. The absolute range in value is represented by the vertical columns, the upper and lower limits of which are equal to the highest and lowest value associated with a function at any of the sample centers respectively. The top of the figure corresponds to the value 100 percent; *ergo* it is a diagrammatic representation of the peak lot. For our purposes, we assume that an establishment is able to compete for any location along the value range. When a function occurs only once at the sample centers, and consequently has no range in values, it is plotted on the figure by its mean value only.

The extent of overlap between functions in the real world is more complex than was indicated in the conceptual discussion of threshold ranges above. Although it is difficult to generalize about the diagrams, functions can be arbitrarily and loosely classified into two basic types according to the extent of their range in value. One type consists of those functions associated with a relatively wide range in value, and

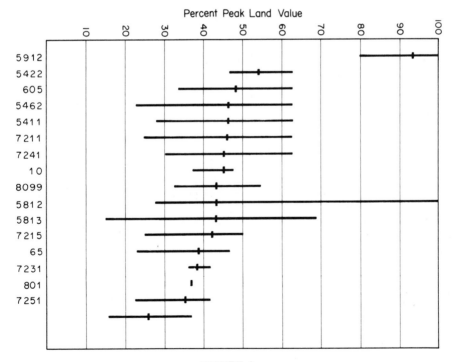

FIGURE 1

Range in Land Values of Neighborhood Functions at the Neighborhood Level

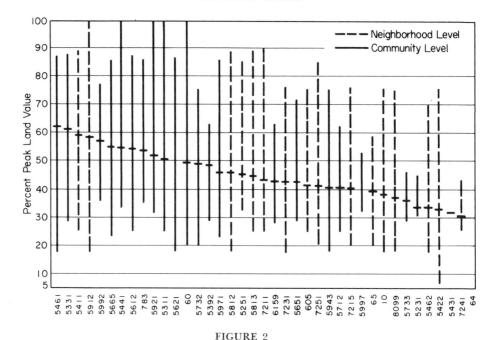

FIGURE 2

Range in Land Values of Functions at Community Level Nucleations

hence are dispersed in varying degrees throughout the nucleations. The other type comprises functions with a somewhat more limited value range and which are therefore relatively concentrated within certain parts of the nucleations.

Concentration may occur in the inner, middle or outer peripheral parts of centers. For instance, in the neighborhood center, drugstores (5912) are concentrated in the high value innermost area; meat markets (5422) are on sites between 46.0 percent and 62.0 percent of the peak, or roughly in the middle part of the center; shoe repairs (7251) are, on the other hand, found only on lower value land toward the periphery between 15.0 percent and 37.0 percent of the peak value. As a result, these three functions are not in competition with each other for sites in those parts of the nucleation. In

other words, the threshold ranges for these functions do not overlap.

The threshold ranges for these functions do overlap, however, with the ranges for certain other types. In particular, overlap occurs with those functions which are characterized by wide value ranges, and which are relatively dispersed within centers. Thus, for instance, the range in values for eating places (5812) extends from the peak value down to 28.0 percent of it. Thus, it overlaps with the entire range for drugstores and meat markets, and with the uppermost part of the range for shoe repairs. Competition presumably exists between these functions for sites at different parts of the nucleation.

In general, there is a marked increase in the range of values for most functions as order in the hierarchy increases. This is to be expected since it has already been shown that functions

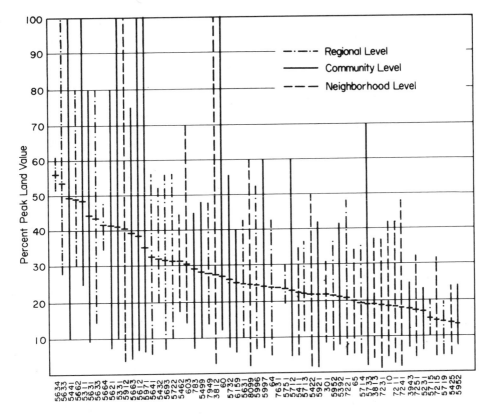

FIGURE 3

Range in Land Values of Functions at Regional Level Nucleations

occur most frequently at higher order centers on account of the larger portion of the urban markets serviced by them. Wide differences in tastes, needs and preferences of the individuals comprising this demand presumably allows scale shifts and a greater degree of product differentiation between establishments.

Thus at higher order centers, thresholds for any given function extend over a greater range. This is expressed geographically by the increased dispersion of lower order functions within high order centers. For instance, neighborhood functions by and large are more dispersed—or extend over a wider range of values—when they occur at the community level. Drugstores, which were notably concentrated on high value land or neighborhood level centers, are found on land as low as 18.0 percent of the peak value at the higher order center. The resulting effect is an increase in the number of different functions competing for sites at any single part of the nucleation.

This is clearly illustrated by the increase in the type of functions competing for peak lot locations at the higher order centers. At the neighborhood level, only drugstores and eating places are in competition for peak lots. Five functions compete for these at the community centers. Drugstores are again represented, and are joined by candy, liquor and department stores, and banks. It appears that eating places are unable to meet the increased competition for these high value sites at this level, although their absence probably reflects sampling variability. Competition is even more acute at the regional level where nine functions occupy peak lots. Apart from liquor stores, which are not represented at this level, hosiery, variety, women's clothes and jewelry stores are added to those functions present at the community level. It is interesting to note that eating places reappear as peak lot occupants at this level although they were absent at the previous one.

NEIGHBORHOOD CENTERS. Figure 1 shows that eating places and bars extend over the greatest range in values at this level center. Their ranges do not, however, overlap at the highest and lowest extremities. Eating places are in competition with drugstores at locations valued at above 80.0 percent of the peak; whereas bars compete with shoe repairs on the lower value land below 23.0 percent of the peak. Most functions at this level are in competition for sites between 30.0 percent and 60.0 percent of the peak, although the range for individual functions does not always extend fully between these limits. For instance, supermarkets and beauty shops appear relatively concentrated between 37.0 percent and 49.0 percent, and 36.0 and 41.0 percent of the peak value respectively where they are in competition with other types.

COMMUNITY CENTERS. The major difference at this level is the greater geographical dispersion of functions, as shown in Figure 2. Although the range in value varies considerably between individual types, only four functions

are characterized by ranges which are small enough for them to be considered concentrated within the nucleation. These are gift shops (5997), music stores (7235), paint and glass stores (5231), and to a lesser extent, barber shops (7241). Other functions, generally speaking, extend between 25.0 percent and 85.0 percent of the peak value. Five functions occupy peak lot locations. At the periphery, meat markets (5422) stand in isolation on land below 18.0 percent of the peak. It is significant that the range in values increases for all the neighborhood level functions when they occur at the community centers.

REGIONAL CENTERS. Figure 3 shows the distribution of functions at the highest order center. The down-shift in value is reflected in the extension of virtually all functions onto land valued below 20.0 percent of the peak value. There is, consequently, less competition for high value sites.

Apart from the nine functions mentioned as peak-lot occupiers, only a handful of other activities extend onto land above 60.0 percent of the peak. These consist of representatives of the clothing group of functions, although not all types in this group are included. For instance, children's clothes (5641), apparel accessories (5631), children's shoes (5664) and millinery stores (5631), all have upper limits below the 60.0 percent level. Apparel accessories and children's shoes are the most concentrated of all the clothing functions. The former are concentrated between 60.0 percent and 52.0 percent of the peak; the latter between 48.0 percent and 35.0 percent. They are the only two clothing functions for which value ranges do not overlap, and which are therefore not in competition for site utility.

Other notably concentrated functions include hardware stores (5251), located between 20.0 percent and 30.0 percent of the peak; and two regional level representatives of the furniture group, china and glassware stores (5715) and miscellaneous furnishings (5719), both of which are found below 20.0 percent of the peak at the periphery of the nucleation. In general, other functions at this level show varying degrees of geographical dispersion.

WORKINGMEN'S CENTERS. Figures 4 and 5 show the range in values for functions at the minor and major centers respectively. The data are much more incomplete at minor centers because many functions occur only once at sample centers. In spite of this, some generalizations can be made.

At minor centers there is a distinct difference in the extent of value ranges between the high and low mean value functions. A somewhat similar situation was noted at the neighborhood level. High value functions tend to be more dispersed; whereas lower value functions are usually more concentrated. Dispersed high value functions include drugstores (5912), bars (5813), banks (60), men's clothes (5612) and family clothes stores (5651). Family shoe stores are exceptions to this generalization. Although they are a high value function in minor centers, they are relatively more concentrated on higher value land between 45.0 percent and 65.0 percent of the peak value. The only lower value function characterized by such dispersion is eating places (5812), which extends from the peak lot out to the periphery. Five peak lot uses are recognized: drugstores, family clothes stores, bars, eating places and candy stores.

The remaining functions are concentrated in varying degrees toward the periphery of minor centers between approximately 10.0 percent and 40.0

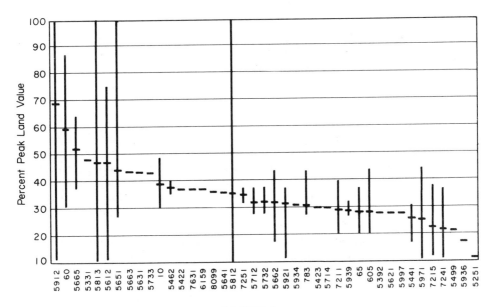

FIGURE 4

Range in Land Values of Functions at Minor Centers

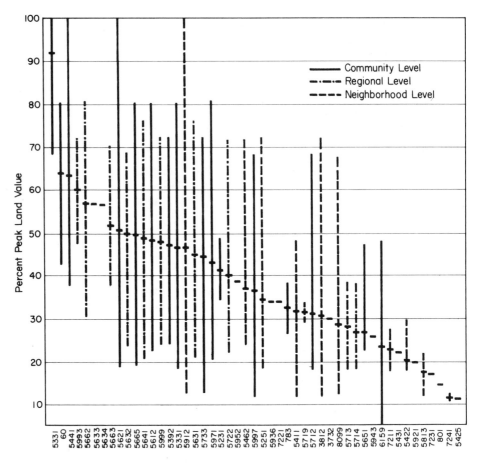

FIGURE 5

Range in Land Values of Functions at Major Nucleations

percent of the peak. Considerable overlap in ranges exists and all functions except family shoe stores (5665) are in competition with each other for sites at different parts of the center. This is especially marked in the lower value part of the nucleation. However, on land above 50.0 percent of the peak, competition is restricted to high mean value types.

The pattern at major centers in many respects is similar to that at the community centers. There is a notable increase in the range in values for all

functions. Unlike those in the minor centers, the relatively high mean value functions are more concentrated. Thus, for instance, department stores (5311) only extend out as far as 70.0 percent of the peak value, and overlap between its range and others takes place notably between 70.0 percent and 80.0 percent of the peak. Other functions concentrated on higher value land include banks (60), women's shoe stores (5663), candy stores (5441), cigar stands (5993), and to a lesser extent, men's shoe stores (5662).

Most functions are fairly well dispersed between 70.0 percent and 20.0 percent of the peak value. Functions overlap considerably between these limits. Two functions stand out as being relatively more dispersed within this area. Women's clothes stores (5621) and drugstores (5912) both extend onto higher value land and occupy peak lots. Other peak-lot functions are department stores (5311), and candy stores (5441). It is interesting to note that the number of functions in competition for peak lots at the higher level center is the same as at minor centers. This is directly reverse to the situation at centers in the Rest of the City, where there was an increase in the number of peak lot uses as order in the hierarchy increased.

Functions at the lower value locations tend to be relatively concentrated. The degree of concentration generally increases toward the periphery as it does at the other centers. However, eating places (5812), optometrists (8099) and furniture stores (5712) are more dispersed than the other low value functions.

Relative Variability in Land Values

Comparisons of the variability in values between individual functions is not meaningful unless reference is made to the size of the mean about which variation occurs. The coefficient of variation is normally used to take this into account. However, because insufficient data are available to calculate the necessary standard deviations the index of variability used here is simply based upon the absolute range in values. The resulting indices for individual functions at each of the five levels of center are shown in Table 18.

In both the Rest of the City and in

TABLE 18
Variability in Land Values by Function [1]

S.I.C. Code		R	C	Center N	Major	Minor
R	5231	1.00	.45	—[2]	.34	
N	5251	.43	1.17	—	1.55	—
C	5311	1.54	1.50		.35	
C	5331	2.18	.97	.71	1.33	—
C	5392	1.60	.70		1.03	—
N	5411	1.32	1.07	.74	1.14	—
N	10	2.03	1.48	.25		.46
N	5422	2.09	2.00	.29	.53	—
N	5423	1.39			—	—
C	5431		—		—	—
C	5441	1.83	1.21	—	.99	.54
N	5462	.80	1.52	.84	1.31	.11
C	5499	.83	.95		—	
C	5612	2.44	1.12	.19	1.20	1.35
C	5621	1.77	1.35	—	1.63	—
R	5631	1.39	.68		1.25	—
R	5632	.92		—	.90	
R	5633	1.33			—	
R	5634	.14	—		—	
R	5641	1.54	1.11		1.14	—
C	5651	1.60	.96		.93	1.63
R	5662	1.02	—		.88	.81
R	5663	1.50	—		.60	—
R	5664	.31				
C	5665	1.79	1.15		1.23	.51
R	5671	—	—		—	
R	5699	1.80	—			
C	5712	2.35	.91		1.29	.29
R	5713	1.07	.44		.71	
R	5714	1.57	.54		.74	—
R	5715	.66	—			
R	5719	1.06	.61		.16	
R	5722	1.43	.86		1.15	
C	5732	1.87	1.11	.36	—	.29
C	5733	3.42	.48		1.37	—
N	5812	3.47	1.53	1.65	1.97	2.52
N	5813	1.71	1.40	1.23	.54	1.88
N	5912	2.35	1.41	.22	1.91	1.27
C	5921	1.76	1.35	.83	—	.81
R	5942		—			
C	5943	.93	1.37		—	
R	5952	1.42	.02		—	

TABLE 18—Continued

S.I.C. Code	R	Center C	N	Major	Minor
C 5971	2.65	1.32	—	1.39	1.27
C 5992	1.29	.71	—		
R 5993		—		.42	—
R 5996	1.79	.66			
C 5997	1.34	.51	.98	1.55	
R 5999	2.51	.75		1.01	
C 60	3.17	1.61	—	.59	.75
N 605	1.83	1.19	.60		.83
C 6159	1.33	.78	1.10	1.84	—
R 64	1.54	—			
N 65	1.41	.98	.61		.61
N 7211	2.10	1.45	.81	.44	.68
N 7215	1.63	1.34	.29		1.10
R 7221	2.10	—		—	
N 7231	1.78	1.28	.13	—	
N 7241	2.47	.76	.69	.06	1.19
N 7251	1.92	1.56	.81		.14
C 7631			.63		—
C 783	1.24	.93	—		.53
R 7949	1.21				
N+ 801	1.05	1.24	.52	—	—
N+ 8099	2.25	1.53	.48	1.95	—
Vacant	2.57	1.27		1.78	.98

Notes: (1) The numbers represent an index of variability derived from:
$$\frac{absolute\ range\ in\ value}{average\ value}.$$
(2)—indicates no variability in value.
N+ typical of the neighborhood level and all higher levels in the hierarchy.

the Workingmen's area, variability increases directly with order in the hierarchy. For instance, neighborhood functions show an increasing index of variability at community and regional level centers. Similarly, community level functions have increased indices at regional centers. This regularity is to be expected since number of establishments for any given functional type increases directly with order in the hierarchy.

It follows from this that higher order functions will be associated with lower indices of variability than lower order functions. An example will make this point clear. Clothing functions are divided into community level and regional level types. When these occur at the regional centers, the lower level community types have larger indices of variability than the higher order regional types. Similar ratios obtain for the different level types within the other functional groups.

In certain cases this regularity does not apply. In the Rest of the City, five functions are associated with lower variability indices at higher order centers. These are: hardware (5231) and bakeries (5462), stationery stores (5943) and delicatessens (5499). These all show a decrease in relative variability at regional centers. Eating places (5812) decrease in variability at community centers.

At major and minor centers, the regularity is less clear, and a greater number of functions shows a smaller index of variability of higher level centers. These include: men's clothes (5612), family clothes (5651), eating places (5812), bars (5813), banks (60), dry cleaners (7211) and barber shops (7241).

Summary

When the range in land value is used as an approximation of threshold range, a complex picture of overlap in thresholds between functions is revealed. Assuming that functions are able to occupy sites at any point within their value range, many functions are able to compete for locations at various parts of the retail nucleations. Thus, the extent of zones of overlap envisaged in the more complex model above must be considered a gross oversimplification of the pattern, but one that is necessary in order to comprehend the real world situation.

Both absolute and relative variability in land values increase directly with order in the hierarchy. This is expected since more establishments of any given type are found at higher order centers. Variations in the market served enable greater degrees of product differentiation between establishments, an extension of the threshold range, and result in wider geographical dispersion within centers. Some functions are, however, notably more concentrated within any given level center, and although product differentiation must also exist for these, they presumably are able to compete for higher or lower value land as the case may be.

Factors Affecting Commercial Land Values:
An Empirical Study of Milwaukee, Wisconsin

Paul B. Downing

Land rent and hence land value can be defined as the excess of total revenue over the total costs of production (exclusive of land) at that site. This excess is the result of the natural productivity of the site and the activities of man which alter the site's productivity. Man alters the natural conditions of urban land by building improvements on it, supplying it with public services such as water, sewer and roads, and altering the productivity of the sites surrounding it. Several writers have statistically explored the importance of various factors in determining urban land value.[1] For the most part both these empirical studies and existing theoretical analyses deal only with residential land value. Commercial and industrial land has been largely neglected in recent empirical analyses. The purpose of this paper is to explore the factors which affect the value of urban land in commercial uses.

Measuring Urban Land Value

Most previous studies have had to rely on a third party's opinion of the value of a site (typically the city assessor). This study uses actual sales prices as the measure of land value. Thus, we are regressing the model against actual market sales rather than someone's opinion of market value.

In view of typical assessment practices, the use of assessed value of land in a study such as this could lead to incorrect conclusions. Assessed value of land may actually include some influence from the existing improvements to that site. Furthermore, the existence of over- and underassessment of land varies with its location within the city.[2] Underassessment of land is likely to be most severe in areas of active redevelopment. Decaying areas where redevelopment is not taking place may have overassessed land values due to lags in reassessment as the market

Reprinted from *Land Economics*, February 1973, by permission of the author and the Regents of the University of Wisconsin Systems.

[1] See, for example, Eugene F. Brigham, "The Determinants of Residential Land Values," *Land Economics*, November 1965, pp. 325–334; Duane S. Knos, *Distribution of Land Values in Topeka, Kansas* (Lawrence, Kansas: Center for Research in Business, University of Kansas, May 1962); F. Gerard Adams, Grace Milgram, Edward W. Green, and Christine Mansfield, "Underdeveloped Land Prices During Urbanization: A Micro-Empirical Study Over Time," *Review of Economics and Statistics*, May 1968, pp. 248–258; and Paul B. Downing, "Estimating Residential Land Value by Multivariate Analysis," in Daniel Holland (ed.), *The Assessment of Land Value* (Madison, Wisconsin: University of Wisconsin Press, 1970), pp. 101–124.

[2] I am indebted to the reviewer for this suggestion.

changes. Assessed value is also likely to mask variations in value due to micro-locational characteristics of interest such as distance from a corner.

For this study, data have been obtained on the actual price paid for the purchase of urban commercial land. The land value data were obtained from the Office of the Assessor of the City of Milwaukee.[3] In addition to the selling price of the land, the address, the size of the lot, and the type of zone and intensity of use allowed were recorded. Data were collected for all confirmed sales of commercially zoned land for the years 1958 through 1962. The total sale price of each site was divided by the number of square feet sold to determine the land value per square foot. This value is used as the dependent variable in the regression models reported here.

Commercial Land Value

Many urban land value models have been presented in the literature. Many of these have their main emphasis on one aspect or another of location or transportation costs. These models often include consideration of lot size

as well.[4] Several studies have added other variables to location and lot size such as amenities, social overhead capital, taxes, topography, land use, and zoning.[5] The purpose of this section is to develop a hypothesis about the factors which determine commercial land values which considers all of these factors.[6]

The amount a firm bids for a site depends upon the discounted sum of anticipated future net returns when operating at the site. Anticipated revenues depend upon several factors. Primary among these is the accessibility of the site for potential customers and primary among accessibility measures in the literature is distance from the Central Business District (CBD) of a city. The straight line distance from the site to the CBD is used in the regressions. A more appropriate measure would be the time it took to travel from the site to the CBD, but this measure was not available. However, in the period studied no expressways existed nor were any under construction. All traffic traveled over conventional streets. Furthermore, the city had many angle streets which fed into the CBD. Thus, we feel that the straight line measure of distance to the

---

3 Thanks are due Mr. William Weisler of the Research Branch, Office of the Assessor, for collecting these data and making them available. The data were collected under a research grant to M. Mason Gaffney by the Urban Land Institute and thanks are due him for allowing me to use them for this study. Before including an observation, the sale and price were verified by Mr. Weisler.

4 See, for example, W. Alonzo, *Location and Land Use* (Cambridge, Massachusetts: Harvard University Press, 1969); John Meyer, John Kain, and W. Wohl, *The Urban Transportation Problem* (Cambridge, Massachusetts: Harvard University Press, 1965); E. S. Mills, "An Aggregative Model of Resource Allocation in a Metropolitan Area," *American Economic Review*, May 1967, pp. 197–210; Richard Muth, "The Centrality of Urban Land Values," *Land Economics*, August 1963, pp. 275–284; and Lowdon Wingo, *Transportation and Urban Land* (Washington, D.C.: Resources for the Future, 1961).

5 These studies include: Adams, et al., *op. cit.*; Brigham, *op. cit.*; J. P. Crecine, O. A. Davis, and J. E. Jackson, "Urban Property Markets: Some Empirical Results and Their Implications for Municipal Zoning," *Journal of Law and Economics*, October 1967, pp. 79–100; Downing, *op. cit.*; and R. Harris, G. Tolley, and C. Harrell, "The Resident Site Choice," *Review of Economics and Statistics*, May 1968, pp. 241–247.

6 A general theory of commercial land value is presented in the Appendix.

CBD is a reasonable approximation of the preferred time–distance measure. In addition to its effect on anticipated revenues, the distance to the CBD might be associated with the firm's cost of obtaining goods and services. In Milwaukee most of the wholesale operations and transportation points (rail and water) are near the CBD. Thus, the measure of distance to the CBD also measures access to wholesalers and major transportation links. Greater accessibility for customers and to transportation and wholesalers are both expected to increase land values (value declines with greater distance from the CBD).

Another factor which is likely to affect the anticipated revenue a firm can earn is the knowledge potential customers have of the firm's location and existence. One would expect that more well known locations and locations with opportunities for visual advertising of the firm's location would increase sales and, therefore, land values in commercial uses. Three separate measures of this influence have been included: distance from a regional shopping center (defined as any retail sales area with at least one department store), traffic level on the main street, and corner influence.[7] A fourth factor, distance from the main street, was also to have been included but when the data were collected it was found that there were virtually no sites that were more than a few paces from a main street. The greater the distance a site is from a regional shopping center, and from the corner, the lower the land

value, while more traffic would be expected to increase land values.

A retail sales firm can be expected to draw much of its business from the population in the general area. Thus, it was expected that a larger population in the area surrounding the site would increase anticipated sales and thus land values. Since the relevant market distances from which firms may draw their customers were not known, populations within a one-, two-, or three-mile radius were used and three separate regressions were run.

The total value of sales anticipated at a particular site is also likely to increase with greater income of its potential customers. Since it was expected that most of a firm's customers live fairly near the site, median income in the Census Tract surrounding the site was included to measure this influence.

The amenities of the site and the area surrounding it are expected to affect the anticipated revenues of the firm. The percentage of the population in the surrounding Census Tract which was non-white was included to measure the disutility members of the white population might attach to visiting an area with substantial non-white population. This variable might also be a proxy for the risk of loss through theft of merchandise. In either case its influence would be negative. The percentage of the dwelling units in the block which were deteriorating or dilapidated was used as a measure of visual amenities and was expected to have a negative influence on land value.

---

[7] Corner influence is measured by determining the last two digits of the site address, subtracting them from the last two digits of the estimated middle of the block address, and squaring the result. Thus addresses near the ends of the block would have higher weight than near the center. This measure is subject to measurement errors since the middle of the block address could only be guessed at with the available information.

Let us now look at the cost side factors which affect the bid price of a firm. In theory a site would be used as intensively as is justified by its locational value and the relative costs of constructing multi-story versus single story improvements.[8] Zoning regulations on the intensity of use would be meaningless if such regulations were not binding. That is, if the most valuable use of the site were to build a single story building, zoning which allowed multi-story development would not affect the value of the land. On the other hand, if the most valuable use of the site was for multi-story development, but the zoning regulations allowed only single story development, site value would be reduced. In Milwaukee there are several intensity zones. Four of these are used in connection with "Local Business" use. Zone A is the most intense use allowed and intensity allowed generally diminishes through B and C to D zone, although the intensity relationships between B, C, and D zones are not entirely clear.[9] It is expected that many sites have potential uses which exceed the current intensity allowed and the intensity regulation provides a restraint on development to these more intense new uses. Furthermore, less restrictions on the development of a site are in themselves valuable because the developer has more freedom to adjust his design to meet his needs. To test this hypothesis three dummy variables were used for A, B and C zones. Thus, each variable measures the value of an allowed increase in the intensity of use over the least intense D zone. It is expected that each variable will have a positive influence on land value and the value of the regression coefficients should increase with the intensity of use allowed.

A trade-off exists between the size of the lot purchased by a firm and the cost of constructing improvements. Large lots allow for more ground floor improvements which are less expensive per square foot of usable space than second story construction which is in turn less expensive than third story construction. Thus, increasing the size of a site will reduce improvement costs. The greater the increase in site size, the smaller will be the marginal improvement cost savings because more construction will be on the lowest cost ground floor. Thus, it is expected that the value of land per square foot decreases as the size of the lot increases.

Other factors which affect operating costs include the direct cost and availability of public utilities and other social overhead capital. No direct measures of these factors were included but they were held relatively constant by using data for areas covered by one government and hence one general level of service and taxes. Another part of the operating costs is the cost of insurance (or the losses incurred if insurance is not available) for fire and

---

[8] Intensity is used here to refer to the height, setbacks, and other attributes of an improvement on a site and does not necessarily imply a greater population density or value of improvements per square foot of land.

[9] See, City of Milwaukee, Municipal Reference Library, *City Zoning Code* (Milwaukee, Wisconsin, 1967). Our contention is that these zones do in fact provide an effective constraint on the intensity of the development of various sites. The reasoning behind this contention is as follows. These "intensity of use" restrictions were placed on each site in 1951 and at that time they reflected the current use for the most part. As the city has developed, the bid prices and desired intensity of use of sites have changed and for the most part increased.

theft. This influence may be included in our amenity measures.

The general conditions of the market for land, such as the value of the dollar, interest rates, and other factors which change over time have not been explicitly included in this study. Since the study is an attempt to explain the value of commercial land at a given point in time, no attempt was made to quantify changes over time. However, the data cover a five-year span over which the level of land prices may have increased. The data for any year are not necessarily equally distributed geographically. Hence, in an effort to standardize the observations over the five-year period, time was introduced as a proxy for the sum of these dynamic influences. Time was set at 0 if the sale took place in 1958 and increased by 1 each year.

Pooling the cross section data for five years involves some assumptions about the stability of the relationship between the independent and dependent variables over time. Implicit in the decision to pool the data is the assumption that the relationship was steady over the period.[10]

In summary, this study hypothesizes that commercial land value varies over sites because of variations in the total revenue that can be earned at different sites and because of variations in the total costs of producing a good or service at different sites in a city. Further, it has been suggested that both revenues and costs vary systematically with certain locational factors.

DIFFERENCES AMONG LAND MARKETS. Most general urban land value theories make the assertion that land is allocated to that use which is the highest bidder for the site and hence each site is allocated to its highest and best use. This theory implies that the urban land market is a single market in which all users and uses are competing for each site. However, there are at least two reasons why residential, industrial, and commercial land markets can be treated as separate for the purposes of determining the factors which affect land value.

First, there are certain barriers and institutional restraints to the transfer of land from one use type to another. Zoning can prove to be an effective restraint on land use changes. One of the avowed purposes of zoning is to modify land use choices. Thus it is often necessary to obtain a variance or change in zoning in order to change uses. There is much discussion about the ease with which zoning can be changed especially for people with "friends" on the local zoning board or legislative body. There are certainly many such cases. But it is also true that there are many unrecorded cases where zoning was not changed upon request. Furthermore, even when zoning is changed the process is expensive and time-consuming.[11] Thus, it is argued that zoning can be and often is an effective restraint on the transfer of land use.

Second, even if the land market were one market, there is every reason to believe that the different possible uses

[10] A Chow test was run on the stability of the non-time variables. See, J. Johnston, *Econometric Methods* (New York: McGraw-Hill, 1963), p. 137. The observations were divided into 1958–60 and 1961–62 samples. The Chow test confirmed that the two samples could be considered to be from the same population and thus the non-time variables are stable over the 1958–62 period.

[11] In one recently revealed case it cost $7,000 and took six years for one person to get a zoning change in Los Angeles. *Los Angeles Times,* Sunday, April 23, 1972.

would bid for the land for different reasons. Thus, the relative importance of the different factors will vary among types of land use. In order to test this hypothesis two Chow tests were run. Using a residential land value model previously developed, a test was run on the residential and commercial land value sales.[12] An F of 4.31 was calculated for the test so that we would reject the hypothesis (at the 1% level) that the residential and commercial data come from the same population. A similar test was run between commercial and industrial sales based on the commercial land value model used here. Again the hypothesis that they were from the same population was rejected (F of 37.62). Based on these arguments and test results the three land markets will be treated as separate.

ASPECTS NOT INCLUDED IN THIS STUDY. There are many factors which can be thought of as influencing the value of urban land, but which have not been included in the regressions reported here. One such factor is the level of the property tax. Since all observations are for the City of Milwaukee and since the city has only one property tax rate for all property, differences in legal rates need not be considered. The level of government services varies widely among political jurisdictions. However, all the sales in the sample are located within one political jurisdiction. This includes the school district and the water and sewage utility service areas as well as the services provided by the City of Milwaukee. The typography of

a site can have an influence on its value. In Milwaukee, however, topography is not a major factor except in a few small areas, since the land is generally flat or gently rolling. Another physical factor influencing land value which may be of significance in Milwaukee is the esthetic attributes of the site. A view of Lake Michigan or of one of the river parkways can materially increase the esthetics of a site. The smell of a brewery or tanning operation would reduce esthetics. No consistent and uniformly available measure of such attributes was found. Thus, this factor is not included in the study.

Regression Results

There are several use zones in the City of Milwaukee which allow commercial or business uses. However, enough data were obtained for analyses in only the "Local Business" and "Major Commercial" use zones. The "Local Business" use allows most retail sales uses except sales of dirty items such as coal or lumber as well as residential uses, although in practice such uses are rare in new construction.[13] "Major Commercial" use allows essentially all wholesale and retail sales *and* light manufacturing. This being the case, we hypothesized that "Major Commercial" sites would not fit our commercial land value model and should be included with other manufacturing uses in an industrial land value analysis. A Chow test was run to determine if data on "Major Commercial" and "Local Business"

---

12 The model is described in Downing, *op. cit.*

13 Since the sales data employed are for commercially zoned vacant land, only the many mixed use dwellings which exist in the older parts of Milwaukee through conversion of residential structures are irrelevant.

uses could be considered to be in the same population. This test denied the hypothesis that these two zoning classification samples could be expected to come from the same population ($F = 7.25$). Thus, the following analysis deals only with the "Local Business" use zone.

RESULTS. Table 1 presents the results of the three city-wide regressions run for this model (one each for one-, two-, and three-mile radius). Both linear and non-linear forms of the distance to the CBD and distance to the nearest shopping center were run, but the results were unaffected by functional form. Since the non-linear form is more consistent with traditional theory and was found to substantially improve the fit in the residential land value regressions previously reported, it is reported here (Table 1). For distance to the CBD the regression coefficients are not significant. An explanation for this result may be that the land sales we have observed are mostly for retail sales firms which draw their customers mostly from the more immediate neighborhood and are not much affected by the advantages of centrality. Some supportive evidence for this can be found in the population coefficients. While the population coefficient is not significant for one-mile radius, it is significant for both two- and three-mile radii.

The coefficient for the distance to the nearest regional shopping center is not significant in these regressions but in all cases is of the expected sign. However, there is a problem with this result because only two regional shopping centers are within the City of Milwaukee and only one of these has enough observations close to the center to be useful. Since it is expected that the locational advantage of being near

a regional shopping center diminishes rapidly, lack of close observations may wash out this effect.

Additional light can be shed on this and other issues in Milwaukee's commercial land market by partitioning the data by geographic "neighborhoods." The City was partitioned into five geographic areas which roughly represent neighborhoods of similar characteristics and separate regressions were run for each area. The results for the Near North Side and the Northwest Side are presented in Tables 2 and 3. The East Side, Near South Side, and Southwest Side results are not presented because there were insufficient observations to provide meaningful results. The single regional shopping center which was both new in the period studied and wholly contained within the city boundaries (called Capitol Court) is contained in the Northwest section of the city. As the results of Table 2 indicate, this new regional shopping center exhibits a powerful attraction to customers and hence a strong locational advantage. This advantage declines rapidly as distance from the regional shopping center declines. The reason for the significance of the shopping center variable in the Northwest section can be explained by the shopping opportunities available. Several of the major arterials feed into the area of the large regional shopping center. In other areas of the city there are typically local shopping opportunities in various directions from residential sites. These are usually of the old strip shopping type. In the newly developing Northwestern section these local centers are relatively scarce. Thus, we find a greater orientation toward the regional shopping center and commercial establishments located at a substantial distance from it are at a competitive disadvantage in attracting customers.

TABLE 1
Land Value Regressions for Local Business, City of Milwaukee: Total City

Variable	One-Mile Radius		Two-Mile Radius		Three-Mile Radius	
	Regression Coefficient	t Statistic	Regression Coefficient	t Statistic	Regression Coefficient	t Statistic
Constant	1.910		1.214		1.287	
Distance to CBD (reciprocal) (miles)	0.462	1.30	0.450	1.27	0.456	1.29
Distance to shopping center (reciprocal) (miles)	0.067	1.63	0.053	1.29	0.061	1.48
Traffic level on main street (1000's of veh/24 hr)	0.691 D-4 †	6.35 ***	0.609 D-4	5.30 ***	0.616 D-4	5.34 ***
Corner influence	0.823 D-4	0.90	0.706 D-4	0.78	0.772 D-4	0.85
Population within ___ mile radius (people)	0.278 D-5	0.93	0.322 D-5	2.31 **	0.182 D-5	2.12 **
Median income in census tract ($)	−0.185 D-3	−1.93 *	−0.121 D-3	−1.21	−0.137 D-3	−1.40
Per cent non-white in census tract	−1.280	−2.42 **	−1.412	−2.78 ***	−1.227	−2.48 **
Per cent deteriorating or dilapidated in the block	−0.753 D-2	−2.26 **	−0.746 D-2	−2.27 **	−0.755 D-2	−2.29 **
A zone (dummy, 1 if site is in A zone, 0 if not)	3.065	3.42 ***	3.106	3.52 ***	3.052	3.46 ***
B zone (dummy, 1 if site is in B zone, 0 if not)	0.226	0.78	0.227	0.80	0.187	0.65
C zone (dummy, 1 if site is in C zone, 0 if not)	0.807	4.40 ***	0.774	4.27 ***	0.729	3.90 ***
Lot size (square feet)	−0.111 D-4	−3.25 ***	−0.100 D-4	−2.93 ***	−0.106 D-4	−3.13 ***
Time (1958 = 0)	0.199	2.88 ***	0.206	2.99 ***	0.198	2.88 ***
R²	0.439		0.445		0.444	
Std. error	1.315		1.307		1.309	
N	406					
Mean LV ($/sq. ft.)	2.344					

† For coefficients in this format move the decimal point to the left the number of places shown. Thus, this number is 0.0000691. *** Significant at .01 probability level.
** Significant at .05 probability level. * Significant at .10 probability level.

Sources: Traffic Level on Main Street was derived from Traffic Flow Map, City of Milwaukee 24-hour Volume (Weekdays), 1957 as updated to 1960. Population, Income, Non-White, and Deteriorating and Dilapidated data were derived from the 1960 Census of Population and Housing, Block Data and Tract Data.

341

TABLE 2
Land Value Regressions for Local Business, City of Milwaukee: Northwest and West

Variable	One-Mile Radius		Two-Mile Radius		Three-Mile Radius	
	Regression Coefficient	t Statistic	Regression Coefficient	t Statistic	Regression Coefficient	t Statistic
Constant	−0.171		0.325		−0.308	
Distance to CBD (reciprocal) (miles)	5.970	3.59 ***	7.192	3.09 ***	7.226	2.88 ***
Distance to shopping center (reciprocal) (miles)	0.249	3.84 ***	0.284	3.51 ***	0.258	3.89 ***
Traffic level on main street (1000's of veh/24 hr)	0.485 D-4†	3.68 ***	0.495 D-4	3.76 ***	0.501 D-4	3.77 ***
Corner influence	0.195 D-3	2.14 **	0.202 D-3	2.21 **	0.197 D-3	2.17 **
Population within ___ mile radius (people)	0.427 D-7	0.02	−0.170 D-5	−0.72	−0.089 D-5	−0.65
Median income in census tract ($)	−0.513 D-4	−0.31	−0.411 D-4	−0.25	−0.400 D-4	−0.24
Per cent non-white in census tract [1]	—		—		—	
Per cent deteriorating or dilapidated in the block	−0.013	−2.05 **	−0.014	−2.16 **	−0.014	−2.15 **
A Zone [2]	—		—		—	
B zone (dummy, 1 if site is in B zone, 0 if not)	0.016	0.03	0.046	0.10	0.060	0.13
C zone (dummy, 1 if site is in C zone, 0 if not)	−0.119	−0.59	−0.107	−0.53	−0.102	−0.50
Lot size (square feet)	−0.762 D-5	−1.98 **	−0.777 D-5	−2.03 **	−0.788 D-5	−2.05 **
Time (1958 = 0)	0.198	2.84 ***	0.203	2.90 ***	0.201	2.88 ***
R^2	0.444		0.446		0.445	
Std. error	0.922		0.920		0.920	
N	198					
Mean LV ($/sq. ft.)	1.793					

*** Significant at .01 probability level. † For coefficients in this format move the decimal point to the left the number of places shown. Thus, this number is 0.0000485.
** Significant at .05 probability level. [1] Virtually no non-white population in the area. [2] No A-zoned sites in sample.

342

TABLE 3
Land Value Regressions for Local Business, City of Milwaukee: Near North Side

Variable	One-Mile Radius		Two-Mile Radius		Three-Mile Radius	
	Regression Coefficient	t Statistic	Regression Coefficient	t Statistic	Regression Coefficient	t Statistic
Constant	0.511		−2.780		−2.315	
Distance to CBD (reciprocal) (miles)	−0.022	−0.03	−0.102	−0.16	0.053	0.08
Distance to shopping center (reciprocal) (miles)	0.107	0.80	0.092	0.75	0.078	0.58
Traffic level on main street (1000's of veh/24 hr)	0.994 D-4†	3.27 ***	0.983 D-4	3.28 ***	0.939 D-4	3.07 ***
Corner influence	0.981 D-4	0.29	−0.291 D-4	−0.08	0.311 D-4	0.09
Population within ___ mile radius (people)	0.546 D-5	0.42	1.143 D-5	1.51	0.681 D-5	1.09
Median income in census tract ($)	−0.144 D-3	−0.58	−0.733 D-6	−0.00	−0.808 D-4	−0.32
Per cent non-white in census tract	−0.913	−0.99	−1.036	−1.27	−0.622	−0.78
Per cent deteriorating or dilapidated in the block	−0.303 D-2	−0.47	−0.391 D-2	−0.61	−0.384 D-2	−0.59
A zone (dummy, 1 if site is in A zone, 0 if not)	4.225	2.61 **	4.721	3.05 ***	4.054	2.74 **
B zone (dummy, 1 if site is in B zone, 0 if not)	0.447	0.64	0.469	0.68	0.272	0.39
C zone (dummy, 1 if site is in C zone, 0 if not)	0.520	1.03	0.459	0.92	0.195	0.33
Lot size (square feet)	0.212 D-4	0.48	0.321 D-4	0.73	0.304 D-4	0.68
Time (1958 = 0)	0.329	1.29	0.393	1.55	0.357	1.41
R^2	0.504		0.518		0.511	
Std. error	1.717		1.693		1.705	
N	85					
Mean LV ($/sq. ft.)	3.136					

† For coefficients in this format move the decimal point to the left the number of places shown. Thus, this number is 0.0000994. *** Significant at .01 probability level. ** Significant at .10 probability level.

343

The distance from the CBD also has a significant positive coefficient in the Northwest regressions. Sites in this area are at least three miles and up to ten miles from the CBD. Thus, it appears that distance from the CBD is an important factor when the distance is substantial but not when it is relatively short.

Corner influence, which is measured as the square of the distance from the center of the block and thus is non-linear, is of the expected sign but not significant in the general regressions of Table 1. However, the corner influence variable is significant and of the expected sign in the Northwest section. One reason for the significance of this variable in this area but not in other parts of the city could be that the length of blocks along main streets is longer than is typical for other areas. It is probably easier to find parking or to make left turns into or out of a firm's parking lot if the site is on a corner rather than in the middle of a long block. The effect might be accentuated by the existence of center dividers in many of the main streets in the area which would prohibit left turns in the middle of the block. Measurement problems may also account for its non-significance in the Total City regressions.

The traffic level on main streets is a highly significant positive influence on commercial land values in all the regressions run as expected.

The population coefficient is positive as expected for all three Total City regressions but it is significant only at the two- and three-mile radii. Thus, it appears that a more general drawing area population is more important than the immediate neighborhood. The median income variable has a curious result. It is consistently of the wrong sign and significant at the 6% level for the one-mile radius

(Table 1). There are several alternative explanations for this. One is an exploitation hypothesis. It could be argued that business establishments are more able to charge high prices in low income areas because the people are less informed and less mobile. Another explanation could be that lower income people spend a greater proportion of their income on necessities which they do not travel great distances to acquire. A third might be that it is picking up some of the negative amenity effects attributed to the non-white and deteriorating and dilapidated variables.

The two amenity variables are negative and significant as expected. The results for the Near North Side (Table 3) are of some interest. This area is the Black ghetto of Milwaukee. In this area both the percentage non-white and percentage deteriorating or dilapidated are not significant although of the expected sign. This might indicate that the people patronizing commercial establishments in this area are more accustomed to the presence of non-whites and the view of poor quality houses. Since we expect that a high percentage of the customers of firms in this area would be Black this might be a reasonable argument. An additional reason for this result might be that the residents of this area neither have the desire nor ability to shop elsewhere due to financial or social restraints.

The zoning variables are measures of difference from the D zone. All three zones allow more intense (less restricted) development and their coefficients are positive as expected. However, only the coefficients for the A and C zones are significantly different from the D zone. Also, the A zone coefficient is larger than the C zone as expected from their allowed intensities of use. B zone is apparently not significantly different from D zone. This result can be interpreted in two ways. One is that the rules for B zone do not allow for a substantially different level of development than is allowed in D zoning. While it is not made clear in the zoning regulations, this interpretation does not appear to be consistent with the results for A or C zoning or with what one might expect. An alternative explanation is that the requirements for B zoned areas do not constitute an effective restraint on development of these sites.

The coefficients for the lot size variable are negative as expected and significant in the Total City regressions as well as the Northwest regressions. However, they are of the wrong sign and nonsignificant in the Near North Side regressions. One reason for this might be that this is a completely developed area so that all sites are of roughly the same small size and not large enough for construction economies to be significant or if they are significant they are offset by additional site accumulation costs.

The time trend variable is significant and positive as one might expect.

There may be some problems of multicolinearity in these regressions. There are generally high simple correlation coefficients between the population, median income, non-white population, deteriorating and dilapidated housing and distance to the CBD variables. Thus conclusions regarding the variables must be made with caution. However, I feel that most of the results are consistent with [our] hypothesis. Thus, I conclude that the results have not been seriously affected.

Many appraisers claim that commercial establishments are more concerned with the number of front feet of a site than with its depth and overall size while I have contended that lot size is the most important variable. To test these alternative hypotheses two additional regressions were run. First, the number of front feet of the site was used in place of the lot size. While the appraiser's hypothesis would indicate that a greater number of front feet would increase the sales price and thus the value per square foot, the coefficient was negative and significant. Next, both lot size and number of front feet were included in the regression. In this case the lot size variable was negative and significant as expected while the front foot variable was still negative and not significant. The simple correlation coefficient between lot size and front footage was 0.56 which might cause one to falsely attribute front foot influences to lot size. However, these results at least cast some doubt on the conventional wisdom that front footage is a significant factor in determining the value of a site for commercial purposes.

Conclusions

In general, the regressions presented seem to explain a substantial portion of the variations in commercial land values in the City of Milwaukee. However, there remains a large portion of the variations yet to be explained. Analysis of the micro-locational characteristics of each individual site may help substantially. Another factor which might be important is the air quality in the area.[14] The importance of various locational characteristics may differ among types of commercial establishments. Also, the nearness of

---

[14] Such an effect has been shown for Chicago by Thomas Crocker, "Urban Air Pollution Damage Functions: Theory and Measurement," Working Paper #5, *Program in Environmental Economics,* University of California, Riverside, April 1971.

competitors and complementary land uses may be important.[15] The analysis of such factors awaits additional data.

Appendix: A Theory of Commercial Land Value

The maximum price a firm is willing to pay for any site (LV) is a function of its anticipated future returns when operating at the site (R, which is assumed constant for simplicity), the interest rate (i), and the effective property tax rate on the land (t).

$$LV = \frac{R}{i + t} \qquad (1)$$

The annual return can be thought of as the excess of total annual revenue (TAR) over total annual costs for all factors of production other than land including intermediate goods purchased (TAC).

$$R = TAR - TAC \qquad (2)$$

Total annual revenue can be defined as the sum of the prices paid for various goods and services sold at the site in that year (P_a) times the quantities sold (Q_a).

$$TAR = \sum_{a=1}^{n} P_a Q_a \qquad (3)$$

where n is the number of different goods or services sold at the site. The prices paid provide the first locational dimension of the model. For the firm's customer, the price of acquiring a good or service is not just its money cost (P_a), for it is necessary for a customer to travel to the location to complete the purchase. The cost of this travel can be thought of as having three dimensions: the actual dollar cost of travel (out-of-pocket costs plus the value of travel time) (T), the cost and availability of parking (PK), and the dollar value of the aesthetic pleasure or displeasure of the trip (AE). Thus:

$$TP_a = P_a + T + PK + AE \qquad (4)$$

where TP_a is the total cost to the customer of acquiring a good at some unspecified site.

It is obvious that T, PK, and AE can vary among sites. It is also true that P_a can vary among sites. For retail sales, for example, it might be the case that a firm in the CBD sells a good for a lower price than a competitor in a regional shopping center. For many potential customers it could be the case that T, PK, and AE are greater for acquiring the good at the central site than at the regional center. The individual's choice will depend upon which TP_a is less for him and this will vary with the customer's location relative to the two competitors.

Another dimension may be added to the shopper's choice between competing locations. The potential customer must not only assess prices but he must also assess the relative probabilities of finding what he wants at each alternative location. While selection may be better at the CBD than at the regional center, the potential customer may be willing to trade off the convenience of shopping at the regional center for the loss in selection.

The quantity of the good sold by any one firm at various prices (Q_a) is also somewhat dependent on the location of the firm. Of course, the quantity sold by a firm is a function of the total demand for the good and his price

---

[15] Such effects are suggested by Walter Isard, *Location and Space Economy* (Cambridge, Massachusetts: The M.I.T. Press, 1956), p. 200.

relative to that of his competitors. But Q_a is also dependent on the knowledge potential customers have of the firm and its location. A central location is likely to increase customer knowledge of the firm. Likewise, corner lots and locations on main streets are likely to improve customer knowledge of a firm's location and existence as well as provide ease of access.

Let us now look at the cost side of equation (2). At each alternative location being considered by the firm, the total annual cost for all factors other than land is the sum of direct wage payments (W), direct capital costs (C), intermediate good costs (IGC), and other operating costs (OC):

$$\text{TAC} = W + C + \text{IGC} + \text{OC} \quad (5)$$

Some authors have argued that real wages vary with the time of travel from the worker's residence to his place of employment.[16] Travel-to-work costs affect the availability and quality of employee a firm may draw on for its labor force at a given W over different locations.

That portion of capital cost which is spent on site improvements will increase with the value of the site. That is, there exists a trade-off between capital expenditures on improvements and the cost and size of a lot. As a general rule *ceteris paribus* a firm would value a site more as lot size increases but the value per square foot would decline since marginal construction cost savings would decline as lot size increases. Zoning setback and height restrictions may affect the degree to which the height–lot size trade-off may be exercised for any one site.

Intermediate goods are usually sold f.o.b. the producing firm. The cost of transportation will include delivery to a central delivery point in the city and distribution to the firm's location. If the distribution center is located near the center of the city, the IGC will increase with distance from the CBD. If the commercial land use is retailing, then the IGC can be borne in part by the wholesaler. He will store goods at his warehouse which is typically centrally located (although there is a growing trend toward suburban locations) and distribute the goods as they are ordered by the retailer. The cost of delivery to the retailer may be borne by either the wholesaler (and thus redistributed to all retailers) or the individual retailer, depending upon the custom for that type of good.

Operating costs, as we are using the term here, are composed of items other than wages and intermediate goods. One factor affecting operating costs is the price and availability of public utilities and other social overhead capital. The cost of providing these services probably increases with distance from a centrally located distribution point and with reductions in density.[17] To the extent that charges are formulated independently of these distribution cost factors (which is often the case), areas which are more costly to serve (typically outlying areas) may not pay the marginal distribution costs. This would increase rents in such areas relative to other areas that pay greater than the marginal cost of distribution

16 John Kain, "The Journey-to-Work as a Determinant of Residential Location," *Papers and Proceedings of the Regional Science Association*, 1962, pp. 137–169; and Wingo, *op. cit.*, make this argument.

17 This has been shown for sewage service in, Paul B. Downing, *The Economics of Urban Sewage Disposal* (New York: Praeger Publishers, 1969).

to them.[18] Another part of the operating costs is the cost of insurance (or the losses incurred if insurance is not available) for fire and theft. Fire insurance rates depend upon the rating given to the city's fire department and the service provided the particular site. For theft, insurance costs increase with the area's crime rate which, in turn, varies with the socio-economic characteristics of the neighborhood. Contact with other firms has often been cited as a reason for central tendency in commercial firms. This contact is said to increase the flow of information and thus reduce operating costs. Meyer, Kain, and Wohl point out that modern improvements in communications and increased use of computer data processing have reduced this central tendency over the past few years.[19]

In summary, this theory of commercial land value hypothesizes that value varies over sites because of variations in the total revenue that can be earned at different sites and because of variations in the total costs of producing a good or service at different sites in a city. Further, it has been suggested that both revenues and costs vary systematically with certain locational factors.

[18] See, Paul B. Downing, "The Role of User Charges in Financing Urban Development," *Proceedings, American Real Estate and Urban Economics Association,* May 1972.

[19] Meyer, Kain, and Wohl, *op. cit.,* pp. 14–17.

VALUATION OF
PROPERTY INTERESTS

The value of real property interests emanates from the use, utility, wants, needs, and satisfactions of man. It is the service function attributes of real property that principally constitute the basis of value. These factors collectively underscore and manifest themselves in the demand aspect for one of many different kinds of real property interests. In turn, demand, its depth and quality, is a direct link to value; it is one of the principal foundations of the value of real property.

Measures of Demand

Prior analysis pertained to matters of urban growth dynamics, trade area analysis, location analysis, and consumer behavior, profiles, and preferences, which are essentially surrogates for the total measure of demand for different locations and related facilities. For it is fundamental that a retail designed building has value for a retail use only if the critical supporting elements reflect positive aspects concerning the purchasing power of consumers, trade area qualities and dimensions, and so forth.

In ascribing value to a retail facility, existing or proposed, new or old, the matter of future productivity of the property at the given location is paramount. Transaction (sales) analysis and competitive rental studies are valid elements of evidence for a value estimate, but they are by definition retrospective evidence of value. Accordingly, because market value is prospective in nature by definition (present worth of future benefits), it is the future productivity of the property, whether leasing to a prospective

349

tenant or owner use is contemplated, that is central to the value question.

For example, a 20-year old, small, freestanding, one-story store-room building on a secondary strip commercial street has value for continued use only if potential users can be ascertained based on location, area trends and developments, and so on. Prospective rental values should be predicated on such potential users (say, a barber shop or shoe store) and the current and anticipated intensity of utilization of the standing inventory of competitive properties. Intensity of utilization and absorption levels of new or existing facilities comprise a *pressure index of area need*. Suppose that two- and three-year leases that have expired in the last several years are not renewed for similar or longer periods, but, rather, one-year or month-to-month leases represent the state of renewals. This then can serve as an index of one of several crucial things: lack of confidence in the location(s) for the particular lines of business and/or services, shifting trade areas and consumer patronage, and perhaps undercapitalization or noncompetitiveness of current retailing–service functions. Frequently, these trends also reflect a weakened rental rate structure.

Since change underscores all economic activity, leases and sales of a year or two ago, in and of themselves, represent marginal evidence of value today. They are essentially a permanent record of transpired economic activities and the corresponding perceptions and evaluations of owners–lessees *at that time*. Failure to recognize and draw these distinctions places an analyst–appraiser in one of a number of positions, to wit, that change is not a basic ingredient of economic activity, that market demand can be assumed or is irrelevant, that financial markets are static, which in turn suggests adequate equity and mortgage funding resources, and so on. Furthermore, even if all these important factors were assumed not to be important, complete reliance on retrospective evidence (sales–leases) suggests an error-free marketplace; that is, market participants simply did not over- or underpay via one of several obligations at that point in time.

Since expectations represent an important part of the fabric of economic activities, measures of expectations are basically a recognition of a fundamental real property principle—anticipation.

Some direction for the expectation–anticipation matrix can be obtained from data as shown in Table 1. These national forecasts can be related to the local areal unit appropriate to the location of the property under study. Studies of the degree of correlation between national and local trends can suggest the most probable direction of specific activities at the local level. Translations of

TABLE 1
Consumer Spending Trends

Product group	1960	1970	1973	1979	1984
Food and tobacco	26.9	22.9	22.2	21.7	20.6
Clothing and accessories	10.2	10.2	10.1	10.0	10.2
Personal care	1.6	1.7	1.5	1.4	1.3
Housing	14.2	14.7	14.5	14.1	13.9
Household operation	14.4	14.1	14.6	13.9	13.8
Medical care expenses	5.9	7.7	7.8	8.1	8.2
Personal business	4.6	5.7	5.6	6.6	7.6
Transportation	13.3	12.6	13.6	14.3	14.6
Private education and research	1.1	1.7	1.6	2.0	2.2
Recreation	5.6	6.6	6.5	5.7	5.4
Religious and welfare activities	1.5	1.4	1.3	1.3	1.3
Foreign travel and other, net	0.7	0.8	0.7	0.8	1.0
Durable	13.9	14.8	16.2	14.0	13.6
Nondurable	46.5	42.7	42.0	41.6	39.9
Services	39.6	42.5	41.8	44.4	46.5
Total	100.0	100.0	100.0	100.0	100.0

Source: National Planning Association, 1975.

expenditures into per capita or per household units interfaced with current competitive firms provide a sound foundation for determining entry or nonentry of a new retail facility.

Manifestly, demand over time, its rate of change and direction, collectively with expectations, uncertainty, and risk comprise important dimensions of the economic value of real property interests. The time factor is foremost because use, utility, and the like are encompassed in a short-run or long-term frame. In turn, revenues and expenses give viability to the notion of the time value of money.

Thus, money in a time–dimension context remains central to all premises, concepts, methodology, and techniques utilized or promulgated in reference to the valuation of real property interests for one of many uses, be they retail, service-oriented, or otherwise.

Capital Structure Analysis

Since most real estate of an investment nature, such as retail stores and office buildings, is developed or purchased on the basis of the kind, extent, cost, and availability of mortgage financing, realistic and responsive valuation methods integrate this aspect into the process. Additionally, the investor-contemplated retention or holding term of an investment is an important element for consideration.

Suppose that an investor is planning to construct a building for a discount variety chain on a site which he owns. The lease is noncancelable for 10 years with level rent. The owner is obligated under the terms of the lease to pay taxes, insurance, and for the exterior maintenance of the building, including the off-street parking area. The elements of this contemplated investment are as follows.

1. Cash flow: Net income after expenses for the 10-year period.
2. Reversionary value: Value of property at expiration of lease period.

Assume that the following facts on financing and equity investor yield requirements prevail.

1. Financing: 80 percent loan, 9 percent interest, 30 years (payable monthly).
2. Holding period of investment (by investor): 10 years.
3. Investor's equity yield (20 percent equity) requirement: 14 percent.
4. Anticipated value of property at end of 10 years: increase 20 percent.

The property is estimated to cost $4,000,000 and the net income after expenses is ascertained to be about $37,500 per year. The lease, however, is still under negotiation.

The derivation of a capitalization rate that includes all these factors and assumptions is shown in Figure 1. The factual data is entered as noted with the table data obtained from any one of many financial tables.

Capitalizing the net income indicates an investment value of $4,142,300. Suppose the investor further analyzes the assumptions, in particular the 20 percent increase in property value after expiration of the lease, and would like to know a range of expectations of future value versus the net income stream.

Further analysis, as shown in Table 2, indicates that, all assumptions remaining the same except for the future property value estimate, the rental might have to be increased (to derive a higher net income) if the investor is to achieve a 14 percent equity yield over the investment period.

Implicitly, this example indicates that a single point estimate of investment value might be misleading because of the many assumptions contained therein. A range of probable values under modified assumptions permits a closer look at alternatives and

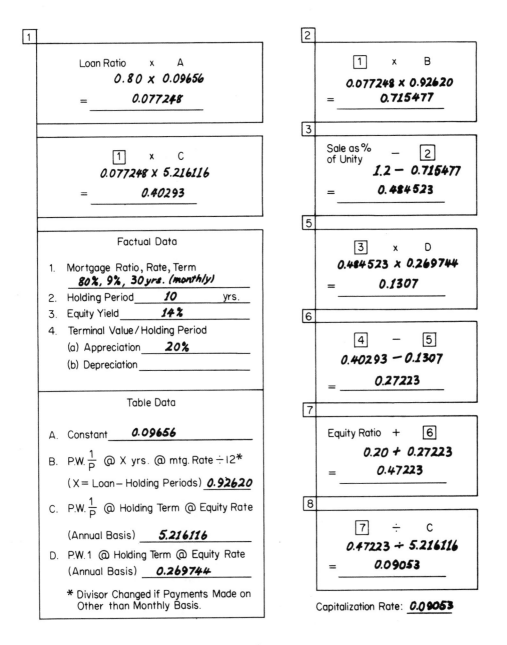

1

Loan Ratio   x   A
0.80×0.09656
= 0.077248

$\boxed{1}$ x   C
0.077248×5.216116
= 0.40293

Factual Data

1. Mortgage Ratio, Rate, Term
   $80\%,\ 9\%,\ 30\,yrs.\ (monthly)$
2. Holding Period 10 yrs.
3. Equity Yield 14%
4. Terminal Value / Holding Period
   (a) Appreciation 20%
   (b) Depreciation _____

Table Data

A. Constant 0.09656

B. P.W. $\frac{1}{P}$ @ X yrs. @ mtg. Rate $\div 12$*
   (X = Loan − Holding Periods) 0.92620

C. P.W. $\frac{1}{P}$ @ Holding Term @ Equity Rate
   (Annual Basis) 5.216116

D. P.W. 1 @ Holding Term @ Equity Rate
   (Annual Basis) 0.269744

   * Divisor Changed if Payments Made on
   Other than Monthly Basis.

2

$\boxed{1}$ x   B
0.077248×0.92620
= 0.715477

3

Sale as %
of Unity   − $\boxed{2}$
$1.2 - 0.715477$
= 0.484523

5

$\boxed{3}$ x   D
0.484523×0.269744
= 0.1307

6

$\boxed{4}$ − $\boxed{5}$
$0.40293 - 0.1307$
= 0.27223

7

Equity Ratio   + $\boxed{6}$
$0.20 + 0.27223$
= 0.47223

8

$\boxed{7}$ ÷   C
$0.47223 \div 5.216116$
= 0.09053

Capitalization Rate: 0.09053

FIGURE 1

Capitalization Rate Computation (Investment Capital Structure)

TABLE 2
Investment Decision—Strategy Matrix

Property Value Change End of Lease (%)	Capitalization Rate	Investment Value	Minimum Net Income Required *
+30	.08536	$4,393,200	$34,144.00
+20	.09053	4,142,300	36,212.00
+10	.09570	3,918,500	38,280.00
None	.100871	3,717,600	40,348.00
−10	.106042	3,536,300	42,417.00
−20	.111213	3,371,900	44,852.00
−30	.116385	3,222,200	46,554.00

* Before debt service.

revised courses of action. For example, if the cost of the subject development could be scaled down to $3,500,000, the minimum net income requirements, before debt service, would be $37,114 (.106042 × $3,500,000), even though the property was assumed to depreciate 10 percent for the term of the lease.

After-Tax Yield Analysis

In a total context, real estate investment decisions are made not only on gross and net cash flows and credit of lessee, but also are predicated on the tax impact on the eventual sale of the investment property. More attention in this area has been generated as a consequence of the upward surge of rentals, property values, and individual tax liabilities of investors. Manifestly, concern about yield, over a given period of investment retention, includes the rate of return considering the tax shield of depreciation during the course of holding the investment, but also the tax consequences on sale, disposition, or liquidation.

The illustration in Table 3 concerns a proposed purchase of an investment property for $390,000. Equity requirements total $97,500, with financing of $292,500 for 25 years at 10.5 percent interest. Improvements are valued at $253,500, the depreciable asset of the investment, which will be amortized on a 30-year straight-line basis; investor's tax rate is 40 percent.

On the assumption that the property will sell for the acquisition price, the capital gains tax is computed at $16,900. Net to equity position after taxes and mortgage balance is $132,266, thus indicating an IRR (internal rate of return) of 15.0857 percent before taxes and 11.1971 percent after taxes. The basic assumption

TABLE 3
Pro Forma After-Tax Analysis

Year	Cash Flow	Mortgage Amort.	Book Deprec.	Taxable Income	Income Tax	After-Tax Cash Flow
1	$ 12,616	$ 2,549	$ 8,450	$ 6,715	$ 2,686	$ 9,930
2	12,616	2,830	8,450	6,996	2,798	9,818
3	12,616	3,142	8,450	7,308	2,923	9,693
4	12,616	3,488	8,450	7,654	3,062	9,554
5	12,616	3,872	8,450	8,038	3,215	9,401
6	12,616	4,299	8,450	8,465	3,386	9,230
7	12,616	4,773	8,450	8,939	3,576	9,040
8	12,616	5,299	8,450	9,465	3,786	8,830
9	12,616	5,883	8,450	10,049	4,020	8,596
10	12,616	6,531	8,450	10,697	4,279	8,337
	$126,160	$42,666	$84,500	$84,326	$33,731	$92,429

Depreciation method: straight line   1st year eq. div.: 12.9395%

Sale price at end of 10 years	390,000
Capital gains tax	— 16,900
Excess deprec. tax	— 0
Mortgage balance	—249,834
After-tax eq. revenue	$123,266

underscoring this yield is resale of the property at its acquisition cost ($390,000) and mortgage financing with a constant of .113302. Any change in these factor inputs will of course result in modifications of equity yields on a before- and after-tax basis.

Sensitivity Analysis

A number of variables converge and are synthesized into an investment proposal that may eventually serve as a basis for acquisition of property. Some of these variables are fixed (deterministic) and may remain constant, like the acquisition cost of a site; others are random, frequently for the economic life of the improvements. Operating expenses fall in this category.

In the study of a proposed project, a series of analyses can be undertaken to include the sensitivity of input factor changes on equity yield and overall rate of return; such analyses may raise questions concerning the feasibility of the project as constituted.

In some instances, mortgagee underwriting requires additional equity funds or participation on the part of the lender during periods of escalating interest rates or other long-term investment uncertainties. The following examples illustrate several of a number of sensitivity assessments that may be made on a proposed new development contemplated for retention as an investment.

TABLE 4
Project Development Costs

Construction Costs		
Total building cost (34,406 sq. ft. at $12.50)		$430,075
Construction contingency		21,504
Subtotal construction		451,579
Architecture fees	at 2.0%	9,032
Engineering fees	at 1.0%	4,400
Loan origination fees	at 2.0%	9,032
Legal and closing fees	at 1.0%	4,516
Taxes and insurance	at 0.2%	700
Cumulative subtotal		479,258
Interim interest–construction ($479,258 at 11.0% for		
12 months compounded)		29,538
Total construction costs		508,796
Land Costs		
85,000 sq. ft. at $1.75		148,750
Interim interest–land ($148,750 for 12 months at		
11.0% compounded)		17,213
Total land cost		165,963
Total land and construction cost		$674,759

The total cost for constructing a one-story building proposed for occupancy by a supermarket are $674,759, which includes interim costs of financing and the like. The total construction period, as noted, is judged to be 12 months.

The investor would like to consider all viable options available in the market for financing the project. Accordingly, the analyst–appraiser has prepared a schedule, as noted in Table 5, indicating various loan ratios, terms, related constants, and the corresponding debt service. Each of the 25 financing plans represents a defined capital structure situation.

With these capital structure parameters, a series of sensitivity analysis can be made. One such run is illustrated in Table 6. Here the constant factors include an assumption of a 75 percent ratio loan at 10 percent for 20 years, with a total equity of $168,690.

TABLE 5
Capital Structure Parameters

Amount financed $472,331
Equity $202,428
Loan ratio 70.0%

Interest	Term	Constant	Debt Service
10.00	20.0	11.5803	54,697
9.50	25.0	10.4844	49,521
9.00	15.0	12.1712	57,488
10.50	27.0	11.1636	52,729
11.00	28.0	11.5378	54,496

Amount financed $506,069
Equity $168,690
Loan ratio 75.0%

Interest	Term	Constant	Debt Service
10.00	20.0	11.5803	58,604
9.50	25.0	10.4844	53,058
9.00	15.0	12.1712	61,595
10.50	27.0	11.1636	56,496
11.00	28.0	11.5378	58,389

Amount financed $539,807
Equity $134,952
Loan ratio 80.0%

Interest	Term	Constant	Debt Service
10.00	20.0	11.5803	62,511
9.50	25.0	10.4844	56,595
9.00	15.0	12.1712	65,701
10.50	27.0	11.1636	60,262
11.00	28.0	11.5378	62,282

Amount financed $573,545
Equity $101,214
Loan ratio 85.0%

Interest	Term	Constant	Debt Service
10.00	20.0	11.5803	66,418
9.50	25.0	10.4844	60,133
9.00	15.0	12.1712	69,807
10.50	27.0	11.1636	64,029
11.00	28.0	11.5378	66,174

TABLE 5—Continued

Amount financed $607,283
Equity $67,476
Loan ratio 90.0%

Interest	Term	Constant	Debt Service
10.00	20.0	11.5803	70,325
9.50	25.0	10.4844	63,670
9.00	15.0	12.1712	73,914
10.50	27.0	11.1636	67,795
11.00	28.0	11.5378	70,067

TABLE 6
Sensitivity Analysis: Rental Rates Versus Vacancy

	Annual Cash Flows				
	Vacancy Allowance (%)				
Rental Rates Annual ($/sq. ft.)	0	5.0	7.0	10.0	12.0
2.00	−9,713	−13,085	−14,434	−16,457	−17,805
2.25	−1,284	−5,077	−6,594	−8,870	−10,388
2.50	7,146	2,931	1,245	−1,284	−2,970
2.75	15,575	10,939	9,085	6,303	4,448
3.00	24,005	18,947	16,924	13,889	11,866

	Break-even Rental Rates				
	Vacancy Allowance (%)				
	0	5.0	7.0	10.0	12.0
Rental rates Annual ($/sq. ft.)	2.29	2.41	2.46	2.54	2.60

Assumptions for the derivations:

Fixed Parameters

Site	85,000 sq. ft.
Building	34,406 sq. ft.
Efficiency	98.0% of gross
Loan ratio	75.0% of $674,759
Equity	$168,690
Financing	20 years, 10.0%
Other income	$0 annually
Expenses	$0.55/sq. ft.

The interfacing of various potential rental rates with different levels of vacancies suggests the feasible and infeasible regions of Table 6. As noted, the indicated minimum rental must be $2.50

per square foot. This is further confirmed by the break-even study in the lower portion of the tabulation. The indication here is that the rental rate should not be less than $2.50 per square foot with a vacancy rate not to exceed 7 percent to achieve a positive cash flow.

Another sensitivity test relates the loan–cost ratio to debt service. This tests for the extent of leverage possible under various financing options. The feasible and infeasible zones have been outlined in Table 7. In this analysis, the highest cash flow would develop at an interest rate of 9.5 percent with a loan ratio of 70 percent for 25 years, followed by a 27 year loan at 70 percent ratio and bearing an interest rate of 10.5 percent. Thus, extending the payout period increases the cash flow, provided the rate of interest does not exceed 10.5 percent at a loan–cost ratio of 70 percent.

TABLE 7
Sensitivity Analysis: Loan–Cost Ratio Versus Debt Service

| | *Annual Cash Flows* | | | | |
| | *Loan–Cost Ratio (%)* | | | | |
Financing	*70.0*	*75.0*	*80.0*	*85.0*	*90.0*
20 yr., 10.0%	6,838	2,931	−976	−4,883	−8,790
25 yr., 9.5%	12,014	8,477	4,940	1,403	−2,135
15 yr., 9.0%	4,047	−60	−4,166	−8,272	−12,379
27 yr., 10.5%	8,806	5,039	1,273	−2,493	−6,260
28 yr., 11.0%	7,039	3,146	−747	−4,639	−8,532

| | *Break-even Rental Rates* | | | | |
| | *Loan–Cost Ratio (%)* | | | | |
Financing	*70.0*	*75.0*	*80.0*	*85.0*	*90.0*
20 yr., 10.0%	2.29	2.41	2.53	2.65	2.77
25 yr., 9.5%	2.12	2.24	2.35	2.46	2.57
15 yr., 9.0%	2.37	2.50	2.63	2.76	2.89
27 yr., 10.5%	2.23	2.34	2.46	2.58	2.70
28 yr., 11.0%	2.28	2.40	2.52	2.64	2.77

Assumptions for the derivations:

Fixed Parameters

Site	85,000 sq. ft.
Building	34,406 sq. ft
Efficiency	98.0% of gross
Revenue	$2.50/sq. ft.
Vacancy	5.0% of leasable
Other income	$0 annually
Expenses	$0.55/sq. ft.

From the prior sensitivity analysis, indicating a rental rate of $2.50 per square foot, the subject break-even study would indicate a 75 percent loan at 15 years and interest at 9.0 percent, or any extension of term or increased loan–cost ratio as noted in the break-even part of Table 7.

With fixed parameters of financing at the 75 percent ratio, with interest at 10 percent and term of 20 years, and assuming a basic rental of $2.50 per square foot, a series of net changes in parameters was undertaken as shown in Table 8. The principal object was to ascertain what changes in factor inputs could be made to increase the cash flow. The most substantial was decreasing the total cost of the project by $100,000, or by $1 per square foot, followed by the obvious step of increasing the rental rate by 10¢ per square foot. As noted in Table 8, just increasing the construction period by one month results in decreasing the cash flow by $685,000.

TABLE 8
Sensitivity Analysis: Fixed Parameter Changes

Parameter Change	Increase in Cash Flow	Effect on Construction
Decrease construction cost $100,000	$13,048	−$112,670
Decrease construction $1.00/sq. ft.	4,489	−38,765
Increase construction period 1 month	−685	5,915
Decrease const. and land interim 1%	524	−4,522
Increase building efficiency 1%	629	
Increase rental rate 10¢/sq. ft.	3,204	
Decrease vacancy rate 1%	844	
Decrease operating rate 10¢/sq. ft.	3,371	
Decrease permanent rate .25%	1,002	
Decrease permanent loan term by 1 year	−986	
Decrease permanent loan term by 5 years	−6,655	
Decrease the loan ratio by 5%	3,907	

Assumptions for the derivations:

    Fixed Parameters

Site	85,000 sq. ft.
Building	34,406 sq. ft.
Efficiency	98.0% of gross
Loan ratio	75.0% of $674,759
Equity	$168,690
Financing	20 years 10.0%
Revenue	$2.50/sq. ft.
Vacancy	5.0% of leasable
Other income	$0 annually
Expenses	$0.55/sq. ft.

Construction and land cost $674,759
Construction interim rate 11.0%
Construction period 12 months
Land interim rate is 11.0%

Another assumption in a sensitivity analysis was to assume that the annual cash flow would be increased $3,500. The results of this are outlined in Table 9, with a series of options that might be attractive, provided the assumptions are valid and achievable.

Finally, with all these norms formulated from various sensitivity assessments, a pro forma investment analysis was completed. See Table 10. The findings suggest a marginal and perhaps an infeasible project. The realism of the high interest rate (10 percent) and short payout period (20 years) makes excessive demands

TABLE 9
Equivalent Effects to Yield (a $3,500 increase in annual cash flow)

Decrease construction cost by	$0.78/sq. ft.
Decrease construction period by	5.1 months
Decrease interim interest by	6.68%
Increase building efficiency by	5.57%
Increase rent rate by	$0.11/sq. ft.
Decrease vacancy by	4.15%
Decrease expense rate by	$0.10/sq. ft
Decrease permanent rate by	0.87%
Increase permanent loan term by	2.6 years
Decrease loan ratio by	4.5%

TABLE 10
Pro Forma Cash Flow Analysis: Parameter Norms

Gross square feet in building	34,406
Building efficiency	98%
Net leasable square footage	33,718
Land and construction cost	$674,759
Loan–cost ratio	75%
Original loan amount	$506,069
Equity requirement	$168,690
Permanent interest rate	10%
Term of loan	20 years
Annual debt service	$58,604

	Annual Dollars
Gross income: 33,718 sq. ft. at $2.50	$84,295
Less: vacancy allowance of 5.0%	4,215
Gross effective income	80,080
Operating expenses: 33,718 sq. ft. at 55¢	18,545
Net operating income	61,535
Debt service (11.58% constant)	58,604
Pro forma cash flow	2,931
Return on equity: 1.74%	

on cash flow, thus indicating a potential equity yield of 1.74 percent on a total capital structure of 25 percent equity investment.

Simulation Analysis

Simulation is defined as a method of evaluating alternative courses of action predicated on a mathematical model depicting the actual or proposed situation involving a decision. Essentially, it is an experiment performed with a mathematical model that depicts the interrelationship of a group of key variables.

A simulation analysis can serve as a decision-making technique because it outlines a series of probabilities within defined limitations of input data. Repeated runs of a simulation improve the confidence factor since statistical errors tend to average out over repeated trials. The kind of distribution selected (normal probability, uniform, etc.) depends on the analyst's perception of the real life problem and other empirical evidence.

The following equation represents a capital structure model relating equity return as a dependent variable to gross income multiple, expense ratio, and mortgage terms as the independent variables.

$$r = \frac{1}{x_4}(1 - x_1) - x_2 / x_3$$

where $x_4 =$ gross income multiple
$x_1 =$ expense ratio
$x_2 =$ loan constant $\times$ loan ratio (%)
$x_3 = (1 -$ loan ratio)
$r =$ equity return

Assume that a property is financed with a 10 percent loan, 25-year term, at 8 percent interest, with a loan constant of 0.0927. The operating ratio is expected to vary between 38 and 42 percent and the GIM (gross income multiple) between 6.0 and 6.5; that is, the purchaser is considering paying six to six and one-half times current gross income for the property.

For example, if a purchase is consummated at six times gross income and the operating ratio is 0.38, then under the above capital structure model the equity yield will be 14.57 percent; with GIM $= 6.25$ and the operating ratio at 0.42, the equity yield will be 9.3 percent. In essence then, a 56.9 percent variance in equity yield might occur simply with an increase of 10.5 percent in operating ratio and 4.2 percent in the direct conversion factor (GIM).

A simulation was undertaken utilizing a QIKSIM program (03-1589; version 3). The simulation suggests, as indicated in Figure 2, that 43 percent of the time (43/100) the yield is likely to be between 11.5 and 12.4 percent; at the extremes are an 8 percent chance of an equity yield of 9.6 percent and a 7 percent chance of obtaining a yield of 13.8 percent.

This is further illustrated in the cumulative frequency distribution shown in Figure 3 and tabulated in Table 11; as indicated in the table, there is at least a 50 percent probability that the equity yield will be at least 11.94 percent. The probability of exceeding a 13 percent equity yield is 15 percent (1 — .85). As noted in Figure 2, the highest chance is for a 12.4 percent yield.

The simulation of the problem was further extended with only one change in the previous parameters: the GIM was estimated in the range of 6.0 to 6.5. Assuming that a purchaser might consider paying between six and six and one-half times the gross annual income, what are the probabilities of equity yield, their range, and so on? The histogram of Figure 4 suggests that the most likely equity yield would be 9.9 percent (20/100), with a range up to 10.5 percent (17/100). The cumulative distribution is shown in Figure 5 and the tabular form in Table 12.

In the first paper of this section, the function of an appraisal in the context of investor decision making is outlined by Edwin M. Rams, along with basic real property principles, data requirements, and correlative analysis. This is followed by the new real

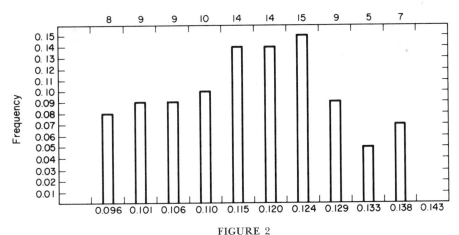

FIGURE 2

Histogram of $Y = ((1/X1)*(1 - X2) - .0742)/.2$

TABLE 11
Reduced Tabular Summary of $Y = ((1/X1)*(1-X2)-.0742)/.2$

I	$Y(I)$	Probability of $Y(I-1)$ to $Y(I)$	Cumulative Probability
1	.100116	.05	.05
2	.102301	.05	.1
3	.104735	.05	.15
4	.106857	.05	.2
5	.109804	.05	.25
6	.111059	.05	.3
7	.113316	.05	.35
8	.117687	.05	.4
9	.11849	.05	.45
10	.119431	.05	.5
11	.120918	.05	.55
12	.122454	.05	.6
13	.124194	.05	.65
14	.12557	.05	.7
15	.126441	.05	.75
16	.128977	.05	.8
17	.130805	.05	.85
18	.136245	.05	.9
19	.138353	.05	.95
20	.142649	.05	1.

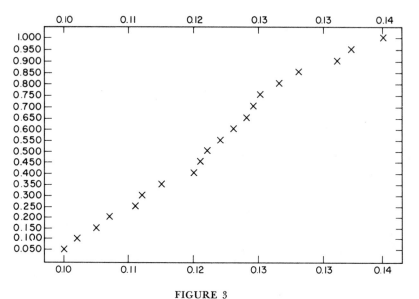

FIGURE 3

Cumulative Frequency Plot of $Y = ((1/X1)*(1-X2)-.0742)/.2$

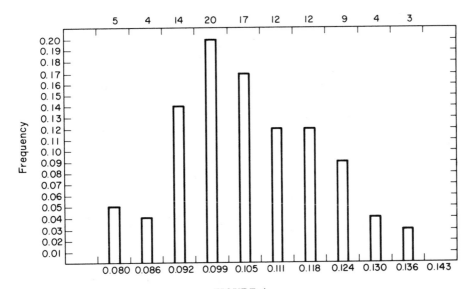

FIGURE 4

Histogram of $Y = ((1/X1)*(1 - X2) - .0742)/.2$

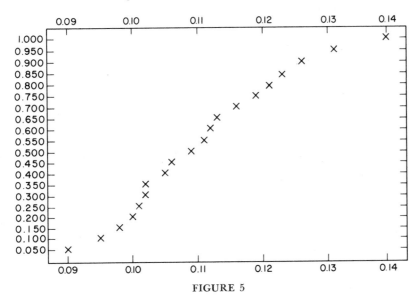

FIGURE 5

Cumulative Frequency Plot of $Y = ((1/X1)*(1 - X2) - .0742)/.2$

estate process that provides a realistic forum for deriving the value
of real property interests.

In a capital structure analysis of a real estate investment, the
final estimate of value is based on the reliability of key data infor-

mation and forecasts. David W. Walters outlines the priorities that should be assigned in such an appraisal endeavor. His study provides insight into the extent of leverage in a mathematical investment model of holding term, mortgage and equity rates, and the like. Continuing in the same frame of reference, Lloyd D. Hanford illustrates the impact of changes in net income on property value through the use of discounted cash flow analysis. Examples are provided that highlight the use and application of this method in real property analysis–valuation.

In retail property analysis–valuation, the leasing of facilities represents a typical problem situation. The impact of leases on value is a subject under consideration by a number of authors. A definitive and substantitive presentation is made by Keith B. Johnson and Thomas B. Hazuka; they explore, compare, and analyze the techniques of leading authorities on the matter of lease or buy. What are the right criteria and basis for measurement and evaluation? Some interesting answers and comparisons are outlined in this presentation.

James E. Gibbons analyzes the components of value in a leased property, changes in value parameters where below market leases prevail, and the confluence of these factors in the processing of income and risk rate selection, with proper attribution to competing forms of investments.

Finally, as discussed by Adolph Koeppel, the matter of eminent domain, the lessee and property owner and their interests and related property values, draws attention because of its impact via displacement.

Collectively the essays provide the why, how, and when of retail property valuation. While not exhaustive in coverage of typical and atypical situations, the material represents definitive solutions to prevailing appraisal problems. The papers are worthy simply for the aggregate, multi-vantage point of illustrations and perspectives outlined and provide an immediate privity of application to most similar everyday problems of the analyst–appraiser of real property facilities.

The Function of Valuation for Articulating the Investment Decision-Making Process

Edwin M. Rams

Every investment decision involving the contemplated purchase of real property, and related assets, involves consideration of two basic ingredients common to an entrepreneur's decision-making process. These two future aspects are uncertainty and risk. Their consideration and measurement, whether made explicitly or intuitively, may involve fundamental valuation processes and techniques. The quality and comprehensiveness of such an evaluation can determine to a large degree the optimum use and return from the property and this is in fact the investment making process.

This paper will endeavor to discuss the attributes inherent in an investment decision process and the role and function that property valuation can play for attaining and insuring entrepreneurial objectives and expectations.

The Investment Decision Process

A basic dilemma confronting every investor is one common to all investment decisions, i.e., an imperfect knowledge of the future. Notwithstanding the presence of this partial vacuum, an investment decision must be made within the realm and framework of the available evidence and the related outcome or expectations to flow from the decision—to purchase the property, or not. Accordingly, an investor is faced with an initial evaluation, i.e., the extent of evidence and supporting knowledge that he presently has or can possess prior to even making a tentative commitment to invest. Such evidence and knowledge may be constituted from present similar investments, prior experience in purchase and sale, etc.

However, one basic truth is inescapable—a minimum amount of evidence must exist prior to making the investment judgment. For we know *ispo facto* that investment decisions continue to become less perfect as supporting evidence and knowledge are reduced. Consequently, an investment decision made by astute men occurs within the polar constraints of knowledge and experience; one minimum and the other optimum. Outside of this continuum of knowledge and experience are defensive policies to negate any possible affirmative action. While a negative course of action represents a *decision* it does not necessarily represent the *best decision*.

Reprinted from *Valuation*, Vol. 20, No. 1, May 1973, by permission of the editor (Copyright American Society of Appraisers).

Accordingly, astute investors follow a positive and aggressive course in their decision making process. This kind of policy necessitates proper consideration and evaluation of a proposed property investment in terms of risk and uncertainty as concerns the investment under consideration.

Study of Risk

A study of risk encompasses two vital aspects; these are concerned with

1. prediction of the productivity of the property, and
2. the degree of certainty of such prediction.

From this it is apparent that risk can be evaluated, i.e., it can be quantified and measured in terms of possible loss or gain. Further, the quantification of risk and its attendant prediction results in a derivation of the contingencies or eventualities possible from a contemplated investment.

It is evident then that an evaluation of risk is objective; a comparative study of the productivity of property along with a determination of the certainty of the prediction, results in a finding of the attendant risk in undertaking a given property investment. This risk is insurable; provisions and certain actions can be undertaken to minimize losses thereby reducing risk.

Study of Uncertainty

A study of uncertainty is subjective because it is evaluated in an environment of *incomplete* knowledge; therefore, uncertainty is not insurable. Consequently, uncertainty cannot be absorbed into an investor's property portfolio's cost structure as risk can.

Uncertainty stems from and is related to the following aspects of a property investment.

1. Profit uncertainty
2. Production uncertainty
3. Cost uncertainty

Other classes of uncertainties related to the three noted above are: demand uncertainty, price uncertainty, economic and political uncertainty, and capital uncertainty.

We can see that uncertainty is a very vital matter in terms of long-term commitments in investing in real property. By far the most important point to be noted about uncertainty is its relevancy to the investment decision process; this is the degree of uncertainty which exists relative to demand, profit, production, etc. Thus the degree of uncertainty on several aspects of an investment proposal may be the pivotal point weighing against the undertaking. In any event, identifying the degree of uncertainties of the many aspects of an investment venture increases the supporting knowledge for sound and reliable decision-making.

The Function of Valuation

The central theme of valuation is market value—the *present worth of future benefits*. Valuation is concerned with forecasts; forecasts of the future use and productivity of the property under study.

Property valuation is a vital part, where properly used and understood, in the sequential decision making process of management. Viewed in proper context and coupled with correct use, property valuation enables management to arrive at a terminal decision, i.e., sale, purchase, or exchange. Property valuation represents an important step and segment of managerial decision. The principal reason is readily apparent as the central problem of an investor–purchaser is to forecast future benefits *before* making a decision to invest.

Property valuation can encompass all of the following classes of property, where sale, purchase, or exchange is contemplated.

1. Market value of real property
2. Market value of personal property
3. Market value of other assets (patents, franchises, etc.)

In other instances, dictated largely by the type of property under consideration and the needs of a specific investor, property valuations might be oriented to any of the following pertinent concepts and determinations.

a. *Current Market Value of Property*—this type of study and analysis develops a market frame of reference in terms of probable sale–purchase; included in the analysis is a study of number and frequency of similar properties at the local, regional, or national level; type, extent and availability of financing and re-financing; trends in equity requirements and related returns; volume of transactions, anticipated productivity and best use of property, etc.

b. *Future Pattern of Value*—forecasts and predictions of the future pattern of value of the property enables an investor to make certain tentative decisions about the property prior to purchase. For example, if the outlook for maintaining the prevailing gross and net income is poor, any purchaser must of necessity think in terms of added investment for modernization and/or modification of the property. On the other hand, a property which is modern and in excellent condition places a prospective purchaser in another frame of reference as to needed improvements, etc. Both concepts of appreciation and depreciation of the property are important in terms of maintaining optimum equity position, yield on equity after satisfying all charges including mortgage amortization payments.

Prospective appreciation, in a growth situation venture, can be quantified and assessed in a short-run outlook should a re-sale of the property be considered within several years.

In any event, a forecast of future patterns of value of a property really reflects the market value concept—the present worth of future benefits; the duration and durability of future benefits in the form of net income are the essence of value today.

c. *Absorption Capacity*—the type, class, incidence of a property, and extent to which it is traded in the market has a bearing on its absorption capacity.

Absorption can be viewed from two distinct perspectives. In one case, the matter of absorption is vital where a new development is under way. Whether an apartment project, shopping center, or industrial production facility, the principal query is: can this facility, assuming it is competitive, get its share of the existing or forecast market? Or further, if displacement in the activity is necessary, what will the cost be to displace one or several competitors? In the second instance, absorption is viewed in terms of liquidation of the investment, this becoming necessary for one of many reasons. From this perspective the matter is viewed as to the lower or lowest range of value which must be met to effect disposal. Obviously, any liquidation requires time; therefore, where a sale is contemplated, schedules of asking prices based on market exposure, extent of market penetration, etc., must be developed. Finally, a lower limit or liquidation price might be established should all other efforts fail after proper exposure time in the market.

Fundamental Valuation Principles

Many of the present day concepts and principles utilized in the valuation of real property were developed by classical economists. The contributions of Ricardo on land rent, Fisher on interest and Von Thunen on industrial location are well known to students of valuation.

Real estate as a heterogeneous commodity, a combination of land and the technology of man, is susceptible to market forces as are all other commercial products. Its uniqueness stems from immobility; therefore, real estate markets to a large degree are local in nature. Collectively, the attributes of immobility, indestructibility, and environmental bias make real estate a distinct market commodity.

Against this backdrop, the following principles and concepts find application in the study and analysis of real property.

1. *Demand*—some principal determinants influencing the demand for real estate are: (a) population, (b) employment, (c) income/family ratio, (d) personal debt, (e) family formation, (f) housing-building costs, (g) mortgage/ratio, (h) foreclosure rate, (i) lessee/ownership, (j) rental vacancies, (k) rate of demolitions, (l) number of substandard units, (m) construction costs, (n) interest rates, (o) mortgage ratios, (p) land prices,

(q) technological innovation, (r) sociological changes, and (s) political trends.
2. *Supply*—while supply of real estate is influenced largely by the same forces as demand, the following factors represent the more important in point of time: (a) high construction costs, (b) high land prices, (c) high financing costs, (d) labor shortages, (e) excessive vacancies, (f) excessive number of units for sale, and (g) high rates of foreclosures.
3. *Principle of Highest and Best Use*—the most profitable legal use at the time of appraisal. The most profitable use means that use which produces the greatest net return in money to land, during the foreseeable future. The use must be within the realm of probability.
4. *Principle of Surplus Productivity*—the value of land tends to be fixed by the present and anticipated net income attributable to it within the *present* economic environment.
5. *Principle of Anticipation*—future benefits anticipated are translated today into so many dollars that reflect value of the property.
6. *Principle of Economic Size* [1]—relationship of size and value; a commodity in size resulting in maximum aggregate and/or unit value(s), a point in size that imputes decrements in aggregate and/or units value(s) for added increase in size.
7. *Principle of Economic Division* [1]—related to optimum use—allocation of land, buildings, etc., where the cumulative value(s) of the parts exceeds the value of the whole; that increment in total value attributable to the division of the whole (spatial units of land, improvements, or combination thereof) into feasible optimum economic size units thereby maximizing net return and values.
8. *Principle of Change*—changes which affect the utility and value of real estate, i.e., change in the surrounding neighborhood, technology, etc.
9. *Principle of Contribution*—the incre-

ment or decrement in value generated by adding or deducting some of the amounts of the several agents of production (land, capital, labor, etc.).

10. *Principle of Increasing and Decreasing Returns*—essentially the concept of "increasing returns to scale."

11. *Principle of Balance*—concerned with the proportionality of the agents of production.

12. *Principle of Utility*—value of property and its use equated in terms of time and location; usefulness of property.

13. *Principle of Conformity*—concerned with compatibility of land uses, architectural design, and the socioeconomic background of areas and neighborhoods.

14. *Principle of Integration*—concerned with the nucleation of compatible and complementary urban land uses.

15. *Principle of Substitution*—the value of a commodity is limited and controlled by the cost of an alternative and equivalent commodity that is available for purchase.

16. *Principle of Competition*—competition is synonymous with an existing market; the extent of competition depends on the degree of a market, i.e., the scarcity or abundance of a commodity.

17. *Principle of Regression*—concerned with the decline in utility, desirability and consequent marketability of real property; the forces of time, innovation, technological progress, changes of locational patterns and their individual and collective effect on the value and marketability of real estate.

Methods of Valuation

As earlier noted, the process of property valuation is utilized to measure market value, i.e., the present worth of future benefits. While the history of a property can be meaningful, it is the future use of the property, actual and anticipated, which generates value today.

The beginning point of a valuation

is the collection of data and information which may have a bearing on the value of the property. The following represents the minimum of information needed to properly analyze a typical real property investment.

1. *Data involved in the study of productivity.*
   a. Data relating to revenue productivity.
   b. Data relating to operating expenses.
   c. Data relating to new technology, methods, etc.

2. *Data involved in the study of utility.*
   a. Data relating to obsolescence (plant equipment, processes).
   b. Data relating to urban and regional growth.
   c. Data relating to architecture.
   d. Data relating to long-term prospect for property, products and services.

3. *Data involved in the study of investments.*
   a. Data relating to general market for investments.
   b. Data relating to financing of new ventures.
   c. Data relating to equity trends and public ownership.

4. *Data concerning the property.*
   a. Data relating to physical attributes of property.
   b. Data relating to ownership, leases, etc.

5. *Data concerning value distribution.*
   a. Data relating value allocation among land, buildings, equipment, patents, licenses, and franchises.
   b. Data relating to other short term costs and incomes.

Manifestly, the ascertainment of market value begins with a number of important analyses. These include:

Study of Productivity

An analysis of the productivity of property involves a forecast of future returns. Such an analysis involves an evaluation and identification of value creating attributes of the property.

A forecast of the productivity necessitates a study of the significant factors contributing to the value of the property; the components thus contributing to value are evaluated in terms of the most probable level of productivity, in point of time, up to the terminal end or productive life of the property. Accordingly, a study of productivity of the property terminates when the analysis reveals that costs of operation equal revenues.

Productivity analysis may also signal the end of the economic life of the property. Following this premise to its logical conclusion, such a study may identify the point in time when the value of the original property is less than the value of a new enterprise less the cost of the new land improvement.

A vital area of productivity analysis involves a detailed study of the components of the property which generate value. For example, where a large industrial firm is under consideration, property component productivity analysis may reveal significant obsolescence in some departments or divisions. The obsolescence may be significant to the point of necessitating early replacement or re-design. In some instances immediate replacement is feasible with sale of existing equipment for alternative and less intensive use.

Another instance where a study of the production capability of property contributes to sound managerial decisions is the matter of expanding markets. A given industrial firm may or may not have capability for expanded production. Manifestly, a component productivity study might reveal production constraints of sub-production industrial units. Given this type of analysis, management can evaluate a firm's

future competitive position in terms of expanding markets, probable production costs, revenues, profits, etc.

Finally, productivity analysis yields an important by-product, i.e., it develops a basis for judging the most probable liquidation price of the property. While perhaps secondary at the time of purchase, a tentative finding of the probable liquidation price may have an influence on the price offered for the property, etc.

While the earnings price ratio has its place and is an important tool of management in arriving at an investment decision, productivity analysis of a property goes several steps farther. Essentially it reduces to components all value generating aspects of a property, and further, identifies the probable economic life of each vital component. Implicit in these findings and determinations are forecasts of production capability over time, probable competitive position, timetable for terminal points of use of some parts of the property, etc.

Study of Utility

A study of the utility of a property is not independent of productivity analysis heretofore discussed, but rather is undertaken concurrently as part of a broad economic analysis and study.

Utility analysis is concerned with evaluating the usefulness of all the property; like productivity analysis, it also is concerned with the various components of the property under analysis. This facet of property valuation provides an insight into matters of superadequacy of equipment or portions of property, the extent of under investment in some phase of income generating units, and the extent of contribution that the several operating phases of the property make to the total income value pattern.

Accordingly, a study of the utility and related value of property can identify those segments that have use-value only; the remainder of the property may have feasible alternative use. For example, a study of a small industrial enterprise might reveal that the land and buildings are not only adaptable for an alternative use but that relocation to a new location is economically feasible since costs (including relocation) are less than the capital yield from an alternative use.

Study of Highest and Best Use

This highlights the central issue of property valuation. The issue is to identify the highest and best use of the property assuming the site is unimproved or with present improvements available for use and occupancy. A study of the highest and best use of property is made with the principal objective being the maximizing of net returns and resultant values.

The analysis identifies the best program of land use, possible succession of land uses, or a modification and/or modernization of the structure contemplating a new utilization program. The pivotal point in all analysis is economic feasibility of one program of use versus another which are pertinent matters of interest to every investor; *time, timing,* and probable *net return* from each identified course of action are formulated.

Within these circumscribed valuation findings management can make positive investment decisions as to sale, purchase, or retention and moderniza-

tion. The three vital elements of time, timing, and net return are of utmost importance. Collectively they reflect present and anticipated market conditions. Manifestly, the study of market conditions is difficult because market analysis is a deductive process. Therefore, the degree of change in markets is not as susceptible to a definitive prognosis as one might hope for in a critical situation.

However, plausible schedules concerning these important elements can be derived thereby providing a range of possibilities which reflect the best and most realistic courses of action.

Investor Oriented Value Findings

The process of property valuation facilitates a number of value derivations which can serve as guidelines for investor decision making. These value findings are (without order of preference or importance):

a. *Replacement Cost*—this concept reflects the current replacement cost of property under study. The well-founded economic principle states that the value of a thing should not exceed, as an upper limit of value, the present cost of production and/or substitution, all other things being equal. Accordingly, the replacement cost concept seems to provide a tentative ceiling on the value of property, assuming of course that replacement and/or production of a new facility is not unduly long, and further that construction costs are not increasing significantly. Either condition can make this value finding vulnerable.

b. *Investment Value*—this essentially represents the upper limit of an investor's bid; it reflects the individual investor's tax position, financial situation, interest in the investment, etc. It may reflect the present worth to the investor of the future returns capitalized at a rate acceptable to him predicated on his evaluation of the investment characteristics of the property.

c. *Market Price*—frequently referred to as the earnings–price ratio; this reflects what the property would probably sell for in the market under present conditions.

d. *Market Value*—reflects the present worth of future benefits derived from ownership of the property; more specifically defined as: the highest price estimated in terms of money which the property will bring if exposed for sale in the open market by a seller who is willing but not obliged to sell, allowing a reasonable time to find a buyer who is willing but not obliged to sell, allowing a reasonable time to find a buyer who is willing but not obliged to buy, both parties having full knowledge of all uses to which it is adapted and for which it is capable of being used. The following critical factors exist under the concept of fair market value.

1. A demand for the property exists, i.e., a reasonable number or buyers are in evidence.
2. The property will be exposed in the open market.

3. A reasonable time will be allowed to find a buyer.
4. Both buyer and seller have full knowledge regarding the adaptability and capability of the property for various uses.

e. *Value-in-Use*—this concept is applicable where the value of property results from the use to which it is put, and varies with the profitableness of the use, present and prospective, actual and anticipated; further, there is no pecuniary value outside of that which results from use of the property. Specifically, the attributes of the value-in-use concept are:

1. That the value of the property stems from use.
2. That value is not cost.
3. That value is not market price since in most cases no market, in the accepted sense, exists.
4. That value, generally, is not economic value.

The concept is implemented by an analysis to determine the cost to acquire a substitute property having equal facilities and utility which will provide similar services, amenities, etc. The technique has special adaptability where value findings are necessary concerning special-purpose property; these may be steel blast furnaces, airport runways, certain types of public utility properties, etc.

.   .   .

The *New* Real Estate Appraisal Process

Edwin M. Rams

All human activities and endeavors which require training, skill, and related adaptation and application of knowledge are in a constant state of change and evolution. In some disciplines, change in the state of the art, or the way of doing things, is traceable to internal or group concern or dissatisfaction; in other instances, externally generated research and development accelerates change, directly or indirectly, occasioned by the evolving state of knowledge. Additionally, client and market needs may also represent compelling incentives for progress.

The principal vantage point of this paper is prospective in nature, rather than retrospective in evaluation. For it is basic to progress in any field of interest, to take lessons of the past and form and construct building blocks of knowledge for the future. Such positivism is necessary to avoid entrapment in any proverbial "criticism for the sake of criticism" with no net gains or potential progress forthcoming.

Accordingly, those matters needing special attention, embellishment, or modification become the central point of any re-examination of the real estate appraisal process. An important *a-priori* is to ask just what is appraising, what does it entail, its discipline-parameters, etc. From this vantage point the functional activities of real estate appraising are examined; this in turn serves as a forum to formulate a new real estate appraisal process model.

Definitional-Functional Criteria

The real estate appraisal process can be simply defined as a mental process of ascribing the worth and value of real property interests through a series of steps and operations predicated on the attributes of the property. The combining of a mental activity related to a physical object and environment places a premium on the perceptual process. For it is what one sees, compares and evaluates that provides the foundation and input data for resolution of the worth and value of real estate.

Real estate appraisal is an observational-quantifying and accounting of human behavior as personified and translated via economic transactions (sales) in the marketplace. Consequently, visualizing, relating, and comparing are basic attributes and functions of real estate appraisal; these are also the keystones of the perceptual process. Therefore, in a definitional and functional context, perception can be considered

Reprinted from *Right of Way*, Vol. 23, No. 1, January 1976, by permission of the Editor.

the most important and demanding mental skill in the valuation of real property.

How an appraiser perceives and assesses an environment, location, neighborhood, competitiveness of adjacent housing projects, potential consumer acceptance of new office space, remaining economic life, et al, are just a few of the critical aspects and surrogate factors which provide the elements and the evidence for a resolution and final synthesis reflected in an opinion of value.

The general rubric of "experience" really means relating and identifying the present facts and circumstances with prior exposure of a similar nature. The mental process "retrieves, relates, sorts, rejects, and accepts" facts, figures, data, and relationships to delineate a congruency of the past to the present. The resultant is a series of thought-forms and mind-sets which when further differentiated and evaluated outline the basis of differences and similarities of present and past problems and situations. Because of these characteristics, perception is both subjective and probabilistic in nature.

The Resource Allocation Function

A basic modus operandi of the valuation function involves the analysis of scarce resources to optimize their utilization. Resources include land, capital, land improvements, etc.

As an example, a farm on the edge of an urbanized area is proposed for conversion to residential use. A basic inquiry and related analysis concerns what kind of residential use (single family, apartments, etc.), when should the development begin, proceed at what speed (absorption rate), at what prices, etc. Fundamentally, it is a highest and

best use study relating the allocation of land to the most viable uses profiled against markets and the time value of money to maximize yield from the undertaking and minimize risk, or potential failure of the venture.

Resource-best use assessments might be termed scenario analysis, i.e., alternative and/or sequential possible choices and conditions affecting land utilization and culminating in an optimum value of the property.

Manifestly, in the appraisal of real estate, every act of ascribing a value with supporting data and analysis does in fact, either expressly or by implication, attest to the proper or improper use of resources. An overimprovement or improper improvement signals a level of property dysfunction with increased and attendant functional risk. Conversely, statements in an appraisal that the subject use is in fact the highest and best use means that the appraiser has tested and analyzed all resources involved or required, and has determined that the present allocation/distribution /utilization of resources is optimum as of that time. In some instances, inputs of additional resources are valid assumptions of a final estimate of value. Whether these conclusions are derived via differential analysis, incremental analysis, or any other technique, this is what in fact the "message" of the report is conveying.

Resource allocation, and its analysis in the context of land utilization, represents a foremost activity and responsibility in the appraisal of real estate interests.

Value Links and Relatives

The value judgment concerning the worth of any real property, whether expressed by a layman or a highly qualified real estate appraiser, is subjective; it lies in the eyes of the beholder.

Basically then, the art of appraising real estate and ascribing a value (one of many kinds depending on purpose, objective, assumptions, etc.) involves the analysis of the linkage and relative assessments by others who are or were market participants at one time or another (buyers, sellers, etc.), based on their perception and consequent probabilistic resolution of value (price paid, offered, et al). This tangible evidence (market transactions) which has a series of probability profiles, a product of a state (S1) of economic-social-political-monetary environment, must be linked and related to a new state (S2) of environment; its relevancy and credibility must be judged, differentiated, and resolved for eventual use or nonuse.

A viable, meaningful, and operational real estate appraisal process is a model representing fundamental components which have influence, directly or indirectly, on the value of real property. The model should depict and recognize the practices, thinking, and motivations of the marketplace; a recognition of the interlocking actions of the several economic agents like financing and equity participation. Paralleling the realities of the marketplace is a prime requisite. Any model development or input data selection must also recognize its operational context, i.e., it must be structured in a fashion with proper qualification concerning the locational-competitive-environmental parameters which are central to the value of real property.

The real estate appraisal as an activity and its connectivity in a total market context is illustrated in Figure 1.

The interrelationships are a recognition of the competitive nature of real estate, i.e., the property in a neighborhood vis-a-vis other properties-neighborhoods in the city and urbanized areas. Essentially, it is an interfacing of an area or neighborhood, where a property is located, to the total market complex, thus giving credence to supply/demand in a spatial framework and the competitive attributes of the real estate marketplace. Each of these connecting links of the fabric of the marketplace can be briefly described as follows.

(a) Total Market Complex

Analysis of population, employment, income trends, and market segments quantified over time and profiled against supply/demand (consumer market alternatives) of similar facilities, houses, apartments, et al to formulate forecasts of demand. An important facet of this inquiry is the intensity of utilization (by kind, quality, location) of the standing inventory (surpluses/deficits of resources).

(b) Sub-Market Context

Study of the area/neighborhood vis-a-vis the city-metro area. Within this framework value attributes, as identified and differentiated, of the property are ascertained. This analysis, plus an assessment of market transactions, provides key inputs to the final phase, i.e., the property context.

(c) Property Context

This analysis and final synthesis is predicated on inputs of supply/demand (function of potential marketability) which has as a foundation the trends, developments, and expectations of the basic fabric of a real estate market, i.e., population, employment, and income of the residents. Quantification is accomplished with this backdrop and concerns the best probable use of the property,

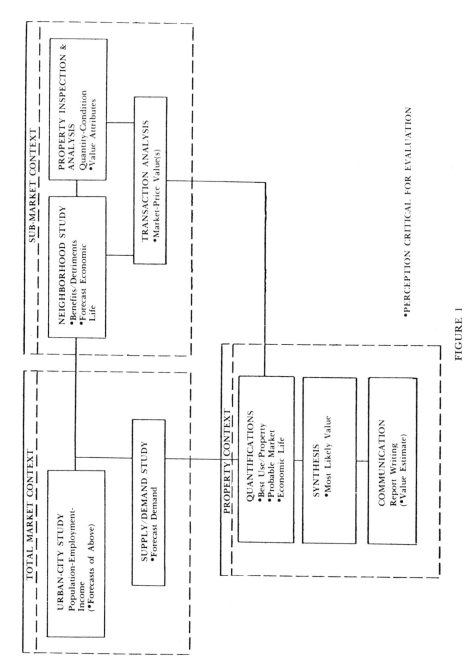

FIGURE 1

Functional Activities of Real Estate Appraising (From *Rams' Real Estate Appraising Handbook.*
© 1975 by Prentice-Hall, Inc. Reproduced by permission.)

probable market(s), economic life, etc. A synthesis of all these factors, forces, trends, and developments is resolved into a most likely value for a particular real property interest. Finally, a report is formulated.

What should be noted in this flow diagram of real estate appraising activities is the linkage of the various components which generate value in the marketplace. Also, significance of two factors which have pre-eminence in the total sphere of activities, i.e., perception and forecasting. They address themselves to the central issue of real estate appraisal and circumscribe the concept of market value—the present worth of future benefits.

These then can be viewed as functional activities of real estate appraising.

Formulating A New Model

The evaluation of real estate appraising activities, from a functional viewpoint, serves as a foundation to formulate a new model appropriate to the importance of major and subdominant matters of inquiry and analysis. A viable and relevant model is not predicated on rote or a formula-approach. Rather, integration of important components into a system which requires: (a) attention and priority to those elements and factors about a property which have a high degree of correspondence to any ultimate conclusion of value, and (b) the market demand for the property, having identified its distinctive qualities and attributes in a locational context.

A credible real estate appraisal process model must satisfy four principal elements of a problem solving context, i.e., genesis, diagnosis, analysis, and synthesis. For it is elementary that a query, what is the market value of a given property, is a question proposed for consideration and solution—a problem.

The genesis of an appraisal problem concerns the perception and identification of the problem based on (1) the purpose of the value estimate, (2) the kind of value estimate (definition and underlying assumptions) to be ascertained, and (3) the physical-environmental-economic-social setting and parameters of real property interests which are the subject of an estimate of value.

Diagnosis of an appraisal problem involves the refinement of objectives and related description and understanding in terms of major components of the total property under study. This may involve aspects of physical improvements, their adequacy-inadequacy and condition, property interests, locational attributes, etc. Problem diagnosis is crucial simply because any failure to clearly understand an assignment, may subsequently result in introducing redundant or circuitous assumptions, conditions, premises, or methodology, and lead to fuzzy, chance, or simply wrong solutions.

Problem analysis of data, trends, and components of a substantive nature is necessary to avoid error—simply not knowing enough about the key factors of the marketplace and their pervasive influence on the value of property. Research of the market is the answer. However just gathering sales and drawing of inferences is not research; developing market insight of the "what, where, and WHY" of economic activity (sales) and related economic forces and their degree of impact on value is the forum and substance of analysis.

Problem synthesis involves the integration, via translation and quantification, of the indexes of value into a final solution (value estimate). To synthesize means to build up and form a composite into a unified entity; the selection of plausible and believable evidence with sufficient connectivity to provide a solid foundation for ultimate resolution. However, all value synthesis must be underscored by an important caveat, i.e., quantitative and quantified data only has relevance in terms of plans, preferences, decisions, states of information, and expectations of the real estate marketplace as of the date of the appraisal report. Manifestly, realistic appraisal methodology must transcend the property-neighborhood-sales transaction matrix and include the catholic vantage point of analysis of urban dynamics and economics.

The new real estate appraisal process model, as depicted in Figure 2, is the author's concept of a systems approach consistent with the problem solution matrix discussed. The centrality of the process revolves around two foremost interdependent elements, market supply and demand analysis, and highest and best use studies.

The following is a brief discussion of the ten step process.

I. Identification of rights and interests which are the subject of appraisal. A concurrent activity is a physical inspection of the property, area, and perception of the locational environment. This stage also addresses itself to the legal aspects (zoning, deed restrictions, etc.) of the present, permitted, or contemplated use(s).

II. This stage involves the first proximation, or first judgment, based on an appraiser's perception of the best use of the property. It is a hypothesis at most —subject to testing, validation, analysis, etc.

III. The next stage involves a consideration of the physical-locational-environmental attributes of the subject property, whether vacant or improved, against thirteen basic and important real property value principles. The comparison of each principle is predicated

on a point of reference (which is a requirement for making all kinds of measurements) called a *value parity index*. Simply stated, a value parity index is a market derived basis which shows the attitudes and actions of the marketplace towards various property attributes and characteristics by kind and quality of property. For example, the abutment of an old run-down and cheap house to a railroad right-of-way may be an acceptable locational factor, however marginal. On a newer and more expensive house, the market may find this either unacceptable or at most tolerable at huge discount of price. There is a market central tendency of values/prices equated out over property location-quality-condition, etc. Each of these represent value parity indexes for a particular kind of property under study.

Experienced and knowledgeable appraisers know from the performance of various markets and market segments that value of real estate is either inhibited or propelled, depending on market attitudes, their differentiation, and the kind, quality, and location of real property. The indexes change over time largely attributable to available and competitive (product-price-location) market alternatives, neighborhood changes, technological innovations, broad socio-economic development, etc. In a contemporary context, the energy crises could in the near future, change the mode from large spacious single family housing life styles to more compact and densely developed energy saving housing.

IV. At this step a summary of the shortcomings and positive characteristics of a parcel of real estate can be formulated. A second stage hypothesis of highest and best use can be evolved. The basis, though still tentative, has been market derived and predicated on the applicable value parity indexes. For

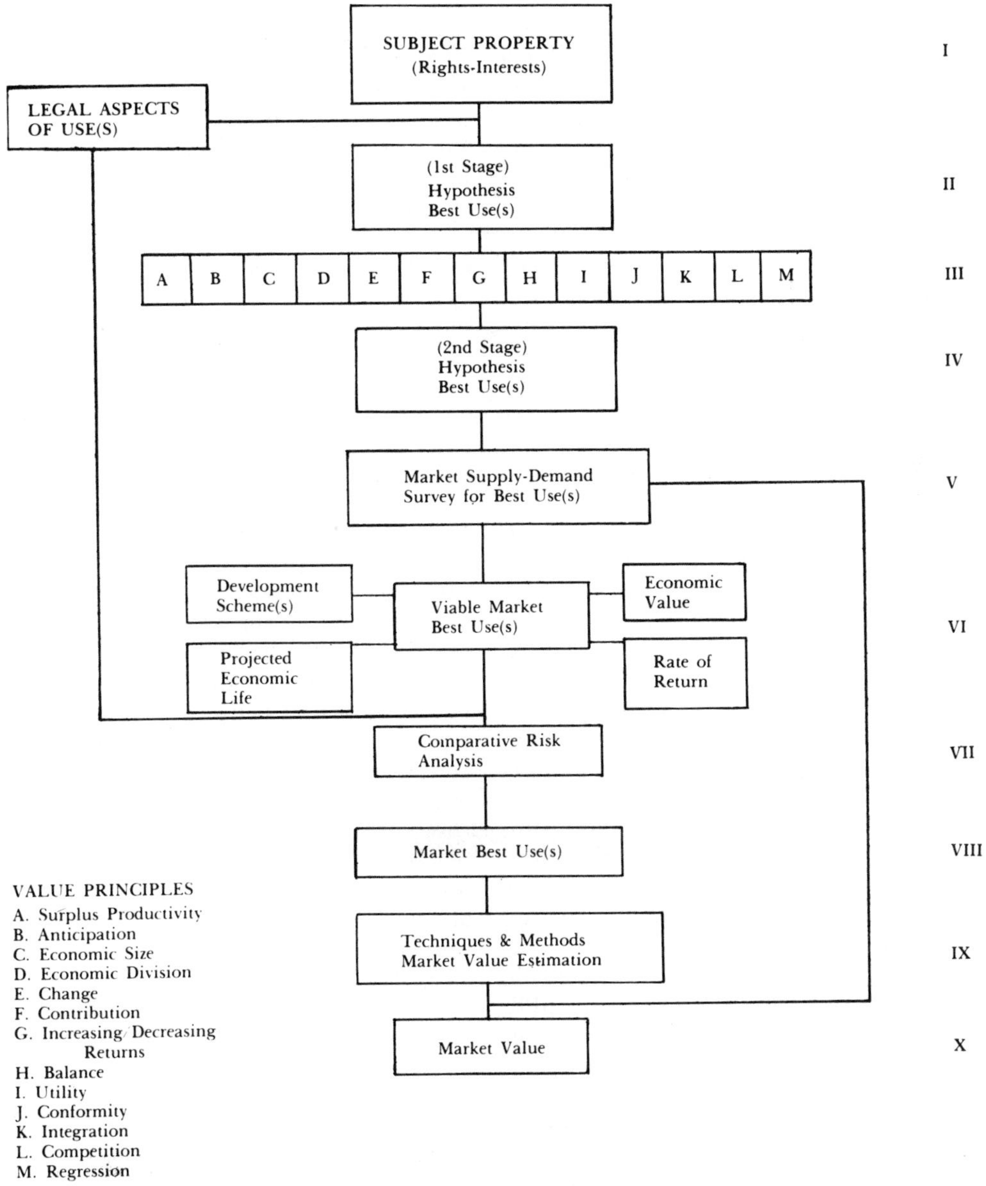
SUBJECT PROPERTY
(Rights-Interests)
I
LEGAL ASPECTS OF USE(S)
(1st Stage)
Hypothesis
Best Use(s)
II
A B C D E F G H I J K L M
III
(2nd Stage)
Hypothesis
Best Use(s)
IV
Market Supply-Demand
Survey for Best Use(s)
V
Development Scheme(s)
Viable Market
Best Use(s)
Economic Value
Projected Economic Life
Rate of Return
VI
Comparative Risk Analysis
VII
Market Best Use(s)
VIII
Techniques & Methods
Market Value Estimation
IX
Market Value
X
VALUE PRINCIPLES
A. Surplus Productivity
B. Anticipation
C. Economic Size
D. Economic Division
E. Change
F. Contribution
G. Increasing/Decreasing Returns
H. Balance
I. Utility
J. Conformity
K. Integration
L. Competition
M. Regression

FIGURE 2

The Real Estate Appraisal Process (From *Rams' Real Estate Appraising Handbook.* © 1975 by Prentice-Hall, Inc. Reproduced by permission.)

example, a newer house in an old neighborhood might be readily marketable with some discounting of price; however, the anticipation principle, via value parity indexes, suggests a significant "downside trend," thus necessitating a much larger discounting for the implied marketability under a fair market value concept.

V. A market supply-demand study of similar and competing properties, *having the same or similar highest and best use(s)* is made to test the marketability of the tentatively hypothesized use(s). This can signal, verify, or confirm, the extent of "upside," "no-change," or "downside" of market trends and implications of marketability as related to the best use premise derived and the future of the property (if improved). On vacant land, modifications to the best use or change of use may be indicated along with formulating client advice concerning one of several postures i.e., wait, develop, or sell. An analyst-appraiser must particularize both supply and demand in terms of the specific location vis-a-vis the property and its environs.

VI. Step six results in a delineation of the viable best use(s) for testing their respective economic feasibility. Factor tests might include, but are not limited to, rate of return (yield on equity cash flows, etc.), economic value, economic life, and related development/rehabilitation/property modification schemes as appropriate to the property under analysis. An important feedback concerns the legal aspects of the proposed use(s).

VII. Since all futures involve risk of various kinds, a comparative study of risk (potential loss in value, failure of investment, etc.) of the highest and best use is undertaken. On improved properties, the extent of property dysfunction (functional risk) may be important;

in other instances, the kind of property may reveal the principal market being constituted with largely risk-averters, thereby signalling price concessions to facilitate marketability within a reasonable period of time. In any event, a number of different measures of risk are accomplished, as appropriate, on the type of property under appraisal.

VIII. At this state the market best use(s) are ascertained based on: (a) the quality, kind, and locational-physical-environmental attributes of the property, (b) a realistic view of the market for and the competitive environment (supply-demand studies), (c) economic viability of the use(s), and (e) the least risk, on a comparative basis to alternate best use or uses.

IX. Measures of value of the best use are utilized which are applicable and credible. An important feedback, and as a further confirmation of market viability, are the findings derived under the market supply-demand survey. This builds a bridge between retrospective market evidence (sales transactions), current state and expectations of the market (asking price-offers), and prospective value (market value)—all placed within a competitive framework, i.e., market supply and demand of similar, available, and alternative properties.

X. Based on all prior data, trends, analysis, interpretation, and derivations, a market value estimate of a given property is ascertained.

Conclusion

The outlined new real estate appraisal process formulates a distinct trilogy of: resource—market—value.

The resource is the property, improved or vacant, with distinct characteristics, qualities, and attributes. As resource analysis and allocation is central to marketability, a clear understanding of this facet (via value parity indexes) is necessary to measure levels and potentials of marketability.

The market element of the trilogy concerns the potential receptivity of the resource in the market. Mere resource presence does not ipso facto assure or assume, by any means, its marketability.

Value being the third and last element of the trilogy is a consequence of the other two elements, resources and markets. For it is basic to our economic system that resources-products (the Ed-

sel for example) do not in themselves have value. Rather, it is the needs and wants of consumers, commensurate with their financial abilities, which give rise to value of products and commodities.

The worthiness of any method, technique, process, or model should be evaluated on a scale of relevancy and analogy to the real world and its likelihood to improve the scope of knowledge and quality of performance of its users. Whether the recommended model meets the stringency of this criteria can only be evaluated through application, adaptation and use, and consequent results.

Priorities in Appraisal Analysis

David W. Walters

Real estate appraisal is a complex process requiring the estimation of many parameters. Certain of the parameters which must be determined have more influence on the accuracy of the valuation estimate than others. However, there is little quantitative information to aid the appraiser in deciding which variables must be estimated with greater care. This article presents results of a computerized study of the relative importance of various inputs to the income capitalization approach to appraisal. It indicates which variables require careful estimation and which variables can be merely approximated with little effect on the accuracy of the value estimate.

The Problem

The process of real estate valuation frequently requires the real estate analyst to make and justify various assumptions concerning the subject property. In applying the cost approach to value, he must estimate current construction parameters and account for physical deterioration. In applying the market approach, he must select suitable comparables and estimate corrections in their values to account for differences in size, amenities and style. In using the income capitalization approach to value, the analyst must predict future property value appreciation, current money market conditions and typical capitalization rates.

The fact that real estate valuation requires many assumptions concerning input variables has made real estate appraisal subject to criticisms from those unfamiliar with its methodology. However, skilled appraisers are quick to point out that there are many checks within the appraisal process. For example, by using a combination of all valuation methods, certain discrepancies can be dealt with. In addition, the experienced analyst knows that certain inputs are more critical than others, and he devotes more time and effort to estimating those inputs than less significant factors.

For example, in applying the cost approach to value, the analyst spends more time estimating the cost of the building shell than estimating the cost of door knobs. He knows that the careful calculation of shell costs is more important to the overall accuracy of his appraisal than an exact door knob price determination. Similarly, in applying the market approach, the analyst spends more time in selecting comparables in terms of location and size than in accounting for differences in roof pitch or room color. He knows that certain attributes are more significant than others.

The fact that certain variables are more important to the overall estimate of value is a phenomenon intuitively understood by all appraisers, but rarely documented by hard facts. Within the cost approach, there is some degree of quantification because comparative component costs are available. However, in applying the other methods of appraisal, many appraisers focus their efforts on certain factors without justification for their choice. Present studies using regression analysis on market data are beginning to reveal that many variables which appraisers believed to be important in the market approach to value are not as significant as some less obvious variables.[1] In the use of the income capitalization approach, analysts know that correct estimate of future value appreciation and of current interest rates are important; however, few are aware of which inputs have more effect on the accuracy of the value estimate.

Methodology and Results

The purpose of this study is to demonstrate the relative importance of factors used in the income capitalization approach to value. With the knowledge of which factors are most significant in an income capitalization estimate of value, the analyst could more effectively allocate his time, energy and resources. He would also be able more easily to defend his valuation, knowing which errors in estimation can be ignored and which errors are truly crucial.

The author believed that the relative importance of each input to the income capitalization approach to value could be determined by measuring the effect of a ten percent change in each variable on the project's value. If, for example, a ten percent change in the project's net income has a greater impact on the value than a ten percent change in the available interest rate; then the analyst would know that more attention should be spent estimating future income streams than in predicting interest rate conditions.

To measure the impact of changes in each of the variables necessary for the income capitalization approach to value, the author postulated a typical real estate income project. The characteristics of this project are listed in Table 1. Computer programs developed at the Center for Real Estate and Urban Economics at The University of California, Berkeley, were used to

TABLE 1

Variable	Value
Net income (dollars)	$100,000
Desired equity yield (%)	15.00%/yr.
Interest rate (%)	8.00%/yr.
Loan-to-value ratio (%)	75%
Holding period (years)	10 years
Appreciation (%)	30%
Mortgage term (years)	30 years

---

[1] For a thorough analysis of use of regression analysis and computer techniques in assessment and appraisal, see "Computerized Assessment Administration" by Jerome Dasso (IAAO: Chicago, 1973) and "Automated Mass Appraisal of Real Property" a compilation of papers from a seminar sponsored by IAAO, the John C. Lincoln Institute and the International Tax Program of Harvard Law School (IAAO: Chicago, 1973).

generate values, using the Ellwood or internal rate of return capitalization process.[2] The value of the project was first determined using the characteristics listed in Table 1 ($1,187,242). Then, additional values were determined by changing each factor plus and minus ten percent. Tables 2 and

TABLE 2

Variable	+10% Change	Change in Value (%)
Net income	$111,000	10.00
Desired equity yield	16.50%/yr.	7.00
Interest rate	8.80%/yr.	6.60
Loan-to-value ratio	82.5%	6.44
Holding period	11 years	2.19
Appreciation	33%	1.79
Mortgage term	33 years	.40

TABLE 3

Variable	−10% Change	Change in Value (%)
Net income	$90,000	10.00
Desired equity yield	13.50%/yr.	6.23
Interest rate	7.20%/yr.	5.73
Loan-to-value ratio	67.5%	5.71
Holding period	9 years	4.06
Appreciation	27%	1.73
Mortgage term	27 years	.54

3 contain a summary of the changes in each factor and the corresponding changes in value.

Figure 1 is a graphic display of the changes in value corresponding to ten percent changes (plus and minus) in each variable. An examination of Figure 1 indicates that changes in certain

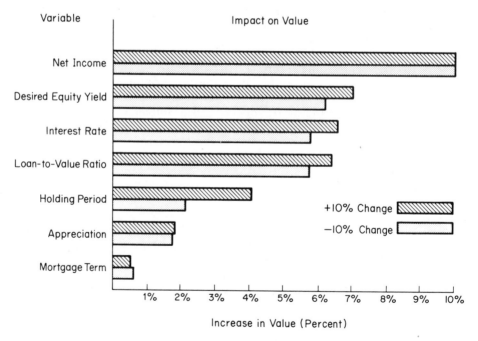

FIGURE 1

[2] See "Ellwood, Inwood and the Internal Rate of Return" by Paul F. Wendt, *The Appraisal Journal,* October 1967.

variables have a great effect on value while changes in other variables have less effect. This suggests that errors in estimating certain variables would have more effect on the accuracy of the value determination than errors in estimating others.

It is clear that the single most important component to valuation by the income capitalization method is, of course, net income. Since all capitalization rate formulae apply some rate to net income, it would be unusual not to have a one-to-one change in value as net income is changed. However, it is important to note that the great impact of changes in net income implies that errors in the estimation of net income streams have a greater impact on the value than do errors in estimating any other variable. This suggests that the analyst should allocate substantially more resources, time and effort to establishing the net income stream than any other input to the income capitalization method.

The desired equity yield of the investor also has a great influence on the value of the property. Changes in the investor's yield requirements from 15 percent per year to 13.5 percent per year increased the value of the project by 6.23 percent. Similarly, changes in the desired equity yield from 15 percent per year to 16.5 percent per year changed the value estimate by 7 percent. Appraisers have long known that each appraisal is closely linked with the buyer's or user's characteristics and expectations. Indeed, it may very well be that there ought to be a fourth method of appraisal called the "who is going to read this report" method. However, even more important is the fact that a misjudgement of the desired equity yield to be applied to the income capitalization process can result

in large value discrepancies. Any appraiser using the income capitalization method should carefully justify any equity yield assumptions.

Financing parameters have always been considered an important input to income capitalization appraisal methods. Figure 1 indicates that errors in interest rate and loan-to-value estimates can have substantial effects on the accuracy of any value estimate. A variance in the interest rate from 8 percent per year to 8.8 percent per year results in a 6.60 percent change in value. A variance in the interest rate from 8 percent per year to 7.2 percent per year results in a 5.73 percent change in value. Similarly, a change in the loan-to-value ratio from 75 percent to 82.5 percent results in a 6.44 percent change in value, while a change from 75 percent to 67.5 percent results in a 5.71 percent change in value. The relatively great effect of changes in financing characteristics suggests that the analyst should devote much time to his estimate of mortgage market conditions.

The relatively small impact of changes in the holding period of the property suggests that less attention can be spent determining the optimum holding period than in estimating other variables, such as net income or desired equity yield. An increase in the holding period by 10 percent only affects the value by 2.19 percent. Similarly, a decrease in the holding period only affects the value by 4.06 percent. While an accurate estimate of the holding period is certainly important to income capitalization methods, the analyst can provide a better overall appraisal by devoting less time to estimating the optimum holding period and more time to estimating the net income or desired equity yield. Errors in determining the holding period are less significant than errors in estimating the net income or desired equity yield.

A somewhat surprising result of this study is the small effect that changes in property value appreciation have on the value of the project. A 10 percent change in the project's appreciation over ten years (from 30 percent to 27 percent or from 30 percent to 33 percent) resulted in very small changes in the value (1.79 percent and 1.73 percent respectively). While appreciation potential has long been associated with real estate investment, the relatively small impact of changes in the appreciation projected on the value of the property suggests that there are other more important components to overall real estate value. So long as there is some appreciation, it is more important accurately to estimate shorter term income and financing parameters than to forecast value growth far into the future.

Figure 1 indicates that the factor with the least effect on value is the mortgage term (life). This, again, shows a priority system in allocating the analyst's time and effort. Very large errors can be made in assigning a suitable mortgage life without materially affecting the accuracy of the value estimate. Therefore, the analyst should be justified in spending very little time and effort on estimations of mortgage terms. The time saved could be spent estimating income streams or financing parameters.

Summary

The results of this study demonstrate that certain variables are more important in the income capitalization process than others. The estimation of net income is an activity which should be given the most effort and time in any appraisal process. Similarly, the analyst should devote considerable effort to an accurate determination of the investor's required equity yield and the interest rate and loan-to-value ratio. Errors in estimating those variables could materially influence the accuracy of the value estimate. However, the determination of the optimum holding period, future value appreciation, or the life of the mortgage can be done with less precision. Errors in the estimation of those variables has relatively little impact on the value estimate.

While accurate appraisal requires careful attention to the details of estimating each and every variable, the realities of the world prevent the appraiser from devoting as much time and effort to all possible variables as he would like. The results of this study indicate that the appraiser can be justified in spending little time in the calculation of some variables. The time saved can be reallocated to the more careful estimation of other, more significant variables, with a resulting improvement of the overall quality of the appraisal and the appraiser's product.

EDITOR'S NOTE

For a more incisive study of discount rates and risk in the context of discounted cash flow analysis, a series of risk-rating tables is included in the author's *Real Estate Appraising Handbook*, Prentice-Hall, Inc., Englewood Cliffs, N.J., 1975.

The tables also permit the development of risk profiles on the cash flows and the reversion based on discount rates used versus those of competitive properties exhibiting less than or more than the risk attributable to a given property under analysis.

The Use of Discount Cash Flow Analysis

Lloyd D. Hanford, Jr.

Discount cash flow (DCF) analysis is growing in popularity as an appraisal tool. It is important to recognize at the outset that DCF in its modern context *is not* a market value appraisal method or approach except in certain limited appraisal problem areas. The principle of DCF is not new to the real estate appraisal field. Research on the Inwood Premise will reveal that appraisers have been employing the discounting concepts for quite some time. The term *Discount Cash Flow Analysis* is somewhat new to appraisal jargon and deserves being placed in proper perspective.

Many seasoned practitioners recall using the Inwood Premise as an approach to market value in and of itself. The criteria generally employed required that the income stream have the character of an annuity. Thus use of the Inwood Premise was generally restricted to long-term leases at fixed rates except in those instances where a lessor's or lessee's interest in a lease was being valued.

There was much to be said for the Inwood Premise as it did attempt to reflect the present worth of an investment by reducing the income stream and reversion to their respective present values. The inherent weakness in

the Inwood Premise as a valuation method lay not in the process but rather in the assumptions surrounding selection of reversionary value. It was generally accepted that the reversion be valued, for the purpose of discounting, at its future depreciated value. Hence, if a property costs $150,000 with building representing $100,000, future value might have been set at $37,500 based on a 40-year life and a 25-year lease term. Thus, reversionary value would have been fixed at $87,500 at the end of the twenty-fifth year.

Appraisers have long recognized that, while the Inwood Premise was not the magic answer, the assumptions employed in direct capitalization also had some limitations. Unquestionably the practice of capitalizing the present stabilized net income into value is limited by the fact that an increasing or decreasing income stream over the holding term is more probable than a level income. Purchasers of investment property acquire the right to the future benefits of the property which are generally expressed in terms of cash outflows from the property. That these periodic cash flows will vary from period to period is a probability as well as a possibility. Hence, using a discount cash flow analysis would, on

Reprinted, with permission, from the November/December 1973 issue of *The Real Estate Appraiser*, Society of Real Estate Appraisers, Chicago, Illinois.

cursory examination, appear to provide a more reliable picture as it allows the variable income flows to be valued at given points in time.

Unfortunately, the DCF analysis does not qualify as a market appraisal approach or method for two primary reasons:

1. In order to make a study of future income streams, the analyst must make *assumptions* about the quantity and quality of the future income stream. This involves making a prediction under circumstances of great uncertainty. Unless the quantity of net income is fixed by lease contract as to its variability, a prediction of future rent levels and operating expenses is an educated guess under conditions of uncertainty. Who can say with certainty that net will increase 1 percent, 2 percent, 5 percent or 10 percent each 1, 2, 3, 5 or 10 years? Failing to be able to predict with certainty limits the utility of DCF analysis as a method or approach to market value. This would not be the case under the circumstance of a long lease with full operating cost escalation plus a fixed increase in base rental each 3, 5 or 10 years. Then the amount of net could be accurately established as to the future. Further, the discount rate used only relates to the present and reflects the opportunity rate for capital today. Application of today's opportunity rate to futures has some limitations. The assumptions inherent in employing DCF analysis can produce distortion as will be demonstrated in examples to follow.

2. Appraisers must try to reflect market thinking in arriving at market value. Purchasers do not usually purchase based on the discounted present worth of future benefits. Rather, where present stabilized net is *at market* purchasers emphasize net, not future net in reaching the price to be paid for a property. For this reason appraisers must heavily rely on present stabilized net in forming a market value opinion.

In making a discount cash flow analysis the analyst makes a prediction of the reversionary value at the end of the holding period. These predictions or assumptions can cause substantial variations in the answers produced. To demonstrate this point the following example will be useful:

Fact Situation: Office building.

Loan: $1,500,000, 8.25 percent interest, 25 years.

Payable: $141,921 per annum with a remaining balance of $964,248 at the end of the fifteenth year.

Current net income: $160,000 after vacancy and operating expenses.

Net after debt service: $18,079.

Leases are 5-year term.

Holding period: 15 years.

Discount rate: 9 percent.

Analyze using the assumptions that net will increase at 5 percent simple each 5 years and 10 percent simple each 5 years and that the reversion would be based on a capitalization of net at 9 percent.

| | Five Percent | | Ten Percent | |
Period	Net	After Debt	Net	After Debt
1–5	$160,000	$18,079	$ 160,000	$18,079
6–10	$168,000	$26,079	$ 176,000	$34,079
11–15	$176,000	$34,079	$ 192,000	$50,079
Reversion: Sixteenth year income $184,000			$ 208,000	
at 9%: $2,045,000			$2,310,000	

Present value (PV) of cash flow discounted:

	Five Percent			Ten Percent		
1. PV years 1–5, $18,079 @ 9%		$ 70,321		$ 18,079 @ 9%	$	70,321
2. PV years 6–10, $26,079 @ 9%				$ 34,079 @ 9%		
$101,438, 5 years deferred @ 9%		65,927		$ 132,555		86,152
3. PV years 11–15, $34,079 @ 9%						
$132,555, 10 years deferred @ 9%		55,993		$ 50,079 @ 9%		
				$ 194,790		82,281
4. Reversion	$2,045,000			$2,130,000		
Less loan bal. (rounded)	—945,000			—965,000		
Net reversion	$1,080,000			$1,345,000		
PV 15 years delayed @ 9%		296,501				369,254
Total		$ 488,742				$ 608,008
5. Original loan		1,500,000				1,500,000
Present value for purchase price purposes		$1,988,742				$2,108,008

In this example the first 5 years of income is valued based on the PV of the 5 years income stream discounted at 9 percent. The second 5 years income is first valued based on a 9 percent discount; however, the resulting value is delayed 5 years and thus must be further discounted to reflect the present worth of a future income stream. The same process applies to the third 5 years except that it is delayed 10 years and must thus be discounted to reflect that delay.

The reversion occurs at the end of the 15-year holding period and its value is predicated on the income for the years 16–20. The gross value of the reversion is adjusted by deducting the remaining loan balance at the end of the year 15 reflecting the net cash. The present worth of this reversion is based on discounting at 9 percent based on a payment that is 15 years delayed. It is a single payment that will be received in 15 years. Thus its value is the price that would be paid today for a payment of that amount to be received in 15 years with money worth 9 percent (discount rate).

This example should demonstrate that the basic assumption of the quantity of future income (or reversion) is very influential on the result. In general one could, under present economic conditions, predict a growth in income of up to 20 percent or more each 5 years without departing from *reasonable* anticipation based on past rental growth rates. These basic assumptions permit too wide a variation to permit estimating market value based upon them.

With these limitations qualified, what is the appraisal use of the discount cash flow analysis? With the exception of certain special applications DCF analysis is primarily an analytical tool that provides an assumptive basis for *buy–sell* decision making. DCF analysis *does not* provide the answer to present market value. Appraisers will find DCF analysis an invaluable consulting tool to be used in advising clients on *buy–sell* decisions. Consider the following examples:

1. **Fact:** Retail store currently leased at $25,000 per year net with 5 years remaining; current appraised value is $275,000. An offer is received for $250,-

000 after 5 months of good exposure. The owner asks the appraiser for advice as to whether the offer should be accepted. The appraiser's records indicate that the present income is below market and all available data strongly indicate that 5 years hence net will increase to $28,500 and a new 10-year lease would be reasonable to expect. The property has a remaining economic life of more than 25 years and is well located for growth purposes. Based on the increase in net to $28,500, the property should increase in value to $315,000.

PV 5 years income $25,000 @ 9% discount	$ 97,241
PV of $315,000 reversion 5 years delayed @ 9%	204,729
Present value of future benefits	$301,970

Advice: If the owner concurs with the assumption that income will increase to 28,500 and that worth will increase to $315,000 in 5 years, then it is better to hold than to sell at $250,000. The value of the property to its owner exceeds its value to the purchaser.

2. In the foregoing example, assume that the seller is offered a trade into a property net leased for 20 years at $22,000 for the first 5 years, $26,000 for the second 5 years and $40,000 per year for the last 10 years with the reversion at $445,000.

1. PV $22,000 for 5 years @ 9%	$ 85,572
2. PV $26,000 for 5 years @ 9%, 5 years delayed	65,728
3. PV $40,000 for 10 years @ 9%, 10 years delayed	108,435
4. Reversion $445,000, 20 years delayed at 9%	71,372
Present value of future benefits	$331,107

Advice: Even though the present income would be reduced, the exchange would appear justified as the value benefits to be received from the new property exceed the value of the benefits from the present holding.

3. In the first example assume that the appraiser's data indicated that at the end of 5 years, changes taking place in the neighborhood would support an assumption of declining rents and that the probable future re-leasing rate would be $21,000 per year with the future capitalized value at $235,000.

1. PV of current 5 year $25,000 income stream @ 9%	$ 97,241
2. PV of $235,000 5 years delayed @ 9%	152,734
Total	$249,975

Advice: Even though the present income net would indicate a market value presently of $275,000, an offer of $250,000 is consistent with long-term projections and should be considered provided the seller agrees with the assumed probability of declining rents and value.

4. A client is offered a retail property at $1,275,000, netting $102,000. Current opportunity rates indicate that the purchaser should purchase to yield 9 percent. Serious negotiations at a price of $1,135,000 produced the firm counter offer of $1,275,000. The purchaser likes the property and could advantageously move his own business into it at the end of the current 3-year lease term. The purchaser currently operates out of space 75 percent the size of subject and pays $105,000 on a volume of $2,100,000. The purchaser feels that in the subject property with the added space, volume could be in-

creased to $2,835,000 based upon which a net rent of $141,750 would be indicated.

Forecasts indicate that the purchaser could only use the subject for 10 years at which time it would have to be leased to others or sold. There is no market information to support a market rent value above $102,000 per year and the market rent is more probably $100,000 per year. There is no indication that would support a prediction of increasing market rent value over the foreseeable term. Value at the end of 10 years would probably fall to $1,-100,000. The best available loan is $850,000 at 8¼ percent 20 years with payments of $86,911 per year. Loan balance at the end of 13 years would be $460,985.

Analysis:

1. PV $102,000 less $86,911 loan payments or $15,089 for 3 years at 9%	$ 38,195
2. PV $141,750 less $86,911 loan payments or $54,839 for 10 years @ 9% 3 years delayed	271,760
3. Reversion $1,100,000 less loan $460,985 or $639,015 delayed 13 years at 9%	208,433
Total PV of future benefits	$518,388
Beginning equity required $1,275,000	
—850,000 loan	
	$425,000

Advice: Even though the property would be acquired at a price in excess of market at an initial yield of less than 9 percent and even though the future value 13 years hence will be less than current acquisition cost, the purchaser's special use would justify an equity investment of $425,000 as the

discounted present worth of the future benefits to the purchaser are in excess of the $425,000 equity cost.

In these brief examples the use of DCF analysis as an investment decision tool is demonstrated. It should be realized that the answers resulting from these analyses are subjective and represent worth to a specific party to the transaction rather than worth to a market in general. It would not be reasonable or proper under present market behavior patterns to use this format as a market valuation method. Some day in the future purchasers may establish the price they would pay for an asset by discounting all of the future benefits to a present value or worth. When and if this becomes an established market behavior pattern then DCF analysis may become an appraisal approach or method.

There are numerous special cases where DCF analysis can be in part employed as a market valuation approach:

1. A net leased property with a 10-year prime term at $100,000 per year is being valued. The lease contains a renewal option at $75,000 per year for 10 years. The market capitalization rate is 9¼ percent.

1. PV $100,000 for 10 years at 9¼%	$634,763
2. PV of the reversion $75,000 @ 9¼% $810,810 delayed 10 years at 9¼%	334,737
Total	$969,500

If the current net of $100,000 is capitalized at 9¼ percent, value is indicated at $1,081,080. However, recognizing that the option is at $75,000 does not permit overall capitalization of the current net. Rather, both the current income and future income come into play.

2. A property currently nets $90,000 per year. Three leases provide for automatic rental increases. The first is a $1,500 per year increase to take effect two years hence. The second is a $1,000 increase to take effect three years hence; and the third is a $2,000 increase to take effect four years hence. Operating cost escalation provisions in all leases stabilize expenses at current levels. This type of property sells to yield 9½ percent overall. None of the increases will cause the effective rents to exceed market rent levels.

1. Capitalized value based on $90,000 net at 9½%	$947,368
2. Capitalized value of $1,500 at 9½% = $15,789 postponed 2 years at 9½%	13,168
3. Capitalized value of $1,000 at 9½% = $10,526 postponed three years at 9½%	8,017
4. Capitalized value of $2,000 at 9½% = $21,052 postponed four years at 9½%	14,643
Total value	$983,196

In this example the current net income was capitalized at 9½ percent; however, because of rental increases programmed into the *existing* leases the base capitalization does not reflect all income components. In the fact situation the increases would, in effect, be net. Thus, the value of each increase at 9½ percent is determinable. The values determined, however, must be discounted since each is not due immediately but rather at a future date. The discounted present values of each increase plus the capitalized value of the present net more accurately reflect market value than the traditional brokerage method of showing the average annual rent as the stabilized rent.

3. A property developed on leased land nets $175,000 per year. Ground rent is $15,000 per year net. The lease terminates in 25 years. The ground has a current free and clear market value of $375,000. The present market rate of return is 8¾ percent (capitalized rate).

A. What is the value of the leasehold position?

(1) PV $175,000 per year less $15,000 land rent or $160,000 per year for 25 years at 8¾%	$1,603,987

B. What is the value of the fee interest to the fee owner assuming a reversion worth $2,000,000 in 25 years?

(1) PV $15,000 per year 25 years @ 8¾%	$150,374
(2) PV $2,000,000 due in 25 years @ 8¾%	245,640
Total	$396,014

It would be difficult to sell the fee interest at $350,000 or $396,014 because 25 years is too distant a future date to influence purchasers. If a purchaser wanted 8¾ percent on his investment, the market value of the fee subject to a 25-year fixed income lease at $15,000 per year would probably be $171,500. However, its value to the owner predicated on a $2,000,000 reversion would be $396,000.

4. A lease at $23,000 per month with 42 months remaining is to be settled.
A. What price should the lessor take in settlement if the rate were 9 percent?

---

(1) PV $23,000 per month for 42
   months at .0075 (.09 per annum) $826,015
   If the lease went to maturity the
   total received would be
   $23,000 × 42 $966,000

---

5. An equity sold for $150,000 based on a seller carryback of $700,000 at 6 percent 30 years payable $50,854 per year. Current loans are 8¾ percent 30 years.
A. How would this sale be adjusted?

---

(1) Equity price $150,000
(2) Present value of $50,854 per
   year for 30 years discounted
   at 8¾%   534,260

   Adjusted price $684,260

In this example favorable financing at sub-market rates created a *paper* sale price of $850,000. However, the discount value of the cash flow to the seller on the loan carried back was $534,260 based on conventional rates and not $700,000 as indicated on the face.

6. A retail property is being condemned. The tenant has sued for a portion of the award based on a leasehold interest. Rent is $725 per month with 51 months of an original 10-year term remaining. The current market value of the space is $900 per month.
A. Assuming a rate of 8½ percent, what is the value of the lessee's interest?

---

(1) Space value $900; rent $725;
   lessee interest $175 per month
(2) PV of $175 per month for 51
   months at 8½% per annum
   (.0070833 per month) would
   represent the lessee's interest $8,909

---

7. A condominium development consisting of 100 two-bedroom, two-bath apartments costs $3,300,000 to develop. Average sales prices will net $43,875 after sales expenses. Total sell-out will net $4,387,500. It is forecast that 3 units per month will sell during the first twelve months after completion and 2 units per month thereafter. Thus, 3 years and 8 months will be required to sell out. Carrying costs are 12 percent including debt.

---

(1) 3 units × $43,875 = $131,625/
   month for 12 months at 12%
   per annum PV $131,625 for
   12 months $1,481,450
(2) 2 units × $43,875 = $ 87,750/
   month for 24 months 12
   months delayed   1,654,300
(3) 2 units × $43,875 = $ 87,750/
   month for 8 months 36
   months delayed   469,280

   Total discount value $3,605,030
   Cost   -3,300,000

   To profit $ 305,030

In this example, which is much like a subdivision study, it is indicated that sellout will be $4,387,500 against a cost of $3,300,000 indicating a profit of $1,087,500. However, since 100 percent of sales will not occur immediately, profitability must be measured against the discounted present value of future cash flows from the project. Discounting these futures indicates a present worth of future sales at $3,605,030 and thus real profit is $305,030, not $1,087,-500.

In working discount cash flow analysis, some terms and processes should be amplified.

1. Present value (present worth, PV) represents the value today of future cash flows. The value is dependent on:
   A. The amount (quantity) of cash flow
   B. The selected discount rate
   C. Term of years (periods) over which the flow is to be received (or number of years until the payment is received).
2. Discount rate: For real estate appraisal purposes, depending on the problem, the discount rate could be the debt interest rate, the equity cash flow (dividend) rate, or the overall market capitalization rate.
3. Future value: Future value is the future worth of an asset. It is the sum to be received at a future date.
4. Reversion: The amount/value (future value) of the asset at a future date.
5. Processing:
   A. Present value of an income stream is calculated by obtaining the *present value of 1 per period* factor from the tables indicating the preselected number of periods and rate. For example, the factor for a 5-year term at $9\frac{1}{2}$ percent is 3.8397087865, which rounded becomes 3.83971. This factor multiplied by the income in dollars per period will give the present worth.
   B. If the income being measured does not start immediately, then its present worth is calculated as per A above and future discounted to reflect the waiting period. Thus, the table used would be *present value of 1* due in the future which at $9\frac{1}{2}$ percent 5 years would produce a factor of .6352276653, or .635228 rounded.
      (1) Assuming an income stream of $1,500 per year for 5 years due

to commence 5 years hence, what is the present value at $9\frac{1}{2}$ percent?
$1,500 × 3.839709 = $5,759.56
$5,759.56 × .635228
(present value of 1, $9\frac{1}{2}$%
5 years) = $3,658.63
   C. If the item being measured is a reversionary interest (land and building at the end of a lease term or holding period), then the *present value of 1* would be the table to be used.
      (1) Assuming a reversion 15 years hence worth $1,000,000 at the time of reversion, what is the PV at $9\frac{1}{2}$ percent? Using the PV of 1 table for 15 years at $9\frac{1}{2}$ percent indicates a factor of .2563233748 or .256323 (rounded). $1,000,-000 × .256323 = $256,323
   D. Thus, the two tables most ordinarily used are:
      (1) *Present Value of 1 per Period* or what $1 payable periodically is worth today.
      (2) *Present Value of 1* or what $1 due in the future is worth today.
   E. The minimum tools necessary to run DCF analyses are a book of financial tables plus a calculator. The longhand math is too time consuming and cumbersome. More sophisticated analysis will use computer programs and/or financial computer calculators. However, these expensive tools are not necessary to the practitioner who has only occasional need to make discount cash flow studies.

Summary

The term *discount cash flow analysis* should be no stranger to appraisers. The term sounds complicated; however, the process is rather simple to apply and understand. It is not necessary to understand the mathematic formulas used to develop the factors reflected in the various tables used. It is only necessary to learn how to use the tables. The process is one of simple multiplication made even easier by a calculator. The concept of discounting involves no more than an understanding that the present value of an income stream is less than the sum total of dollars to be received. Stated more simply, a prudent man would not pay $100,000 today for an income of $10,000 per year for 10 years. At worst the $100,000 could be deposited in a bank at $4\frac{1}{2}$ percent compounded and would be worth $155,297 in 10 years.

Application of DCF techniques to investment real estate analysis requires acceptance of the assumption that over a period of years the income can be either greater than or less than the currently stated income. The appraiser need only select the time span to be measured, the amount of income per period during that time span and the discount rate to be applied. DCF analysis permits viewing the worth of a property under a variety of income assumptions with relative ease.

As stated at the outset, DCF analysis *is not* currently *an appraisal approach or method*. The uncertainty surrounding the predictions of quantity of income at future dates or time periods limits the market valuation utility of DCF techniques save for special situations.

DCF analysis is, at best, a technique for processing assumptive data into a measurable value and as such its best appraisal applications are as a tool to be employed in the decision process.

An analysis leading to decision making only has validity to the person making the study and the ultimate decision. The results of studies based on assumptive data are wholly subjective and any correlation between these results and market value as appraisers define market value would be coincidental. If a stock sells at $27.50 based on 11 times earnings of $2.50 per share with earnings historically compounding at 12 percent per annum, then the stock should be worth $48.50 per share in 5 years based on earnings of $4.41. The decision to purchase is based on an assumption of futures. The same is true in predicating real estate *buy–sell* decisions on a DCF analysis.

The sum total of future income and reversion as discounted to present value must exceed the purchase price today if the purchaser seeks a growth real estate investment. Conversely, if an owner is offered a price today that appears to him to exceed the discounted present worth of future income and reversion then sale would be indicated.

DCF analysis will prove to be an invaluable analytical tool for appraisers working in the investment segment of the economy. It is useful as a feasibility study tool and is extremely useful in study of subdivisions or condominium developments. As time goes on, the appraisal profession should witness greater need to employ DCF analysis in counseling clients.

The NPV–IRR Debate in Lease Analysis

Keith B. Johnson and Thomas B. Hazuka

Over the last decade or so a number of methods have been proposed to facilitate analysis of lease or buy decisions. Most of the methods suggested are variations of discounted cash flow approaches which have found increasingly wide acceptance in capital budgeting. The purpose of this paper is to review the evolution of net present value (NPV) methods in leasing starting with Vancil [6, 3, 7, 4] and to compare internal rate of return (IRR) methods proposed relatively recently by Beechy and Mitchell [1, 2, 5]. It would be more appropriate to call them internal rate of cost (IRC) methods, but for our purposes here the more familiar (IRR) terminology will be retained.

After noting potential advantages of leasing, this paper summarizes and contrasts significant contentions and contributions to lease analysis set forth in the journal literature and a leading textbook. These analytical approaches are also compared using a common illustrative problem. It will be shown that, although none of the methods is theoretically flawless, the IRR methods are superior to the NPV methods from both a theoretical and a practical viewpoint. This conclusion should be of interest to academicians and practitioners alike, since the literature has predominantly favored NPV. The material developed here is generally applicable to service or operating leases as well as financial leases, and hence no distinctions are drawn.

Potential Advantages of Leasing

Most potential advantages of leasing over buying an asset can be summarized in the following categories:

1. Tax advantages related to the amount and timing of tax payments;
2. Cost advantages related to the ability of the lessor to acquire, maintain, and/or dispose of the asset more efficiently;
3. Reduction of risk or uncertainty related to the determination of estimates such as salvage value by the lessor in setting up the lease proposal;
4. Credit advantages related to the terms of the lease under consideration and the future borrowing capacity of the lessee.

The effects of tax and cost advantages can be evaluated relatively objectively; reducing uncertainty and evaluating credit advantages require more subjec-

Reprinted from the *Mississippi Valley Journal of Business and Economics*, Vol. IX, No. 2, Winter 1973–1974, by permission of the authors and editor.

tive analysis. Neither the possible credit advantages nor the uncertainty reduction as defined above are incorporated explicitly in any of the methods dealt with here. These two potential advantages are alleged to be declining in magnitude, and their consideration is beyond the scope of this paper. The focus is on the evaluation of tax and cost-related factors.

Net Present Value Approaches

Most people are familiar with the advantages associated with the use of discounted cash flow techniques, and in particular net present value (NPV), to analyze lease or buy decisions. NPV approaches have been widely advanced in the literature, starting with Vancil; through Bower, Herringer, and Williamson; and subsequently, Weston and Brigham. More recently these NPV approaches have been summarized and criticized by Johnson and Lewellen.

Vancil [6] was the first to attempt to provide an analytical framework for the buy or lease decision using present values in his Basic Interest Rate (BIR) approach. Bower, Herringer, and Williamson [3] subsequently proposed a present value method quite similar to Vancil's and developed a standard computer program for the computations. Both of these methods assume that the interest cost implicit in the lease, an unknown, is equal to the firm's marginal borrowing cost—a rough approximation at best. Since finance charges are excluded from cash flows which are discounted in capital budgeting, the interest cost at the rate applicable for marginal borrowing is removed from the lease payments in their analyses. The remaining cash flows associated with leasing and own-

ing an asset are then discounted at the firm's after-tax cost of capital. The lower present value cost is superior when the present value cost of leasing is compared with the present value cost of owning.

The present value approach advocated by Weston and Brigham [7] differs from the previous approaches mainly in that only the salvage value of the asset is discounted at the cost of capital. All other differential cash flows are assumed to be certain or riskless and therefore are discounted at the after-tax cost of debt. In the Weston and Brigham approach, the cost of leasing is compared with the cost of a loan having the same repayment schedule.

In their present value approach, Johnson and Lewellen [4] properly argue that the inclusion of a charge for interest as a cost of owning is inconsistent with the general normative framework for capital budgeting. They then devise a method wherein interest is excluded from the cost of owning by considering the purchase price to be an initial cash outflow, as is normally the case in capital budgeting. However, they fail to exclude interest from the cost of leasing. It would seem that the inclusion of interest is just as inappropriate in the case of the lease alternative as it is in the case of the purchase alternative. Unfortunately, there is no effective way to exclude interest from the lease alternative using present value methods when the implicit interest cost of leasing is not equal to the (interest) cost of borrowing. In addition, the effective interest rate associated with leasing is unknown.

Another major inconsistency is inherent in the method proposed by Johnson and Lewellen. They correctly state that if a present value technique is utilized, it is appropriate to use different discount rates when dealing with cash flows of unequal riskiness. In their illustrative calculation, after-tax lease payments are discounted at the cost of debt, and tax savings on depreciation are discounted at the cost of capital. There is little reason to believe that these cash flows are of unequal riskiness, however, and consequently there appears to be no basis for the use of different discount rates in this case.

All the proposed present value methods account for risk in some fashion by the use of two discount rates. However, for risky cash flows, the implicit assumption is made that the risky flows are in the same risk class as the overall risk of the firm when the firm's overall cost of capital is used for discounting. In those cases where risk reduction is a primary reason for leasing, as is often suggested in the case of high technology items such as computers, it would seem inappropriate to use the firm's overall cost of capital in discounting very risky cash flows such as salvage value. Weston and Brigham use the firm's overall cost of capital in their calculations to discount the salvage value, but they do make note of the fact that, in certain cases, other discount rates may be more appropriate.

Internal Rate of Return Approaches

Although they have not had as wide an exposure as the NPV methods, a number of internal rate of return methods have been proposed to analyze the buy or lease decision. Two of the more recent IRR methods have been developed by Beechy [1, 2] and Mitchell [5]. The Beechy and the Mitchell methods provide, respectively, a before-tax and an after-tax effective cost of leasing in terms of an interest rate.

In proposing his method, Beechy points out that the cost of capital is the result of financing decisions. He argues that the main theoretical objection to the use of present value analysis in evaluating buy or lease decisions is that one is using the cost of capital to determine the cost of one of its components, i.e., the cost of leasing. In principle, the cost of capital should not be utilized in the determination of a component of the cost of capital. Beechy also argues against the use of present value to evaluate the cost of leasing on the practical grounds that decision makers almost universally think of the cost of debt-related financing in terms of a specified interest rate.

Accordingly, Beechy proposes that an IRR method is more appropriate for lease evaluation, and, since debt financing costs are usually quoted as pre-tax interest rates, he generates a before-tax rate. This nuance may prove confusing to some, but obviously before-tax and after-tax approaches produce the same decisions if applied consistently. Beechy refers to his method as the Effective Interest Method of Analysis. First, the interest cost implicit in the lease is assumed to equal the interest cost on a term loan to the lessee, with repayments following the same pattern as the lease payments. He then computes the net cash flow of the lease payments by adding or subtracting all differences in cash flow which are caused by changes in tax effects and by any changes in operating costs associated with the asset. Finally, Beechy determines the discount rate at which the present value of the resultant cash flows is set equal to the base cost of the asset. This is the effective before-tax interest cost (rate) of the lease. The lease is favorable if this rate is less than the borrowing rate.

The IRR method proposed by Mitchell calculates the cost of leasing in terms of an after-tax interest rate. To obtain this rate, Mitchell takes the yearly after-tax lease payments, subtracts from each payment the depreciation tax shield lost by not purchasing the item, and then solves for the rate that will set the present value of the resultant yearly cash flows equal to the purchase price of the item.

Although both methods give equivalent answers, the Mitchell method is simpler and more straightforward computationally than the Beechy method. Beechy's calculations are relatively complex, because he is attempting to obtain a before-tax cost of an item (leasing) that is treated differently from owning for tax purposes. Beechy must therefore adjust for differences in timing of taxes between leasing and owning, while being careful to exclude differences in amount of taxes paid between the two alternatives. Accordingly, the simpler after-tax calculation would be preferred in practice. If one agrees with Beechy's argument that businessmen think of borrowing costs in terms of *before-tax* interest rates, it is an easy task to adjust the after-tax cost of leasing by dividing it by one minus the marginal tax rate to obtain the before-tax cost of leasing:

$$\text{Before-tax Cost of Leasing} = \frac{\text{After-tax Cost of Leasing}}{1 - \text{tax rate}}$$

It is important to note that, by using IRR methods, the implicit effective interest payments on the lease are discounted at the effective cost of leasing. This procedure avoids the prob-

lem, inherent in the present value methods, of discounting at one rate (i.e., the cost of capital or the cost of borrowing) payments that had been implicitly compounded at a different rate (i.e., the relative interest cost of leasing). By definition, IRR methods discount the lease payments at the same rate at which they were implicitly compounded in the first place, thereby effectively excluding financing from the calculations.

IRR methods of lease or buy analysis account for risk by excluding it. As with IRR methods in general, no provision is made for taking into account any differences in the risk characteristics of the various cash flows. This leaves the decision maker free to make a subjective evaluation as to whether the trade-off between cost and risk is equitable. Subjectivity may also enter into risk evaluation using present value methods if the discount rate is chosen explicitly to account for risk. If the cost of capital is chosen as the cutoff rate, this indicates that the decision maker feels that the risk of the project is equal to the average risk of the firm. It would seem that the IRR approach to lease evaluation accounts for risk intelligently, by tacitly acknowledging that it must be evaluated subjectively.

Illustrative Calculations

Four of the more recently proposed methods of analyzing the buy or lease decision (two NPV methods and two IRR methods) have been selected to analyze a specific buy or lease decision. The example used below is that of Johnson and Lewellen [4], since it is a general example, incorporating both annual operating savings and salvage value.

. . . consider the case of a piece of equipment having a five-year useful life and costing $15,000 which can, as an alternative to purchase, be leased for five years for a payment of $4,200 per annum. Assume that the equipment would be fully depreciated on a sum-of-years-digits schedule, is expected to command a $1,500 cash salvage price at the end of year 5, and will require $1,000 more in annual (pre-tax) operating costs if it is owned rather than leased. Finally, assume the corporate income tax rate to be 50 percent, the capital gains rate to be 30 percent, that the firm in question estimates its overall cost of capital to be 12 percent after taxes, and that it has been confronted in its recent borrowings with an 8 percent pre-tax (hence 4 percent after-tax) effective interest rate demand by lenders.

Although all four methods produce the conclusion that the lease is preferred, the illustration serves to explain the several computational assumptions and methods more clearly.

Table 1 shows the analysis of this buy or lease decision using the Johnson and Lewellen method. Johnson and Lewellen's actual calculations have been modified to reflect that, because of depreciation recapture, the gain on disposal of the equipment (salvage value) is not taxed at the capital gains tax rate but rather at the ordinary tax rate. According to the calculations in Table 1, leasing has an NPV advantage of $1,214 over buying; therefore, leasing is the preferred method of acquisition.

In Table 2, the same example is analyzed using the Weston and Brigham method. Again, leasing turns out to be the preferred alternative, but by a much smaller margin. The NPV advantage to leasing is $600 by the Weston and Brigham method. The main reason for this difference is that the depreciation tax shield under the borrowing alternative is discounted at the after-tax cost of debt by Weston and Brigham, while Johnson and Lewellen discount the same cash flow at the firm's cost of capital since they assume it to be a riskier amount. The objection to this Johnson and Lewellen procedure was noted above. This serves

TABLE 1

Johnson and Lewellen Example as Analyzed by Johnson and Lewellen (Modified)

Year, i	Tax Savings on Depreciation, tD_i (1)	After-tax Added Operating Costs $0_i(i - t)$ (2)	Salvage Value Net of Taxes, $S - t_g(S - B)$ (3)	After-tax Lease Payment, $L_i(1 - t)$ (4)	Present Value of (1) minus (2) plus (3), at 12%	Present Value of (4), at 4%
1	(.5) (5,000)	(.5) (1,000)	—	(.5) (4,200)	$1,786	$2,019
2	(.5) (4,000)	(.5) (1,000)	—	(.5) (4,200)	1,196	1,942
3	(.5) (3,000)	(.5) (1,000)	—	(.5) (4,200)	712	1,867
4	(.5) (2,000)	(.5) (1,000)	—	(.5) (4,200)	318	1,795
5	(.5) (1,000)	(.5) (1,000)	(.50) (1,500)	(.5) (4,200)	425	1,726
					$4,437	$9,349

Equipment purchase price = $15,000.
Therefore: NPV = $4,437 − $15,000 + $9,349 = −$1,214.
Conclusion: Leasing is *better* than purchase.

TABLE 2
Johnson and Lewellen Example as Analyzed by Weston and Brigham Method

Computing Net Cost of Owning

| | Applicable to Loan | | | | | | | | |
Year (1)	Total Payment (2)	Interest (3)	Amortization Payment (4)	Remaining Balance (5)	Maintenance Cost (6)	Depreciation (SYD) (7)	(3)+(6)+(7) Tax Deductible Expense (8)	1/2 (8) Tax Saving (9)	(2)+(6)−(9) Cash Outflow if Owned (10)
1	$3,757	$1,200	$2,557	$12,443	$1,000	$5,000	$7,200	$3,600	$1,157
2	3,757	995	2,762	9,681	1,000	4,000	5,995	2,998	1,759
3	3,757	774	2,983	6,698	1,000	3,000	4,774	2,387	2,370
4	3,757	536	3,221	3,477	1,000	2,000	3,536	1,768	2,989
5	3,757	278	3,477		1,000	1,000	2,278	1,139	3,618
5		Salvage Value (After-tax)							(750)
Totals	$18,785	$3,783	$15,000		$5,000	$15,000	$23,783	$11,892	$11,143

Lease Cost After-tax (11)	(11)−(10) Advantage to Owning (12)	4% Present Value Factor (13)	(12)×(13) Present Value of Advantage to Owning (14)
$2,100	$943	.962	$905
2,100	341	.925	315
2,100	(270)	.889	(240)
2,100	(889)	.855	(760)
2,100	(1,518)	.822	(1,248)
	750	.567	425
$10,500	$(638)		$(600)

Note: 12% present value factor applied to the salvage value.

Assumptions:

1. The firm can borrow $15,000 to be repaid in 5 equal annual installments. The annual payments are computed as: (a) Interest Factor for 5 years, 8% Annuity = 3.993; (b) Required Annual Payment = $15,000 ÷ 3.993 = $3,757.

2. The firm can arrange to finance its $15,000 equipment purchase under a 5-year lease plan calling for an annual rental of $4,200.

3. The equipment is worth $750 (after-tax) at the end of 5 years. This $750 is added to column 10 as a cash inflow for the owning option.

4. The firm uses sum of the year's-digits depreciation.

TABLE 3
Johnson and Lewellen Example as Analyzed by Beechy Method (Before-tax Effective Cost of Leasing)

Year (1)	Net Lease Payments * End of Year (2)	Equivalent ** Loan Payment End of Year (3)	Loan Balance During Year (4)	Interest @ 8% on Loan Balance (5)	Principal Payments End of Year (6)
1	$3,200	$3,478	$15,000	$1,200	$2,278
2	3,200	3,478	12,722	1,018	2,460
3	3,200	3,478	10,262	821	2,657
4	3,200	3,478	7,605	608	2,870
5	4,700	5,109	4,730	379	4,730

Tax Deductions

Year	Interest @ 8% (7)	Depreciation (SYD) (8)	(7)+(8) Total (9)	Equivalent Loan Repayment (10)	(10)−(9) Difference (11)	1/2 (11) Tax Effect (12)	Net Lease Payment (13)	Net Lease Cash Flow (13)−(12) (dollars) @ 0%	@ 5.9%	@ 6.0%
1	$1,200	$5,000	$6,200	$3,478	$(2,722)	$(1,361)	$3,200	$4,561	$4,307	$4,303
2	1,018	4,000	5,018	3,478	(1,540)	(770)	3,200	3,970	3,540	3,533
3	821	3,000	3,821	3,478	(343)	(171)	3,200	3,371	2,838	2,830
4	608	2,000	2,608	3,478	870	(435)	3,200	2,765	2,198	2,190
5	379	1,000	1,379	5,109	3,730	(1,865)	4,700	2,835	2,129	2,119
	$4,026	$15,000	$19,026	$19,021	0	0	$17,500	$17,502	$15,012	$14,975

Notes: Asset cost = $15,000; r = 5.93%.
Some columns do not add to totals due to rounding.
* Gross lease payments of $4,200 have been reduced by the $1,000 savings in operating costs in years 1 through 5 and increased by the $1,500 lost salvage value in year 5.
** PV of net lease payments @ 8% = $13,799.

Equivalent loan payment = lease payment $\times \dfrac{\$15,000}{\$13,799}$ = lease payment $\times$ 1.087

405

to make borrowing less attractive under the Johnson and Lewellen analysis
relative to the Weston and Brigham
analysis.

Table 3 evaluates this example using the Beechy method. The before-tax
cost of leasing is 5.93% compared to
the 8% before-tax cost of borrowing.
Unless the risk of leasing due to a
noncancelable contract outweighs cost
considerations, leasing is the preferred
alternative.

Table 4 determines the after-tax
cost of leasing to be 2.95% for the
example using the Mitchell method.
In a manner analogous to Beechy's,
this cost is compared to the 4% after-
tax cost of borrowing. Thus leasing is
again the preferred alternative. It is
apparent that the Mitchell method is
computationally simpler than the
Beechy method and conversion of the
2.95% to a before-tax rate produces
an identical result, aside from rounding error.

Conclusion

It has been shown that the IRR methods of lease evaluation are superior to
NPV approaches from a theoretical

viewpoint in that they: (1) effectively
separate the finance charges associated
with leasing from the calculation by
discounting lease payments at the cost
of leasing and (2) do not utilize the
cost of capital to calculate a component
of the cost of capital. From a practical
viewpoint the IRR methods provide an
effective cost of leasing in terms of an
interest rate, which is a common
method of expressing financing costs.
For subsequent discussions of lease
evaluation methods, we suggest that
"internal rate of cost" (IRC) is more
appropriate terminology than "IRR
method."

IRR methods also handle risk in a
superior manner by allowing (or forc-
ing) the decision maker to account for
risk subjectively. There may be a
temptation in using NPV methods to
account for risk in an arbitrary or
routine manner by using the firm's
average cost of capital to discount
more or less risky cash flows. In view
of their theoretical and practical su-
periority, IRR approaches to analyzing
the buy or lease decision deserve more
favorable attention and greater use
than they have been receiving, relative
to the more widely publicized NPV
approaches.

TABLE 4

Johnson and Lewellen Example as Analyzed by Mitchell Method (After-tax Cost of Leasing)

Year (1)	Net Lease Payments (2)	Depreciation (SYD) (3)	(2) — (3) Difference (4)	1/2 (4) Tax Difference (5)	(2) — (5) Net Lease Cash Flow @0%	@2.9%	@3.0%
1	$3,200	$5,000	$ (1,800)	$ (900)	$ 4,100	$ 3,984	$ 3,981
2	3,200	4,000	(800)	(400)	3,600	3,400	3,393
3	3,200	3,000	200	100	3,100	2,845	2,837
4	3,200	2,000	1,200	600	2,600	2,319	2,310
5	4,700	1,000	3,700	1,850	2,850	2,470	2,458
					$16,250	$15,018	$14,979

Asset cost = $15,000; $r = 2.95\%$.

REFERENCES

1. Thomas H. Beechy, "Quasi-Debt Analysis of Financial Leases," *The Accounting Review,* XLIV (April, 1969), 375–381.
2. Thomas H. Beechy, "The Cost of Leasing: Comment and Correction," *The Accounting Review,* XLV (October, 1970), 769–773.
3. R. S. Bower, F. C. Herringer, and J. P. Williamson, "Lease Evaluation," *The Accounting Review,* XLI (April, 1966), 257–265.
4. Robert W. Johnson and Wilbur G. Lewellen, "Analysis of the Lease-or-Buy Decision," *The Journal of Finance,* XXVII (September, 1972), 815–823.
5. G. B. Mitchell, "After-Tax Cost of Leasing," *The Accounting Review,* XLV (April, 1970), 308–314.
6. Richard F. Vancil, "Lease or Borrow—New Method of Analysis," *Harvard Business Review,* XXXIX (September–October,˙1961), 122–136.
7. J. Fred Weston and Eugene F. Brigham, *Managerial Finance,* fourth edition (New York: Holt, Rinehart and Winston, Inc., 1972), pp. 459–469.

Leases and Their Effect on Value

James E. Gibbons

A lease is a legal instrument used by an owner of real estate, the landlord, to convey some of his rights in the property to another party, the tenant. In simplest terms, the tenant is given, for a limited time, rights of occupancy and use conditioned upon his meeting specified requirements, chief among which is periodic payment of rent. The lease creates and transfers to the tenant restricted rights, generally called the leasehold estate, and reserves to the landlord the residue of property rights, called the fee estate. It is obvious that interests created, limited, transferred, or reserved in lease transactions are desired by potential purchasers. Hence, they have values which are frequently objects of appraisal studies. For appraisers, therefore, a vital field of inquiry and study is the influence of lease terms on valuation procedures.

While there are many definitions of the term value, the most acceptable from a broad viewpoint is that value is the present worth of future benefits. It is also described as the relationship between a thing desired and a potential purchaser. More than by any other factor, the quality of this relationship must be influenced by the purchaser's estimate of benefits he will enjoy through acquisition of the desired object. The record of past productivity is of interest to him only if it projects some light into the darkness of the future, assisting in preparation of forecasts. It is evident that a valid and thoroughly practical philosophy of valuation is expressed in the basic economic principle of anticipation. Value lies in futures.

If one accepts the proposition that value is the present worth of future benefits, he should agree that valuation is a discounting process. In real estate, whenever possible, benefits of ownership are estimated in monetary terms. For example, during his tenure, an owner of realty is entitled to receive its net income earnings, and upon disposal of the parcel, the proceeds of sale. Both benefits are customarily expressed in dollar amounts. It is also true that when an owner leases his property to a tenant, the future he anticipates are rental collections during the lease term, and at its conclusion, a reversion of all property rights free of any lease encumbrance. Again, these items are customarily estimated in dollar amounts.

The present worth of an anticipated future receipt of money can be calculated by reducing the expected amount to the extent of the loss of compound interest occasioned by the waiting period. It is reasoned that if the money

Reprinted, with permission, from the July/August 1970 issue of *The Real Estate Appraiser,* Society of Real Estate Appraisers, Chicago, Illinois.

were immediately available, it could be invested and earn compound interest. Hence, the present worth of an expected future receipt is its amount discounted or reduced by such lost interest. The heart of the valuation problem is clearly the selection of the rate at which loss of interest should be computed. This is a discount rate, or as it is frequently referred to in appraisals, a capitalization rate. Valuation, then, is a discounting procedure in which future benefits estimated in terms of money are discounted to express their present worth.

The body of knowledge identified as the science of real estate appraisal has been properly developed from foundations in fundamental economic principles. Among the more important of these basic propositions is the bundle of rights theory. It advances the notion that the desired objects of potential purchasers are not physical characteristics of property, but the various rights that may be exercised with respect to it. Among such rights are: the right to occupy and use, the right to sell, the right to mortgage, the right to lease, the right to give away, etc.

This multitude of rights is embraced in ownership of real estate, and the type of title known as fee simple is said to represent the entire bundle. It is clear that the owner of the bundle can break it down in many ways, conveying away some of the rights and retaining others. In view of these possibilities, a foundational element in any appraisal is identification of the property rights to be valued. Not in every instance will the objective be valuation of all rights in a fee simple; instead one may be required to appraise a leasehold estate, an undivided interest in a property, a remainder interest, a life estate, or other property rights.

Essentially, the solution of any real estate appraisal problem is accomplished in a few steps. There must be an identification of the property rights to be valued. These rights must then be studied in the context of time, location and economics for the purpose of forecasting the benefits that will accrue to their owner. Such anticipated benefits, generally expressed in terms of money, must then be discounted to achieve an estimate of their present worth, which is termed value.

Consideration of the effect of leases on value must involve exploration of several areas. First, how does the lease contract divide property rights between its parties? Second, which rights are to be valued? Third, how do the terms and covenants of the lease instrument reveal the magnitude and limitation of monetary benefits which will flow to the owners of the various property rights conveyed or reserved? Fourth, how does a knowledge of the terms of the lease or the identity of the parties thereto, assist the appraiser in making a selection of the appropriate rate of discount to be applied to such future benefits in the estimation of their present worth?

Probably the best exemplification of the bundle of rights theory is a typical lease transaction. In its most common form, the owner of real estate, the landlord, conveys for a limited time some of his property rights, usually those of occupancy and enjoyment to another party, the tenant, while reserving to himself the right to receive rent during the lease term, and at its conclusion, to have the property revert free of all lease encumbrances. A lease term is limited in duration and may be quite short or extend for many years. The tenant's occupancy, use and enjoyment of the property are usually exclusive and subject only to his payment of rent, all or part of the property's operating expenses, and possibly performance of some service. Unless prohibited by the terms of his lease, the tenant has the right to sub-let the property, or assign his rights to another party. In so doing he conveys away his rights of occupancy and use, and reserves the right to collect rent from his sub-tenant.

In simplest terms, therefore, leases divide property rights by allocating to the owner of the fee rental income during the lease term, and at its conclusion, reversion of all rights. To the tenant, for the lease term, goes the use and enjoyment of the property subject to required rent payments. In modern real estate practice, various lease instruments have been developed making possible great diversification in modes of property rights divisions; and to guard against misapprehensions one must study carefully the many covenants drafted to effectuate such arrangements. Above all, the conclusion is inescapable that the validity of an appraisal rests on adequate and accurate identification of property rights to be valued.

After a clear identification of property rights to be appraised, the next appraisal step is a forecast of future benefits that will accrue to the owner of such rights. In the ordinary lease transaction the rights reserved to the owner of the fee are receipt of rent payments and, at the conclusion of the lease term, property reversion. The appraiser must assign dollar amounts to the benefits flowing from these rights. The terms of the lease will clearly indicate the amount of anticipated rent collections, but the value of reversionary rights must be estimated. This entails projecting the unencumbered value of the property as of the last day of the lease term. It is clear, then, the value of the fee estate is the present worth of income plus present worth of anticipated property reversion.

Rights conveyed to the tenant are customarily referred to as the leasehold estate. The estimation of benefits flowing to such rights is accomplished by first estimating, on an unencumbered basis, the property's market net income earnings capacity. If this amount exceeds the rent obligation of the tenant, ownership of the leasehold estate carries with it an economic advantage. For example, if the property is capable of earning a net income of $50,000 per year and the tenant must pay a rental of $30,000 per year, the leasehold estate would enjoy earnings of $20,000. Value of the leasehold estate, therefore, is estimated by finding that there are no reversionary rights available to the leasehold estate. At the conclusion of the lease term, all rights of tenancy are extinguished. In the event the tenant decides to sublease, property rights are conveyed to a sub-tenant and may produce monetary benefits to the extent that the market net earnings capacity of the property exceeds the sub-tenant's rent obligation. If such is the case, he has an anticipated monetary benefit and the value of his interest is the present worth of such benefit. With the existence of a sublease, the benefit that will accrue to the first tenant is simply the difference between rental collection from the subtenant and rental payment to the fee owner. Value of this prime tenant's position is, therefore, the present worth of such differential. In all cases, the value of lease interests is found by first estimating the present worth of income the interests are expected to earn. Then in the case of the fee estate only, the valuation is completed by adding the present worth of expected property reversion. Summarizing, the value of a fee estate is the present worth of income plus present worth of reversionary rights. Value of a leasehold or subleasehold interest amounts to the present worth of the income such interests are expected to earn.

Inasmuch as valuation of lease interests hinges largely upon an accurate forecast of income earnings attributed to such interests, it is necessary to consider the manner and extent to which the lease's many covenants affect income. While a lease will invariably require a tenant to pay some rental, the full amount of this obligation is not always readily discernible. Leases are said to be of two general types, either gross or net. In the case of the typical gross lease, the tenant's sole obligation is to pay the stipulated rental amount and the landlord must pay all property operating expenses. Hence the net income earnings to the fee estate are not the total rent collections, but such amount less operating expenses. The leasehold estate's net income earnings are the difference between the property's earning capacity and the tenant's specified rental obligation.

In the case of a net lease, however, the obligation to pay operating expenses is passed, in whole or in part, to the tenant. This allocation of expenses materially influences the estimated earnings of both fee and leasehold estates. The rent payments specified in the lease are truly net income to the fee owner, and the leasehold estate's net earnings are reduced by the amount of the tenant's required payment of operating expenses.

In modern real estate leasing practice, there are a great variety of arrangements for sharing property expenses. For example, in many leases there are tax stop provisions which require the landlord to pay taxes up to a point, or fixed amount, and pass to the tenant the obligation to pay any additional

taxes. In many leases there are clauses dividing the burden of other operating expenses.

It must be noted that the rent obligation is not always fixed. Leases may provide for graduating or declining rent payments. The frequency and degree of changes can be stipulated contractually in which case the lease is either a step-up or step-down contract. In other cases, rent payments are established on the basis of a fixed minimum amount against a percentage of a gross volume of business transacted at the property. In long term land leases, the rent is frequently fixed for a limited period of time, with provisions for future adjustments measured as percentages of then appraised land values.

In all cases, lease covenants are of vital appraisal importance. Value is said to be the present worth of future benefits, and such benefits are clearly influenced by lease terms. On the basis of the few examples presented, it is obvious that lease arrangements can either enhance or diminish earnings of fee or leasehold estates. Then, too, of great importance are lease provisions relating to possible future property condemnation, or damages caused by fire or other hazards. In most jurisdictions, apart from separate contractual arrangements, the general rule is that condemnation terminates a lease, and serious damage to the property by fire or other hazards has the same effect. Since projected benefits attributable to a leasehold estate depend wholly upon the existence of a lease, in the valuation of such an estate the possible termination of the lease through condemnation or damage must be carefully considered and weighed. The appraiser must closely study lease covenants to ascertain stipulated arrangements for distributing condemnation and damage awards. Since the flow of benefits to both fee and leasehold estates may be regulated by these terms, the appraiser's final value estimate must reflect their potential influence.

The identity of the parties to the lease can be another matter of substantial importance. In most instances, an appraiser is estimating market value which should be a function of a property's market income producing capability. The rental stipulated in the lease may or may not be at such true market level. The appraiser must then decide whether he can base his value on the stipulated contract rent or predicate his appraisal on an estimated market level of rents. In the valuation of a fee estate, the market value is limited by and is a function of the terms of the lease creating such estate, provided the contractual rental is equal to or less than the rent one could expect to obtain through negotiation in a free market. If the rental is equal to such potential market income, there is a clear identification with the market and no further questions need be raised.

If the lease rental is less than potential market rate, the fee estate has yielded to the leasehold estate a portion of the benefits it should receive. Under such circumstances, it can be said from a market valuation viewpoint, the leasehold estate encroaches upon the fee position. The holder of such a leasehold, or his successors, will certainly guard such advantage, hence the value of the fee estate flows from and is strictly limited by rent specified in the lease.

If the lease rental is greater than potential market rate, the fee estate encroaches on the leasehold position. In such case, the appraiser must give some consideration to the credit standing of the tenant. If the tenant is a major corporation or entity of top rating, the contract rent generally can be accepted, as a strong, responsible lessee could be compelled to honor the disadvantageous rent requirements. If the tenancy is not substantial, then for valuation purposes it would be appropriate to adjust rent downward and closer to market level.

The foregoing discussion, concerning the acceptability of a contractual rental for purposes of appraising a fee estate relates to the situation where the realty is unimproved. Where, however, leasehold improvements have been erected, a different condition may exist. In order to protect his investment in the improvements, the leasehold tenant, or his successor in interest, will obviously continue to meet contractual rental obligations even though they represent more than potential market rate. As long as the leasehold estate enjoys a net operating profit, the fee estate is in no substantial danger of suffering a rental default. The more extensive the leasehold improvements, and the greater the prospective net earnings therefrom, the less need for the appraiser to investigate the market character of the specified lease rental. These comments, concerning the relationship of contract rent to market potential, are directed to situations involving long term leases.

Where lease terms are short, the customary appraisal procedure is to base valuation on market level of income and either add or subtract an increment to reflect the limited advantageous or disadvantageous contract rent. The magnitude of the increment is usually estimated by capitalizing the rent excess or deficiency at a relatively high rate.

Having established the monetary benefits expected to accrue to lease interests, valuation is accomplished by discounting such benefits to express their present worth. The appropriate amount of discount is the loss of interest occasioned by deferral periods involved in income and reversion collection. The value of the fee estate is said to be the present worth of future income earnings, plus the present value of anticipated property reversion. A major problem is the selection of the proper rate of discount or capitalization. This can be accomplished by using risk rating reasoning and procedures. This involves analyses of the nature and quality of risk in the investment and comparison with other opportunities with rated risks and known earning abilities. In any situation an investor looks for an attractive, competitive return on capital and provisions for its recapture. Attractiveness of yield is assessed against risks involved, and as hazards increase, higher and higher yields are required to attract capital.

Above all, one must recognize that an investor with money to put to work has available to him a vast array of opportunities. He is certainly not restricted to real estate interests, but may turn to a variety of bond situations, common stock, and other business ventures. All such investment situations compete for capital. Before committing his money to any project, the investor will first study all possible moves judging attendant risks and examining prospective yields. This provides a picture of the available range of investment opportunities. In making a decision concerning the appropriate rate of earnings for a real estate investment, the investor will first judge its risk quality and relate it in the spectrum of opportunities analyzed. By so doing he will have a good indication of earning rates available for comparable risks.

This risk rate procedure constitutes the only valid approach to rate selection in that it reflects influences from all segments of the economy and gives particular weight to the competitive element. To describe more fully discount rate selection through risk rating, a typical example can be analyzed. In recent weeks many market transactions revealed that long term U.S. government obligations were selling at prices to yield normally 8%. The full significance of this yield is appreciated when one recognizes that the investments must be deemed to be virtually riskless. Further observation indicated that U.S. government agency obligations or bonds yielded approximately $8\frac{1}{2}\%$. These bonds would be considered to have a somewhat greater element of risk than direct U.S. government obligations, but they would nevertheless be judged relatively risk free.

Market reports for the same period revealed long term, high grade corporate obligations were priced to yield approximately $8\frac{3}{4}\%$. These are rated riskier than U.S. government agency obligations, hence a somewhat higher yield is needed. Corporate obligations with a lower quality rate were priced to yield 9% and up. Moving to the real estate field, first mortgage transactions indicated interest rates of 9% to 10% with additional interest earnings from equity participations. Throughout this entire analysis, there is clearly observable a pattern of higher and higher yields as degree of risk increases.

In real estate, investments are invariably composite situations made up of mortgage and equity capital. The trend is to acquire as much of the capital as possible in the form of mortgage funds with the balance being provided as an equity contribution. These segments of financing are available in the market at costs which are expressed as rates. To determine the appropriate rate factors at any given time, one would simply look at the total picture of then existing competitive situations in the money market. Such an observation will reveal the going rate for long term forecasted income capital, such as mortgage money, and the more hazardous venture capital, known as equity funds. Observing the proper discount or capitalization rate must be the weighted average of these two rates.

In the valuation of lease interests, it must be recognized that appraisals cover not the entire bundle of rights, but portions thereof. One may start the problem of rate selection with the rate appropriate for the overall property, and then make adjustments for the differences in risk involved in investments in various component parts created by lease instruments. In this light, the safest investment is clearly a fee estate which has first claim on the productivity of the property. The leasehold estate involves somewhat more risk in that while it is entitled to the earnings of the property, it is nevertheless subject to the obligation to pay lease rent. A sub-tenant position is, of course, even more hazardous than the original leasehold. In capitalizing the monetary benefits flowing to these various lease interests, successively higher capitalization rates are appropriate to reflect the increasing hazards.

In present day real estate projects, the lease arrangement is utilized as a financing technique. All investors strive to enjoy the benefits of maximum leverage. In so doing, they attempt to acquire as much as possible of an investment's required capital in the form of mortgage and keep the equity relatively thin. To achieve such a situation a device frequently used is

the sale of land to an institutional investor with a leaseback of the fee estate to the developer. A leasehold mortgage is then obtained by such developer with which he finances the erection of building improvements. In this manner he frees up capital that would normally be tied up in a land investment, leaving it available for leasehold equity. The arrangement has tax advantages in that land may not be depreciated for income tax purposes, but ground rent is a legitimate tax deduction. Currently, owners of highly rated urban sites are creating leases whereby they divide property interests into fee and leasehold estates and place their interests in entities, all of which they control. Thereafter, both the fee and leasehold are financed. This accomplishes the same advantages as the purchase leaseback, but does not necessitate relinquishing the fee title.

On the basis of information presented in this article, it is obvious that leases and lease terms have a material influence on valuation. As investments, under the influence of current tax pressures, grow increasingly complex, appraisers strive to interpret realistically and accurately the various property rights distributions flowing from commonly used lease instruments. In all difficult situations the best approach to the solution of a problem is to resort to fundamentals.

First, there should be clear understanding and identification of the property's rights to be appraised. Where leases are involved the instrument should be studied to determine how it breaks down the rights within the total bundle, and to whom they are distributed. With rights identified and allocated, information is gathered to forecast future benefits that will be enjoyed by the owners of such rights. These benefits are rental collections and reversionary rights, and they are expressed in terms of money. Value is the present worth of these futures; therefore, the valuation process entails discounting. A rate of capitalization or discount is selected on the basis of attendant risks and then applied to forecast future payments. The resulting discounted present worth is what appraisers have always characterized as market value.

Sample Condemnation Clauses for Various Leases

Adolph Koeppel

In the condemnation of leased premises, the obligation of the condemnor to pay just compensation is exactly the same as if the premises were not leased. The condemnor pays the fair market value of the real property on the title vesting date. Whom he must pay it to really doesn't concern him. He pays no more nor less in either case.

However, where the premises are leased at title vesting, the scramble for the award between landlord and tenant really begins.

Generally, the Landlord is entitled to that portion of the award for the land that is known as the reversion—or the present value of the land which will be returned to him at the end of the term (had the condemnation not occurred). This can vary from 99.9% to zero depending upon the time the lease still had to run on title vesting date.

In addition, *all* the improvements belong to the Landlord, except any Tenant fixtures that have not become (in law or by contract) part of the building.

The Tenant would be entitled to his fixtures and the present value of the right to enjoy the premises for the unexpired term if the contract rental were less than the fair market rental.

The Printed Clause

Option to Terminate by Tenant

The standard New York Real Estate Board Lease (store and loft) is the one we most often run into.

> If the whole or any part of demised premises shall be acquired or condemned by Eminent Domain for any public or *quasi* public use or purpose, then and in that event, the term of this lease shall cease and terminate from the date of title vesting in such proceeding and Tenant shall have no claim against Landlord for the value of any unexpired term of said lease.

Where does such a clause place the parties in the lawsuit?

Now things for the Landlord (he drew the lease, of course) have changed for the better. He still gets the reversion and the improvement value—but, in addition, he, the Landlord, gets the full present value of the land since the Tenant has agreed to give this up to the Landlord. This holds true for a

Reprinted from the *New York State Bar Journal*, Vol. 41, No. 5, August 1969, by permission of the author and editor.

total or a partial taking, since the clause is very specific ("if the whole or *any* part").

The Tenant should seek, especially where he runs a small business and location and good will are often a major asset, a clause giving *him* the option to terminate the lease in the event of a partial taking. This would give the Tenant a choice—depending how untenantable the premises become after the vesting—of staying at a reduced rental (and this should also be apportioned, if possible) or terminating and seeking new space elsewhere.

Making Your Own Hand-Tailored Clauses

Definitions

Always include; we rarely see this, yet it is vitally important to tell the condemnation judge *exactly* what we mean by:

1. condemnation proceedings,
2. title vesting,
3. building improvements,
4. land improvements,
5. fixtures (Tenants')
6. contract rent v. economic rent,
7. value of the land,
8. partial taking,
9. cessation of the obligation to pay rent.

The definition of some of these terms may be self-evident and yet the English language has a way of evolving and taking on different though related meanings over the years. What harm in spelling it out? How much easier you will make the job of the trial practitioner if you, for instance, take the trouble to say:

(1), (2) that title vesting in a condemnation proceeding is the date, fixed by the appropriate law, when the condemnor became vested with title and specifically includes a vesting of *title de facto*—as well as *de jure*—whichever occurs earlier. "Condemnation proceeding shall also include within its definition a private purchase in lieu of condemnation."

(3) *Building Improvements* include, but are not limited to, stores, offices, apartments and all structures on the land which can be rented or leased for the production of income to the owner.

(4) *Land Improvements* can be defined to include water and sewer mains and connections, telephone and electric lines, blacktop paving of parking areas, water storage tanks, etc.

(5) *Tenants' Fixtures* can be defined and listed generally (where not known at time of execution of lease) and specifically where known as: plumbing, heating, air conditioning, special water lines, the installation costs of heavy machinery, built-in cabinets, safes, panelling, ceilings and floors (to name a few).

(6) *Contract Rent versus Economic Rent* is defined by a long line of cases but why not spell it out: "The tenant shall have no claim in any condemnation proceeding in the event of a total or partial taking unless the rental specified in this lease (contract rent) is *less* than the economic or market value rental for this space on the date of taking."

(7) *Value of the Land* simply means: "The value of the leased premises as if vacant, unencumbered and unimproved on the date of vesting."

(8) *Partial Taking*—Do not use this phrase unless you further define it; to wit, how much of a partial taking do you desire before the lease term (and the obligation to pay rent) comes to an end? Perhaps a partial taking that

does *not* touch any of the improvements should be the cut-off point where a partial taking shall result in an automatic termination of the lease. But with office and shopping center space, the parking becomes significant and so, if you represent the Tenant, you had better insist that loss of a certain amount of parking spaces should give the Tenant the right to cancel.

(9) *Obligation to Pay Rent*—You must nail this down. Tell us, in the event of a total, or a substantial partial, taking, *exactly when* the obligation to pay rent ceases.

Some Standard Clauses

I. Termination—Partial Taking Defined—Parking Loss to Office Building or Shopping Center

"If, at any time during the initial term or any renewal term of this lease, title to the whole or substantially all of the demised premises shall be taken in condemnation proceedings or by any right of eminent domain, then and in that event, this lease shall terminate on the date of such taking and the rent and any additional rent reserved herein shall be apportioned and paid to the date of such taking."

"*Substantially all of the demised premises* shall be deemed to have been taken if the portion remaining cannot reasonably be used, after restoration, to complete architectural units, for the conduct and operation of a bank and office building, including necessary accessory parking."

(The term *"necessary accessory parking"* may be *"reasonable"* despite the fact that such parking no longer complies with the appropriate zoning ordinance.)

"The parties agree that there are now 250 on-site parking spaces accessory to the building. As a result of the taking, it is agreed that the portion remaining cannot reasonably be used for the conduct of a bank and office building if the on-site accessory parking spaces fall below 150 on-site parking spaces."

(Alternatively, *"substantially all of the demised premises"* can simply be defined as more than 50% of the land and buildings thereon.)

II. Total or Substantial Partial Taking; Distribution of Proceeds; (Various Types of Leases)

"In the event of a total taking or of a substantial partial taking as hereinabove defined, the rights and interests of the Landlord and Tenant in and to the entire award (including interest) or the aggregate of any separate awards (made by the Court or otherwise), after payment of all reasonable fees and expenses incurred by both parties in connection with the establishing and collection of such awards, shall be apportioned as follows:

[(A) Short-Term Lease—No Building Improvements Made by Tenant; Fixtures Defined]

Landlord shall be entitled to receive and retain such portion of the award as shall represent compensation for the value of the land and improvements thereon, including severance and consequential damages to the remainder. The tenant shall receive no compensation for its leasehold value, if any, and it shall be entitled solely to compensation for fixtures owned by it at title vesting.

Tenant's fixtures shall *not* include electrical wiring, air-conditioning ducts, heating units and conduits, floors and ceilings, all of which items shall be included in the landlord's share of the award."

[(B) Short-Term Lease—Improvements Made by Tenant]

(Landlord still is awarded that portion of the award that represents the land.)

(Tenant still obtains *his* fixtures.)

"That portion of the award that represents the improvements shall be apportioned between Landlord and Tenant as follows:

(i) The first $50,000 thereof shall belong to the Tenant.

(ii) The Landlord shall then be entitled to receive and retain such portion of the award (with interest thereon) as the number of months elapsed since the commencement of the initial term bears to the number of months from the commencement of the initial term to the then scheduled expiration date of the term, initial or renewal as the case may be, during which the taking occurs.

(iii) The balance of this award shall then belong to the Tenant."

[(C) Long-Term Lease—No Building Improvements Made by Tenant—Option to Renew]

(Tenant is awarded his fixtures.)

(Landlord is awarded his building improvements.)

"That portion of the award that represents the value of the land shall be apportioned between Landlord and Tenant as follows:

(i) The first $50,000 thereof shall belong to the Landlord.

(ii) The Tenant shall then be entitled to receive and retain such portion of the award (with interest thereon) as the number of months elapsed since the commencement of the initial term bears to the number of months from the commencement of the

initial term to the then scheduled expiration date of the term, initial or renewal as the case may be, during which the taking occurs.

(iii) The balance of this award shall then belong to the Landlord.

Option to Renew—Any option to renew contained in this lease shall, on the date of the taking, be deemed to have been exercised by the tenant so as to be computed as part of the initial term for the purposes of this condemnation clause."

[(D) Long-Term Lease—Building Improvements Made by Tenant—Tenant's Right to Participate in Condemnation Proceedings]

(Tenant is awarded his fixtures.)

(Building improvements apportioned as in Case B.)

(Land award apportioned as in Case C.)

"Notwithstanding any language of limitation on the Tenant's rights to any awards in condemnation as set forth in these condemnation clauses, it is specifically understood and agreed that the Tenant has reserved the right to notice and to participate in the trial of the condemnation proceedings, any settlements thereof and in any negotiations that lead to acquisition by purchase in lieu of condemnation. The Landlord specifically covenants not to settle any such proceedings without the prior written consent of the Tenant."

III. Unsubstantial Partial Taking; Tenant (or Landlord) to Make Repairs—Depending on Who Made the Improvements; Term and Rental Not Abated; Allocation of Award

"In the event of taking of less than the whole or less than substantially all of the demised premises, the term of this lease shall not be reduced or affected in any way and the Tenant shall restore the improvements constructed by it in accordance with subdivision (c) hereinafter set forth. The award shall be apportioned as follows:

(a) The Landlord shall first be entitled to receive and retain such portion of the award or awards with the interest thereon as shall represent compensation for the value of the land or the part thereof so taken considered at the option of Landlord as vacant and unimproved, or based on an economic value at the time of the taking, plus severance and consequential damages (but after giving effect to the completion of the restoration by tenant) to the remainder considered as vacant and unimproved.

(b) If the balance of said award or awards shall be in an amount of Fifty Thousand ($50,000) Dollars or less, such award shall be paid to the Tenant for application by the Tenant to the restoration and repair of the improvements constructed by it on the demised premises. If the balance of the award be an amount in excess of Fifty Thousand ($50,000) Dollars, then and in that event, said sum shall be paid to the Landlord as Condemnation Trustee for application pursuant to the terms of subsection (e) of this clause.

(c) The Tenant, at its sole cost and expense and whether or not the award payable under subsection (b) of this clause shall be sufficient for the purpose, shall proceed with reasonable diligence to construct, repair, alter and restore the remaining part of the demised premises so that said premises will contain complete architectural units for use as one banking and office building and related parking facilities with that combination of rentable space and facilities for the on-site parking of automobiles which will result in the greatest number of square feet of rentable space permitted by the law of the appropriate municipality or other governmental unit having jurisdiction thereof. (Such construction repairs, alterations or restoration, including temporary repairs, are sometimes referred to in this section as the "Restoration.")

(d) The conditions under which the Restoration is to be performed and the method of proceeding with and performing the same shall be covered by all of the provisions of this lease relating to restoration after fire. The cost of the Restoration shall include the reasonable fees of an architect, if any, employed by the Landlord for the purpose of examining and passing upon the plans and specifications and supervising the Restoration.

(e) If the awards are deposited with the Landlord as Condemnation Trustee under the provisions of subsection (b) of this clause, the Landlord shall hold, apply, make available and pay over to the Tenant the award in the same manner as is provided with respect to insurance proceeds under the appropriate provisions of this lease; provided that any balance of the award not used for the Restoration shall be divided between Landlord and Tenant as follows:

(i) The Landlord shall be entitled to receive and retain such portion of the balance of the award or awards with interest thereon as the number of months elapsed since the commencement of the Initial Term bears to the number of months from the commencement of the Initial Term to the then scheduled expiration date of the term, Initial or Renewal as the case may be, during which the taking occurs.

(ii) The balance of any award or awards shall belong to the Tenant.

(f) In the event of a taking as de-scribed herein, there shall be no abate-ment of rent allowed to Tenant."

IV. Temporary Easement Taking

"If the whole or any part of the demised premises or of Tenant's inter-est in this lease shall be taken in con-demnation proceedings or by any right of eminent domain *for a temporary use or occupancy,* the term of this lease shall not be reduced or affected in any wise. Tenant shall continue to pay in full the rent, additional rent and other charges herein reserved, in the manner and at the times herein specified with-out reduction or abatement, and, ex-cept only to the extent that Tenant is prevented from so doing by reason of any order of the condemning author-ity, Tenant shall continue to perform and observe all of the other covenants, agreements, terms and provisions of this lease as though such taking had not occurred.

"In the event of any such taking, Tenant shall be entitled to receive the entire amount of any award made for such taking whether such award is paid by way of damages, rent or otherwise, unless such period of temporary use or occupancy shall extend beyond the ex-piration date of the term of this lease. In such latter case, the award, after payment to Landlord therefrom of the estimated cost of restoration of the de-mised premises to the extent that any such award is intended to compensate for damage to the demised premises, shall be apportioned between Land-lord and Tenant as of such date of expiration in the same ratio that the part of the entire period for which such compensation is made falling be-fore the date of expiration and that part falling after, bear to such entire period provided, however, that if the portion of the award payable to tenant

is made in a lump sum or is payable to Tenant other than in equal monthly installments, Landlord shall have a right to collect such portion of Ten-ant's award as shall be sufficient to meet:

(a) The payments due to Landlord from Tenant under the terms of this lease during the period of such tem-porary use or occupancy and Tenant's obligations with respect to such pay-ments shall abate to the extent of the receipt of such portion of the award by Landlord; and

(b) The estimated cost of restora-tion of the demised premises, if such taking is for a period not extending beyond the expiration date of the term of this lease, which amount shall be made available to Tenant when and if during the term of this lease, Tenant shall have restored the same as nearly as may be reasonably possible to the condition in which the demised prem-ises were immediately prior to such taking."

V. Special Clauses for Percentage Lease (Stores)

"(A) In the event of a total taking, the lease shall terminate on title vest-ing date and the *entire award* in con-demnation shall belong to the Land-lord.

(B) In the event of a partial taking, which taking exceeds more than ten (10%) percent of the ground floor of the leasehold premises, either party may terminate the lease by written notice (etc.), written ten days after the date of title vesting. This ten (10%) percent proviso shall not be applicable if the lease has less than three years to expiration date on the date of title vesting. In that latter event, either party may terminate in the same man-ner as hereinabove set forth.

(C) If neither party exercises the

option to terminate (in a partial taking), then and in that event, the Landlord agrees at his own cost and expense to restore and repair the demised premises."

VI. Special Clauses for Tenant—Good Will, Business Damage

"Nothing contained in this lease shall be deemed a waiver by Tenant of its right to present a claim in the condemnation proceedings for loss of business profits, loss of good will and moving expenses, should these items then be compensable as subsequently determined by settlement or after trial, as long as the ultimate compensability of these items to Tenant does not diminish any award to the Landlord."

VII. Termination by Valid Non-compensable Exercise of the Police Power

This is tricky. The operation of the Tenant's business (under the lease) might be curtailed, limited or destroyed by a non-compensable exercise of the police power such as sandmining in a residential area, loss of access with no taking, loss of business to gas station or roadside stand due to limited access highway, one-way street, roadway divider or loss of curb cuts.

In such cases, Tenant will want a reasonable option to terminate. Landlord will tend to be unreasonable. It is best to spell this out in detail in each specific case.

ANNOTATED BIBLIOGRAPHY

1. *Baker,* Condemnation: Concepts and Consequences of Public Intervention in the Landlord–Tenant Relationship, 9 Kansas Law Review, 393 (1961).
    A scholarly and concise review of the legal effect of condemnation on the interests of the parties; contains indicated areas to be covered by lease draftsman.
2. *Bonner,* Appraisal of Short Term Leaseholds, Appraisal Journal, Vol. XXIII (Jan. 1955), p. 59–62.
3. *Boyer and Wilcox,* An Economic Appraisal of Leasehold Valuation in Condemnation Proceedings, 17 Miami Law Review, 245 (1963).
4. *Broadman,* Providing in the Lease for Possible Condemnation, The Practical Lawyer (Association of the Bar of the City of New York), May 1968; reprinted New York Law Journal, 11/21, 22/68.
    A concise, exhaustive review of the problems to be encountered in the condemnation of leased property. Clauses are suggested, but a warning that they must be adequately tailored for the precise situations. Catchalls and ambiguities are to be avoided. Partial takings—the provisions for repair and renovation of buildings partially taken—termination clauses in the event of a valid non-compensable exercise of the police power—are all suggested.
5. *Comment,* The Lessee's Rights in Eminent Domain, 31 Conn. Bar Journal, 156, 158 (1957).
6. *Friedman,* Handbook of Real Estate Forms, p. 124 (1957).

7. *Garrett,* Contemporary Real Estate Leases, University of Illinois Law Forum (Fall 1952), p. 407–13 (condemnation).

   Excellent practical suggestions for clauses in specific situations. Does not contain actual clauses but covers (1) the taking of the entire property including the estate of both tenant and landlord, (2) condemnation of part of a building and part of the leasehold, (3) condemnation of all or a part of the leasehold estate and (4) damage without actual taking of the property itself.

8. *Gill,* Condemnation of Leased Property in Arkansas, 14 Ark. Law Review 326, 330 (1960).

9. *Gleaves,* Leasehold Problems in Eminent Domain, 31 Los Angeles Law Bulletin 3 (1955).

10. *Hershman,* Compensation—Just and Unjust, 21 Business Lawyer, 595, 604–06 (1966).

11. *Hitchings,* The Valuation of Leasehold Interests and Some Elements of Damage Thereto. Southwestern Legal Foundation p. 61 (1960).

12. *Horgan,* Some Legal and Appraisal Consideration in Leasehold Valuations under Eminent Domain. Hastings Law Journal, p. 34 (1953).

13. *Kizer,* Valuation of Leasehold Estates in Eminent Domain, 67 W. Va. Law Review, 101, 102 (1965).

14. *Kuehnle,* The Appraisal of Leasehold, The Appraisal Journal, Vol. XIX, No. 2, April 1951.

15. *Lieberman,* Effective Drafting of Leases for Real Property, p. 249–264 (1956).

16. *Matheny,* Leasehold Interests, Appraisal Journal, Vol. XXVII (July 1959), p. 375–385.

17. 2 *Nichols,* Eminent Domain Section 5.23 (3d ed. 1964).

18. 7 *Nichols,* Eminent Domain, Section 11.06, 11.07, 11.08. Condemnation Clauses in Leases, and generally Chapter 11 (1968).

   The most detailed work to date. Actual clauses for specific leases.

19. *Note,* A Survey of Landlord and Tenant in Eminent Domain, Williamette Law Journal, Vol. 3, 1964 p. 39–51.

   A student note. Contains a paragraph on the effect of a condemnation clause.

20. *Note,* Condemnation and the Lease, 43 Iowa Law Review, 279 (282–3).

21. *Note,* Eminent Domain: Compensation for leasehold interest where no provision in lease (Note) 48 Marquette Law Review 90 (1964).

   Wisconsin statutes analyzed. Common law rule compensating lessee for fair market value of leasehold—partial or total. Discusses "market value" test versus "intrinsic value" test of damages. Special items of tenant loss such as OPTION to PURCHASE, OPTION to RENEW, FIXTURES AND IMPROVEMENTS, COST of RELOCATION and LOSS of PROFITS, are treated.

22. *Orgel, Valuation,* Section 121 (2d ed. 1953).

23. *Polasky,* The Condemnation of Leasehold Intents—48 Virginia Law Review 477 (1962).

   Verbose, standard law school treatise—interminable sentences where short ones would not only suffice, but would clarify.

Interesting hypothetical cases of allocation of awards between landlord and tenant—he has studied the appraisal process.

Concludes that careful and lengthy drafting of condemnation clauses is vital—else we get some of the absurd decisions he has analyzed. The clause must cover:

(1) award for balance of term to tenant,
(2) especially where he has made substantial improvements,
(3) fixtures,
(4) options to renew and
(5) options to purchase.

24. *Practicing Law Institute,* Condemnation Clauses in Leases—Panel discussion 3/12/64—by Herman Cohen, Benjamin Pollack, Robert H. Schaffer.

A one-page pamphlet containing six suggested provisions covering condemnation. The panel made suggestions for over a dozen additional clauses.

25. *Purnell,* The Valuation of the Leasehold Estate, Southwestern Legal Foundation (1959), p. 79–99.

Another review of the applicable Texas law—but does include a three page discussion on the importance of a proper condemnation clause.

26. *10 Rabkin and Johnson,* Current Legal Forms (1966).

27. *Roe,* Leasehold Interests, Appraisal Journal, Vol. XXVI (Oct. 1958), p. 531–36.

28. *Sackman,* Compensation Upon The Partial Taking of a Leasehold Interest: Southwestern Legal Foundation (1961) (p. 35–77). The old professor does it again. The author and editor of *Nichols* presents the definitive work in this field to date. **A must.**

29. *Sando,* Appraisal of Leasehold Interests, Southwestern Legal Foundation p. 79–97 (1961).

An excellent analysis of the types of leases; the interests to be appraised and principles of valuation. The capitalization process is discussed in detail as it relates to the leased fee and the leasehold interest.

30. *Schmutz,* George, Condemnation Appraisal Handbook—Chapter 15, Leaseholds, p. 226–33 with citations (fifth printing, Jan. 1967).

Standard reference work.

31. *Skeer,* A Lessee's Interest in Condemnation, Appraisal Journal, Vol. XXIV (April 1956), p. 266–269.

32. *Soles-Cohen, Jr.,* Appraisal of Leaseholds, The Encyclopedia of Real Estate Appraising, Chapter 20, p. 465–482.

Excellent coverage.

33. *Speir,* Allocation of the Recovery Between Lessor and Lessee, Southwestern Legal Foundation (1968), p. 159–174.

A fine review of the problem as it projects itself into the courtroom. Interesting examples for the appraiser including a gasoline station.

34. *Wilcox,* Valuation of Leasehold Interest Under Law of Eminent Domain, The Appraisal Journal, Vol. XXXI (Oct. 1963), p. 453–471.

Professor Wilcox presents a scholarly, but realistic analysis. A classical work for every library.

35. *Woodruff,* Legal Damages in the Partaking of a Leasehold Interest, Southwestern Legal Foundation (1963), p. 137–158.

Fairly detailed exposition of the Federal and Texas decisions—emphasis on non-compensable items—i.e., good will, business damage. Fixture problem is analyzed.

INDEX